Migrating Meanings

Migrating Meanings
Sharing Keywords in a Global World

'Europe, The Citizen, The Individual, The People'

James W. Underhill and Mariarosaria Gianninoto

EDINBURGH
University Press

Edinburgh University Press is one of the leading university presses in the UK. We publish academic books and journals in our selected subject areas across the humanities and social sciences, combining cutting-edge scholarship with high editorial and production values to produce academic works of lasting importance. For more information visit our website: edinburghuniversitypress.com

© James W. Underhill and Mariarosaria Gianninoto, 2019, 2021

First published in hardback by Edinburgh University Press 2019

Edinburgh University Press Ltd
The Tun – Holyrood Road, 12(2f) Jackson's Entry, Edinburgh EH8 8PJ

Typeset in 11.5/13 Monotype Ehrhardt by
Servis Filmsetting Ltd, Stockport, Cheshire

A CIP record for this book is available from the British Library

ISBN 978 0 7486 9694 9 (hardback)
ISBN 978 1 4744 8138 0 (paperback)
ISBN 978 0 7486 9695 6 (webready PDF)
ISBN 978 1 4744 4737 9 (epub)

The right of James W. Underhill and Mariarosaria Gianninoto to be identified as the authors of this work has been asserted in accordance with the Copyright, Designs and Patents Act 1988, and the Copyright and Related Rights Regulations 2003 (SI No. 2498).

Contents

Introduction	1
Global Concepts	2
Migrating Meanings	5
Europe and Global Politics	6
Which Languages?	10
Why Chinese?	12
Methodology	16
Our Sources	20
Objectives	21
1 The People	23
English Ideals of the People	24
What 'the People' Means to Us	26
Dictionary Definitions	28
Corpora Findings	32
Encyclopaedias and Quotations: The People is Elsewhere	48
MyEnglishCorpus	49
Other European Peoples	55
The People in Radical Politics	65
人民 Rénmín	85
2 Citizen	114
Introduction	115
Scope of the Corpus-based Study	118
Criteria for Citizen in English	119
Origins and Evolution of the Concept	120
Synonyms, Antonyms, and Related Terms	124
Corpus Analysis	125

Compounds and Collocations	131
Limits of Corpus Analysis for 'Citizen'	133
The Rights of Man, and Exclusion from Humanity	135
Scottish Citizens	141
Comparing Citizens in Cultures	145
Citizens in Chinese	172
Concluding Remarks	192
3 Individual	196
Dictionary Definitions	196
The Individual as a Conceptual Problem	205
Corpora	206
Words for Individual and Individualism in Chinese	239
4 Europe	264
Europe in English and Other Languages	266
English Corpora	269
Personal Corpora	285
Does the Press Misrepresent Europe?	291
Metaphors for Europe	294
Europe in Europa	300
Provisional Findings	303
Introducing Europe to China, or China to Europe?	306
A Final Word	334
Glossary	340
Bibliography	363
Corpora and Databases	363
Books and Articles	364
Websites	388
Index	390

Introduction

孟子曰：諸侯之寶三：土地、人民、政事。寶珠玉者，殃必及身。

Mencius said, 'the precious things of a prince are three: the territory, the people, the government and its business. If one values as most precious pearls and jade, calamity is sure to befall him.'[1]

In 2001, the [American] president accounted for the 9/11 attacks on the basis that terrorists do not respect or value individual human rights. (Jan Hancock, *Human Rights and US Foreign Policy*, 2007, quoted in the American Corpus of Colloquial English (COCA)).

China sees improved relations with Japan as an opportunity to try to burnish its credentials as a good global citizen. (Minxin Pei, 'Out Into the World; China is Ready to Become a Good Citizen- But On Its Own Terms', article in *Newsweek*, 31 December 2008, quoted in COCA).

In marked contrast to her predecessor Alex Salmond, who regularly describes [Scottish] independence as inevitable, the first minister [Nicola Sturgeon] said that the fate of a second referendum lay in the hands of the Scottish people (*The Guardian*, 15 October 2015, http://www.theguardian.com/uk).

欧洲人的政治目标似乎首先就是保护"欧洲生活方式"。这一欧洲式的"政治性"很有些特别。通常，政治目标是要保护某种政治制度，或者说对权利和权力的分配制度，一般并不包括全部生活内容，而欧洲梦所表达的政治性却是包括全部生活内容在内的政治性，它要捍卫的是一个完整的生活体系。[2]

The European political goal seems first of all to protect the 'European way of life'. This is very specific to Europe. Often, the political goal is to protect a political system, or the distribution of rights and power. This generally does not encompass all aspects of life. On the contrary, the political nature expressed by the European dream includes all dimensions of life: what it wants to defend is a complete system of life.

GLOBAL CONCEPTS

When Alex Salmond and Nicola Sturgeon, the First Minister of the Scottish Parliament, debate the fate of 'the Scottish people', we are dealing with one take on a shared cultural concept – the people – evolving over time within a specific social and historical context. Any context will produce a specific form steeped in its own particular tradition. Take the related ideals of 'freedom', 'liberty', 'autonomy', 'independence', and 'revolution'. The way these ideals are venerated, and the way they maintain patterns of feeling and thinking within any given worldview, any language and culture, depends on what is happening within the linguistic community, on its status within the world, on its history, and on the fears, hopes, and aspirations of that community.

The North Americans defined themselves by revolting against their English aristocratic overseers. Consequently, not only do they venerate revolution and the republic, they also tend to sympathize with the Scottish and Irish independence movements and other 'freedom fighters', as they themselves selectively define them. Americans can identify with the Scots and enter into their worldview, more easily than the English can. Why is this significant? Because it enables us to understand both something universal and something specific about what a people is, what it does, and whether national and global forces enable it to develop and express itself, and ultimately to govern itself. This depends, of course, to a great degree on global forces. Scottish nationalism and the Scottish people are not perceived by Europe or the United States as a threat. Throughout the twentieth century, Europe had a very different relationship with German nationalism and the *Deutsche Volk*. Wars affect worldviews and sympathies.

At regional, national, and global levels, politics clearly affects how we perceive shared concepts. When the Chinese speak of 'serving the people' we realize that we are moving into a communist worldview, but we all, nonetheless, appreciate that we are dealing with a meaningful concept. All cultures must negotiate the relationship between the group, the nation or the State and the individual person. And this involves a definition of the single person, their rights and responsibilities. In all states, individuals form part of the people. Individuals contribute to the identity and culture of the people, just as most of us hold that the people should recognize the freedom necessary for individuals to creatively, collectively, and individually, express and realize themselves. In doing so, individuals sustain the people. This is why it is often argued that it proves counterproductive to force individuals to conform to norms and modes of thinking and expression with which they cannot identify.

Hence, the meaning we attribute to the 'individual' and to 'the people' turn out to be both existential and political questions. At the most objective and neutral level, they refer to those mutually dependent opposites, the smallest unit, and the largest collective unit within a State or nation. No modern State can avoid these universal concepts. But as soon as we begin to consider the rights of individual citizens within the State, we are forced to recognize that the way we organize individuals within 'the people' is never neutral, politically speaking. The way we define who belongs to the people, who does not, and who is relegated to the status of an 'enemy of the people' is clearly ideological.

Who belongs within the State? The citizens? This question seems simple enough, until we realize that the term 'citizen' is always defined in time and space, and by interest groups with political power and influence. In the 1930s, Algerian women were 'subjects' of France but not 'citizens' (*sujets*, but not *citoyennes*). British feminists of the 1970s also spoke of women being treated as 'second class citizens'; citizens without the same rights as men. But Algerian women were doubly *déclassées*. As members of France's colonies, they were not attributed the same rights as French women. But even French women did not obtain the vote until 1944. In one fell swoop, Charles de Gaulle liberated French women from both German occupation and patriarchy. They became fully entitled voting citizens. This was a long process, however, and various conceptions of rights and responsibilities, various so-called 'ideals' of woman come into play in complex narratives that helped sustain the pre-war exclusion of women from the status of full democratic citizenship.

The question of citizenship and the rights of individuals takes us to the heart of our project. We want to try to understand how we think together as a global community. This means investigating both what we share and what we understand about our differences: cultural differences, traditional differences, linguistic differences, political and ideological differences, and those specific differences related to individual perspectives and personal sensibilities. The authors of this book, an Italian sinologist, and a Scottish ethnolinguist, both live in France and work in a number of languages, travelling widely within Europe and beyond the frontiers of Europe. We have spent six years trying to understand what meanings belong to 'citizen', 'the people', and 'the individual'. What we propose to offer in the following chapters, in the clearest possible terms, is a rigorous account of our painstaking attempts to gain an accurate impression about how these keywords, the citizen, the individual and the people, are used in written texts by individuals of various European nations. We seek to grasp the associations related to the English concepts and logics and cultural narratives they are bound up in. And we contrast the perception of these English words with the way other peoples use their own keywords for these concepts, intuitively apprehending them in their own ways within the framework of their own traditions.

We are Europeans. But as 'foreigners' in France, we are 'migrants' of a sort, inhabiting parallel worldviews. This has enabled us to set up together a stimulating dialogue. And our shared dialogue has been nourished by our ongoing exchanges with a wide network of scholars and friends around the world. Similarly, our ideas and impressions have been contradicted or confirmed, and critically appraised and modified during our encounters with both academics and individuals from all walks of life who have done us the favour of sharing their own ideas and impressions with us. The Rouen Ethnolinguistics Project (http://rep.univ-rouen.fr/), with its conferences and online videoconference papers, proved an important forum for discussion for European academics from Germany, Italy, Spain, Poland, the Czech Republic, France, China, and Australia. The lively debates and discussions we have had make us hope that this book will not only read as an academic treatise, but will also open up a space for reflection on the words we live among.

What stimulates us is the meaning of words and the way people make meaning out of language: the way individuals give a sense of meaning to their lives and to their own experiences. We are fascinated by the way their words open up their worlds for them. And as migrants, we have tried to bear witness to the way meanings migrate from culture to culture. We have observed the way migrating meanings take up new roots in foreign soil, allowing people to express their perspectives and affirm their positions.

MIGRATING MEANINGS

On the whole, our research and reflection have led us again and again to the conclusion that meanings are anything but neutral. Meanings are generated within shared cultural mindsets. They circulate in society, as individuals take stances in discussions, and express their own individual worldviews and their changing perspectives. Consequently, what people feel about 'the people', and what they mean by that word, tells us something about each people. How peoples feel about other peoples is equally significant. The associations that peoples conjure up in other peoples' minds when they use such terms reveals something about their times, about their social circumstances, their relations, and about the way their languages, their cultures, and their traditions evolve together.

Tracing and tracking down the meaning of words means accepting that the whole is made up of more than the sum of its parts. The individual and the citizen go hand in hand. For this reason, individual is often an adjective; we speak of 'individual citizens'. And citizens are considered as 'individuals' with rights. Words are not atoms, isolated individual entities. Like individuals, words interact with words. And we see our task to be unravelling the unique way broadly similar keywords interact within the patterning of each culture and language.

One of the main conclusions that our work on 'migrating meanings' led us to, was that the simple words invariably prove anything but simple. The people is complex conceptual construct, and our relationship to the people, in all the various meanings of the word, is complex. As linguists, translators, and thinkers, the authors of this book were not surprised to find that concepts come in a vast variety of forms. We anticipated that our keywords would take on a kaleidoscope of shades and hues. Philology, translation studies, and literary scholarship, for many generations now, have amply explored the diversity of meanings in cross-cultural studies. But we were forced to recognize the limits of our own languages and worldviews during the course of our investigations. We were forced to admit how those worldviews conditioned the kind of questions we asked ourselves about citizens, individuals, peoples, rights, and responsibilities. As Europeans, we had to learn to accept that our own modes of conceptualizing the people, the individual, and the citizen are bound up in feelings and values. We evolve among words, just as words evolve among us. We can no more escape our times or our cultures, than words can escape their socio-historical contexts. Thinking and feeling prove inextricable.

We set out to track down the meanings of words. But what exactly do we mean when we speak about tracking the trajectories of migrating meanings? We mean entering into linguistic patterning, and trying to trace some of the major highways and avenues that each language opens up to reflection. It will be clear for ethnolinguists, sociolinguists, and linguistic anthropologists that we are using a Humboldtian conception of language here. Language is not considered a neutral means of denoting universal abstract meanings. Thinking is thinking-in-language. And we want to know how various cultures think and feel differently.

EUROPE AND GLOBAL POLITICS

Political scientists, politicians, or journalists would have a very different idea in mind if they spoke of 'Europe and global politics'. But we are linguists. For people interested in society, ideas come first, and words are considered the mere means by which ideas are given expression. The very word, 'expression', metaphorically implies giving an outer voice to inner meanings. Linguists see things differently. They work from words towards meanings. We are specialists of semantics. We move from definitions to discourse strategies. We observe how we all think in language by using words to define things in order to position ourselves in debates with overt and covert objectives in mind.

This is the approach we have adopted to try to understand the way citizens of nations, as individuals, have begun speaking of themselves as 'global citizens'. This has become standard practice in a world in which global governance is debated and promoted. But it is paradoxically both new and ancient. For centuries, Americans and Frenchmen have spoken of being 'world citizens', *citoyens du monde*. Irish aesthetes, such as Oscar Wilde, aspired to such an ideal. And among the Germans, the great poet-dramatist, Wolfgang von Goethe (1749–1839), and the enlightened linguist, Wilhelm von Humboldt (1767–1835), and his brother the famous naturalist explorer, Alexander von Humboldt

(1769–1859) subscribe to the ideal of the enlightened scholar as a world citizen (*Weltbürger*). Those late Enlightenment thinkers believed that world citizens would create and maintain a world university that would represent the meeting of minds unhindered by political factions and provincial prejudice.

But are global citizens world citizens? In the opening of this introduction, we quoted the COCA, in which an American journalist claimed that China saw 'improved relations with Japan as an opportunity to try to burnish its credentials as a good global citizen'. This prepared the ground for the criticism that was soon voiced: 'Chinese can just sit back and look like responsible international citizens' (*Newsweek*, 31 December 2008, quoted in COCA). We chose that quote because we wanted to highlight that Americans were trying to understand the strategies of other nations to project an impression of themselves conforming to shared international ideals and requirements. But the ironic tone of the line quoted made it palpable that the Americans felt that they were entitled to question and decide who is authentically living up to norms, ideals, and requirements defined and dictated by a 'global world' in which 'Western models' dominate. The line comes from a right-wing Christian source, *The Christian Science Monitor*, and the speaker quoted suggests that China was trying to promote the idea of tackling the question of global warming rather than 'beating up on the Japanese', because it makes them look better, or as Mr Glosserman, the speaker, put it, 'Improving relations with Japan makes China look like a responsible stakeholder'. Whether China is or is not a good international citizen is clearly a political question. But the politics lies not only in the either/or, the for or against: it lies in the very formulation of the concept. To ask the question is already political. To ask is to take a stance, and address an audience; and neither of these acts can be neutral in the 'global *polis*'.

The famous English historian, born in Egypt, Eric Hobsbawm (1917–2012), a radical political thinker from the left, questions the very concept of global citizenship itself, seeing a covert strategy lying behind it. Eugene D. Genovese put his objection in the following terms:

> As Hobsbawm pointed out, there is no such thing as **global government** or a **global citizen**. In fact, the globe is not a political entity at all, but an abstraction as remote as any other astronomical object--which, when you think about it, is what the globe is. As an economic abstraction, 'global' is meaningful to the heads of

capitalist enterprises, since it is part of the algorithm through which they manipulate the economic machinery, untouched and untouchable by any democratic political process. For ordinary persons, 'global' is an abstraction roughly translatable as 'beyond our influence'. (Genovese 2014, quoted in COCA; emphasis added)

This introduces the question of space and the political spheres of activity and influence. Hobsbawm was closely affiliated with the great Marxist literary scholar, Raymond Williams (1921–1988), whose *Keywords* (1985), first published in 1976, remains a major influence for a generation of thinkers concerned with the relationship between words and ideology. Anna Wierzbicka (born in 1938), a kindred soul, whose Natural Semantic Metalanguage approach (set up with Cliff Goddard) coincides with our objectives to some extent (see Wierzbicka 2014: 22–27, on Underhill), is only one of many academics who have found inspiration in Williams' idea that a culture can be understood by studying it through the prism of its keywords. Discourse analysis, philosophical and political reflection, cultural linguistics, linguistic anthropology, and ethnolinguistics all remind us that, as Williams (1985) demonstrated, everyday words like 'democracy', 'private', 'public', 'class', 'community', and 'empirical' are all deeply entrenched in ideological presuppositions. Meanings take root in mindsets, and mindsets cannot escape ideology. This does not mean that there is no freedom of thought, but rather that freedom is a game in which certain rules apply. Rules, definitions, patterns, and narratives influence the way in which free debates are framed and played out. Individuals take positions in relation to positions. The game is unpredictable, and the players are 'free', but the chessboards they play on have squares traced and defined by tradition.

Our investigation is semantic, critical, and speculative. We ask for example: What is an individual? How does the phrase 'global citizen' work within the frameworks of various debates? What spheres of life does the global citizen belong to? Who uses this concept in English? Are they English-speakers? Or speakers of other languages using Global English in international debates? What speakers of which languages use analogous concepts? And when did they start to circulate? And why? What purpose does 'global citizen' serve? And whose interests? This would ultimately have been Williams' question. And our desire to uncover the underlying logic of cultural narratives means we are in tune with Hobsbawm when he objects that we cannot simply take such terms at face value. We get caught up in values, traditions, and interests. These are the kind of questions that critical discourse analysis would ask (see Toolan 2002). Exponents of metaphor theory would approach these questions from a similar angle with their own modes of questioning (see Musolff et al. 1996; Musolff 2001, 2016; Goatly 2007; Underhill 2011; and the forum for debate on metaphor http://www.metaphor.de).

We have striven to avoid being 'ethnocentric' and 'Eurocentric', but this remains a European book. We have taken up the task of asking how Europeans are speaking about 'peoples', 'individuals', and 'citizens'. But this begs the question: What do we understand by 'Europe'? We wanted to study Europe as part of our conceptual cluster, in order to see how Europe speaks about people, about individuals, and about citizens. But our project also means considering the way we define Europe, and the way we define it from within and from without, as citizens, as individuals, and as individual Member States. This dual perspective is crucial, because many of the speakers of Member States, like many individual citizens of Europe, conceive of themselves as 'insider-outsiders'. We are all 'in' Europe. But many Europeans still see Europe as something 'over there', something abroad. Europe's laws and regulations are imposed upon them, such people tend to think. The policy of Brussels 'penetrates' 'their' spheres of existence, they feel. An alien external force.

Our research involved forcing us to continually question the limits of our own perspectives. Most of all, we were forced, as Europeans, to face up to our own Eurocentrism when we considered the way Europe is defined from without by non-Europeans. Often we take ourselves and our troubles too seriously, seeing storms in teacups each time tensions arise in the European Union (EU). The Chinese are following with interest the various crises that Europe has recently been engaged in: the financial crisis of 2007, the refugee crisis of 2015, and Brexit and the rise of Europhobic nationalism in European Member States. But this does not prevent them from recognizing the power and the potential of the European project as a whole.

For the Chinese, Europe can be both a trading partner and a rival. And this takes us beyond an East–West model. We often represent our Continent as a fragile Europe whose cracks indicate the edifice is in danger of collapsing. The Chinese are lucidly observing Europe's teething pains, but like the Americans, the Russians and the Indians, the Chinese take Europe seriously.

WHICH LANGUAGES?

Given the fact that English is currently the world language, it will seem perfectly legitimate that we have focused on English, and taken it as our starting point. English exports its culture with its language. It exports fragments of its worldview with the words it sends out into the world. 'Democracy', 'legitimacy', 'transparency', and 'empowerment' do not necessarily derive originally from English-speaking cultures, but they do traverse the prism of English, and are reformulated in languages and integrated into other worldviews with translations from English.

We have striven to present a more accurate picture of English by opening up our chapters to the diversity of Englishes that exists. Scottish and American sources have been represented to some degree in each of the chapters. It will, of course, go without saying that there has been no systematic attempt to cover all the various forms of English – a task that would take us into a study spanning several volumes. We have, nonetheless, never stopped stressing that we are always dealing with a complex origin before considering the complex innovations that take place when words and ideas are exported to other languages. This has helped us to avoid presenting misleading schematic oppositions. It has, furthermore, enabled us to illustrate that certain facets of each concept are eclipsed or opened up, played down or highlighted, when words migrate from one context to another both within languages and between languages.

We are, of course, interested in the specific origins and developments of individual words and the way they interact with other words within given linguistic communities. This is not simply because we are two Europeans and our work leads us to dialogue with the people of other languages and cultures in our private and professional lives on a daily basis. This is because we believe that complexity and linguistic diversity is a question that is fundamental for Europe. Europe is by nature made up of a great diversity of cultural traditions. The European Union is perfectly aware of the richness of its cultural diversity and seeks to preserve and promote that diversity with its Language Rich Europe project which encourages its citizens to learn not only their mother tongue but two more languages (usually English plus another European language). In our own way, we hope that our book will do justice the rich linguistic diversity of Europe, and defend that diversity.

We have investigated the languages we read and speak. Contrary to a practice sometimes adopted in comparative linguistics, we have refrained from quoting languages with which we are not familiar. This means that we have limited the European languages quoted to English, French, German, Czech, and Spanish, languages which at least one of the authors reads or translates.[3] Those who speak Czech can – if they make the effort – follow Polish and Slovak, so a certain number of minor references to these languages have been included. This serves to open up our study to debates and definitions in these languages. Inevitably, these attempts provide us with only fragmentary glimpses of how individuals are making sense of the world with words in Europe. But they do make a contribution to trying to help us understand what it means to be European, and think like Europeans. And above all, it should shield the authors from the criticism that this project is Anglocentric.

Our multilingual approach takes a broad perspective, and this should help readers escape from routine modes of thinking and feeling about Europe. German adds another dimension to the worldview of the English-speaker: German words and concepts bring us back to common Germanic origins that persist within English ('burgh', 'borough', in the names of towns and districts, and 'burgher' as opposed to the German *Bürger*, the contemporary word for 'citizen').

Czech may seem a surprising choice to include in our selection of languages. But Czech allows us to investigate questions of identity and ideological questions. Czech allows us to escape the Cold War paradigm that somewhat arbitrarily carved up 'Eastern' and 'Western Europe'. And it allows us to problematize ideological questions by tracing capitalist and communist meanings not when they migrate between cultures but when they evolve within the tradition of a single linguistic community. Most of all, Czech communist texts offer parallels to Chinese communist discourse. So instead of positing a democratic liberal capitalist West in opposition to a communist Chinese East, we find ourselves being forced to integrate the logic of communist arguments concerning the people, and individualism in Czech into our own 'Western' European heritage. Contrary to much of the post-1989 rhetoric, we consider those socialist modes of thinking and feeling to be part and parcel of our evolving European heritage.

Where does this leave us as Europeans? In response to the European Union's utopia of a language rich Europe – and for our part, we do not intend 'utopia' in an ironical sense – we propose a language-rich reflection upon the migration of meanings among the peoples of Europe.

WHY CHINESE?

Those curious readers who share our enthusiasm for linguistic diversity will, nonetheless, be justified in wondering where Chinese fits into the picture, and why we have contributed no less than a third of the work to the Chinese language, and its culture. We should once more stress here that we are all too aware of the limits of our project. This book is certainly not intended as an explanation or even an introduction to the worldview of the Chinese people. That would have been a very different book.

We have opened up our work to take on board the meanings that the Chinese attribute to the keywords we understand as 'the people', 'the citizen', 'the individual', and 'Europe' for reasons which vary for each of the concepts. Europe allows us to get outside ourselves and look in on ourselves. In trying to understand how the Chinese speak about 'Europe' and the 'Europeans' of today and their traditions, we are able to gain a crucial critical distance. We gain insight into our own values, and our ideals. But we also perceive more clearly our own prejudices.

If we have found Chinese to be a source of inspiration and fascination, it is because it has constantly forced us to revise and reappraise the paradigms and oppositions with which we interpret our own cultures and the cultures we work on. The way Chinese receives some European words and modifies them forces us to reflect upon which facets of the concept are highlighted in the discourse of various political factions and social classes in any given European language at a given moment in history.

The citizen, the individual, and the people are, as we have argued, clearly bound up together as conceptual constructs developing over time. But as we begin to enter into the Chinese worldview, things change. Where 'Europe' seemed the odd man out in our choice of concepts, from the European perspective, it is 'the people' that appears to stand out in the context of the Chinese tradition. The 'individual' and the 'citizen' are clearly perceived by specialists as concepts imported into Chinese from Europe in the eighteenth and nineteenth centuries. But this is not the case for 'the people', because there has always been a Chinese people. It was, therefore, crucial for us to trace the origins of that concept. And once more we found this inescapable everyday concept to be anything but neutral. The people can be perceived as both an actor and an object in various discourses in Chinese. The people can become an ideal or a victim. At times, it is the 'glorious fate' of the Communist people which is at stake. And at other times, the people becomes a rallying call for patriots defending the Chinese nation. 'The people' takes on a crucial role in texts concerning the liberation of the Chinese people from invaders (both British and Japanese), for example.

The question is complex. And we trust that our findings do justice to that complexity. By closely studying the way our four words are conceptualized in Chinese, we can hope to move beyond clichés of traditional stances. We are now a little wiser, a little less inclined to fall into the complacent caricatures that are set up when we set East and West in opposition. The East has been amply critiqued by post-colonial studies in the generation that grew up between 1977 – when Edward Said published his famous *Orientalism* – and 2012, when his *Culture and Imperialism* came out. But our study of Chinese has forced us not only to question our conception of the 'East', but also to question the very idea of the 'West'.

We conclude that East and West are both culturally charged concepts that need to be unpacked. Nonetheless, the tendency to promote an East–West dichotomy and to set the two in opposition persists today. And that dichotomy forms the framework and basis of debates. And what does that mean? That it is only another way of saying that we still use the East–West opposition to make sense of the world, or at least to try to interpret it. Once more, it becomes clear that, as Europeans, we are constructing the world within the frameworks of our historically, socially, and linguistically configured worldviews.

If we had been writing a book on the Chinese keywords, then other terms would probably have been chosen. For instance, among the recent studies on Chinese keywords, there is the noteworthy analysis of the word *sùzhì* 素质[4] ('quality') by Andrew Kipnis (2006) adopting a keyword approach.

In *Words and Their Stories: Essays on the Language of the Chinese Revolution* (Wang 2011b), the keywords and expressions of the Chinese revolution, such as 'revolution', 'rectification', and 'socialist realism', are studied. Such expressions as 'let a hundred flowers blossom, let a hundred schools of thought contend', and 'use the past to serve the present, the foreign to serve China' are contextualized in this work. Wang also claims that Raymond Williams' *Keywords* was a major source of inspiration for him (Wang 2011: 1–2).

Ye adopts the Natural Semantic Metalanguage approach (see Ye, https://webtv.univ-rouen.fr/videos/meaning-culture-and-communication-the-natural-semantic-language-approach/), to examine keywords and key expressions of contemporary Chinese (most of all Ye 2013, 2014; Goddard and Ye 2016). Her 'corpus-based lexical-conceptual analysis' (Ye 2018) proved invaluable in explaining how meanings work in Chinese.

Other studies should not be forgotten. Among them, it is worth quoting several studies analysing specific words and concepts which can be considered as keywords in contemporary China or as keywords enabling us to understand its recent history. Fumian's article (2014) posits *fèndòu* 奋斗 (struggle, to struggle) as a keyword in contemporary Chinese. As Fumian (2014: 361) writes:

> the word *fendou* runs like a thread throughout the history of modern China, changing its meanings along with the changes of the ideological paradigms and the mainstream goals of Chinese modernity. Thus after the Darwinian struggle of the late Qing Era, and the individualist struggle of the early New Culture period, we enter the age of the collective 'objectives of struggle' of the Maoist times, to go back to the 'individual struggle for society' advocated by Party ideologists in the wake of Deng Xiaoping's economic reforms.

A parallel can be found in the Czechoslovak communism of the postwar period. In Czech, the concept of 'struggle' ('*boj*', see Underhill 2011: 110–155) got caught up in the patriotic rhetoric of liberation from German occupation, Marxist–Leninist ideology of class struggle, and the dissident rhetoric of individual human rights. 'Struggle' ('*boj*') becomes a Czech keyword that takes root at a crucial period in Czech history, then continues to grow and develop.

Furthermore, the project Language and Politics in Modern China, launched by Jeffrey Wasserstrom in the 1990s, analysed several words in revolutionary political culture (for instance, Schoenhals 1994). The Language and Politics in Modern China working papers formed 'part of a collaborative research project, "Keywords of the Chinese Revolution: The Language of Politics and the Politics of Language in 20th-Century China"', seeking 'to present an account of the ways that the language of politics has shaped and, in turn, has been reshaped by the Chinese Revolution from the early decades of this century to the present' (http://www.indiana.edu/~easc/publications/working.shtml). Among the 'working papers' published between 1993 and 1996, there are publications on the 'Non-People' in the People's Republic of

China (Schoenhals 1994), on the word *guójiā* 國家 ('nation'), *yúlùn* 輿論 ('public opinion') in late Qing China (Judge 1994), and on the changing terminology to designate state administrators in Republican China, from 'lettered officials' (*wénguān* 文官) to 'cadres' (*gànbù* 干部) (Strauss 1995).

Besides these studies, different keywords come into usage in different periods, with social and political changes. For instance, among the numerous 'keywords' (关键词) mentioned by Chén (2008: 14–19) in the volume he edited on the Chinese lexicon in the Reform and Opening up period (post-1978 period), words and expressions like *xià hǎi* 下海 'plunging into business' and *Zhōngguó tèsè* 中国特色 '[with] Chinese characteristics' (for instance in the expression 'socialism with Chinese characteristics', but also in reference to different academic disciplines), and political slogans, such as *héxié shèhuì* 和谐社会 'harmonious society', would merit further investigation.

However, we have chosen to compare three words of the sociopolitical lexicon (the people, citizen, individual), which have been central, or become central, to various languages. This is not a book about 'universal' concepts shared by the Chinese and European languages. It is, ultimately, a book about European keywords, and the way they are conceptualized in Chinese. Each of the words studied has a long history in their European languages. The definition of these words is clearly a political question, but our interests are not confined to politics.

We have insisted that these keywords are crucial for the worldviews of linguistic communities. They cannot be simply limited to the political sphere. Our keywords are personal as much as they are political. Individual freedoms are personal freedoms, the freedoms of citizens within states. And the way a State limits those freedoms is crucial for all of us, as individual persons. For that reason, the questions that have stimulated us for the past half-dozen years are likely to continue animating debates in the global world in the decades to come. To many Western thinkers, communism may appear to be something from the past, but comparing Czech and Chinese forms of citizenship as they evolve in their traditions should help us to define what individuals are, what they can do, what they want to do.

The languages we have studied and the periods we have covered will take us on a long trip through what is uncharted territory for many of our readers. We cannot assure readers that this will make for an easy voyage, but we like to believe that following these migrating meanings will prove to be a memorable adventure. And although we can only introduce readers to the difficulties we have grappled with, we have come to one firm conclusion: comparing and contrasting migrating meanings does make sense.

METHODOLOGY

English

Throughout our study, we have aimed to grasp our four keywords – the people, individual, citizen, and Europe – as they figure in the minds and speech of the individuals in given linguistic communities. We have striven to reproduce an overall impression of the ways vastly different meanings emerge from usage, and how they tie in together in patterned forms of thinking and feeling. This involves understanding the contexts in which they are used, the compounds that they form, and the collocations they figure in. But it also means considering the metaphors and figurative expressions that they are grounded in. It involves trying to determine the complex conceptual clusters these concepts get tied up in when we speak about individuals and peoples. We wanted to try to grasp the way those clusters invite us to think along the lines of overarching or underlying logics. And we wanted to trace the way those logics change from group to group, and change over time. This inevitably takes us into personal discourse strategies and into ideology. The scope of our study also had to open up to take on board questions related to religion and national politics. Ultimately, in practice, citizenship is not only a national and cultural question; it often becomes a question of religious affiliation, and race. Crucial for both our sense of identity and our sense of belonging, the idea of citizenship inevitably draws us into the question of 'Us' and 'Them'. Discourses situate people and us with them, drawing us into debates about 'Them' in 'Our Space' and 'Us' in 'Their Space'.

Although we have included extensive discussion of French, German, Czech and Spanish, ultimately we have chosen to focus primarily upon English and Chinese. The most established online corpora often failed to cover some of the domains in which we believed our keywords were frequently being used. We reaped a poor harvest for 'citizen' in a selection of texts in which literary texts predominated. Our initial choice of texts, therefore, had to be revised. Corpus analysis also presented its own challenges. On the one hand, we found ourselves swamped with statistics, and on the other, we ran the risk of drawing misleading conclusions about the supposed absence of these keywords which are ultimately so central to debates on democratic ideals and the functioning of the modern State.

Although 'citizen' and 'individual' are commonly used words, they do not figure highly in literary texts, so the personal corpora that was originally used, the three million word MyEnglishCorpus and the three million word MyAmericanCorpus, proved insufficient for our purposes. For this reason, the corpus of texts was widened to include more American and more Scottish texts. French, German, and Czech dictionaries, corpora, texts, films, and online media were also widely consulted. But the most significant innovation regarding the studies of 'individual' and 'citizen' was the decision to create a personalized History of Ideas Corpus drawn from texts downloaded from http://www.gutenberg.org. This corpus included entire individual works from Hobbes, Locke, Hume, Smith, Mill, James, and Dewey. It proved revealing for two reasons: it was a good source of information for clarifying the way both 'citizen' and 'individual' are used, and it helped us to the degree to which each keyword is used or neglected. Reading and research based on the downloaded texts also enabled us to determine more clearly which synonyms and related terms our keywords are in competition with: 'individual', for example, can often be replaced by 'self', 'person', or 'personality' by certain authors. In the same way, 'inhabitant' and 'dweller' are often used in the place of 'citizen'.

All in all, we estimate our research into English meanings has covered between 1000 and 1200 usages for each of the English keywords considered. These usages were drawn from:

1. dictionaries, and online dictionaries such as the *Oxford English Dictionary* (*OED*) and *Merriam-Webster*;
2. encyclopaedias;
3. dictionaries of quotations;
4. political and philosophical texts, both online and written;
5. novels, poems, and songs;
6. films and online media;
7. established online corpora (British National Corpus (BNC), COCA, but also the Leipzig Wortschatz);
8. MyEnglishCorpus;
9. MyAmericanCorpus;
10. MyHistIdeasCorpus.

Chinese

As for the Chinese keywords analysed, great attention was paid to the etymology of each word and the trajectories they followed. Where possible, the first usages were retraced, with the help of an etymological dictionary (*Cíyuán* 辭源) and by consulting the Chinese Text Project (*Zhōngguó zhéxué shū diànzǐhuà jìhuà* 中国哲学书电子化计划, http://ctext.org/zh). Developed by Donald Sturgeon, this is 'the largest database of pre-modern Chinese texts in existence', bringing together 'over thirty thousand titles and more than five billion characters' (http://ctext.org/). We also consulted the 100 million-character corpus of Classical Chinese (*Gǔdài hànyǔ yǔliàokù* 古代汉语语料库) of the State Language Commission Corpora (国家语委语料库, http://www.cncorpus.org/ACindex.aspx). These corpora and this database – whose sources cover many centuries – not only provided us with details about the first usages of the Chinese word forms, but also allowed us to follow the way these forms persisted or were modified over time.

We made great use of the Modern Chinese Scientific Terminology database (hereafter abbreviated as MCST; 现代汉语学术用语研究, http://mcst.uni-hd.de/search/searchMCST_short.lasso), 'a repository of Chinese scientific, philosophical and political terms coined in the nineteenth and early twentieth century', created by M. Lackner, I. Amelung and J. Kurtz. This resource contains 'roughly … 136,000 words or expressions that were or may have been coined as equivalents of European and/or Japanese terms used in many different branches of knowledge' (http://mcst.uni-hd.de/helpMCST/wscdb.lasso).

It also became evident to us that it was crucial to take into account the related Japanese and European keywords, because of the 'massive (unidirectional) interactions between Chinese, Japanese and modern European languages' which took place after the latter half of the nineteenth century (Liu 1995: 17). Lackner et al. (2001a: 2) underscore this process, affirming that 'in less than one hundred years, the Chinese language absorbed, or indeed "devoured" the nomenclatures of the most diverse branches of Western knowledge, the formation of which had taken millennia – including several periods of cross-cultural translation – in the occident'. Hence, numerous sources of the late imperial and early republican period have been taken into account in order to identify and retrace the semantic stratifications, the facets, and the connotations of our selected keywords.

As for the usages of these words in recent decades, we compared the different editions of two reference dictionaries for Modern Chinese (*Xiàndài hànyǔ cídiǎn* 现代汉语词典 and *Xīnhuá cídiǎn* 新华词典). In addition to these, we consulted the ten billion character Beijing Language and Culture University Corpus Center (BCC) corpus of Modern Chinese (*Běi Yǔ hànyǔ yǔliàokù* 北语汉语语料库, http://bcc.blcu.edu.cn/hc); the Peking University Center for Chinese Linguistics (CCL) corpus of Modern Chinese (581 million characters), and the CCL Chinese–English parallel corpus (6 176 546 characters, 3 934 609 words), both compiled by the Institute of Linguistic of Peking University (*Běijīng dàxué hànyǔ yǔyánxué yánjiū zhōngxīn yǔliàokù* 北京大学汉语语言学研究中心, http://ccl.pku.edu.cn:8080/ccl_corpus/); and the twenty million character 'Corpus of Modern Chinese' (*Xiàndài hànyǔ yǔliàokù* 现代汉语语料库) of the State Language Commission Corpora (国家语委语料库).

For the more recent usages, we wanted to ensure we had a large spectrum of sources, so we made great use of the website of an influential Chinese newspaper, the *People's Daily* (*Rénmín wǎng* 人民网, http://www.people.com.cn), and a database of human and social sciences academic writings (http://www.nssd.org/). Blogs and other social media were also consulted, in order to gain a wide range of the usages of words as they appear in various kinds of discourse.

We also had recourse to native informants and to specialists of the Chinese language and culture in both Asia and Europe. We would like to thank in particular the specialists and PhD students who have read various chapters and have shared their useful comments and insights with us, notably:

- Professor Huáng Yáng 黄阳 from the School of Humanities of Southwest Jiaotong University in Chengdu (China);
- Professor Giorgio Casacchia from Naples Oriental University (Italy);
- Miss Yuán Zhōngjùn 袁中隽 PhD student (Institute of Oriental Languages and Civilizations, Paris, France);
- Mr Zhū Bīng 朱冰 (PhD student) from the Department of Applied Linguistics of Nagoya University (Japan).

We also would like to thank Professor Hilary Chappell from the School of Advanced Studies in the Social Sciences (Paris, France) for the useful comments on the sections of this work which were included in Gianninoto (2017).

Our native speakers from various Chinese regions enabled us to confirm or modify the working hypotheses that we set out with, and most of all to ensure we did not make rash or unfounded statements about the way Chinese-speakers perceive the various connotations evoked by each of the keywords discussed.

In fairness, it is important to stress that, for reasons of scope and space, only Mandarin Chinese has been taken into account. We focused on mainland China usages, as we soon came to feel that it would be impossible to enter into detailed discussions about the specific ways various vernaculars handle our keywords, and how the meanings they generate contrast with each other. These are fascinating questions which deserve further research, and we trust that scholars will extend our investigative project by researching particular regions, and by working together in comparative research projects. But all scholars and all books must recognize their limits.

Gathering together our impressions, by analysis and synthesis, we aim to generate an intuitive overall impression of our English and Chinese keywords, one that will supplement dictionaries of both a general and a subject-specific kind, such as dictionaries of sociology, politics, and philosophy. The examples quoted in this book are intended to give a deep and insightful understanding of the way our keywords are used.

OUR SOURCES

Our sources are too numerous to acknowledge, but credit should be given to Humboldt, Williams, Bartmiński, Abramowicz, Wierzbicka, and many others. Besides the above-mentioned authors, various key authors have helped us to understand the way keywords migrate to Chinese. Among these, we can include the essay on the different meanings of 国民 (國民) in Chinese and Japanese by Guō (2011) and Burtscher (2012); the essay by Guō (2013) on the notion of 'citizen'; and Huáng's (2004) study on the translation of 'individualism'. Because we are interested in following the trajectories of socio-political terms, the two volumes edited by Lackner et al. (2001b) and Lackner and Vittinghoff (2004) devoted to the lexical change following the introduction of new notions in late imperial China proved very useful. The essays on 'liberty', 'president', 'right', and 'power' are particularly enlightening in this respect.

The Chinese of the late imperial period were engaged in developing Chinese equivalents for Western-inspired notions (see Lackner et al.

2001b). But this was no straightforward process. The idea of 'transposition' does not work as a framework for explaining what was going on in this period. Concepts and categories were reconceptualized within the framework of long-standing traditions. The West may have provided 'food for thought', but the Chinese worldview absorbed and digested that food, transforming it into very different, culturally specific forms of thinking and feeling. Zarrow (2012: 95) points out the adaptive and accommodative character of this process in reference to the political lexicon. In his terms, 'the Chinese political vocabulary expanded dramatically not through mechanical translation but a process of adapting usage to conditions'. The context transformed the migrating meanings. Lydia Liu sees this more as a process of reinvention than appropriation. She explains this as a process of 'domestication of words, categories, discourses, and modes of representation'. For her, meanings 'are not so much "transformed" when they pass from the guest language to the host language as invented within the local environment of the latter' (Liu 1995: 26).

It will be clear then that each of the languages we have studied offered different resources for investigating broadly similar questions. In considering Europe, the citizen, the individual, and the people as keywords and as concepts, we made use of the appropriate resources to ask in what ways these keywords and related ideas were being used in the everyday language, journalism, politics, and academic literature. In English and Chinese, and in the other languages we have considered, we took into account dictionaries, corpora, and a wide variety of texts drawn from newspapers, online sources, and political speeches.

OBJECTIVES

We believe our objectives are coherent. In investigating these keywords, we hope to make a contribution to semantics, comparative linguistics, linguistic anthropology, ethnolinguistics, and translation studies. We have a single aim that can best be described in terms of seven related objectives:

1. To better understand the diverse facets of our keywords in English.
2. To understand the diversity of traditions that exist in English, and the multiple and complex ways keywords are used in different forms of English.

3. To compare the traditions in which our keywords were formed.
4. To compare the ways analogous keywords have evolved in a selection of other European languages.
5. To see how indigenous Chinese words were transformed or replaced when foreign borrowed words started to enter into usage.
6. To try to understand how borrowed words introduced new concepts into the Chinese worldview, and how the Chinese creatively modify and domesticate the concepts they adopt and integrate.
7. To understand the way the process of integration gives rise to transmutations, and the way transformed keywords open up new trajectories for the Chinese culture.

NOTES

1. Chinese text and James Legge's English translation quoted from the Chinese Text Project database: http://ctext.org/mengzi/jin-xin-ii/zh?en=on
2. Interview with Zhào Tīngyáng 赵汀阳, researcher at the Institute of Philosophy of the Chinese Academy of Social Sciences (中国社会科学院哲学研究所), by the journalist Mǎ Jìng 马静, *People's Daily Tribune* (人民论坛 2011), http://paper.people.com.cn/rmlt/html/2011-09/23/content_930576.htm
3. All translations in the text, therefore, are ours unless stated otherwise.
4. We use the *pīnyīn* transcription system, that is, the official transcription system adopted in the People's Republic of China. Whenever a different system is used in the quotation, the original transcription is maintained.
  The simplified forms of Chinese characters are used, except for quotations, the choice between traditional and simplified forms of the characters being determined by the source itself.

CHAPTER I

The People

民為貴，社稷次之，君為輕。

The people are the most important element in a nation;
the spirits of the land and grain are the next;
the sovereign is the lightest.[1]

Ce soir c'est à vous tous que je m'adresse. Vous tous ensemble, le peuple de France. ... Je défendrai la France, ses intérêts vitaux, son image, son message, j'en prends l'engagement devant vous, je défendrai l'Europe, la communauté de destins que se sont donnée les peuples de notre continent. C'est notre civilisation qui est en jeu, notre manière de vivre, d'être libre, de porter nos valeurs, nos entreprises communes et nos espoirs. (Emanuel Macron on Election Night, http://www.parismatch.com/Actu/Politique/Le-premier-discours-d-Emmanuel-Macron-president-de-la-Republique-1250729)

Tonight, it is you, that I address, all of you together as one, the people of France. ... I will defend France and its vital interests, its image and its message; this oath, I hereby take before you: I will defend Europe, the community of fates that the peoples of our continent have taken upon themselves. It is our civilization that is at stake, our way of living, to be free, to hold up our values, our shared undertakings and our hopes.

Smile at us, pay us, pass us; but do not quite forget.
For we are the people of England, that never have spoken yet.
(Chesterton: 'The Secret People', *Oxford Dictionary of Quotations*: 199)

ENGLISH IDEALS OF THE PEOPLE

The question of the people is always political. Brexit can be considered an opportunity or a catastrophe, but it was certainly a question about how the English people are governed and who governs them. Rejection, revolt, and the rights of the people were at the heart of the debates framed by Farage's UK Independence Party (UKIP). The Scottish people voted to remain within Europe. The English people voted to force Britain as a whole to break away. How are we to understand the way this keyword, the people, resonates within the English imagination? How are we to understand the way it functions within the patterning of the language? And how are we to contrast it with alternative conceptions of the people in other European traditions? In the following sections of this chapter, we shall take into consideration dictionary definitions, corpora findings, literature, quotations, and newspaper articles, and popular myths, in order to suggest tentative answers to these complex questions.

Brexit may not seem to many critics much of a 'happy ending', but mythology starts with a happy beginning, at least. Several folk traditions celebrate 'the English people'. Robin Hood protects the people against corrupt governance of the evil King John. And if that myth has stood the test of time, it is because the story flatters various political sensibilities. For the free-thinkers, anarchists, and socialists, Robin can be seen as a proto-communist, redistributing wealth and resisting monarchy and capital accumulation, an enemy of taxation and the banks. But Robin Hood also reassures monarchists that there are good kings and bad kings, false monarchs and real rulers who love, and are beloved by, their people. The 'true monarch', in this fairy tale, Richard the Lionheart, loves his people. His return is supposed to re-establish the natural order, joined in the secure bond between the regent and the ruled. The king is the loving and beloved monarch of his loyal people. The people's love of themselves, their love of the land, and their love of their monarch fuse in this fairy tale. And indeed, throughout literature and popular mythology, the 'staunch yeoman' who incarnates the loyal, stoic, but freedom-loving Englishman, resolute in defending his strip of land against invaders, is regularly celebrated as an English ideal.

This is a resilient tradition that the Romantic poets were to reawaken. In his 'The Lay of the Last Minstrel', Sir Walter Scott regularly links 'bold' to 'free' when celebrating the quintessential English qualities of the yeoman (Scott 1845: 138, 166, 167 for example). And Lord Byron reactivates the idea of 'the staunch yeoman' in *Childe Harold* (Byron: 2012: 33). Curiously, however, Scott was not English. As his name suggests, Scott was a Scot. And Byron was half-Scottish. Nevertheless, they were both all too conscious of the effect this keyword, the people, would have in reawakening deep sentiments in the English psyche.

Nostalgia and romanticism continues to fuel the popular imagination today. When Nigel Farage railed against enslavement to Eurocrats and foreign rules, he was making the case that he was the true champion of 'the English', and 'the English people'. On both the left and the right in the French 2017 elections, similar arguments were being made by Le Pen, the leader of the Front National, and Mélenchon, with his movement for a France that would not be 'put down' or 'bridled' ('*Une France insoumise*'). Two things are striking about these populist movements. Firstly, the power such arguments have to trigger reactions and generate support on the one hand, among the people. And secondly, the seeming blindness of the mainstream political parties to this power. Both British and French politicians seemed at first deaf to claims that the people must be taken into account, and then, as a wave of populism rose up, they appeared ill-equipped for debates with the people. The political elites of France were taken by storm as this mounting populism swept aside the two major political parties in the French elections in May 2017. And Brexit came as a shock to the Tory government and the Home Counties that had counted on reason keeping Britain in Europe.

How are we to understand this? If we are to begin to understand the way the people works within the English worldview, we must take into account not only the myths and conceptions of the people, but also the diverse ways the people are marginalized and forgotten by the political elites. The populism of Farage, Le Pen, and Mélenchon are distasteful to the political elites of Britain and France, and this distaste has a long tradition, as we shall see. Populism and pandering to the people goes against the grain of the established English parties on both the left and the right. But, arguably, it was this very lack of taste, and the refusal to take popular sentiment seriously that led to Brexit, on one side of the Channel, and the eradication of the right-wing parties and *les socialistes* in France's 2017 elections, on the other. This reveals the true complexity of our questions. When we try to understand a keyword like 'the people', we clearly need to understand what Raymond Williams (1985) called those 'structures of feeling' that involve myths, ideas, ideals, and sentiments.

WHAT 'THE PEOPLE' MEANS TO US

The meanings of keywords are anything but neutral. How could they be neutral? If they are woven into our 'structures of feeling', if they involve our relationships with ideas, myths, ideals, and sentiments, surely it would be absurd to suppose that keywords could be reduced to objective realities that mean the same thing for everyone. Meanings are generated within shared cultural mindsets; they circulate in society as individuals take stances in discussions and express their own personal worldviews and their changing perspectives.

Consequently, what people feel about 'the people' tells us something about those people, their times, their social circumstances and about the way their languages, their cultures, and their traditions evolve together. The associations they evoke for other people when they use 'the people', and the intentional way they harness those associations when they speak about them tells us a lot about how they feel others should feel about 'the people'. And, crucially, it tells us who is supposed to belong to 'them', in their opinion.

'People' is a commonplace everyday word. But as we shall see, 'simple words' invariably prove anything but 'simple'. And this will become palpably obvious as we explore the different ways 'the people' are celebrated, extolled, idealized, flattered, despised, ignored, or forgotten. Three overriding attitudes to 'the people' can be posited: idealized, despised, or forgotten. We contend that the place of the people in cultural mindsets can be analysed in terms of the associations, the conceptual clusters, and the dynamic oppositions that organize the way different cultures at different times represent 'the people' or the way they avoid evoking 'the people' as a keyword.

In our semantic approach to the question, we have investigated corpora and texts in order to try to reveal the way our complex ideas and feelings, meanings, and associations related to the people can be uncovered. And we hope to demonstrate the way associations and underlying logics enable arguments to be made to represent the people as an ideal or a danger. We have tried to understand the ways meanings, associations, myths, metaphors, and arguments are used in discursive strategies in order to maintain and promote certain relationships with 'the people'.

As linguists, we believe that this is always a question that involves language, culture, and individuals. Ideologies and political parties may promote certain structures of feeling. They may frame the people and individuals within their own cultural mindset, but it is, ultimately, always individuals who position themselves in debates and discussions. This means we refuse a deterministic conception of language and meaning. Meanings are not forced upon us. Individuals negotiate meanings. And for that reason, we hope to identify and outline the scope individuals have for opposing and transforming existing representations of 'the people' and various relationships that are taken up with 'them'.

We are not slaves to tradition, and we can resist it. Nonetheless, when we question overarching ideologies and implicit attitudes, we are resisting conventions and constraints. And we learn the concepts with which we think, as we are socialized into language, society, and culture. This is what it means to start getting to grips with our shared linguistic worldview. As we consider in the way 'the people' is represented over the following pages, we will be investigating both:

- culture-specific paradigms; and
- conceptual patterns that transcend the boundaries of specific linguistic communities.

As we shall see, Chinese, French, English, and American attitudes and perspectives tend to opt for a limited number of attitudes. From our research, we can posit six fundamental conceptions of the people. The people is understood to be:

1. society as a whole, an identified group, whose individuals are subject to rights and responsibilities according to state legislation;
2. a political force;
3. an ideal, an actor in society and in history;
4. the others, the masses, an object of fear and contempt;
5. a group that is marginalized or ignored;
6. a word that loses meaning and begins to fade away in the language system.

What trends will assert themselves in the various languages we have studied? What attitudes will predominate? Let us return to the world language: English. English opens up the world to around 400 million speakers. And to a little under one billion speakers, it opens up a second world as those speakers learn English as their second language. What attitudes and perspectives does English allow in the various forms of English in use? And what modes of thinking and feeling about 'the people' is English promoting as it daily influences the various cultures around the globe?

DICTIONARY DEFINITIONS

As Samuel Johnson argued, the best dictionary is imperfect, but the worst is better than none. And although we will need to move beyond dictionaries to reach deep into discourse and literature to begin to understand the roles 'the people' plays in the English imagination, dictionaries remain a good starting point. So what can they tell us about how we think and feel about the people?

Merriam-Webster

America is in many ways a country that celebrates the democratic will, in its constitution and in its political rhetoric, but if we consult the *Merriam-Webster* online dictionary (http://www.merriam-webster.com), we find a rather perplexing definition. *Merriam-Webster* provides a rather unflattering definition of the people, a negative definition: the people are those excluded from power and privileges:

> the ordinary people in a country who do not have special power or privileges <She is well-liked as a senator because she listens to *the people.*> <*the* common *people*>. (*Merriam-Webster*)

The people *is* represented here, and this is fundamental. In the example given in the entry, the Senator is praised for listening to the people. But, crucially, she is not praised for being part of the people. She can stand next to them, but not with them. The people, furthermore, are powerless, and unprivileged in this representation. This is only one conception. *Merriam-Webster* also reminds us that the people is: 'used to refer to the government of the U.S. or of a particular state in the name of a legal case <*The People* vs. John Doe>'. This partly explains why 'the people' appears so much more frequently in official texts in American English than in English ones, and is especially frequent in the language of legal cases.

OED

The *OED* (http://www.oed.com) mirrors *Merriam-Webster* in referencing the legal use that applies in Irish as well as US law. Similarly, the *OED* retains a negative definition of the people:

Those without special rank or position in society; the mass of the community as distinguished from the nobility or the ruling classes; the populace.

A negative image of the people is asserting itself in both American and English dictionaries, it would seem. Once more, however, it would be unfair to reduce the people to this single story of a powerless populace. Traces of other narratives are clear in the examples quoted by the *OED*. The people as a concept, used to refer to a united body, a folk, and a nation, is clearly established in the *OED*. Indeed, examples can be found going back as far as the middle of the fourteenth century:

ffor þe peoples speche. (1325)

So hadde Vortiger the hertys of the peple, and he knewe well that thei heilde hym worthy and wise. (1500)

The People in England are universally discontented with the daily new Taxes imposed on them. (1650)

I speak to the people as one of the people. (1771)

He caught the ear of the people by using the people's own speach. (1854)

These examples show that the concept is clearly in use and that, in some respects, it has undergone very little change over 800 years. The following example quoted by the *OED* from *The Guardian* in 2000 works very much in the same way as the examples above:

King George was famously out of tune with the mood of the people.

It is clear enough that King George is being criticized here. Apparently, the leaders of the country and its regents are supposed to be in tune with the people. But it is, nonetheless, worth noting that the Nobility and certainly not the Monarchy should not *be* part of the people. Here we are dealing with the same dynamic opposition that is set up with the American Senator above. As members of 'the ruling classes', monarchs and senators should both ideally remain separate from the people, but in contact with them.

It would be difficult and perhaps pointless to give a representative sample of the great number examples provided by English dictionaries, but in general, the Oxford Dictionary online resources (https://en.oxforddictionaries.com/definition/people) coincides by and large with the *OED*'s extended definition. When people are considered to be 'of the people', they are considered to be of 'the common people', and the common people are not the people in general, a definition which refers to citizens or nationals; the common people are negatively defined as being 'without rank or position' (https://en.oxforddictionaries.com/definition/people)

Taken as a whole, what impression do we form the *OED* examples consulted? All in all, the impression is perplexing. Firstly, representations of the 'the people' are not frequent, they form part of a marginal use of the concept of 'people' in general, and the general often seems to degenerate into 'the common' people. Secondly, when the people is taken into account in the examples quoted, it is not a man or woman of the people who represents the people and its interests, it is a ruler condescending to enter into contact with the people. The ruler interacts with a separate body of people to which he or she, by definition, does not belong.

In this conception, we evaluate and judge the degree to which the ruler can listen to and respond to this alien body. In the example above, King George is blamed for not having a place in his heart for the people. He should be able to descend to his people; his power depends on this ritualized bonding. In contrast, to this we have the example above, dating from 1500, concerning another regent who is being extolled for being able to gain the hearts of his people: 'So hadde Vortiger the hertys of the peple' (*OED*). Two things are crucial for our studies, however. Both examples consolidate the ideology of monarchy by promoting the ideal of a monarch capable of responding to and winning the hearts of his people, a people that belongs to the monarch. Judging from the *OED*'s examples, Vortiger appears to be the exception rather than the rule.

Shakespeare appears to be more representative of the English imagination, when he portrays a people easily hoodwinked and misled by populist demagogues and self-interested agents hostile to legitimate power. This is the sentiment found in the quote from his work cited by the *OED*:

Our People, and our Peeres, are both mis-led. (1616, Shakespeare *Henry VI, Pt. 3* (1623) III, iii, 35)

The rich resources of the *OED* should not be reduced to caricature. Examples in defence of the people can be found. And yet, if we consider these examples, even they tell a perplexing tale:

> He also accused the Government of not trusting the people, of shrinking from an appeal to the people. (1884, *Spectator*)
>
> The Euro-zealots appear unable to cope with the voice of the people or deal with democratic decisions. (1992, *Daily Express*)
>
> The need to take people's views and experience into account was hammered home in 1975. (1993, *Canadian Geographic*)

In these examples, the media in both the late nineteenth and the late twentieth centuries are represented here as a counter-balance for a government in Britain or in Europe that is hostile to the interests of the people. And the example that quotes the need to insist on taking the views and experience of the people into account, though quoted by an English dictionary, is drawn from a Canadian source, as if few such examples were to be found in English sources.

Despite occasional celebrations of the people, the people is invariably identified in implicitly negative terms in the entries in the *OED*. The people must be dealt with. And this sets up an 'Us' and 'Them' dynamic in which authority does not identify with 'the people'. 'We' must enter into contact with 'them' and negotiate with 'them'. At times, it is necessary to negotiate with 'them' on their terms. This is clear in the 1771 example above referring to the importance of being able to speak the language of the people. But using the same language does not imply adopting the same worldview. When we speak of the people, the perspective is clearly not that of the people; 'we' are not part of the people in these examples.

Neither is the perspective particularly sympathetic on the whole. There is little trace of a dialogue with the people in the *OED* examples. We are clearly dealing with the 'inclusive we' of the ruling classes, speaking in their language to their own class. The people are neither speaking, nor being spoken to. 'We' are never confused with the people. The inclusive 'we' is, of course, profoundly and irrevocably exclusive. Even the idea of taking the people into account is absent in the majority of these examples.

Is this specific to monarchic traditions? Certainly, there is a spatial dimension to this perspective which is specific to monarchies and class-based societies and the hierarchies they espouse and promote. The 'upper class' remains 'above', looking down. Although it is at times forced to descend among the people, the ruling class stages this symbolic descent in performed rituals. Architecture has its role to play in physically manifesting the spatial logic of this dichotomy. Addresses from balconies are traditional modes of address. But the stairways in palaces and government buildings enact a symbolic meeting between the two classes. And this is a two-way process. Just as the rulers enact their spatial descent, those belonging to the people are invited to mount the stairways to the palaces of power. The people are lifted up and invited in. But does this involve inclusion? Or does it not rather reaffirm exclusion and force 'subjects' to 'subject themselves' to the power structure in place, by accepting the 'invitation'?

The ideology of the true king who wins the hearts of his people is clearly a powerful narrative that runs from the tales of the absent Richard the Lionheart to King George. Royalty may fail the people, but even in the darkest days there remains the fantasy of a day of justice that will be reinstated when the true ruler returns to put things right for the people, as their legitimate sovereign. This conception reinforces both the ideal (above) and the subjects (below). The spatial logic of this relationship does not appear particularly conducive to defending the people as an ideal. And it could be argued that the examples furnished by the *OED* do not reflect well upon the health of British democratic tradition. But do these dictionary definitions really give a fair impression of the English-speakers' worldview? To what degree is everyday English capable of generating a democratic rhetoric of the people for the people? To answer this question, we clearly have to carry out further research. And corpora and texts will be used to help us form a more subtle and accurate idea of how 'the people' functions within the English worldview and within the patterning of the English language.

CORPORA FINDINGS

BNC

From the very outset, speaking about 'the English people' turns out to involve a political attitude in the most famous English corpus, the 100 million word British National Corpus that came out in the early 1990s. In a great many of the examples the BNC lists, to speak about the English, is to speak about the Empire, and to assume that the English belong to that ascendant culture that towers above the other nations of the British Isles. The English are, besides, widely recognized throughout the nineteenth and twentieth centuries as the culture that gained control over North America, Australia, and India. For more than a century, the English controlled the oceans around the world. Britannia ruled the waves. This is the English people upon whose colonies the sun never sets.

It would certainly seem reasonable, therefore, to imagine that the English people and their status would be reflected in their own language as they are reflected with such brilliance in the literature of peoples around the world. The famous French novelist, Jules Verne (1828–1905), wrote his adventure novels about world explorers and adventurers, but when, in 1874, he chose the hero he wanted to send around the world in eighty days, he chose Phileas Fogg, an Englishman. Why? No doubt because he required a man of superb calm, resourcefulness, dignity, and courage: an Englishman in short, the kind of man who could build an empire.

To the authors of this book, it seemed judicious to begin our study by looking for examples of 'the people' in the BNC's examples drawn primarily from English literature, politics, and the media. We encountered one sizable problem from the very beginning, however. It proved very difficult to get searches to distinguish between 'the people' as a concept, a unified group, identified with the nation, on the one hand, and people in general. Searches kept providing examples such as 'the people standing there', 'the people who want', 'the people concerned'. Consequently, many of the first hundred examples generated from the 10 673 examples listed in the BNC proved unusable for the purposes of our study. We were forced to reject examples such as 'the people at the launch', 'the people who matter', 'the people within the group', 'the people who come regularly', 'health care for the people in the area', and 'the people around them', 'the people who are on low income', and 'the people behind them are white, middle-aged career criminals'.

We persisted in searching for examples of the people as a unified social body, and extended our search to 300 examples. This generated only a limited number of examples, however. Those such as the following, we considered as half-way-house examples:

make an impact on **the people of Harlow**. (Emphasis added)

The Park is an important recreational resource for both **the people of Edinburgh** and visitors to the city. (Emphasis added)

34 MIGRATING MEANINGS

We were once more forced to admit, however, that proper examples of 'the people' were scarce. In fact, the following quotes are not a sample of those found. They form the sum total of the examples found in the 300 examples selected. They have been arranged into groups in terms of claims to defend the people and claims to represent their interests.

Defending the interests of the people:

> **The people want** something to believe in. (*The Daily Mirror*; emphasis added)

> [If] Patten lies to the people of Hong Kong as much as he **lied to the people** of Britain, then God help them when the Chinese take over. (*The Daily Mirror*; emphasis added)

> Indeed, provided you can keep the bodyguards and the cars, it doesn't really matter whether you're in power or out of it. You just write WORLD LEADER in your passport, charge a fortune to **expound views rejected by your people,** and **let the world, and the people, go to hell**. (*The Daily Mirror*; emphasis added))

> As long as an MP [Member of Parliament] declares he or she is on the take these payments somehow are deemed acceptable. So ... the chairman of the Home Affairs Committee can be on the payroll of a private security firm without anyone thinking there might be the tiniest conflict. I remain astonished that this state of affairs is allowed to exist. MPs are elected **to represent the people, not companies and organisations who pay them**. And if MPs on the take are not parroting the opinions of these companies what can we suppose the money they receive is for? (*The Daily Mirror*; emphasis added)

> The Prime Minister's job is **to do what the people of his country want**, not what the leaders of other countries want. (Emphasis added)

> **the people want to know**. (Political meeting; emphasis added)

> **to expend money** on a project over, that is going to last thirty forty years, **and expect the people today to pay for it**. Erm,

when their paying for it, not necessarily with money, but in some cases with their lives, with misery. ... **The people** of this county, were suffering from it, through crying, because of the lack of crime prevention work being done. (Lincolnshire County Council: board meeting; emphasis added)

As I said before on Thursday, that the idea is that **the people outside there, the public, are the ones that are important.** When it comes to an-- announce the fact that we're gon na have er er council elections. (Labour Club meeting; emphasis added)

the people put their trust in the Tories [pause] and I don't think they'll ever do it again. (Leicestershire County Council: council chambers; emphasis added)

You can trust us to protect the people:

we are being **diligent in safeguarding the environment of ... and the quality of life of the people,** and we are not merely interested in financial gain. The fact remains, if this ... development is allowed, it will have an irreversible detrimental effect on the fiscal environment of the town centre and **the amenities of the people for generations to come.** (Town council meeting; emphasis added)

I intend, during my year of office, to get out and meet the people. In particular, I would like to try to visit as many schools as possible. (Bradford Metropolitan Council meeting; emphasis added)

the gentleman who's taping the meeting would like a sort of signature for **the people**'s consent to tape it. (University of York Student Union Entertainments Committee meeting; emphasis added)

The people are learning:

now at least **the people** are becoming more aware ... of the environment. (Lincolnshire: board meeting; emphasis added)

The people are elsewhere:

> The living is cheap and **the people are friendly**, with a large contingent of British who have chosen to make a permanent home here. (Advert for Lanzarote, in a travel magazine, for Club 18–30; emphasis added)

> It's called The Road to Damascus, Chiros and Conversion [pause] and it's a document signed by Christians from all sorts of countries … And it's more than that, mainly because **the people in Africa, and Asia and Latin America particularly, … are being sacrificed to the idol**. (Emphasis added)

These examples contrast somewhat with the sombre picture portrayed by our dictionary definitions. In many of these examples, the people is indeed clearly defined as a homogenous whole that should be served by government. The people have rights. They pay taxes and should by rights be able to expect services to be provided for them, now and in generations to come. These examples should be borne in mind as we progress in our study. Nonetheless, it must be conceded that they are few in number, and even in those they fail to coincide with the prototypical meaning of the people as a unified nation. Often, we are dealing with town councillors referring to their constituents. The university student refers to the public, but more to the public in the audience than the public as a whole. Moreover, the peoples of other countries were referred to almost as much as the British or the English people.

On the whole, the context remains ominous. Many of the examples referring to the people do not so much affirm 'the people' as an unquestionable democratic ideal: they reveal a sentiment that 'the people' are being short-changed, not served. The examples demanding rights and respect for the people came largely from local meetings or from the popular press. The press clearly still has a role to play in democracies. Indeed, the fact that one of the main popular tabloids is still called the *Sunday People*, reminds us of the importance of the free press in the British tradition. With a readership of half a million (http://www.newsworks.org.uk/Sunday-People), this and other newspapers act as a pressure group that questions government action, the policies of the European Union, and manipulation by big business.

The 'people of Europe' was found in one interesting example. Going against the tabloids' habits of disparaging and denigrating

Europe, one speaker lamented that lobbies in Britain were seeking to get round European measures designed to protect the people of the Member States. The speaker argued against the manipulative strategies of such lobbies with energy and conviction at a Lincolnshire board meeting:

> I mean, it disappoints me that we are the country in Europe that that's always dragged, kicking and screaming to the table, to discuss things like this, which are **the benefit of the majority of the people in the in the European Community**. It's just those few, committed capitalists that see profits as the only, the only motive to be on this earth, that seem to ... have the influence in this in this country, and and like er, I'm I'm hoping that this ... British Government objection to the Court of Justice does fail ... (Emphasis added)

Elsewhere, when the people were spoken about as a whole, the examples referred to specific countries. When a clinic was opened in a troubled area between Katesbridge and Castlewellan, in Northern Ireland, for instance, one spokesman, Mr Sherwani, affirmed: 'I realise I'm taking a chance, but **I believe the people of Northern Ireland are now ready for this**' (emphasis added). This was printed in *The Belfast Telegraph*, and recorded by the BNC.

Some of these examples may seem somewhat outdated. The BNC's examples remind us of the 1980s, because the corpus resources are drawn from texts collected up to the early 1990s. This resource does provide us with a fairly accurate overall impression of the way lexemes are used in general over a long period of time. But we obviously require more recent examples.

The most revealing thing was that, as far as 'the people' is concerned, our study provided us with a rather small catch. And those we did find, provided little evidence that the people was considered to be an active force in political life. The people as a concept does not seem to be particularly dynamic in the English worldview, judging from these examples.

The evidence provided by a Google Books Ngram search tended to confirm this conclusion. Despite a peak in usage of the phrase 'the people wants' in the 1870s, the 1890s, and the 1940s, the phrase proved scarce, and rarely exceeded 0.000000200 per cent in word frequency (https://books.google.com/ngrams/graph).

Similarly, when we tried to find examples of 'the people wants' in the BNC, we were perplexed to find only nineteen examples in this 100 million word corpus. And even those examples we did find gave a rather sombre picture of the way 'the people' is represented. Often 'the people' and their 'wants' were spoken about, but the people rarely took the floor or were given a voice. Indeed, at times the desires of the people were openly disparaged, as in the following example:

> **if the people want to wallow in sin**, they should be permitted to do so. (Bruce 1990, cited in *OED*; emphasis added)

In general, the desires and rights of the people were often either portrayed as arbitrary, and of little importance, or they remained unknown or uncertain. The following examples are therefore representative:

> I've told my promoter Dan Duva that **I want to fight all those contenders that the people want me to fight**. (BNC; emphasis added)

> Because nobody is proud of them, the whole principle is undermined -- even lefties are now saying **the people want to buy their own homes? Do they?** Most of the council estate dwellers I meet don't. (BNC; emphasis added)

These examples do not reflect Abraham Lincoln's ideal of democracy as the rule of the people by the people for the people. The case should not be overstated. Individuals did stand up for the people in the BNC examples. The following one can be considered a model counter-example:

> This is **what the people want** and money must not interfere [pause] with their wishes. (Leicestershire County Council: debate; emphasis added)

One writer even went as far to defend the law as the law of the people, and argued that the legal system would be nothing if it did not uphold the welfare of the people:

> A self-consciously strict conventionalist judge would lose interest in legislation and precedent at just the point when it became clear that the explicit extension of these supposed conventions had run

out. He would then acknowledge that there was no law, and he would have no further concern for consistency with the past; he would proceed to make new law by asking what law the present legislature would make or **what the people want or what would be in the community's best interests for the future.** (Ronald Dowkin, 1986, quoted by BNC; emphasis added)

But as in the case of certain examples we have already seen, often the voices raised in support of the people were the voices of those frustrated by governments that did not listen to the people. The following example is representative of this kind of position:

The Government know what the people want. They are choosing to ignore it. (Bradford Metropolitan Council: meeting; emphasis added)

These are strong words, words uttered in resentment in the face of contempt expressed for the people. All in all, after filtering out all of the inappropriate examples, we were left with only a handful of examples concerning the people. These were taken mainly from the less reliable press and from local council meetings or other political meetings.

When it came to speaking about the people as a whole, it was invariably not the 'the English people' who were referred to. The Lanzarote ad above, for example, generalizes about the Spanish population of the town in much the same way as our 'half-way-house examples' above refer to the people of Harlow and the people of Edinburgh. And to speak of 'the people of' is evidently not the same as speaking about representation 'by the people for the people'.

The crushing majority of the examples of 'the people' consulted referred not to 'the people as a whole' but to individual groups: 'the people in this room', 'the people who benefit from', 'the people in power'. When hospital ambulance drivers spoke of 'going out to the people', they evoked budget cuts that made it impossible for them to serve the community. In English, it would seem that when we speak of the people, we are not designating an indivisible category that we belong to, we are referring to 'the people who', 'the people in', 'the people at', 'the people of', and 'the people from'.

Linguistic research and works that study keywords and cultural concepts should clearly define the scope of their surveys, and should avoid hastily drawing conclusions or making sweeping statements about cultures based solely on lexical studies. It would, for example, be unfair to assume that the English are 'undemocratic' or 'anti-democratic' simply because 'the people' appears to be a stunted concept in the English worldview. In English, democratic discourse often employs alternative terms for the people; 'the public' and 'the community', for example, are widely used.

If we consult the first twelve collocations for 'the community' found in the BNC, we do indeed find 'care', 'institutions', 'within', 'throughout', 'benefit', and 'reform'. All of these indicate engagement with people. This is somewhat reassuring. And the BNC provides 5014 examples of 'the English'. But judging from the examples consulted and from the list of collocations for 'the English', once we have filtered out 'the English press', 'the English King', 'the English lads', 'the English countryside' and 'the English language', there remains little left of the English people as the agent of their democratic destiny. For this reason, the following example drawn from the BNC stands out as an ominous question of grave political importance:

> Is democracy a means of bringing about that the people shall consent to what the government proposes to do, or that the government shall do **what the people want?** (BNC; emphasis added)

COCA

The COCA, the American Corpus of Colloquial American English, provides a much more up-to-date corpus than the BNC. With 450 million words, it is also more than four times the size of the BNC. However, the sources of the COCA differ in one important respect to the BNC. It relies heavily on contemporary media, and as a result it tends to follow fashionable trends, political scandals, and hot political debates of transitory importance. At times, this can lead it to misrepresent the way words are used in general in spoken and written American English. In this respect, in the long term, the BNC can be considered a more reliable tool for reflecting British English than the COCA for American English. Both corpora nonetheless give wonderful insights into the various usages that dominate for any given concept. How does 'the people' compare in the two corpora then?

If we compare and contrast the collocates that are generated by the BNC and the COCA we are left somewhat perplexed. The English collocates are difficult to understand. 'People' collocates first and foremost with 'people' in British English. And in order of importance, few of the first twelve collocates appear to relate to politics: people, what, know, wallow, Alistair, contenders, monarchy, sin, choosing, hearing, fight, and buy. When the collocates do relate to politics, they invoke royalty, tradition, morality, choice, conflict, and consumption.

The American collocates are more blatantly political. In order of importance, the first thirteen collocates were: people, what, hear, regime, fall, topple, peace, vote, whatever, squarely, dealt, Perot, rid. Listening to the people is an American value, judging from these collocates. But there is also evidence of an ominous link between the people, war, and regime change. Judging from these collocates the American people would seem to see itself as being on the side of other peoples in other countries. These are the regimes that are being 'toppled'. And whose people are being 'liberated' in the COCA's examples? Certainly not Americans. In these collocations, the violence is palpable. And even 'rid' and 'peace' leave us feeling uneasy.

Nonetheless, throughout the American examples 'the people' seems to function as a far more democratic concept than its English equivalent. Even given the difference in size, with more than four times the volume, the COCA nonetheless furnished us with more than thirteen times the number of examples of 'the people want' (261 examples in total). These examples were read in their entirety for our study. What can we conclude? The various examples could be assorted into a series of different arguments and discourse strategies.

Democratic rhetoric

The democratic usage dominated. Various parties affirmed that politicians must serve the people, and denounced them when they failed to do so. Journalists joined in on this, and often led the way. Detailed discussion focused upon what the people wanted as a nation and as a specific community. Their needs were listed and their expectations were clarified. In this respect, the following examples are fairly representative of the way 'the people' is used in American English.

> you need to have people work with the President on a constructive basis recognizing that **the people want** this done. (ABC, 2013; emphasis added)

> Ultimately, **the people want** to feel that the person they elect as president particularly is ready to be commander in chief and

protect their security because they know that they can't do it themselves. The mayor can't do it. The governor can't do it. It has got to be the president. (Fox News, 2012; emphasis added)

But, a new NBC Wall Street Journal poll finds that is not what the American[s] want. Only 38 percent support the president's unilateral move on immigration. Greg, do you think that when they say that this is what **the people want**, but [*sic*] that's really what **the people want**. (Fox, 2014; emphasis added)

I think it's Ross' responsibility to fight and stay in office. He was elected by the people, and if **the people want** to remove him, that's their call. (San Francisco Chronicle, 2012; emphasis added)

Peoples throughout the world demand democracy

In the US, there is a strongly held belief that it can play the world's sheriff and sort out the troubles of other nations. This deeply held conviction generated the following arguments:

And on Sunday, scores of residents armed with machine guns and rifles joined in a chant that has become the slogan of pro-democracy uprisings in Tunisia, Egypt, Bahrain, Yemen and across the Arab world: '**The people want** to bring down the regime!' (*The New York Times*, 2011; emphasis added)

An amateur video posted online by activists [in Syria] showed at least two of the observers, including the team's head, Col. Ahmed Himiche, standing outside a U.N. vehicle as dozens chanted, 'Death is better than humiliation!' and '**The people want** to topple the regime!' (Associated Press, 2012; emphasis added)

Hundreds surrounded the headquarters of the pro-regime Palestinian party. Was the regime trying to deflect attention from its own atrocities by trotting these young men off to get killed by Israeli border police? Some threw rocks. A 14-year-old boy was shot dead from the building. The people inside fled, shooting in the air as they left. The crowd stormed the headquarters and lit it on fire. They chanted, '**The people want** the end of corruption' and 'God is great.' (Shane Bauer, *Mother Jones*, 2014; emphasis added)

At times when the US military was engaged in the interventions, it expressed disappointment that their efforts were not appreciated or reciprocated:

> '**The people want law and order but they don't want to get involved in it**,' says Capt. James Dykes, a company commander with the 3rd Infantry Division who regularly leads patrols across a wide swath of central Baghdad. (*Christian Science Monitor*, 2003; emphasis added)

However, when the US was not in favour of military intervention, denounced warfare, or expressed the wish to see an end to hostilities, it once more framed these various attitudes by siding once more with the people of the foreign state, as in the following example.

> 'We don't want a new intifada. **The people want peace**,' says Ayman Mondaher, a financial manager. (*Christian Science Monitor*, 2011; emphasis added)

Questioning democracy: when the politics can't or doesn't provide what the people want

What 'the people' wants was not discussed in naïve terms in the COCA examples. Often, the difficulties of maintaining democracy were taken into account, as in the following examples in which politicians proved reluctant or quite simply incapable of providing what the people wanted:

> George Washington behaved like he was walking into a presidential penitentiary. Presidents are expected to perform miracles but lack the instruments to achieve them. Harry Truman wrote in his diary about the 'great white jail' where the disconnect between what **the people want** and what the Constitution allows a president to deliver was so strong it caused the ghosts of his predecessors to roam the halls: 'The tortured souls who were and are misrepresented in history are the ones who come back.' (John Dickerson, *Pittsburgh Post-Gazette*, 2014; emphasis added)

> 'Basically, this is the big guys telling the little guys what is going to happen – big guys from the city and oil companies,' said resident Dick Warkentin, a homebuilder living next to where wells would

be drilled. 'They don't do what **the people want**. They do what they want because they all have their fingers in it.' (*Denver Post*, 2013; emphasis added)

If you look, federal and state government seems to be paralyzed and they work at a policy level. Cities, who are all having economic problems, have to do things better and cities are where mayors work day in and day out and they know what works, what **the people want**. And so we're trying to find out what's the best ideas. Each mayor can have a different idea that may be transferable to another city. And we're all in this together. (*CBS This Morning*, 2012; emphasis added)

The people want you to speak from your heart and soul. Tell us where you want us to go. Tell us what you expect from Congress. Tell us what's on your mind. That never happened. (On the President's failure to take a position when the financial sector defaulted, ABC News, 2011; emphasis added)

Speaking in the name of the people: appropriating 'the people'

The demagogical strategy of using the people to justify advancing your own ideas or policies proved to be a common strategy in US politics, and above all in the media. Fox News was not alone in this, but it did provide various examples, such as the following one:

We want conservatives, conservatives that are going to do what **the people want** them to do and get this country back on track! (Fox News, 2011; emphasis added)

Dubious affirmations about the people in advertising

A certain number of the examples studied referred to trade and commerce. And in this field, the market rules and the customer is king. Producers, promoters, and even analysts accepted this way of thinking, as the following examples show:

In a sense, Snoop is venturing where few rappers have gone, attempting to retain his street cred while setting aside the mantle of High Priest of Hedonism. And if he chooses to turn a blind eye to the contradictions in his life choices, well, chalk it up to the realities of commerce. Like a traditional mafioso [*sic*], Snoop draws a clear line between his life as a family man and the often unsavory nature of his business dealings. **If the people want sex, money, and murder fantasies, he'll serve' em up** -just so long as there's still time for his son's football practice. (*Entertainment Weekly*, 2002; emphasis added)

The people want to give me money that's great, what they're doing is hiring a CEO. (Political election debate, 2015; emphasis added)

If we consider these cynical comments, and the complaints related to the failure of democracy in certain cases, we might be inclined to be reticent regarding the place of 'the people' in the American worldview. On the other hand, the market is important for people in America. A nation which places a high value on materialism and material well-being will inevitably have materialist ideals and desires, and will expect any form of government to cater to them. The COCA also provides a great number of examples contesting government policy. And it could be argued that such criticism testifies to the fact that free speech is still working in the US. The question of whether the people gets what the people deserves or at least what it wants certainly appears to remain central to government action and elections. When American foreign policy in Iraq or Iran is criticized, it is criticized in terms of a 'people' that wants 'a government that tends to their needs rather than international adventures' (*The American Spectator*, 2009, cited in COCA).

Many of the COCA's examples tend to indicate that the Americans see themselves as a pragmatic, problem-solving people. The people demand 'solutions'. As citizens and as consumers, they appear to want elected politicians and state employees to provide them with solutions regarding a wide variety of issues, including gun control, security, and business issues. They expect their rights to political protection, justice, and freedom, to be upheld. The people want to be informed. And it is worth noting that in the COCA's examples, they often declare that they are willing to help, to take part in serving the people.

If we compare and contrast the frequency with which the people collocates with 'allow', we can grasp the degree to which the American people tends to represent itself as a more active empowered people than the British one (Table 1.1).

Table 1.1 Comparing the empowerment of the people

Collocate	UK (BNC)	US (COCA)
the people allow	0	1
people allow	3	26
allow the people	6	41
allow people	74	698

Further research would be necessary to supplement these findings, and to verify the hypothesis that the people is represented as a more active force in the American worldview than in the English worldview. Nonetheless, it seems not unreasonable, at this stage, to posit that what the people are allowed to do and even what the people allow others to do is more central to the American worldview than the English worldview. Political discourse and appeals to the people certainly seem to reflect this, at least. Indeed, the fact that Americans require politicians to cater to their needs was even parodied in comics. Comics disparaged over-eager politicians as 'people pleaser' politicians, which suggests at least that the pressure to please the people is something that cannot be ignored in American politics.

Even those who we might expect to give up on the democratic process seem to refuse adamantly to give up on the people and the democratic process. Down and outs, women, and African Americans, in various examples, stressed that the US should not neglect the people. Referring to the great contemporary writer, Toni Morrison (1931–), one person quoted by the COCA cited, 'Barbara Jordan, elegant orator from the Lone Star State whose legacy lies in tiny truths: "**What the people want** is very simple. They want an America as good as its promise."' (*Essence*, 2000, quoted in COCA; emphasis added)

Such examples do not reflect the tone or the content of the examples found in the BNC. Was this a question of period? Have things changed since the early 1990s? Have the people become more empowered in English-speaking countries with the fall of the communist regimes? How has the consolidation of Europe altered our attitude to the people? We will take up these questions later. To verify whether our findings derived from the COCA and the BNC accurately reflect two different attitudes to 'the people', at this stage we considered it useful to compare the examples with findings drawn from the Leipzig Wortschatz corpus.

Leipzig Wortschatz

With almost fifty million sentences (49 628 862), the English corpus is one of the most frequently consulted corpora provided by Leipzig Wortschatz's selection of 222 languages in its online multilingual corpora (http://corpora.informatik.uni-leipzig.de). It provides a wide selection of examples drawn from British and American texts in a corpus that was put together by 2002. The Leipzig Wortschatz confirms many of the impressions formed by studying English and American corpora. 'The people' is relatively rare. The majority of examples referring to people, refer to 'people who', 'people with', 'people are', 'people in', and 'people have'. Among the most frequent left-hand neighbouring words, 'the' does not figure. Much more common are 'young people', 'many people', 'disabled people', 'older people', and 'other people'.

Of the 200 examples consulted, only five examples could qualify for examples of 'the people' as a nation, a people, or a united community. Two of those referred to the Basque people. One referred to the German people. Two examples were found among texts drawn from British online sources; but neither of those referred to the British or the English people. One referred to 'the people of Oklahoma', and the other referred to a novel about Jesus:

> The previous events at the WTC and Oklahoma don't seem to have **prepared the people**. (agamemnon.co.uk, 30 November 2001; emphasis added)

> Marianne Christian's novel is a vivid portrayal of the times in which Jesus lived, and **the people among whom he preached and worked miracles**. (3lib.ukonline.co.uk, 30 November 2001; emphasis added)

This would seem to indicate that 'the people', if and when it exists, does not exist in Britain. A search carried out on Google Books provided similar findings. Books on 'the people' do exist in English. But in a cursory check, the examples of published literature on the people tended to direct us to works on 'the African people', or 'the people' of the various countries involved in the Arab uprisings. After those, examples such as Bruce Ackerman's *We the People* (1993) confirmed the impression that when English-speaking peoples speak of 'the people', it is usually Americans speaking about the destiny of their people and their nation, rather than Brits talking about the fate of Britain.

ENCYCLOPAEDIAS AND QUOTATIONS: THE PEOPLE IS ELSEWHERE

The absence of 'the people' in the English-speakers' everyday language is even more startling if we contrast it with certain other European worldviews. In contrast to the twenty-six pages of entries for the equivalent term – *Volk* – in the *Enzyklopädie Blockhaus* (Vol 19: 405–430), the *Encylopedia Britannica* provides only six entries amounting to little over a half a column of text. The German word-stem, *volk-*, provides concepts for ethnology, democracy, republican government, folk music, and even genocide. *Volk* is clearly a concept charged with meaning, one that groups fight over and seek to harness and appropriate in their discursive strategies. Not so, 'the people'. The people in the *Britannica* is a term used to refer to peoples of China, Russia, and obscure political groups on the other side of the globe. The online version (https://www.britannica.com) offered the following entries: Congress of the People (political party, South Africa), Father of the People (king of France), Lord of the People (Hindu deity), Bolivarian Alliance for the Peoples of Our America (international organization), Women's Federation of the People's Republic of China (Chinese organization). But it offered nothing from Britain relating to the English or the British people.

Will we find a better crop of examples if we plough through dictionaries of quotations? If we consult the *Oxford Dictionary of Quotations* (*ODQ*) to try to get a grip on more widespread rhetoric used to represent the people, our initial findings prove predictably disappointing: the people proves elusive, examples are rare. Like English dictionaries, the *ODQ* examples give the overwhelming impression that 'the people' is used primarily to refer to 'subjects', 'servants', and 'kinfolk'.

The *ODQ* did provide some interesting examples, however. Edmund Burke (1729–1779), the Whig politician and man of letters, in 'A Tract on Popery Laws' *(ODQ* 1992: 159) unequivocally affirmed: 'In all forms of Government the people is the true legislator.' But this sentiment was somewhat rare among the quotes in the *ODQ*. And Burke was Irish-born. Besides, he himself admitted: 'I am not one of those who think that the people are never in the wrong. They have been so, frequently, and outrageously ...' (*ODQ* 1992: 159).

Among the few English authors cited by the *ODQ* as mentioning 'the people', we can name G. K. Chesterton (1874–1936), the poet, novelist and essayist. But Chesterton obviously feels he is swimming against the tide when he satirically invites his readers to consider their own prejudice and indifference. Those he addresses patently do not associate themselves with 'the people', and that is why, as he argues, 'the people' chide them:

Smile at us, pay us, pass us; but do not quite forget.
For we are the people of England, that never have spoken yet.
(Chesterton: 'The Secret People' *ODQ* 1992: 199)

When the *ODQ* quotes writers or politicians who cry out 'that government of the people, by the people, for the people, shall not perish from the earth', they turn out to be the words not of an Englishman, but of Abraham Lincoln (1809–1865), the US president who fought for the unity of his nation and against enslavement (*ODQ* 1992: 422). The only other entry that evokes the same sentiment in the *ODQ* proves to be from another American, William Tyler Page (1868–1942), in his eulogy of the American Constitution (*ODQ* 1992: 504).

MYENGLISHCORPUS

This proves a poor harvest. And because we were not content to rely on the examples promoted and maintained by these established sources, we decided to generate our own corpus of English texts. This led us to create MyEnglishCorpus, a three million word corpus of texts the authors are familiar with. Our aim was to ensure that the precise nature of usage could be verified by referring to context. This enabled us to remain sensitive to multiple uses of a single word, and most of all ironic uses. What impression did MyEnglishCorpus leave us with? MyEnglishCorpus produced some intriguing examples, but it did tend to confirm the growing impression of a weak or empty concept of 'the people' in the English imagination.

Once more, the writers in texts consulted tended to use 'the people' to designate 'subjects', 'servants', and 'kinfolk'. Throughout the history of England, when a man speaks of 'his people', he speaks of his army or his servants. This meaning is the dominant one in Shakespearean usage (see *Macbeth* and *Twelfth Night*). But even this usage remains rare.

Can this absence be explained in terms of rival synonyms, related or similar terms which compete with existing terms and overshadow them or even push them into disuse? This may, at first sight, appear to be a possibility. 'The people' is contrasted to 'folk' in English. And folk music – music of the people, for the people – would tend to evoke more down-to-earth and democratic associations than the language about the people found in the *OED* or the BNC. But historically, at least, this impression does not bear up to scrutiny. In Old Saxon, Old English, and even in Norman French, the term 'folk' originally referred to the followers, servants, or soldiers of a given person.

In MyEnglishCorpus, 'people' was used neutrally to refer more to the inhabitants of various regions; 'the people of the south' or 'of the north', for instance. But in the texts we considered, there was no negotiation with these people. They were identified and observed. They were described, but not addressed. The people did not constitute an active political force, and they had no voice. We had hoped to find a greater faith in the people in literature. And indeed, Dickens has pity for, and feels a sense of solidarity with, 'the common people'. (*Great Expectations*, 1860, http://www.gutenberg.org/files/1400/1400-h/1400h.htm). But this proves cold solace. In English literature, in Dickens and elsewhere, the common people remain 'common'. They are considered lowly and vulgar. However much we care for them, we still situate ourselves spatially, above, looking down upon the people. Even in expressions of sympathy, empathy and solidarity, the spatial logic of the dominant class seems to assert itself. Perversely, the ruling class would appear to have imposed its spatial logic on the worldview of people. When we feel sympathy for the people, it is more of a pitying kind, than a straightforward sympathy felt for our equals or those close to us. Our pity excludes the people from 'our' space. Prejudice clings to the adjectives used to describe the 'lower' orders.

In other famous novels of the nineteenth century, we search in vain for the people. In Jane Austen's *Pride and Prejudice* (1813, http://www.gutenberg.org/files/1342/1342h/1342-h.htm) 'the people' does not figure: only 'people' exist. And this reveals a great deal about the provincial English worldview of the early nineteenth century, and the way society and the classes were ordered. The questions for Austen's characters are: What will people say? What do most people think? How should people feel about things? 'People' evokes the moral codes and the dictates of the social order. All people are slaves to that social order in Austen's world. And the main objective of the middle class appears to be distinguishing itself from 'the common people'. In order to gain respectability, the middle classes must distance themselves as a group from the supposed moral frailty of 'the common people', their ignorance, and their lack of culture and breeding. In the world of Austen, her characters and her readers prove themselves worthy and gain approval by adhering to the moral code of the reigning ideology. Thereby, they hope to gain acceptance and 'elevate' themselves by marrying into the upper classes, with what is considered to be 'a better class of people'. They transcend their social station, but in escaping from the 'lower orders' and the 'mediocre existences' of the middle classes and 'raising themselves' to the station of the aristocracy or new money, they do not transcend the logic of their aspirations. They remain caught in the logic of spatial hierarchies to which they remain slaves in symbolic terms.

MyEnglishCorpus proved most interesting in forcing us to consider to what extent the concept of the people was significant for the other peoples of the British Isles. True, the people seemed to be absent in English English, but could 'the people' be found elsewhere? To some extent, MyEnglishCorpus did provide evidence that the Irish, Scottish, and Welsh generate different conceptions of people. For this reason, we have stressed the need to distinguish between British Standard English, and English English. Moreover, it was in texts from Irish and Scottish writers that we began to get a hold of what the English people might be. Though such discussions proved rare in English English, discussions about what the nature of the English people is, are to be found in both Scottish and Irish English. This is part of the strategy to define what it means to be Irish or Scottish, in contrast to being English or British.

Stereotypes are set up in contrast to the way speakers like to portray their own identities and cultures. This proved true in our textual analysis. Indeed, we need to turn to Joyce (*A Portrait of the Artist as a Young Man*, 1916, http://www.gutenberg.org/ebooks/4217) to discover the English. The English may ignore them, but the Irish see them (from their own perspective). This means the characters of the novel, Stephen, the protagonist, Dante, and Mr Dedalus discuss the nature of 'the English people' and its relationship with 'the Irish people at home and abroad'. This forms the basis of discussions about politics, religion, and identity. In addition to this, Joyce uses 'your people', and 'his people', to speak of relatives. The characters refer to the community – and more often as not the religious community – as 'the people', for whom the priest is thought to be responsible.

These uses prove rare in English English. Judging from literature, English authors rarely appear to conceive of themselves as either 'a people', or to have any ideal of 'the people'. Neither is Joyce an isolated case. If we compare and contrast the great writers of the British Isles, we find that English novelists such as Thomas Hardy tend to speak of local people, the people of a region (such as his imaginary Wessex), but rarely speak of the English as a people.

The Scots perceive the people differently. Robert Burns (1759–1796), Sir Walter Scott (1771–1832), and Robert Louis Stevenson (1850–1894) all spoke about their regions in relation to the destiny of their nation and the Scots people. The national poet, Rabbie Burns, is often reduced to a caricature, celebrating haggis, whisky, and the highlands, although he himself was very much a lowlands poet. But Burns' dialect poems carved out an elevated poetic voice for the Scots, and helped gain the Scots international prestige in the nineteenth century, and his rousing patriotic songs, like *Scots Wha Hae* are still sung today, as a multitude of YouTube links demonstrate (see for instance https://www.youtube.com/watch?v=o5kE3of1Lzo).

Walter Scott specializes in discovering the Scots through the eyes of outsiders. It is an Englishman that crosses the border to discover the Borders, Glasgow, and the Highlands in *Rob Roy*, 1817, (http://www.gutenberg.org/files/7025/7025-h/7025-h.htm#AlinkCH0021). And there is hardly a page of the novel that does not enter into discussion about the nature of Scots customs, Scots legislation, and the Scots attitudes to themselves and their English neighbours. Robert Louis Stevenson uses a similar narrative strategy. In *Kidnapped* (originally published in instalments in the *Young Folks* magazine, May–July 1886, http://www.gutenberg.org/files/421/421-h/421-h.htm), when Stevenson wishes to depict the people of the Highlands, he sends David Balfour, a lowlander from the Borders there, as the narrator, to act as an intermediary between the Highlanders and a wider readership in England and beyond.

It is difficult to find similar examples in English literature. The theme of the English people was rarely touched upon, in contrast, as far as we could tell from the findings provided by our textual analysis of literary corpora. It would be rash to make sweeping statements about culture and identity, but there seems little evidence to suggest that the English show the same need to define themselves and their project as a people and a nation. It seems as if these questions are part of an attempt to defend their identity for the Irish, the Scots, and the Welsh. Defining and preserving their culture, and defining their identity appear to be part of a project that elevates the people to an ideal as an active political force.

Not only do these peoples speak of themselves as a people, but they are also perceived by foreigners to be different from the English, a people apart. The idea of an Irish, a Scots, or a Welsh people is widely accepted by visitors for example. This was corroborated by online media and the literature and newspapers quoted in MyEnglishCorpus. One American student, for example, put online a YouTube film called *Interviewing the Welsh People* which has been watched by 184 424 people (https://www.youtube.com/watch?v=42NqpUHcw4o).

The independence elections in Scotland in 2015, and the debates following the vote on Brexit in 2016 and the Scottish people's place in Europe, amply demonstrate that the Scots see themselves as a people, a separate people, and a people that must now renegotiate its relationship with both Europe and the rest of Britain. And the European press has, naturally, not shown itself to be indifferent to the desire of Scots to remain within the EU. *Le Figaro*, the French centre-right newspaper, for example, highlighted on 13 March 2017 the news that the Scots were demanding an independence referendum before Brexit went ahead (*L'Écosse réclame un référendum sur l'indépendance avant le Brexit*, 13 March 2017, http://www.lefigaro.fr/international/2017/03/13/01003-20170313ARTFIG00162-1-ecosse-reclame-un-referendum-sur-l-independance-avant-le-brexit.php).

The BBC tends to speak rarely of 'the English people', but examples of the 'Irish people' are often recorded and commented upon on the BBC television or radio stations. The examples do not necessarily show the Irish championing the Irish people or haranguing the English. Often the texts, films, and Internet films consulted commented upon the darker sides of the Irish experience. But what is important for our study is that the Irish people tend to represent themselves suffering their woes and enjoying their successes as a people.

For this reason, when in 2011 the Irish Prime Minister, Enda Kenny, who ousted the government in power for more than eighty years, spoke of the debt crisis which was scourging the nation, he spoke of it in terms of a story that concerned the protagonist, the Irish people. The BBC, in turn, recorded Kenny's words, thereby entering into the conceptual patterning of his worldview, and siding with Kenny's representation of himself as the saviour to an ailing nation and the friend of a suffering people:

Ireland's budget deficit reached an alarming 32 per cent of gross domestic product after a state bailout of the country's banks, which had lent recklessly and fuelled an unsustainable property boom. When Fine Gael and Labour agreed to work as coalition partners, they issued a joint document saying voters had chosen parties 'to begin mending the pieces of a fractured society, a broken economy'. 'It is no exaggeration to say that we now face one of the darkest hours in the history of our independent state. **Our economy and our politics have been shattered. But our people's spirit has not,**' the parties said. (http://news.bbc.co.uk/2/hi/europe/country_profiles/1038581.stm; emphasis added)

Conventional representations often portray the Irish as a people with a certain sense of camaraderie and solidarity: they stick together. Interestingly, this is nowhere more obvious than when Irish individuals are accused (or suspected) of having the typical characteristics associated – rightly or wrongly – with the Irish people. Ireland derives substantial earnings in both commerce and tourism from stereotypes of cosy Irish pubs 'with good crack [*craic*]', but many Irish individuals do not appreciate being considered 'drinkers' either as individuals or as a nation.

In one online story, once again recorded by the BBC, a teacher from the Republic of Ireland, Katie Mulrennan, from County Kerry, was 'turned down for a job in Seoul, South Korea, due to the "alcoholism nature" of Irish people. ... She was told by an agency that their client did not hire Irish people due to their perceived drinking habits.' (http://www.bbc.com/news/world-europe-29929333)

The very fact that this was judged to be newsworthy demonstrates the fact that the Irish tend to perceive themselves – and to be perceived – as a people, as a distinct culture in and of itself. Curiously, this is not contested, but endorsed by the English and their media (the BBC), although far fewer English people appear to speak about themselves in similar terms, as a people. This leads us a curious conclusion. The English language is perfectly capable of generating concepts of the people as an active political force, capable of carving out its own destiny, a culture with its own identity and will, but this capacity is somewhat underdeveloped in English English. This leads us to conclude that, in English, the people is elsewhere: in Wales, Ireland, or in Scotland. Not only that, but when it comes to defining the English, it is these minority forms of English that seem to be preoccupied with the task of defining who the English people are, what they do and what they want. Inevitably then, we are forced to turn to the Scots, the Irish and the Welsh, if we wish to gain a clearer image of how the English are perceived as a people.

OTHER EUROPEAN PEOPLES

As we have seen then, 'the people' in English often compares somewhat unfavourably with other traditions. A marked contrast can be seen in the different ways the Scottish press discuss the destiny of the Scottish people, and both its history and its culture. Likewise, in Scottish literature, the identity of the Scottish people is a vibrant theme that seems to animate the reflection of the great Scottish novelists. English writers often discuss and celebrate the English culture, and the English way of life, and even the English. But it is curious that corpora research has produced few examples discussing 'the English people'.

In German, '*das Volk*' opens up a rich vibrant concept in the imagination of the people: '*das Volk*' is a dynamic concept that proves prodigiously prolific in the way it creates meaning throughout the German lexicon. Words, concepts, and arguments focus upon discussions about the German people. And dictionaries, encyclopaedias, and corpora corroborate this dynamism. In English English, on the other hand, we are left feeling short-changed if we go looking for the same rich patterning in language and thinking, when we ponder texts, dictionaries, and encyclopaedias.

How does this state of affairs compare to other European traditions though? For obvious reasons of space, we can only provide a brief overview of a couple of other traditions; but if we consider the way the people animates the imaginations of the Polish and the French, we should be able to gain a greater grasp of the potential 'the people' as a concept or ideal that takes root in the mindset of a linguistic community and enables it to project itself into the future.

One outstanding contribution to understanding the culturally specific concept of 'the people' was made by the Lublin Ethnolinguistics School by Jerzy Bartmiński and Maciej Abramowicz (Abramowicz and Bartmiński 1998) who compared *lud* in Polish, with *le peuple* in French. Bartmiński and Abramowicz's work is facilitated by the fact that French and Polish do indeed provide a largely analogous concept. As these two ethnolinguists point out (1998: 16–17), the words *lud* and *peuple* cover three main meanings:

1. 'ethnos', a great group of humans that can be gathered together because they inhabit the same area or share the same laws, customs or religion
2. a mass of people, a crowd or multitude
3. the lower social orders, classes of people without rights or privileges. (Our translation from the French original)

Both languages provide a concept that can be characterized as sharing four fundamental characteristics in the imagination: *lud-peuple* is 1. impersonal, 2. united, 3. passive, and 4. laborious. The 'object' designated by the concept forms an indivisible whole which is deprived of individual characteristics, and which is perceived from without. It is not represented as self-motivated or as being inspired by a will proper to itself. This passive representation is somewhat paradoxical, however, because it appears at odds with the fact that the people proves to be the source of great works. How are we to understand this? In French and Polish, 'the people' is a working class; this makes it a force. This tends to contradict the representations of the people promoted by monarchies, democracies, and even communism, at times, which all conspire to consolidate the idea of the people an inert mass moved by external forces. Generals seek to enflame the hearts of soldiers. And Marxism–Leninism does indeed represent the people as a mass that must be 'awoken', and encouraged, or coerced into action.

Up to this point the keywords '*peuple*' and '*lud*' appear to coincide. Bartmiński and Abramowicz uncovered a very different attitude towards the people in the two language-cultures, however. In their corpus-based research, they encountered a great deal of contempt and condescension in French sources. Indeed, '*ça fait peuple*', (that belongs to the people), remains to this day an insult, a gesture of contempt. In their corpus findings, the French '*peuple*' all too often emerged as a concept designating the ignorant, unenlightened, fickle, and insensitive masses. Often, '*le peuple*' was disparaged or referred to with disgust.

On the other hand, the Polish ethnolinguists affirmed that, for them, a people that has often been deprived of its own nation, *lud* was held up as a source of hope in the face of adversity, a rallying cry. The people is celebrated in the Polish worldview as the life and soul of the nation, the essential manifestation and guardian of its culture. Bartmiński and Abramowicz asserted that '*lud*', the Polish people, is clearly endowed with a cultural, national, and historical role. That people fulfils a vocation. This proves to what extent the Polish concept is a socio-historical construct. In many of the traditional English representations of the people, we find a spatial dynamic that depends on a binary opposition: we distinguish between the lower orders and the upper classes – the aristocracy looks down on the people. But for a culture in which the peasants are poor and the aristocracy is disenfranchised, another dynamic is set up. An alliance between the two becomes possible. This goes some way to explaining why the Polish people is incarnated by both the peasantry and by the aristocracy. The Jews and the bourgeoisie, in contrast, were both perceived less favourably in this narrative, as classes that were willing to cooperate and collaborate with the ruling elites of the nations that carved up the Polish nation. Different historical circumstances generate a very different conceptualization of the people. *Lud* is no arbitrary concept. It is a value, of national, political, social, cultural, and historical importance. For that reason, it is a keyword that our Polish ethnolinguistics cannot afford to ignore.

Does this opposition do justice to the concept and provide us with an accurate picture of the '*peuple*' in French? Clearly, further corpus research and discourse analysis is required to answer that question. In fact, as we might imagine, attitudes to the French '*peuple*' turn out to be far more complicated. Despite a certain contempt that sometimes clings to the concept of the people in certain usages in French, a great wealth of other usages counteract and contradict this prejudice.

Frantext and the French '*peuple*'

Using the Frantext corpus (http://www.frantext.fr.ezproxy.normandie-univ.fr/), with just under 300 million words drawn from 5116 texts, we came to the following conclusions. The word '*le peuple*' is clearly in use as of the middle of the fourteenth century. It is not necessarily '*le peuple français*' that is quoted though. References in French are made to the Christian people ('*le peuple créstien*', in old French), to the '*le peuple d'Israel*', and '*le peuple romain*'. Frantext did also generate examples of '*le peuple*' referring to a region, however. We find the same aristocratic conception of the people, but the aristocracy is clearly involved with the people. The king calls upon the people, and addresses them as '*le peuple*', and other persons in power negotiate with the '*peuple*' in French. And although, at times, the people is portrayed as suffering in servitude, at least their perspective is represented in the Frantext's sources.

Predictably, it is with the approach of the French Revolution that the desires of the people assert themselves in the French worldview.

Frantext produced thirty examples in a search for 'the people wants' ('*le peuple veut*') and all dated from the 1760s onwards. The philosopher, Rousseau, is famous for having claimed,

> De lui-même le peuple veut toujours le bien, mais de lui-même il ne le voit pas toujours. La volonté générale est toujours droite, mais le jugement qui la guide n'est pas toujours éclairé.
>
> By itself, the people always wants what is best, but by itself, it does not always see it. The general will is always unswerving, but the judgement that guides it is not always enlightened. (Livre 2, Chapter 6, Jean-Jacques Rousseau, *Du Contrat social*, 1762: 226, quoted in Frantext)

Robespierre, who began as a defender of the constitutional monarchy, but who became a staunch opponent to the monarchy following the betrayal by Louis XVI, was to quote Rousseau in his *Discours* (1793, p. 90, also quoted in Frantext).

Other examples provide a less enlightened image of the people and its will. In *La Chartreuse de Parme*, published in 1839, for example, one character represents the people as a mob that wants to hang a certain character. But on the whole, the Frantext examples refer to a people whose will is reasonable. In his *Thoughts, Essays, Maxims, and Correspondence*, the moralist, Joubert (1754–1824), suggests that the people wish to look at the face of the prince, and to make their own judgement ('*Le peuple veut voir le prince au visage*', Frantext). Once more, this did not necessarily mean that the people sees clearly or even that they are their own best friend: the people can be mistaken, but this is in the nature of things. So, in 1848, when the writer, George Sand, lamented that the people wanted to give the monarchy a second chance, and that there was little to be done to prevent it, she concluded that at least this bad experience would prove more convincing than any advice anyone could give the people. Other examples from Frantext suggest that the people want clear ideas. The people of Athens desire instruction, and the people of France want the king to provide balance in the State:

> That man, the most pretentious that I know, hates the people, because the people want clear ideas. ('*Cet homme, le plus vaniteux que je connaisse, déteste le peuple, parce que le peuple veut des idées claires*', Erckmann and Chatrian in their *Histoire d'un paysan*, 1870, Frantext)

in Athens, the people want to be taught. ('*à Athènes, le peuple veut être instruit*', Fustel de Coulanges, 1864, Frantext)

Do the people want me to counterbalance him as the king? (*Le peuple veut que, roi, je lui fasse équiblibre?*, Hugo, 1865, Frantext)

And one character in Hugo's *Quatrevingt-treize*, published in 1874, champions the people as a united ideal, when he reflects on the necessary evil of characters such as Robespierre and Danton, and argues that it will undermine the movement to attack them: 'Unity, unity, citizens! The people wants us to stay unified!' ('*Union! Union, citoyens! Le peuple veut qu'on soit uni*', Frantext). This is part of the revolutionary history of republican France. And Frantext continues to produce examples of the people's will in the twentieth century. During both the world wars, for example, claims were made that the people wanted peace (Frantext).

MyFrenchCorpus

In our own research based on MyFrenchCorpus, a three million word corpus of selected texts, three intriguing examples could be found of defences of the people. The first certainly runs counter to the general distain expressed for the people that is sometimes expressed by French authors, and which Abramowicz and Barmiński found in their research. In his letters, Napoléon speaks of the people as an active motivated force, a reality. This is the spirit that animates Napoléon's addresses to the people, as we can hear in the following declaration:

Proclamation à l'armée.

Soldats,

Nous allons célébrer le premier vendémiaire, l'époque la plus chère aux Français; elle sera un jour bien célèbre dans les annales du monde. C'est de ce jour que datent la fondation de la république, l'organisation de la grande nation; et la grande nation est appelée par le destin à étonner et consoler le monde. Soldats! éloignés de votre patrie, et triomphant de l'Europe, on vous préparait des chaînes; vous l'avez su, vous avez parlé: **le peuple s'est réveillé, a fixé les traîtres, et déjà ils sont aux fers.** (Napoléon Bonaparte, Au quartier-général à Passeriano, le 26 fructidor an 5 (12 septembre 1797; emphasis added)

Proclamation to the Army

Soldiers,

We are going to celebrate the first *vendémiaire* of the Republic, the first month of the newly revised Republican calendar, the dearest of all periods for the French; in the annals of the world, it will be remembered as a very famous day. From this day dates the founding of the republic, and the organization of our great nation; and that great nation is called by destiny to amaze and console the whole world. Soldiers! – far from your homeland – triumphing over Europe, they had prepared chains for you, you know that, but **the people woke up, and dealt with the traitors, and already they are in irons.** (*Œuvres de Napoléon*, 1821, Tome deuxième, http://www.gutenberg.org/files/12782/12782-h/12782-h.htm; emphasis added)

There is something truly magical and captivating about this. In contrast with English literature, here we find ourselves face to face with examples in which the people are recognized and taken into account. The people are an overwhelming political force with a historical destiny. But it is as much the way the people are perceived as the way they perceive their own power and worth that is startling for English readers. Here a sincere and sensitive attempt is being made to understand and to address the people. This is no longer the aristocracy looking down and pitying or despising the people. In these words, a barrier is clearly being broken down. This opens us a whole new conception of the people for our study. The people have desires, demands, and rights. The people are capable of understanding what is happening in society and what is being forced upon them. They are capable of rising up to defend themselves as an intelligent, self-motivated group. Rather than the despised playthings of history, in the prose and speeches of Napoléon, the people becomes the motor force creating history. The people must be respected.

This can be considered the high point of '*le peuple*' as an ideal. French writers continue to rekindle this love and respect for the people. Indeed, fifty years (1846) later the great historian of the people, Jules Michelet, would write his celebration of the people. This is an inspired and inspiring book that gives a voice to the diverse classes and types of people that the historian describes and analyses with both tenderness and sensitivity. Michelet has a sensibility wholly different from that of the *Ancien Régime*. He is painfully sensitive to the tribulations of the peasant and describes the economic forces bearing down upon the artisan and the shopkeeper. These are the people that make up the *peuple* for Michelet. And he claims his right to tell the story of that people.

In telling the story of the people, however, Michelet is running against the current of the times. When he claims '*je suis resté peuple*' (1946: 24, 'I remain a man of the people'), he knows very well the contempt associated with terms such as 'son of the people' (*fils du peuple*) and 'born among the people' (*issu du peuple*). In Michelet, a voice is heard, the voice of one person speaking for the people. And it has the ring of an authentic voice speaking of a real people. The authenticity of that voice appears much closer to the Polish tradition of *lud*, which Bartmiński and Abramowicz defend. But it is clear from the way Michelet sets about defending '*le peuple*' that it needs defenders in the face of a pervasive condescension that was prevalent in the *Ancien Régime*, and that has, by the middle of the nineteenth century, reasserted itself.

The third example found in MyFrenchCorpus, is curious, if not perverse. La Bruyère, the French moralist (1645–1696) that translates from Greek the great work on the nature of human characters written by Aristotle's student, Theophrasus (around 371–288 BCE), provides us with a perplexing strategy (1775, http://www.gutenberg.org/books/17980). As a moralist, La Bruyère is torn between an admiration for the Greeks and a feeling of distain for his common mortals. As an exponent of the *Ancien Régime*, he has no time for *le peuple*. And yet, ironically, he has great respect for the Athenians of Ancient Greece. Unsurprisingly, as a loyal subject to his king, La Bruyère uses his Greek sources to extol aristocracy as a form of government. Still, he cannot deny the fact that, in Athens, the people acts as a political force: the people demands, the people requires, the people manifests its lack of contentment with political decisions. The people must be catered to and cajoled. And La Bruyère portrays them faithfully.

Yet when it comes to describing his fellow men, the French people, in the second part of his book devoted to, '*Les caractères ou moeurs de ce siècle*', how does La Bruyère portray his own contemporaries? The following example is fairly representative of the attitude he adopts:

Il y a le peuple qui est opposé aux grands, c'est la populace et la multitude: il y a le peuple qui est opposé aux sages, aux habiles, aux vertueux. (La Bruyère 1775)

There exists the people that is the opposite of the great: this is the populace and the multitude. There is the people who are the opposite of the wise, the able and the virtuous.

What does this tell us of La Bruyère's conception of the *le peuple*? The people serves only as the perverse reflection of all that is worthy. If the people is the antithesis of the wise, the able and the virtuous, what qualities can it be allowed? This may sound like *l'Ancien Régime*. It is.

Indeed, the people find no place in the moralist's concerns. In his maxims, either the people simply does not exist, or they have no voice. They certainly have no will. In this way, a gap widens between the way La Bruyère negotiates the translation of the Greek meaning of 'people' into French, and the way he treats the French *peuple*. One is active and full of will. The other is inactive, devoid of expression. This is a kind of ethnocentric inversion: a schizophrenic blindness that prevents La Bruyère from noticing and observing the people around him, although he is perfectly capable of conceiving of a people that acts in its own right, by its own will, in its own interests, in theory. In this way, La Bruyère conforms to the aristocratic worldview of his times in representing the people as a passive mass which cannot be moved without coercion. If self-motivated, aristocrats believe, the people is wild, or mad. If the people become uncontrollable, once more, force must be used to contain them.

The example of La Bruyère is instructive, in that it shows the incapacity of a man to assimilate into his own sensibility and mode of perceiving that he identifies and understands in another culture. As a translator, La Bruyère skilfully contributes to establishing the Greek democratic conception of the people within his own language system. Greek sources expand the comprehension of concepts in French, but they appear to be so perplexing to the translator himself that the Greek conception fails to alter his own prejudice. What appears true for many English writers, appears true for the *Ancien Régime: le peuple est ailleurs*, the people is elsewhere. Perhaps in Athens but not in Paris.

And what of French literature in general? MyFrenchCorpus provided a vivid but perplexing overview of French attitudes to the people. For the great patriotic dramatist Corneille (1606–1684), the people exists, and the characters of his plays speak of the peoples or diverse lands. But 'the people' in *Le Cid* exists to serve a function: to execute the orders of the Aristocracy that reigns over them and directs their will. More importantly, for Corneille, the people exist as the spectators and celebrators of the noble acts of chivalry and bravery those knights see themselves performing. And even in this secondary spectator role, the praise of the people proves stinting. Trusting the people means giving into a naïve illusion, for the characters of Corneille's plays, for the people is a fickle thing. The judgement of the people cannot be trusted. The people lack the faculty necessary for discriminating, his characters tend to believe. For this reason, the Elder Horace, warns Horace, in the play that Corneille devotes to the latter, not to rely on the people or to place too much trust in its judgement. The People, ultimately, is stupid and incapable of discernment.

Horace, ne crois pas que le peuple stupide
Soit le maître absolu d'un renom bien solide:
Sa voix tumultueuse assez souvent fait bruit;
Mais un moment l'élève, un moment le détruit.

Horace, do not believe that the stupid people is the absolute master of solid renown. Its tumultuous voice often makes noise, but in a moment it is raised, in a moment it is destroyed. (MyFrenchCorpus, 1671, http://www.gutenberg.org/files/31628/31628-h/31628-h)

Sadly, this sentiment cannot be attributed to the *Ancien Régime* alone. The great free-thinker, Voltaire himself (1694–1774), speaks of the people with disparagement, claiming they accept religion and laws as they accept money, without discernment. The people, in Voltaire's opinion, are incapable of examining the laws that govern them (Oster 1990: 561).

We might hope for a great schism, a 'before' and an 'after' that comes with the French Revolution, and, indeed, during this period, we can observe a whole series of key phrases related to representation and democracy for the people. Napoléon's address to the people and the republican sentiments voiced by Hugo's characters, and by Jules Michelet in his histories of France, do clearly mark a transitional phase that elevates the people to an ideal. This is short-lived, however. The prejudice proves tenacious. Before the revolution, the characters of the great Classical dramatist, Racine (1639–1699) disparage the idea that the people is capable of recognizing the master who must reign over the masses: to allow them to choose their king is therefore to be excluded (Oster 1990: 387). And the great political thinker, Montesquieu (1689–1755) defends the biological logic upon which the aristocratic class system is based when he warns against allowing the culture of the master-class to be contaminated by 'degenerate' species:

> *Les hommes sont comme les plantes, qui ne croissent jamais heureusement si elles ne sont bien cultivées: chez les peuples misérables, l'Espèce perd et même quelquefois dégénère.* (Montesquieu in Oster 1990: 509)
>
> Men are like plants that are not always fortunately crossed if they are not well-cultivated: among impoverished peoples, the Species is often lost and at times degenerates.

These are certainly the sentiments of the *Ancien Régime*. Even so, seventy years after the revolution, the worldview of the French ruling class has not escaped this contempt for the people. Indeed, it is all too revealing that the quotations found in Oster's second volume covering authors writing from the Revolution onwards through to the twentieth century echo sentiments which are well-anchored in the worldview of the *Ancien Régime*. Society has been transformed, but one ruling class has replaced another, and it seems to have inherited the same prejudices, prejudices that it systematically maintains and propagates in its literature.

Certain of Stendhal's characters speak with disgust of the people in the *Vie de Henry Brulard*. One character, for example, makes no bones about affirming: 'the people are always filthy in my eyes' ('*le peuple est toujours sale à mes yeux*', Oster 1993: 131). In French literature of the period, a sovereign ignorance of people seems to be the rule. The voice of the people is muted or muzzled. Curiously, this attitude was not contradicted by the poets of the Romantic period. When it comes to the people, we are offered disgust and indifference from Baudelaire. The people is a barefoot impoverished bunch, left to die in the gutters below the balcony of the Master (fleursdumal.org/poem/160). At times, in French, the people are represented as a mass, a mob, which only seems capable of showing enthusiasm when it is animated by sadomasochistic spectacles, displays of power and public punishment. The great Victor Hugo, like Dickens, championed the people in his novels, but even he falls short here. Hugo is capable of expressing an authentic sentiment for the people, but the feeling that animates Hugo is more pity than love or admiration: pity and exasperation. 'What is the People', Hugo asks? 'An ass rearing up' (*Le peuple? Un âne qui se cabre!* Ripert: 322). While for one of the world's great short story writers, Guy de Maupassant

(1840–1893), 'the people is an idiotic herd' ('*Le peuple est un troupeau imbecile*' Ripert: 322).

Oster's and Ripert's dictionaries are representative of their kind. In most of dictionaries of French quotations, the people are deprived of all individual characteristics, all rights. The people are even at times denied the right to express their indignation over starving. In the majority of the sources we considered, an overwhelming self-satisfied repulsion for the people was expressed both before and after the revolution.

To sum up, the French tradition provides us with a much more dynamic example than its English counterpart. The ideal of a democratic people who expresses its will and forges its own destiny is perfectly conceivable, and at times it can be raised up as an ideal. The destiny of the people often falls short of that ideal, however, and often the people will be denigrated with a revulsion which is difficult to match, an attitude that proved rare in English. Abramowicz and Bartmiński do not do justice to the ideal of the active will of the French *peuple*. But while the French people can be held up high, they can also be dragged down into the gutter in French representations.

THE PEOPLE IN RADICAL POLITICS

By exploring the linguistic patterning of French and English, our case studies should have demonstrated the various ways keywords in different languages converge in forming similar paradigms and the ways they diverge. It is not simply the core construct of the people that differs: the roots and branches of concepts differ in the associations they evoke. Associations, ideas, and feelings are sustained by the linguistic patterning that gives a meaning and context to words within the language system. Is the 'people' a 'common people'? Is the phrase 'people's hero' used? And what does it mean for a culture to speak of 'an enemy of the people'? The brief consideration of the Polish and German notions of 'the people' should have demonstrated the degree to which a shared concept of the people can reasonably be considered to occupy a place of importance in the languages we have considered, without denying specific cultural, linguistic, and conceptual differences.

This can prove disconcerting. The specific historical, political, social, and cultural forces that go towards forging a unique complex construct in any one language will inevitably perplex people used to their own comfortable, well-worn patterns of thinking and feeling. We can feel at a loss, when faced with conceptual dimensions that are unexplored in our own language. A 'car of the people' makes little sense to English-speakers: but '*Volkswagen*', has its own German logic. And we are capable of grasping that logic. It belongs to a specifically German democratizing tradition that bears much in common with Ford's Model T family car, one of the fruits of American consumerism.

Up until now, corpora findings have revealed the extent to which both the English and the French traditions have often been dominated by thinkers and writers who tended to marginalize and disparage the people. This implicit condescension contrasts with Scottish, Irish, and American celebrations of the people, but it also contrasts with a strong republican sentiment that has marked key periods in French history and culture. And although that sentiment often appears to fade and fall dormant, it has deep roots in the patterning of the French culture and language. French revolutionary sentiment championing the people has a potential that can be awakened. If the roots of the English concept of the people are different, then a different plant will spring forth when populism takes hold of the culture. This is the question we shall now consider. As populism began to wax strong in both France and England in the 2010s, what reserves were tapped, and how did populist discursive strategies flourish? This requires careful investigation, because it will force us to concede that various discursive strategies vie for success in each of the languages. Nonetheless, although competing strategies conflict, they make use of the same conceptual and linguistic resources shared by the linguistic community. This struggle is inevitable, because the stakes are high: keywords are always major stakes in public debates. The ideological rhetoric used by media, political parties, and individuals serves to appropriate and harness the keywords that are capable of moving people. The aim is not only to win over the people, but to make the very concept 'theirs'. How did English and French populists address the people and invite them to join them in adopting their perspectives?

French Populism

The short history of the French people we have recounted should go some way to explaining the diverse discursive strategies adopted by the political parties in the 2010s and the run up to both the 2012 and 2017 elections. In the six years that it took us to write this book, we observed the emergence of various discursive strategies employing 'the people' and populist rhetoric. In 2010 and 2011, during the first years of our research, there was little consideration of '*le peuple*' in the French media, in paper and online newspapers, and in TV debates, all of which we consulted on a weekly basis. Throughout his term in office (2007–2012), Sarkozy and his ministers proved capable of speaking about the 'Tunisian people' and the 'Libyan people', but paid relatively little attention to the French people. Sarkozy's administration tended to reason in terms of 'individuals' or '*les français*'. This was not specific to his administration, however, as the results of a Leipzig Wortschatz search demonstrate.

Expecting to find many examples of '*le peuple français*' in the Leipzig Wortschatz corpus of contemporary French, we ran a check of the right-hand neighbours of '*peuple*'. The results were not encouraging. In the Leipzig Wortschatz sources, the French speak more than four times as much about the Palestinian people than they speak about the French people. They speak almost twice as much about the Jewish people as they speak about the French people. This can in part be explained by the influence of the Bible and biblical stories of the Jewish people's struggle to convert the Nations. But how are we to explain that there are more than twice as many references to the 'Togolais people', or that there are almost as many references to the American people? Why should there be more references to the Algerian and the Iranian peoples than references the French people in a French corpus? Do the French feel for other peoples, but not for their own?

Political crises explain why we find ourselves at certain moments in history speaking about peoples in distress or peoples caught in conflicts. But it does not explain why the French do not speak about the French people. Of a total of 156 466 references in the Leipzig Wortschatz, both the words on the right and the left and the collocations generated reaffirmed the impression that the French look elsewhere when they speak of 'the people'. 'The people' belong beyond French borders. This is clearly not a question of conceptualization, but one of perspective. There is a concept of 'the people' in the French worldview, but in the first decade of the twentieth century it would seem that when the French speak about the needs of the people, they are more often than not speaking about the needs of other peoples elsewhere.

Yet as we saw, a resolute republican rhetoric forms part of the French worldview, and the sentiments that rhetoric evokes can be tapped into when politicians address and celebrate the people. This celebration is not necessarily patriotically optimistic. The people can be represented as a mistreated underdog. But at times this republican celebration of '*le peuple*' proves a powerful rhetoric that does not fall on dead ears. It awakens a latent network of associations that can produce an explosive cocktail in the hands of skilful speakers.

If 'the people' was not being appropriated and given meaning by the left or right, that meant it was open for takers. In the vacuum, it was the Extreme Right, the Front National, who moved in to take over the keyword. Marine Le Pen's party had long defended putting French people first and getting rid of the foreigners that they considered were stealing 'French' jobs. But where formerly the Front National had chanted '*les français d'abord*' ('the French first'), in the early 2010s, they began to hype the slogan '*le peuple d'abord*' ('the People first').

We might describe this as a process of 'semantic evacuation' followed by 'semantic colonization'. A word begins to lose its resonance, and lose its grip on the networks of meaning holding together its place in the patterning of the language; at which stage, the word can be appropriated by marginal uses. The people as a whole, the democratic ideal of a unified and united collective will, is harnessed by minority groups who can integrate it into a nationalistic, racist rhetoric of resentment.

Things were beginning to change in other respects in France regarding the people, however. During the summer of 2011, there seemed little reason to suppose that 'the people' would be at stake in debates and media confrontations leading up to the French elections in 2012. We initially concluded that we were living through a phase in history in which the people was being marginalized or ignored in French politics. But as observers, we were forced to revise our predictions, as the campaign unfolded and brought with it some surprises.

Before the 2012 election, *le peuple* became the rallying call of revolt on both the far right and the far left. On the left, rebellious youth groups protested against the right-wing policies of Sarkozy, which adherents believed excluded segments of society and promoted racism. Sarkozy's policies were blamed for indirectly preventing the children of immigrants from integrating into civil society, and Sarkozy was thus portrayed as going against the founding principles of the Republic, egality and fraternity. This was the point of view promoted by musicians such as Keny Arkana, the twenty-nine-year-old rap singer and her band, appropriately named, *Rage du people* (The People's Rage). This was not a mainstream movement, however. It was very much a minority movement that gained very little interest in the established media whose journalists remained shy of the word, 'the people', throughout the election campaign.

Far more vigorous was the far-right use of the word. Marine Le Pen's Front National used the word '*peuple*' abundantly. The Front National promoted a France reserved for the French people, a France where the French people would feel 'at home' ('*chez eux*'), a France in which the French were not pushed to one side by an 'invasion' of foreigners. When we carried out a youtube.fr search on 12 February 2012, *peuple* called up racist songs. One song, for example, incited the French people to 'rise up' ('*Levez-vous!*'). Pictures of veiled North African Muslims were shown as the singers of the song chanted: '*Marine faut que tu sois à l'Elysée / pour que les arabes on arrive à les virer*' ('Marine, you have to get into Parliament/so we can get rid of the Arabs').

Nicolas Sarkozy had managed to seduce the middle classes in 2007, by promising an increase in spending power for those with modest incomes and easier access to real estate. The economic meltdown of 2007–2009 had put an end to those hopes. Popularity polls showed the people's resentment, and Sarkozy's government was forced, therefore, to seek to expand its popular power base. And this led his right-wing followers to play on resentments in order to gain the support from voters sympathetic to the increasingly popular Front National. What did this signify?

In a cynical tactic, Sarkozy began to make overtures to *le peuple*. But interestingly, this was no longer the people of France. '*Peuple*' had already largely been more or less emptied of its republican content, and was increasingly associated with reactionary far-right resentments. To this extent, the Front National had already won the conceptual battle. The keyword was theirs. Sarkozy seemed to have conceded this, and he was moving in on 'their' territory. He was trying to win back the people, but Sarkozy was no longer addressing the French people as a whole. Many groups were being forgotten. They were not part of 'the people' that Sarkozy began appealing to. *Le peuple* Sarkozy had in mind were the reactionary right, the resentful downwardly mobile white population. Sarkozy thereby consolidated the conceptual conquest of the keyword that the Front National had achieved in redefining the concept of the people in their terms. And Sarkozy's strategy had an impact on contemporary usages of the people as a concept.

This conquest did not go uncontested however. Ideological debates demonstrate the extent to which linguistic communities generate a diversity of perspectives of any one concept. On the traditional left and far left, a new phenomenon had begun to emerge. Jean-Luc Mélenchon began to make a call to the people as a whole, or at least to 'the workers' and '*le peuple de gauche*', the people of the left. This call was inevitably directed mainly at workers who felt disenchanted with the French Socialist Party that had followed a similar path to Blair in adopting neoliberal market-centred policies and which had little more to offer workers than tepid reforms, following with the great swing to the right during the Chirac and Sarkozy presidencies. Mélenchon reactivated the latent republican sentiment that we considered in the quotations from Michelet and Hugo cited above. He harnessed the rhetoric that defines the people as an active force, forging its destiny, an unstoppable historical process, the people Napoléon led into battle as he marched through Europe combatting the Old Order.

Mélenchon was clearly breaking with a socialist party that was no longer in touch with the people and largely incapable of establishing a dialogue with the people. The 2007 presidential candidate for the Socialist Party, Ségolène Royale, in her debates with Sarkozy, did not invoke radical republican sentiment. Royale feels at home speaking about the 'peoples of Europe', but prefers to speak of '*les français*', when it comes to France. The media were generally favourable in the way they presented Royale as a candidate, a woman, and a reformer. But no journalists heralded her as 'a woman of the people'. Royale was clearly a member of the political class, a caste apart, part of what Mélenchon would dub as '*la monarchie presidentielle*' ('the presidential monarchy').

Royale's partner of the time, who was elected President in 2012, François Hollande, seemed to share her uneasiness when it came to the people. He used the word '*peuple*' only once in a two-hour talk given at the Pierre-Mendès University, in Grenoble, 4 February 2011. And when he mentioned 'the people', it was only to affirm that they would be invited to come on election day and vote for his Party. This pragmatic opportunism remained characteristic of the way Hollande spoke of 'gathering people together' ('*rassemblement*') in the first years of his presidency, without ever directly addressing or defining who would be gathered together or why.

Meanwhile, the traditional right-wing in the 2012 election made little concession to populism. They continued to argue that together they would make 'a strong France' ('*une France forte*'), and they celebrated and claimed to defend '*les français*'. In the 2012 election, however, they had no real taste for the word '*le peuple*'. This was to change during the period 2015 to 2016, however, when Jupé and Fillon, the main contenders for leadership of the right in the approaching elections of 2017, both made a concerted effort to win back the keyword, '*le peuple*' from the far right, and win back the alienated electorate with the word.

This seems to suggest that it was the radicals that were redefining the keywords that would frame political debates of the 2017 election.

Debates generated by Le Pen and Mélenchon seemed to have anchored the term *le peuple* once more a little more firmly in the minds of French people. The language of journalists of the time seems to confirm this. A popular weekly magazine, *Marianne* (9–18 May 2012: 14), spoke of François Hollande's electoral victory as an event in which 'a whole people had been shaken up' (*'tout un peuple s'ébroue'*). And it claimed that Parliament (*l'Elysée*) had once more become 'the house of the people' (*'la maison du peuple'*) (idem: 17). Neither was this simply a left-wing knee-jerk reaction following the elections.

Christophe Barbier, representing the right-wing press in his article in *L'Express* (9–15 May 2012), warned the left of their responsibilities to the people: he spoke of 'the anger of the people' (*'colère populaire'*) that would rise up against Hollande if he failed to deliver on promises to protect those suffering in the economic downturn. As the financial situation went from crisis, to stagnation and depression, and as Hollande became increasingly perceived as a lame duck President, these words came to seem prophetic. Hollande became the first post-war President who was forced to stand down without seeking a second mandate from the people.

But this was not simply a criticism of the left but a rejection of the French political class as a whole. The same journalist, Christophe Barbier, was equally hard on the right-wing: looking back on Sarkozy's presidency (2007–2012), he considered that the President had 'distorted his relationship with the people' (*'faussé son rapport au peuple'*, idem: 51). Clearly, the status of the people in political debates was changing: '*le peuple*' was taking on a different meaning, one that was beginning to resound meaningfully in the minds of the far left, the far right, and the traditional right: '*le peuple*' was increasingly being used as a political concept, an analytical tool.

In the media and in political debates, it no longer seemed possible to ignore *le peuple*. This keyword seemed ready to assert itself. *Le Nouvel Observateur* (10–16 May 2012: 43), a centre-left weekly magazine, gave credence to such an idea when it claimed in the weeks between the first and the final rounds of the presidential elections that 'The people, the nation, and the State must be incarnated' (*'Le Peuple, la nation, l'État doivent s'incarner'*).

As it turned out, other events were to take the forefront in the French media. But those events did have a direct impact on rhetoric related to the people. The terrorist attacks in France in 2015 and 2016 encouraged discourse strategies in which '*le peuple*' was recuperated by the State as a means of legitimizing itself as the protector of the people in the face of an external threat. Interestingly, it was more the Prime Minister, Manuel Valls, who began using the keyword, not the discreet Minister for the Interior, Bernard Casseneuve, the main actor in security and internal affairs, who would replace Valls as Prime Minister in November 2016, when Valls ran for leadership as a Socialist candidate for presidency. But even Président Hollande began uncharacteristically adopting the term, as if it had become an indispensable buzzword that he could not entirely avoid. Clearly, Hollande and Valls were seeking to turn around their flagging results in the popularity polls. Indeed, appeals to the people were increasingly made by Valls and Hollande who contended that the government was doing all it could to protect national security. This increasingly became the logic that structured François Hollande's attempt to hang on to power in the course of 2015 and 2016, before he stood down as a candidate for the 2017 elections.

In these years, various improvised discourse strategies were adopted invoking the people. In one *élan* or rhetorical flourish, Manuel Valls called for France to protect its culture against attacks, and he waxed poetical about '*l'âme française*' ('the French soul'). Such outbursts fell flat, on the whole, since the main protagonists of the Socialist Party felt ill at ease with the idea of 'a French soul'. That seemed like something the French Catholic right – represented by François Fillon – would be more likely to celebrate. But despite the Socialists' misgivings about rhetoric addressing *le peuple*, it soon became clear that such addresses could not simply be dismissed as sporadic outbursts of populist rhetoric. They had to be countered by argued appeals to the people. And as the 2017 elections drew nigh, the various parties on the left and the right began to position themselves in relation to the people.

Jean-Luc Mélenchon consolidated his rhetoric of the people. He adopted the slogan '*Avec la force du peuple, tout devient possible*' ('With the might of the people, everything is made possible'). In 2017, he published a book entitled, *L'ère du peuple* (*The Epoch of the People*). His website was called '*La force du peuple*'. And in it he argued:

> *Nous devons séparer la République des lobbies qui menacent l'environnement et notre santé, stopper la toute-puissance de la finance, abolir la monarchie présidentielle et les privilèges de la caste qui dirige tout. C'est le moment de redevenir un peuple souverain et indépendant, libéré des traités européens et des alliances militaires guerrières.* (http://melenchon.fr/2017/04/21/force-peuple-possible/, 2017)

We must cut away the lobbies that threaten the environment and our health from the Republic, and bring an end to the overwhelming power of financial capital, we must abolish the presidential monarchy and the privileges of the cast that directs everything. This is the moment to become once more a sovereign people, independent and free from European treaties and war-mongering military alliances.

And this call to the people did not go unheard. On 18 March 2017, Mélenchon assembled 130 000 militants (according to the organizers) in a march across Paris, calling citizens to rise up against the presidential monarchy (*'une insurrection citoyenne contre la monarchie présidentielle'*, http://www.france24.com/fr/20170318-melenchon-VI-republique-prone-insurrection-citoyenne-contre-monarchie-presidentielle),

Meanwhile, Le Pen continued to consolidate her populist rhetoric, and when she came second in the first round of elections on 23 April 2017, she evoked the people no less than ten times in a speech that was barely 200 words long (http://www.frontnational.com/videos/allocution-de-marine-le-pen-au-soir-du-premier-tour-de-lelection-presidentielle/). Le Pen had narrowly beaten Mélenchon and the right-wing candidate, Fillon, and she had helped to humiliate the Socialists that managed to gather together only 8 per cent of votes in the first round of elections. Le Pen was clearly more in tune with the people than many of the other candidates. She saluted a people that was lifting up its head, a people sure of its values and confident in its future. She spoke of the greatness (*grandeur*) of the French people, and from that moment on, until the day of the election, she resolutely elected herself as '*le candidat du peuple*', the people's candidate.

Once more it appeared all too clear that it was the radicals that were framing the debate. This explains how Mélenchon was able to reactivate anti-monarchic sentiments in a dated rhetoric of freedom from oppression. He was making use of an established rhetoric, one French children learn in history classes in schools, and one that has no real equivalent in English. Authority is monarchy, and monarchy must be smashed by the people. This is a French story, not an English one.

Le Pen, for her part, quoted de Gaulle, the hero of French right-wing republicans, in her celebrations of the French people, and this helped to sell her to voters as the people's candidate. This claim does not bear up to scrutiny, of course. De Gaulle perceived the French people as having a vocation to enlighten the world. In promising to protect the 'greatness' of the French people, Le Pen was more interested in playing on racist resentments, and building barriers and re-erecting France's frontiers. It did, nonetheless, prove an effective tactic, by moving in on the rhetoric of the traditional right and abducting one of its icons.

The left and the right could not remain indifferent to such calls to the people, and they adopted various strategies in their public addresses. In one rally, the right-wing French candidate, François Fillon, celebrated the French people as an 'untiring people':

> *Vous êtes ensemble le peuple qui est tous les jours au travail, qui croit à la famille, à l'ordre juste, qui respecte le drapeau tricolore,* **le peuple qui ne fait pas de bruit, qui a du bon sens.** (7 March 2017, https://www.fillon2017.fr/discours-trocadero/; emphasis added)

> Together you are **the people at work every day**, that believes in the family, in just order, and that respects the blue, white, and red flag of France, **the people that makes no noise, that has good sense.** (Emphasis added)

Certainly, Fillon was addressing another people than Le Pen and Mélenchon. Their peoples were the revolutionary peoples that threatened to transform existing structures and treaties. They went down into the street in a noisy show of strength. Fillon's people kept quiet and got on with their work. Fillon gathered his people together at the Trocadéro in the heart of the richest quarter of Paris, the 16th arrondissement. This was the people of order, the people that did not make a fuss, the traditional people of France, the Catholics who saw the destiny of their culture as inseparable from its past. For this reason, Fillon celebrated the cathedrals of France in his speech. This, however, seemed to alienate him further from the electorate, since in France, the left-wing is primarily atheist or agnostic, and the radical right does not identify with the traditional Catholic right-wing upper classes.

How did the new contender for the presidency, the centrist, Emanuel Macron, respond to this rise in populism? Macron seemed to follow Hollande and Royale in resisting populism. Macron's response to these appeals to the people were tempered and rather lukewarm. In the speech he gave following the first tour of elections which showed him leading by a small margin (https://www.youtube.com/watch?v=oTuJud-kgR4), Macron spoke of the 'profound' and 'organic' and 'profound sentiment' that had 'always carried our people forwards', and he claimed that in voting for him, the people had made a choice for a France that went beyond divisions. He addressed his 'friends' ('*amis*') but made no direct appeal to the people. He claimed that he had heard '*les peurs du peuple de France*' ('the fears of the French people').

But curiously, Macron did not appeal to the people to vote for him. Rather he responded by assuring the people that he would 'accompany' them. This euphemism is not innocent: 'accompany' implies the leader already knows where the people are going and what their ultimate destination is. It supposes that the leader leads those who already adhere to the given destination without discussion. This discursive strategy is difficult to understand for non-natives, but it activates a resilient rhetoric in the French imagination. The idea of 'accompanying' makes reference to the Catholic rhetoric celebrating Jesus the shepherd, a rhetoric that had deep roots in *l'Ancien Régime*. That same conceptual metaphor was taken on by the French State and the education system after the Revolution (see Charbonnel, in Underhill 2011: 34). It was intended to reassure the French, and judging from Macron's success in the second round of elections, this strategy seems to have been successful. But what does such rhetoric imply? The people are sheep, who need protection. The people are looking for a leader to follow. The Shepherd leads the way. The people do not discuss their destiny. Their destiny is not to question, but to follow their course with their saviour at their side.

In the speech Macron gave on the night of his election (http://www.parismatch.com/Actu/Politique/Le-premier-discours-d-Emmanuel-Macron-president-de-la-Republique-1250729), he did address the people directly, but there was a crucial difference between Macron's vision of the French people and the ones presented by Le Pen and Mélenchon. Macron placed the people and its destiny within the framework of the shared destinies of the peoples of Europe, and this was something very new for a French president. De Gaulle believed in Europe, but he believed France would lead Europe; Macron appeared to be arguing that he would lead France back into a pro-European course.

It remains to be seen whether the rhetoric of the people will continue to animate public debates, or whether the radicalism of Le Pen and Mélenchon will peter out. The main parties on the left and the right can be seen as having adopted opportunistic strategies to try to gain popular support in paying lip service to the people during election time. Macron, for his part, remained reluctant to adopt populist rhetoric. He rarely invokes the people, and for the present time, it seems unlikely that he will adopt '*le peuple*' as a keyword, or make abundant use of it in his public addresses. If this is so, perhaps we are witnessing the fall from favour of a concept that waxed strong, but only for a short while. This is only one scenario in the story of '*le peuple*' though, and things may turn out otherwise. The roots of a radical conception of 'the people' exist, and the rise and fall of the people in French political rhetoric reveal the extent to which the French culture shares a vibrant and powerful concept that can provoke strong emotions when it is activated at the right moment.

Brexit: A Victory for 'Real People'?

After a long and hard campaign, and after constant harassment from the mainstream media, Nigel Farage's UKIP movement finally swayed public opinion in favour of the Brexit campaign on 23 June 2016. Understandably moved, on the night of the elections, Nigel Farage welcomed the referendum results by addressing 'the people' that had taken their fate into their hands with the following words:

> Dare to dream that the dawn is breaking on an independent United Kingdom. … If the predictions now are right, this will be **a victory for real people, a victory for all free people, a victory for decent people**. We have fought against the multinationals We have fought against the big merchant banks. We have fought against big politics. We have fought against lies, corruption and deceit. And today, honesty, decency and belief in nation, I think, is now going to win. (https://www.youtube.com/watch?v=k-KolaQhNSQ; emphasis added)

Nigel Farage is a consummate professional public speaker, well versed in the art of rhetoric. The anaphora, repetition at the beginning of phrases ('We have fought …) is typical of his style. He skilfully uses the rule of threes. And even if he is capable of a certain amount of redundant repetition (when for example he rails against lies, corruption and deceit) the rule of threes remains effective. Moreover, his arguments are unquestionably heartfelt. But what people was Farage addressing?

Farage addressed people who he considered to be 'real', 'decent', and 'patriotic'. And these were the people, he claimed, who had won a battle against lies, corruption, and deceit. The banks, the multinationals, and the mainstream political parties were all set up as the would-be liars and tyrants. But in the story Farage was telling, the little man had not been daunted. And together, the little men and the little women of Britain had shown their strength. David had won against a row of Goliaths. The binary oppositions are important here. This story sets up an opposition between falsity and reality, dishonesty and decency.

For the purposes of our study what is important here is that Farage won by addressing 'the people'. This involved cleverly countering condescending reflexes when speaking about the people. Clearly, nobody wishes to consider themselves 'ordinary' or 'common'. To this extent, Farage was simply being respectful and polite in his public addresses. Farage generally refused to speak of or to the electors as 'ordinary people' or 'common people'. By avoiding these two key expressions that systematically marginalize the people and implicitly denigrate the democratic process, Farage managed to establish a rapport with more than half of the voters of Britain. The racist content of his speeches and his policies on immigration have attracted sufficient criticism to make it unnecessary to quote the arguments here. The logic of his discursive strategy does, on the other hand, deserve further consideration. What we have to measure is the extent to which Farage was able to transform the dominant frames of reference concerning the people. This entails not only elevating a part of the people (his supporters) to 'the people'. It also involves setting up sectors of society that must, for the purposes of his rhetoric, be excluded from 'the people'. And the list all of the people excluded turns out to be long.

The 'real people' are not the bankers, the multinationals, or the people working in either of these sectors. They are not the politicians on the left or right, or the people who traditionally vote for them. But more than that, the idea of 'real people' brings into play a curious geopolitical narrative. In popular stereotypes of the north of England, the people of the Home Counties, the affluent south, are regarded to be cold, selfish, individualistic, and pretentious: they are not 'real', as the northerners consider themselves to be. For this reason, the idea of 'real people' brings to mind Northern accents. 'Real people' resounds with the same insistence as 'real ale'. Ale is not lager or beer, it is 'ale', English, old, traditional, real.

The popular narrative that the people of the north are real while southerners are pretentious is inevitably met with incomprehension by the great variety of people living in the south. Nonetheless, this is the cultural stereotype that is familiar to anyone in Liverpool, Leeds, or Hull. Significantly, it is a narrative that proves baffling for Scots as much southerners. It is a specifically English myth. Scotland sets up national stereotypes between Scots and the English, and that sets up internal divisions between the Highlands and the islands and the central belt that links Glasgow to Edinburgh. But it leaves no place for a north–south divide that hinges upon a popular belief in the 'real people'. Who in Scotland would give credence to the idea that Glaswegians are not 'real people'?

Interestingly, Farage is not a northerner. Farage was born in Downe, just south of London, where he went to university. But evidently he understood the usefulness of exploiting this cultural divide between the north and the south. This explains why he pronounced 'real' as a diphthong, almost a double vowel, as northerners do, when he welcomed the referendum results (https://www.youtube.com/watch?v=k-KolaQhNSQ). This is the consummate populist addressing the people in their language.

Farage triggers a set of cultural stereotypes that sets up the banks, the upper classes, the upper-middle classes, and the multinationals of global capitalism as the enemies of the working people, striving to keep their families and communities together, the people trying to keep their jobs faced with cheap labour produced by poorer European member states, by delocalization, and economic and financial crises. Farage is addressing the unemployed, the downwardly mobile middle classes, and those living in provincial towns and cities that suffered from decades of depression following the decline of industry during Thatcher's three terms in office: an electorate eager to believe that a Robin Hood had come to set things aright. Farage therefore addresses the electorate in much the same terms as Scott and Byron when they speak of the self-respecting, freedom-loving good yeoman, the salt of the earth.

Focusing on real people is a discursive strategy that works in two phases. Firstly, a model is set up for the average Englishman; secondly, that model is lifted up and celebrated as an ideal: these two processes – essentialism and elevation – are inextricable. Communist rhetoric of the 1920s and fascist rhetoric of the 1930s employed similar techniques when they celebrated and elevated the average man to the leader of the nation. No longer the 'common' man, the communist man and the Aryan hero of the Nazis were both celebrated as the noble, decent human who believed in his native soil, and was closely bound to his fellow men by a fraternal bond. That man would be an inspiration to generations to come.

Fascist and communist rhetoric both speak of 'enemies of the people' (Underhill 2011: 101–102, 152, 169). Some people walk hand in hand with the people, some people stand in their way, and obstruct the path to the future that the people must construct. Such people do not grasp the historical role of the people, and so they are, inevitably, mowed down by the people. As the Czechoslovak Communist newspaper (*Rudé Právo*) put it: can you blame the train if it cuts your legs off, when you lay down on the tracks of history (Underhill 2011: 99)?

These parallels are interesting from a rhetorical and semantic point of view in that they reveal shared underlying reflexes and strategies, but they should not be overstated. It would be absurd and misleading to set up Farage as a fascist or a tyrant. He stood down from politics after fulfilling his goal to sabotage Britain's partnership in the European project. He had no plans for gulags and concentration camps. Farage may favour strict quotas on immigration, but his party employed people of various ethnic origins, and his wife is German. Nonetheless, his discursive strategy masterfully marshals various populist techniques designed to position the 'people' on one side against the 'non-people' on the other. He negates his opponents and excludes them. He celebrates 'his people' and relegates his opponents to the status of 'non-people'. As UKIP's self-elected pope, he 'excommunicates' such persons from the people. And in one fell swoop he stigmatized them, and excluded them from the community at home, while ensuring Britons excluded themselves from the European community.

This was a powerful victory for Farage, and one that was won by rhetoric. Farage took the risk of believing he was capable of winning over the people. And to the horror of mainstream politics and the media, he succeeded. The media and the leaders of the mainstream political parties did not take Farage seriously until it proved too late. Before and after the referendum they tended to side with Voltaire's and Burke's position, in believing that 'the people' are 'frequently, and outrageously' mistaken in their judgement (*ODQ* 1992: 159). But Farage was countering with powerful strategy. He was banking on the backlash that Chesterton evoked when he warned the ruling classes against forgetting the people. As Chesterton implied, the people will remind their rulers that 'we are the people of England, that never have spoken yet' (Chesterton: 'The Secret People', *ODQ* 1992: 199).

Brexit was not a violent people's revolt or a revolution. Indeed, Farage congratulated the movement on the peaceful means by which it had achieved its aims: 'Without a bullet being fired, we have done it' (https://www.youtube.com/watch?v=k-KolaQhNSQ). This was very different from the radical spirit of revolt that involved the people rising up and taking power, the sentiment Le Pen and Mélenchon were appealing to. That was a French narrative. The English narrative activated a patriotic sentiment that shared much in common with appeals made to the 'staunch yeoman', the loyal, patriotic, freedom-loving Englishman, that the kings and queens of England urged to be resolute in defending their strip of land against invaders.

Nostalgia and romanticism continue to fuel the popular imagination today. And this allowed Nigel Farage, for his part, to play the man of the people, just as Le Pen in France was tailoring herself for the role of 'the people's candidate'. The stakes were not the same, and neither were the narratives the two leaders needed to activate in telling their own stories about how they would save the people and the nation. Farage had to discredit the establishment, and reinvest 'the people' with a political role, a destiny, a vocation. He needed to escape the language of the establishment to change the balance of power. This meant forcing 'the people' and 'real people' into the political arena and forcing other expressions out. What were the keywords of the language of the establishment?

Democratic discourse in Britain at the level of local and national politics tends to make use of the concept of the 'community' or 'the public' rather than 'the people'. Corpus research provides a great many examples referring to how government responds to the needs of the community. If we consult the first twelve collocations for 'the community' found in the BNC, we do indeed find 'care', 'institutions', 'within', 'throughout', 'benefit', and 'reform'. All of these indicate the government's engagement with people. This is somewhat reassuring.

Understandably, far-right populist movements in England, from the British National Front to the British League and UKIP, tend to play down this discourse concerning the community. Far-right rhetoric focuses on 'the English'. It tends to set the English up in a power play that alternates between portraying them as a dominant cultural or racial force, or as a victim of foreign aggression. In most forms, the island mentality is consolidated by spatial metaphors of insides that must be protected against outsiders: and the insider–outsider dynamic opens the way to various forms of racial, cultural, and national exclusion.

Most importantly for our study, 'the people' did not figure highly within conceptions of the community or 'the English'. The BNC provides 5014 examples of 'the English'. But judging from the examples consulted and from the list of collocations for 'the English', once we have filtered out 'the English press', 'the English King', 'the English lads', 'the English countryside', and 'the English language', there remains little left of the English people as the agent of its own democratic destiny. This meant that 'the English people' was 'up for grabs'. After a process of semantic evacuation, it was ripe for colonization. And the master stroke of UKIP was to seize the moment and win the concept over.

Former far-right parties did not grasp this point. The British Defence league rejects other cultures, and celebrates their own idea of 'English culture' (http://www.englishdefenceleague.org.uk/we-are-proud-of-english-culture/). In the Manchester terrorist attack of 22 May 2017, for example, the British Defence League was eager to celebrate the community spirit of the community. They praised:

> **The courage of first responders**
> The first responders included **ordinary people** who courageously and generously stopped what they were doing and joined official police and ambulance staff to help in every way they could. (http://www.englishdefenceleague.org.uk/edl-statement-on-the-attack-at-manchester-arena-a-plea-for-change/; emphasis added)

These lines demonstrate the extent to which the British Defence League adheres to the expressions generated by a class-based conception of 'the people'. The British Defence League is brutal in its racial stigmatization, but somewhat predictable and even timid in the way it adopts currently accepted keywords. It tends to position itself using the keywords in play in traditional mainstream politics. However radical the British Defence League tried to be, it could never hope to win over more than a minority of people in debates using words like 'culture' and 'community' which were so fully entrenched in the language of local politics and bureaucracy. And in this context, celebrating 'the common people' seems absurdly out of place and at odds with populist rhetoric.

Blair and Cameron both promoted the discourse of the 'community'. The term tends to evoke ideals of a traditional rather than a radical kind. Cameron took on the left-wing, when he tried to pose as the defender of 'the big society'. Thatcher had sided with the individual, and disparaged 'society', because 'society' was perceived to be a left-wing concept, a concept of the welfare state that her government set out to transform if not dismantle. Cameron's claim to take on board the concept of 'society' was a bold rhetorical move to try to take over foreign political territory, but it proved somewhat short-lived, and Cameron soon reverted to speaking about 'community'. For example, Cameron's government proposed the 'localism act' of 2011 as part of the 'Big Society' project, which contained a section designed to promote and defend 'community empowerment'.

'Culture', 'community', 'society', 'individuals', and 'private freedoms', these were the keywords in currency in public debate. Farage knew he must radically reframe the debate, if he was to be able to convince the electorate to force Westminster to withdraw from Europe, and that meant moving beyond 'communities', 'individuals', 'cultures', and 'societies'. Blair had won over middle England and addressed the 'middle classes' who appeared to prosper under his administration's government until the financial crises of 2007 and 2008. Cameron continued to preach to the public about individual engagement in the community. But little was done to convince either the north or Scotland that the policies of the City being proposed by either the Chancellor of the Exchequer George Osborne (2010–2016) or the Mayor of London Boris Johnson (2008–2016) had much to do with communities in the midlands or the north.

In this respect, Farage was more attentive to the geopolitics of Britain. He clearly perceived the main pivot of power as being middle England, and he managed to exacerbate and profit from the north–south antagonism, thereby swaying the midlands towards the stereotypes of the north. Farage was making an attack on the centre of Britain's political powerbase. The National Front is still based in Hull, but traditionally it had support bases in Leeds and Liverpool, rather than in London. The National Front marched on London in the 1970s in much the same way as the Nazi party stigmatized Berlin in the 1920s and 30s. Marine Le Pen acts in a similar way when she whips up anti-Parisian sentiment in the South-East and in the North-East of France. Poverty, downward mobility, and resentment against the capital, and against the capital's contempt for the 'provinces' is a powerful cocktail, and one that propagandists like Goebbels, Le Pen, and the National Front can exploit for their purposes. Antiestablishmentarianism and Euroscepticism today can replace former forms of collective paranoia. It is no longer possible to move people with appeals to antisemitism as politicians did in the 1930s. Fanning fears of the 'red terror' kept the Germans in a state of paranoia in the 1930s, and similar rhetoric terrorized the Americans in in the 1950s. But such enemies can no longer be harnessed by extremists looking to curry favour with the people.

What Destiny for the People?

Should we consider Brexit an aberration as it has been represented in many mainstream media accounts, or should it be considered a turning point in the history of Britain and of Europe? Does it come out of the blue, or is it the logical conclusion to a series of developments? Can it be considered a purely English story, or does it reveal a more fundamental European-wide scepticism? If we consider that Boris Johnson's nostalgic *The Churchill Factor*, published in 2015, was translated the very same year into many European languages, we might be inclined to conclude that the problem of Euroscepticism is not restricted to the British Isles. If European readers can be invited to share in a nostalgia that celebrates Churchill's stoic 'go it alone' style, it would appear many Europeans today feel that they are being ignored or despised by politicians at home, while their rights are not being respected or represented in the Europe that is currently being set up.

Farage stood down after the referendum, and left the people to their politics. Where does that leave them? Having whipped up support and enthusiasm, he quit politics, leaving the left and the right ill at ease, and uncertain as to how to address 'this people' that had voted for him, and most of all voted against their policies and against Europe. Having little experience in addressing 'the people', Theresa May's Conservative government was forced to set about putting into effect 'the will of the people', but this proved no easy matter, and a whole host of forces hostile to Brexit and the government joined forces against that process.

In the face of this, the language Theresa May adopted is significant. Her government put a brave face on it, and argued that it would pursue a policy that was solid and stable. This involved 'getting Brexit right' (https://www.youtube.com/watch?v=I_-ZpsFmXoM). May focused on 'young people', 'individuals', and 'communities' and promised: 'I'll make sure that this is a country that our children and grandchildren are proud to call home.'

But she also affirmed again and again that she would respect 'the will of the people'. Speaking on *Question Time* in the spring of 2017 (https://www.youtube.com/watch?v=CNfD-IIT-Vg) the Prime Minister refused to go against the will of the people as expressed in the Brexit referendum. May herself had sided with Cameron in calling voters to vote against Brexit, but when a member of the audience at the *Question Time* debate claimed the public had been misled by Farage and Johnson, and that a second referendum should be held, she resisted that claim.

She said that often in European politics, when the people of a member state voted against European policy, the bureaucrats in Brussels called for a second vote to be held to incite them to vote in accordance with their expectations. In this instance, May sided with what she called 'the will of the people', and she affirmed: 'The people in the UK said, collectively, "That's not the way to behave." If the people have given their choice, let's listen to the people and deliver on it.' In the same *Question Time* debate, May reasserted her faith in the British people: 'If we get it right, and I'm optimistic for the British people, because I believe in the British people, but we've got to get it right' (https://www.youtube.com/watch?v=CNfD-IIT-Vg).

May's turnaround on Brexit was increasingly portrayed as a lack of firm convictions, the proof that the 'strong and stable' policy was sham. Nevertheless, her language is interesting for our study in that it does recognize that Farage had forced politicians to listen to the people and to begin dialoguing more with the people. We cannot propose solutions to political questions here. In this book on the semantics of migrating meanings, we must limit ourselves to analysing discursive strategies and the keywords that they harness. And within those limits, it seems fair to conclude that 'the people' had once more entered public debate as one of the major issues at stake in the future of Britain and its relationship with Europe.

Whether Brexit will culminate in a victory for the people will depend very much on how we define the people, how we treat them, and above all, whether we consider ourselves to be part of the people. For a time at least, Farage managed to convince people that he and they were 'real'. He addressed the people that other parties failed to take into account or blatantly ignored. He spoke to 'them' as 'one of them', and that proved to have explosive effects for England, for the United Kingdom, and for the European Union as a whole.

Will the English people forge a new destiny or withdraw into nostalgia and negation? Will this people that once 'ruled the waves' turn its back on the world and on Europe, and isolate itself? Or will England take the Scottish pro-European vote as a guiding beacon that leads them back into a new relationship with Europe? This is a specifically English story in the middle of a European drama. Will the peoples of Europe join together to form a single people celebrating their unity in diversity, or will they turn from Europe, turn inwards, in nostalgic nationalism, perverted provincialism, and reject a European or global expansionism that seems to leave little place for them as peoples to express themselves?

Only time will tell. Meanwhile, beyond the boundaries of Europe, other narratives structure the worldviews of peoples. How do European traditions compare to those we will find in the long history of the Chinese people?

人民 RÉNMÍN

The Chinese People

Introduction

In his *China in Ten Words* (*Shí gè cíhuì zhōng de Zhōngguó* 十个词汇中的中国), the novelist and essay-writer, Yú Huá 余华 (1960–), decided to place at the top of his list of words characterizing contemporary Chinese culture the word *rénmín* 人民 'the people' (Yú 2010). In the first lines of this chapter Yú Huá writes:

> As I write these characters I have to look a second time to make sure I have them right. That's the thing about this word: it feels remote, but it's so familiar, too. I can't think of another expression in the modern Chinese language that is such an anomaly - ubiquitous yet somehow invisible. (Yu 2013: 3)

Yú's lines bear witness to the complex history and reality of this word, so central in twentieth-century political discourse. *Rénmín* 人民 was adopted in the names of places and institutions, and was used in titles. It is widely used in literature and in the arts, albeit sometimes in an ironic or satirical manner, and yet, it is not particularly common in everyday speech. The word is commonly found in newspapers, in official writings, and in academic discourse. Moreover, the meaning of the word is at times discussed and contested. This leads to ironic uses of 'the people', in phrases like 'for the people' or 'to serve the people'. But the proliferation of the word, and these ironic uses of it, would certainly seem to indicate that *rénmín* does indeed constitute a keyword in the Chinese lexicon.

According to Wàn and Féng (2007), 'the word "the people" [*rénmín*] has become a key term that has deeply influenced modern Chinese society' ("人民"一词成为深刻影响近现代中国社会的关键术语). Wàn and Féng (2007) affirm that this word was adopted by some of the most important intellectual and political figures of modern and contemporary China. However, they stress that the word's meaning and the connotations associated with it have altered over time.

> the meaning of the word 'the people' [*rénmín*] was reinterpreted by Liáng Qǐchāo [1873–1929], Sūn Zhōngshān [also Sun Yat-sen, 1866–1925], Máo Zédōng [also Mao Tse-tung, 1893–1976]; from its original meaning of 'humanity, common people', or 'folks, ignorant people', it was extended to signify the master of the country's destiny ("人民"一词的含义，经过梁启超、孙中山、毛泽东等人诠释后，由最初的"人类、百姓"或"糊涂无知的人"，引申为权力及国家命运的主宰. (Wàn and Féng 2007)

Indeed the keyword *rénmín* 人民 is so productive, it often appears ubiquitous in Chinese discourse. Much of China's modern history has been marked by expressions such as 'the masses of the people' (*rénmín qúnzhòng* 人民群众), 'the people's democratic dictatorship' (*rénmín mínzhǔ zhuānzhèng* 人民民主专政), 'people's communes' (*rénmín gōngshè* 人民公社). And a central moral slogan was 'serve the people' (*wéi rénmín fúwù* 为人民服务). China itself came to be known as *Zhōnghuá rénmín gònghéguó* 中华人民共和国 'The People's Republic of China'. The currency was 'baptized' *rénmínbì* 人民币 (lit. 'the people's currency'). And the word *rénmín* came to be used in a whole host of other expressions and collocations.

Nevertheless, the history of the word *rénmín* cannot be limited to the decades of Communist rule. This keyword can be traced back to imperial China, while the notion of 'the people' occupied an important place in Chinese political thought throughout various historical periods. And it is to try to grasp this concept as a Chinese keyword evolving over time and traversing various historical, social, political, and ideological transformations that we will now give a summary of the way the word's meanings and usages have changed.

Mín 民: *the people in Classical Chinese*

The lexeme *mín* can be considered as pivotal in the political lexicon of various Asian languages, such as Chinese, Japanese, and Korean (see Tsutsumibayashi 2012). It assumed different connotations related to the notions of 'the people', 'nation', and 'citizen' in Meiji Japan[2] and in Late Qing (1644–1911) China. Above all, *mín* has been widely used as an independent word with the meaning of 'the people' in Classical Chinese.[3]

In the *Classic of Poetry* (*Shījīng* 诗经), a collection of 305 poems which dates from the first 400 years of the first millennium BCE (Riegel 2001: 97), and which was to become one of the Five Classics,[4] we can read:

樂只君子，民之父母

To be rejoiced in are ye, noble men,
Parents of the people.[5]

This sentence was quoted and glossed in the 'Great Learning' (*Dàxué* 大学, III BCE), a chapter of one of the Thirteen Classics,[6] the *Book of Rites* (*Lǐjì* 礼记), which became part of another collection of canonical texts, the Four Books:[7]

《詩》云：「樂只君子，民之父母。」
民之所好好之，民之所惡惡之，此之謂民之父母。

In the Book of Poetry, it is said, 'How much to be rejoiced in are these princes, the parents of the people!' When a prince loves what the people love, and hates what the people hate, then is he what is called the parent of the people.[8]

Hence, the benevolent ruler is imagined as the parent of the people, and the relationship between the ruler and the subjects is compared to the relationship between parents and children.[9] According to Lǚ (2003: 16), this political metaphor, crystallized in the current idiomatic expression, *ài mín rú zǐ* 爱民如子,[10] 'love the people as one's own child', reflects the central place of the family in Confucian thought and in Chinese culture. The family is regarded as the basis of the socio-political structure (as synthetized by the expression *qí jiā zhì guó* 齐家治国 'to regulate the family and to rule the state'), and all types of social relations are interpreted by referring to the conceptual framework of the family, or 'familiarized', to use Lǚ's terms (整个社会各种关系都均家庭化, Lǚ 2003: 16).

In the section 'Song of the five sons' (*Wǔ zǐ zhī gē* 五子之歌) of the *Classic of Documents* (*Shūjīng* 书经), another of the Five Classics, we find another central metaphor of ancient Chinese political rhetoric, that of the 'people as the root':

民可近，不可下，民惟邦本，本固邦寧。

The people should be cherished,
And not looked down upon.
The people are the root of a country;
The root firm, the country is tranquil.[11]

This image of the people as the key element in a country was central in early Chinese political thought, and was developed by the early Chinese Confucian philosopher Mencius (*Mèngzǐ* 孟子, 371–c.289 BCE). Mencius wrote (chapter *Jìnxīn xià* 尽心下):

民為貴，社稷次之，君為輕。

The people are the most important element in a nation;
the spirits of the land and grain are the next;
the sovereign is the lightest.[12]

Sabattini (2012: 167) underlines that the idea of the 'people as the root' had 'experienced a revival in China starting from the early twentieth century, when it was introduced into the debate on democracy'. Points of view still diverge on the interpretation of the 'people as the root'. For some scholars, this is to be considered a paternalistic conception of the political relationship. For instance, according to Zhao Yuezhi (2001: 22), 'this earlier concept excludes participation and denotes nothing more than a passive people and a benign ruler'. A more nuanced point of view is expressed by Lǚ (2003: 19), who argues:

民本主义绝不是民主主义，其逻辑起点并非要否定权或推翻王权，而是维护王权。… 但是我们也可以看到，民本主义与参与型的政治文化有相同之处。

The theory of the people as a root is by no means democratic; its logical starting point is not to deny the power of monarchy or to overthrow monarchy, but to preserve it. … Nevertheless, we can see some similarities between the theory of the people as the root and the participant political culture.[13]

Lǚ (2003: 19) mentions, for instance, the role of the *élites*, and the idea of legitimacy and of good government associated with the theory of the

Mandate of Heaven (*Tiānmìng* 天命, i.e. the right to rule given by Heaven to the virtuous ruler, which is lost when the realm is badly ruled). Tze-ki Hon (2012: 12) also underlines the 'paternalist and condescending tone' often associated with *mín* in some of its occurrences in Confucius' *Analects* (*Lúnyǔ* 论语): for instance, *shǐ mín* 使民 (which he translates as 'to dispatch the people'). However, this has also been translated as 'to order the people' (as we shall see in the following quotation), *yǎng mín* 养民 'to feed the people' or 'to nourish the people', *wù mín* 务民, 'to put the people to work', *jiào mín* 教民 'to educate the people'. In the chapter 'Gongye Chang' (*Gōng yě zhǎng* 公冶长), we find two of these expressions, 'to nourish the people' (*yǎng mín* 养民) and 'to order the people' (*shǐ mín* 使民):

> 子謂子產，「有君子之道四焉：其行己也恭，其事上也敬，其養民也惠，其使民也義。」

> The Master said of Zi Chan that he had four of the characteristics of a superior man - in his conduct of himself, he was humble; in serving his superior, he was respectful; in nourishing the people, he was kind; in ordering the people, he was just.[14]

Other scholars and essayists (such as Nuyen 2000) consider the idea of the people as root to be a source of inspiration for a specifically Chinese-style democracy, as distinct from the Western model. In a recent article that appeared in the *Global Times* (*Huánqiú shíbào* 环球时报), part of the official media, and entitled *Mínběnzhǔyì shì gè hǎo dōngxī* 民本主义是个好东西 'The theory of the people as root is a good thing', the Fudan university professor Zhāng Wéiwèi 张维为 (2014) claims that:

> 看来民本主义不仅符合中国政治传统，也代表了世界未来发展的潮流，展现了中国超越西方、超越西方模式的一个核心理念和成功实践。

> The theory of the people as the root can be seen as something that aligns with the Chinese political tradition, but also as a new trend for the future development of the world: it is a core concept and a successful practice for a China surpassing the West and the Western model.

It is clear that 'the people' is a keyword in official discourse and political theory, if we consider the huge amount of four character expressions containing the lexeme *mín*, that were coined throughout China's imperial history and which are still used today as proverbial expressions and in literary quotations. Among those worth quoting are the following:

- *yōu guó ài mín* 忧国爱民 'be concerned with the country and love the people' first recorded in an ancient historical work, the *Strategies of the Warring States* (*Zhànguócè* 战国策).[15]
- *zhì guó ān mín* 治国安民 'rule the country and give the people stability' and *guó fù mín ān* 国富民安 'the country is rich, the people is pacified' both found in the *Book of the Han* (*Hànshū* 汉书, chapters *Shí huò zhì shēng* 食货志上[16] and *Xíngfǎzhì* 刑法[17] respectively).
- *shí wéi mín tiān* 食为民天[18] 'food is the most important to the people' from the *Family instructions for the Yan Clan* (*Yánshì jiāxùn* 颜氏家训) by Yán Zhītuī 颜之推 (531–c.591) of the Norther Qi dynasty.
- *jì shì ài mín* 济世爱民 'help one's generation and love the people', first recorded in Ming dynasty Tú Lóng's 屠隆 (1542–1605) *A Story of Night-blooming Cereus* (*Tánhuājì* 昙花记).
- *guān xīn mín mò* 关心民瘼 'be concerned about people's suffering' from the Qing dynasty Lǐ Bǎojiā's 李宝嘉 (1867–1906) *Observations on the Current State of Officialdom* (*Guānchǎng xiànxíng jì* 官场现形记).

The lexeme *mín* was still to be found in political discourse between the end of the nineteenth and the beginning of the twentieth centuries, when the disyllabic word *rénmín* was already used to refer to the people. For instance, the reformist intellectual Liáng Qǐchāo 梁启超 (1873–1929), one of main figures of the 1898 Hundred Day Reform Movement, was the author of the influential political essay entitled *Xīn mín shuō* 新民说 (1902). The expression *xīn mín* in Liáng's title has been interpreted in various ways. This expression can be understood as either 'the new people' or 'to renew the people', and it was adopted by Liáng to designate the political renewal of China and of the Chinese people. However, Fairbank (1989: 221) underlines that the meaning of this expression in Liáng's political discourse was modified under Japanese influence. Indeed, after Liáng's exile in Japan, this expression assumed a new political dimension, when it was used to refer to the idea of citizenship and citizen's rights. For this reason, this essay has also been translated as 'the new citizen', a term we will be discussing in the second chapter of this work.

The lexeme *mín* was central to the political theory of Sun Yat-sen (Sūn Yìxiān 孙逸仙 or Sūn Zhōngshān 孙中山), who became the first president of the Republic of China in 1911, after the fall of the dynastic empire. Sun's famous *Sānmínzhǔyì* 三民主义 the 'Three People's Principles' (also translated as Tridemism) were first formulated in 1903 (Fairbank 1989: 223), in the last years of the Qing empire (1644–1911).

What do the 'Three principles of the people' designate?

The first principle was the *mínzúzhǔyì* 民族主义, a word formed by *mínzú* 'nation' or 'ethnic group' (Thoraval 1990) plus the suffixoid[19] -*zhǔyì*, 'ism', 'doctrine'. This expression is usually translated as nationalism. In the first formulation of the 'Three principles of the people', it clearly has anti-Manchu (i.e. anti-Qing dynasty) connotations.

The second principle was the *mínquánzhǔyì* 民权主义 (a word formed by *mín* 'the people', *quán* 'power' or 'rights',[20] and *zhǔyì* '-ism' or 'doctrine'), usually translated as 'democracy'.

The third *mínshēngzhǔyì* 民生主义 (formed by *mín* 'the people', *shēng* 'life', and *zhǔyì* '-ism' or 'doctrine') is usually translated as 'people's livelihood', or 'subsistence of the people'.

The three people's principles were reformulated by Sun Yatsen after the end of the dynastic empire and the foundation of the Republic, and this new formulation was influenced by the Russian October Revolution (see Liú and Lǐ 2003: 228). In a series of lectures delivered at the Canton University in 1924, Sun[21] claimed that the three people's principles were to be understood within the framework of a national salvation project (三民主義就是救國主義 'the three people's principles are a national salvation doctrine').

In the so-called 'new three principles of the people' or 'new tridemism' (新三民主义), the principle of 'nationalism' (*mínzúzhǔyì* 民族主义) lost its anti-Qing dynasty connotations and took on an anti-imperialistic meaning (Liú and Lǐ 2003: 229). The principle of 'democracy' *mínquánzhǔyì* 民权主义 progressively came to be associated with forms of direct democracy instead of the Euro-American models of representative democracy. The main objective here was 'to put political power in the hands of the people' (把政权放在人民掌握之中; quoted by Liú and Lǐ 2003: 231). The 'principle of people's livelihood' (*mínshēngzhǔyì* 民生主义, sometimes also translated as 'socialism') evokes the idea of 'control of capital' (节制资本) through nationalizing key industries, and 'land redistribution' (平均地权).

The differences between the earlier and the new formulation of three principles of the people were analysed and commented by Máo Zédōng 毛泽东 in the essay 'On new democracy' (*Xīnmínzhǔzhǔyì lùn* 新民主主义论) in 1940. In that essay Máo defined the 'new three principles of the people' (*xīnsānmínzhǔyì* 新三民主义) as the 'three revolutionary principles of the people' (*gémìng de sānmínzhǔyì* 革命的三民主义).

In subsequent decades, the form *mín* continued to be used in official discourse, in political slogans, and it was commonly found in idiomatic expressions. Nevertheless, during the twentieth century, it was the word *rénmín* 人民 that acquired a central position in official and political discourse, becoming a keyword of contemporary Chinese history and society.

Rénmín 人民: *an ancient form and the contemporary word for 'the people'*

Nowadays, the word used for 'the people', is the disyllabic term, *rénmín* 人民, but this word was found in ancient sources, dating back to the pre-imperial era. The etymological dictionary *Cíyuán* 辭源 (1986: 158) records two meanings for it: the first, is 'folk' or 'common people' (*píngmín* 平民 or *bǎixìng* 百姓), found in the chapter *Dìguān sītú* 地官司徒 'Offices of Earth' of *The Rites of the Zhou* (*Zhōulǐ* 周礼), and the second, 'human kind' (*rénlèi* 人类) is found in the chapter *Qīfǎ* 七法 'The seven standards' of *The Writings of Master Guan* (*Guǎnzi* 管子).

Otherwise, *rénmín* 人民 is widely used in ancient texts. It is found, for example in the lines of the poem 'Yì' 抑 in the *Classic of Poetry* (in the section 'Greater Odes of the Kingdom' *Dàyǎ* 大雅, 'Decade of Dàng' *Dàng zhī shí* 荡之什):

質爾人民
謹爾侯度
用戒不虞

> Perfect what concerns your officers and people;
> Be careful of your duties as a prince [of the kingdom];
> To be prepared for unforeseen dangers.[22]

The word *rénmín* can also be found in Mencius' book (*Mèngzǐ* 孟子, in the chapter *Jìnxīn xià* 尽心下),

孟子曰：諸侯之寶三：土地、人民、政事。寶珠玉者，殃必及身。

> Mencius said, 'the precious things of a prince are three: the territory, the people, the government and its business. If one values as most precious pearls and jade, calamity is sure to befall him.[23]

Rénmín was also used in combination with the quasi-synonym *bǎixìng*, which can be literally translated as 'hundred surnames', the word today used for 'common people'. This is the usage found in the chapter 'Anti-Fatalism, I' (*Fēimíng shàng* 非命上) in Book IX (卷九) of the *Mòzi* 墨子 'Master Mo':

於何用之？廢以為刑政，觀其中國家百姓人民之利。此所謂言有三表也。

How is it to be applied? It is to be applied by adopting it in government and observing its benefits to the country and the people. This is what is meant by the three tests of every doctrine.[24]

While in this context the combination of *rénmín* and *bǎixìng* designates the people, *rénmín* in other passages of the same work can be interpreted as meaning 'the population'. This is the case in the following section from the chapter 'Simplicity in Funerals III' (節葬下) of Book VI (卷六):

是故求以富家而既已不可矣，欲以眾人民，意者可邪？… 是故求以眾人民，而既以不可矣，欲以治刑政，意者可乎？其說又不可矣。今唯無以厚葬久喪者為政，國家必貧，人民必寡，刑政必亂。

Now that the practice of elaborate funerals and extended mourning has failed to enrich the country perhaps it can yet increase the population? … Now that it has failed to increase the population, perhaps, it can yet regulate jurisdiction? Again it is powerless. For adopting elaborate funerals and extended mourning as a principle in government, the state will become poor, the people few, and the jurisdiction disorderly.[25]

The term *rénmín* can be found throughout Chinese pre-imperial and imperial history: 1126 occurrences can be found in the Corpus of Classical Chinese (*Gǔdài hànyǔ yǔliàokù* 古代汉语语料库) of the State Language Commission Corpora (国家语委语料库). This corpus provided sources from the spring and autumn periods (770–476 BCE) up to the Qing dynasty (1644–1911).

The term *rénmín* was destined to take on various connotations in late imperial China, when a massive process of translating Western and

Japanese texts was undertaken in the context of China's modernization process. In this period, a series of 'equivalences' between Western and Chinese notions and terms were 'negotiated' and established (Lackner et al. 2001b). According to the Modern Chinese Terminology Database[26], the disyllable *rénmín* can refer to 'the people' in Wèi Yuán's 魏源 *Zēngguǎng hǎiguó tú zhì* (增广海国图志, 1852). The same usage is found in the *Tetsugaku jii* 哲學字彙 (*Dictionary of Philosophy*), by Inoue Tetsujirô 井上哲次郎 and Ariga Hisao 有賀長雄, published in Tokyo in 1884. The term can also refer to 'mankind in general', in *A Chinese English Dictionary* (Giles 1912), for example. Furthermore, *rénmín* was used to designate the 'citizen' – or *citoyen* in French – as we can see from the *Vocabulaire français-chinois des sciences morales et politiques* (Médard 1927). In contrast to this, Timothy Richard and Donald MacGillivray in *A Dictionary of Philosophical Terms: Chiefly from the Japanese* (1913) remind us that the term could also be used to mean 'the masses'.

As already underlined, the word *rénmín* was also adopted in Sun Yatsen's political discourse. According to Wàn and Féng (2007), Sun Yatsen 'overturned its original meaning' (本义彻底颠覆), conceiving of the '*rénmín*' as a political subject in his writings and speeches. Sun (quoted by Wàn and Féng 2007) claimed, for example:

今日我国为共和国，应以人民为主体。

Today our country is a republic, and must be centred on the people.

Hence, the word *rénmín* progressively assumed strong political connotations and became a keyword of the twentieth-century Chinese political lexicon, as Wàn and Féng (2007) underscore:

20世纪30年代以后，同为政治术语的"国民"、"公民"、"人民"逐渐发生了变化。"人民"一词愈益流行，影响也更大。

After the 1930s, the word 'the people' [*rénmín* 人民] progressively changed its meaning, as well as other political terms such as 'national' [*guómín* 国民, see Chapter 2] and 'citizen' [*gōngmín* 公民, see Chapter 2]. The word *rénmín* became increasingly popular and its impact was even more important.

Moreover, this term was destined to be used more and more in subsequent decades: *rénmín* was destined to become a keyword in communist

China political discourse, especially in Máo Zédōng's speeches and writings.

The people in Chinese communist political discourse

In the speech, 'On people's democratic dictatorship' (*Lùn rénmín mínzhǔ zhuānzhèng* 论人民民主专政), delivered on 30 June 1949 to commemorate the twenty-eighth anniversary of the Chinese Communist Party, Máo described the new regime as a People's state (*Rénmín de guójiā* 人民的国家) that protects the People (*bǎohù rénmín de* 保护人民的). He claimed that 'the people holds in its hands a powerful state apparatus' (*Rénmín shǒu li yǒu qiángdà de guójiā jīqì* 人民手里有强大的国家机器) (Máo 1949a).

Hence, 'the people' (*rénmín* 人民) must undoubtedly be considered one of the cornerstones of Maoist political rhetoric. What does 'the people' designate in his writings and speeches? How was the people defined and described in Máo's discourse?

In a speech entitled 'On coalition government' (*Lùn liánhé zhèngfǔ* 论联合政府), pronounced on 25 April 1945, Máo (1945) presented the people as 'the driving force behind historical development':

人民,只有人民才是改变世界历史的动力。

The people, only the people, are the driving force creating the world's history.

Among the speeches that focus upon the people and its role, one speech deserves to be mentioned: 'Serve the people' (*Wéi rénmín fúwù* 为人民服务), pronounced by Máo on 8 September 1944 for the memorial meeting of the soldier Zhāng Sīdé 张思德 (1915–1944). The title of this speech was destined to become one of the main Chinese political slogans:

中国古时候有个文学家叫做司马迁的说过:"人固有一死,或重于泰山,或轻于鸿毛。" 为人民利益而死,就比泰山还重; 替法西斯卖力,替剥削人民和压迫人民的人去死,就比鸿毛还轻。张思德同志是为人民利益而死的,他的死是比泰山还要重的 (Máo 1944)

The ancient Chinese writer Szuma Chien [*Sīmǎ Qiān* 司马迁] said, 'Though death befalls all men alike, it may be weightier than

Mount Tai or lighter than a feather.' To die for the people is weightier than Mount Tai, but to work for the fascists and die for the exploiters and oppressors is lighter than a feather. Comrade Chang Szu-teh [Zhāng Sīdé 张思德] died for the people, and his death is indeed weightier than Mount Tai.²⁷

According to Wú (2013) *rénmín* had already become a keyword of Máo's political rhetoric in the 1930s. This was clear from his 1935 speech 'On the strategy against Japanese imperialism' (*Lùn fǎnduì Rìběn dìguózhǔyì de cèlüè* 论反对日本帝国主义的策略), in which Máo analysed the attitudes of different classes to imperialism.

Rénmín progressively became a class concept, a historical concept. A detailed definition of Mao's conception of the people can be found in the above-mentioned essay 'On people's democratic dictatorship' (Máo 1949a):

> 人民是什么？在中国，在现阶段，是工人阶级、农民阶级、城市小资产阶级和民族资产阶级。这些阶级在工人阶级和共产党的领导之下，团结起来，组成自己的国家，选举自己的政府，向着帝国主义的走狗即地主阶级和官僚资产阶级以及代表这些阶级的国民党反动派及其帮凶们实行专政，实行独裁，压迫这些人，只许他们规规矩矩，不许他们乱说乱动。

> Who are the people? At the present stage in China, they are the working class, the peasantry, the urban petty bourgeoisie and the national bourgeoisie. These classes, led by the working class and the Communist Party, unite to form their own state and elect their own government; they enforce their dictatorship over the running dogs of imperialism – the landlord class and bureaucrat-bourgeoisie, as well as the representatives of those classes, the Kuomintang reactionaries and their accomplices – suppress them, allow them only to behave themselves and not to be unruly in word or deed.²⁸

The people's class character and historical character were redefined in the speech 'On the correct handling of contradictions among the people' (*Guānyú zhèngquè chǔlǐ rénmín nèibù máodùn de wèntí* 关于正确处理人民内部矛盾的问题), pronounced on 27 February 1957. Máo (1957) specified the different meanings of the word 'the people' and the varying degrees to which the category could be used to include or exclude groups during the anti-Japanese war, the civil war and the ways it could apply in the People's Republic of China:

> 人民这个概念在不同的国家和各个国家的不同的历史时期，有着不同的内容。拿我国的情况来说，在抗日战争时期，一切抗日的阶级、阶层和社会集团都属于人民的范围，日本帝国主义、汉奸、亲日派都是人民的敌人。在解放战争时期，美帝国主义和它的走狗即官僚资产阶级、地主阶级以及代表这些阶级的国民党反动派，都是人民的敌人；一切反对这些敌人的阶级、阶层和社会集团，都属于人民的范围。在现阶段，在建设社会主义的时期，一切赞成、拥护和参加社会主义建设事业的阶级、阶层和社会集团，都属于人民的范围；一切反抗社会主义革命和敌视、破坏社会主义建设的社会势力和社会集团，都是人民的敌人。

> The concept of 'the people' varies in content in different countries and in different periods of history in a given country. Take our own country for example. During the War of Resistance against Japan, all those classes, strata and social groups opposing Japanese aggression came within the category of the people, while the Japanese imperialists, their Chinese collaborators and the pro-Japanese elements were all enemies of the people. During the War of Liberation, the U.S. imperialists and their running dogs – the bureaucrat-capitalists, the landlords and the Kuomintang reactionaries who represented these two classes – were the enemies of the people, while the other classes, strata and social groups, which opposed them, all came within the category of the people. At the present stage, the period of building socialism, the classes, strata and social groups which favor, support and work for the cause of socialist construction all come within the category of the people, while the social forces and groups which resist the socialist revolution and are hostile to or sabotage socialist construction are all enemies of the people.[29]

Whether people were held to belong to 'the people' or to 'the enemies of the people' was thus defined according to the historical context. Schoenhals (1994: 2) underlines that the first decades the People's Republic foundation were characterized by 'a political discourse centered on a distinction between the People on the one hand and the non-People on the other', as 'there were significant segments of China's population that were non-People' (Schoenhals 1994: 3). In the above-mentioned speech, Máo adopted the expression 'enemies of the people' (*rénmín de dírén* 人民的敌人) to describe 'the social forces and groups which resist the socialist revolution and are hostile to or sabotage socialist construction'.

The categories of the 'non-people (fei renmin)' (Schoenhals 1994: 1) and 'enemies of the people' varied in those years, ranging from the *wǔ lèi fǎngémìng* 五类反革命, 'five categories of conter-revolutionaries' (bandit chieftains, professional brigands, local tyrants, special agents, and leaders of reactionary secrets societies), to the five black categories (*hēi wǔ lèi* 黑五类, i.e. landlords, rich peasants, counter-revolutionaries, criminals, rightists), or to the *dìfù fǎn huài* 地富反坏, a four character expression designating 'landlord elements, rich-peasant elements, reactionary elements, and hooligans' (Schoenhals 1994: 9, 12). The official and political discourse concerning the non-people was characterized by the 'use and abuse of political dysphemisms' (derogatory terms) as 'hundreds of new labels were invented to refer to the new non-People' (Schoenhals 1994: 14). Among them, a four-character expression 'rooted in Buddhist demonology' (Perry and Li 1993: 7), *niú guǐ shé shén* 牛鬼蛇神 'ox-monsters and snake-demons',[30] became synonymous with China's non-People (Schoenhals 1994: 12). Another expression was the four-character phrase *yāo mó guǐ guài* 妖魔鬼怪 'evil spirits and monstrous freaks' (Schoenhals 1994: 10). This is to be regarded as an example of the 'dehumanizing terminology' that 'permeated popular and official discourse' in this period (Perry and Li 1993: 7).

The political and official discourse was thus characterized, on the one hand, by an extreme vehemence against the segments of population regarded as 'enemies of the people', and, on the other hand, by the celebration of the 'people', omnipresent in political slogans, formulas, and speeches. For instance, *rénmín dāngjiā zuò zhǔrén* 人民当家做主人, 'the people are the masters' became a slogan, and was also used as the title of well-known song (the entire title being 'the people stand up and become the master', 人民翻身当家作主人).[31]

The following variations on the expression 'serve the people' can be quoted among these political slogans:

> serve the people heart and soul (*quánxīnquányì wéi rénmín fúwù* 全心全意为人民服务). (Wang 2008: 142)

> serve all the people of China and all the people of the world (*wèi quán Zhōngguó rénmín hé quán shìjiè rénmín fúwù* 为全中国人民和全世界人民服务). (Wang 2008: 142)

our literature and art have to serve the masses of the people (*wǒmen de wénxué yìshù shì wéi rénmín dàzhòng fúwù de* 我们的文学艺术是为人民大众服务的). (Máo 1942, quoted by Wang 2008: 134)

'The masses of the people' *(rénmín dàzhòng* 人民大众) was a frequent expression figuring the word *rénmín*. Other examples include *guǎngdà rénmín dàzhòng* 广大人民大众 and *guǎngdà rénmín qúnzhòng* 广大人民群众, both signifying 'the broad masses of the people'.

The word 'the people' was also present in expressions like 'the people's war' (*rénmín zhànzhēng* 人民战争), used by Máo in the abovementioned speech 'On coalition government' (Máo 1945). It was equally to be found in 'the people's revolution' (*rénmín gémìng* 人民革命), in slogans such as 'the People's Revolution under the guidance of Máo Zédōng is the front of the train driving history forward' (毛泽东思想指引下的人民革命是历史前进的火车头) (quoted by Wang 2008: 146). We find it again in the 'revolutionary people' (*gémìng rénmín* 革命人民). And it was also adopted to refer to the peoples of foreign countries, in expressions like 'the revolutionary people of Asia, Africa and Latin America' (亚非拉革命人民). The same usage can be found in 'all the revolutionary people of the world' (全世界革命人民) (Wang 2008: 135). *Rénmín* has also been used broadly as a modifier in the names of political institutions: The National People's Congress (全国人民代表大会), with annual sections held in the 'Great Hall of the People' (人民大会堂).

Nevertheless, various slogans were also formed using the monosyllabic form *mín* instead of the disyllabic word *rénmín*. These include the expressions:

- *yōng jūn ài mín* 拥军爱民 'embrace the army, cherish the people' (Wang 2008: 121);
- *yōng zhèng ài mín* 拥政爱民 'support the government, cherish the people'. This is also found in the longer version *yǒnghù zhèngfǔ, àihù rénmín* 拥护政府, 爱护人民) (Wang 2008: 121);
- *bīng mín shì shènglì zhī běn* 兵民是胜利之本 'the army and the people are the root of success' (Máo 1938, quoted by Wang 2008:114).

These examples clearly demonstrate that *mín* was still present in the Chinese language throughout this period and that it continued to form a productive resource exploited in political rhetoric.

Contemporary definitions and facets of the word rénmín

Rénmín has been central for the greater part of the twentieth century in political history and political discourse, but what place has been reserved for this word in contemporary Chinese society? How has this word been used in the decades following Máo's death in 1976, and in the period following the 'reform and opening up' (*gǎigé kāifàng* 改革开放), the policy that was launched in 1978 and that was to profoundly modify Chinese society and its economy?

The history and the trajectory of *rénmín* are reflected in the definitions and usages listed in contemporary dictionaries. One of the reference dictionaries for contemporary Chinese, the sixth edition of the *Xiàndài hànyǔ cídiǎn* 现代汉语词典 *Dictionary of Modern Chinese* (2015: 1091), gives the following definition of the word *rénmín* 人民: 'the fundamental member of society, essentially composed of the working masses' (以劳动群众为主体的社会基本成). This dictionary entry is followed by compound words and collocations, such as *rénmínbì* 人民币 literally 'the people's currency' (RMB, the Chinese currency), *Rénmín dàibiǎo dàhuì* 人民代表大会 'People's National Assembly', *Rénmín fǎyuàn* 人民法院 'People's Tribunal', *rénmín gōngshè* 人民公社 'people's commune', and so forth.

In a slightly less recent edition of another reference dictionary, the *Xīnhuá cídiǎn* 新华词典 *Dictionary of New China* (2009: 821), we find the same definition (i.e. 以劳动群众为主体的社会基本成员 'the fundamental element of society, essentially composed of the working masses') as the second meaning of the entry *rénmín*, the first meaning being *bǎixìng* 百姓 'common people' or 'folk'. However, the three examples given for this lemma do not seem to refer to this usage. They evoke connotations of a historical or political nature: *rénmín qúnzhòng* 人民群众 'the masses of the people', *zàofú rénmín* 造福人民 'for the benefit of the people', and *wéi rénmín fúwù* 为人民服务 'serve the people'. These are recurrent expressions found widely throughout the discourse of the Chinese Communist Party.

Hence, both dictionaries focus on the 'working character' of the people, rather than the class character. In these editions, no mention is made of the distinction between the people and the non-people.

It is worth stressing that the 1997 edition of the same dictionary (the *Xīnhuá cídiǎn* 新华词典) pointed out that 'the concept of the people differs in different countries and different historical periods in a given country' (人民这一概念在不同的国家和各国的不同历史时期有着不

同的內容), while the last part of this entry's definition coincided with Máo's 1957 definition quoted above ('in our country's socialist period, all the classes, strata and social groups which favor, support and work for the cause of socialist construction all come within the category of the people': 在我国社会主义时期，一切赞成、拥护和参加社会主义建设事业的阶级、阶层和社会集团，都属于人民的范围). The 1985 edition of another reference dictionary, the *Cíhǎi* 辞海 (lit. 'Sea of Words') (1985: 302), also emphasized the historical character of this concept, with a formulation very similar to that of Máo's 1957 definition. The main difference here is the absence of reference to the enemies of the people:

> 在不同的国家和各个国家的不同历史时期，有着不同的内容。如我国在抗日战争时期，一切抗日的阶级、阶层和社会集团，都属于人民的范围；在解放战争时期，一切反对美帝国主义和官僚资产阶级、地主阶级以及代表这些阶级的国民党反动派的阶级、阶层和社会集团，都属于人民的范围；在社会主义时期，一切赞成、拥护和参加社会主义建设事业的阶级、阶层和社会集团，都属于人民的范围。

> The concept of the people differs according to different countries and different historical periods in a given country. For instance, during our country's anti-Japanese war, all the classes, strata and social groups who were against the Japanese, belonged to the category of the people; during the War of Liberation, all the classes, strata and social groups opposing the American imperialism, the bureaucrat-capitalists, the landlord class and the Kuomintang reactionaries who represented these classes, belonged to the category of the people; in the socialist period, all the classes, strata and social groups which favor, support and work for the cause of socialist construction all come within the category of the people.

The ideological dimension in these definitions is evident, and this is clearly inseparable from the history of the Chinese Communist Party. When these references are compared with more recent dictionary editions, it becomes clear that the terms are gradually losing their 'class character'.

Moreover, the usage of the word *rénmín* as 'folk', 'common people' (for instance in the *Xīnhuá* dictionary), which was commonplace in nineteenth-century bilingual dictionaries, and which was overshadowed by the definition of 'the people' as a political force and a political actor, seems to be making a partial comeback in the contemporary lexicon.

Similar conclusions about the progressive weakening of the ideological facets of *rénmín* can be drawn after comparing the examples found in Corpus of Modern Chinese (*Xiàndài hànyǔ yǔliàokù* 现代汉语语料库) of the State Language Commission Corpora (国家语委语料库). This corpus gives 6669 results for the word *rénmín*, in sources drawn from between the 1960s and the 1990s. For instance, among the 1970s' sources, we found the following fairly representative phrases:

- 'the proletariat and the revolutionary people have Máo Zédōng's thought as their sole weapon' (无产阶级和革命人民, 只有以毛泽东思想为武器, 1970);
- 'loyal to the Party, loyal to the people, loyal to President Máo' (忠于党、忠于人民、忠于毛主席, 1978);
- 'to be opposed to our beloved prime minister Zhōu [Zhōu Ēnlái 周恩来, 1898–1976] means to be against Marxism, against the people, against president Mao' (反对敬爱的周总理, 就是反马克思主义, 就是反人民, 就是反毛主席, 1978).

Otherwise, among the more recent sentences we found:

- 'All our country people are unswervingly building socialism under the leadership of the Party' (全国人民在党的领导下坚定不移地建设社会主义, 1991);
- 'ameliorate and enrich the people's lives' (改善和丰富人民生活, 1993);
- 'the need to protect the environment and improve the people's living standards' (保护环境和提高人民生活水平的需要, 1993).

The influential official Chinese newspaper, *People's Daily* (*Rénmín rìbào* 人民日报), proves an invaluable source when it comes to evaluating the more recent developments of the word *rénmín* within the Chinese lexicon. In a keyword search carried out using the online version,[32] we found 7 861 228 occurrences of this word. Besides the copious use of the term in the titles and names of institutions ('People's Tribunal', 'People's Daily', 'People's Daily On-line', 'People's Airforce' among other examples), the word *rénmín* is frequently found in the expression *rénmín qúnzhòng* 人民群众, 'the masses of the people'. Among the 802

967 occurrences, 206 389 come from the section 'Chinese Communist Party news' (中国共产党新闻), and 52 339 come from the section 'Current politics' (时政). Among the examples, we found: 让人民群众满意 'satisfy the masses of the people' and 损害人民群众利益 'harm the interests of the masses of the people'.

The expression 'the interests of the people' (人民利益) proves to be quite frequent, with 57 366 occurrences, which derive mostly from the 'Chinese Communist Party news' section (18 261 references). We also find a relatively high number of occurrences (18 917) for the expression 'the fundamental interests of the people' (*rénmín gēnběn lìyì* 人民根本利益). This expression was used in Máo's political discourse (see Máo 1957). It was, moreover, to be adopted by the former president Jiāng Zémín 江泽民 (1926–) as one of the three main prerogatives. These came to be known as the 'Three Represents'[33] (*Sān gè dàibiǎo* 三个代表). The third of these holds that '[the Party should] always represent the fundamental interests of the overwhelming majority of the Chinese people' (始终代表中国最广大人民的根本利益). Not surprisingly, the majority of the occurrences (7256) are found in the section related to the Chinese Communist Party (中国共产党新闻).

Similarly, the expressions 'the masses of the people' and 'the people's interests' are significantly frequent in the ten billion character BCC corpus of Modern Chinese (BCC现代汉语语料库, http://bcc.blcu.edu.cn/). *Qúnzhòng* 群众 'masses' appears as the most frequent collocative of *rénmín* 'the people': 60 735 occurrences were found for *rénmín qúnzhòng* 人民群众, 'the masses of the people', out of a total 825 161 results for the word *rénmín* 'the people'. 'The interests of the people' (人民利益) was the fifth most frequent collocation, with 3894 occurrences. Among the frequent collocations, we also found 'People's government' (人民政府 32 136), 'People's Liberation Army' (人民解放军, 4915), and 'People's Republic' (人民共和国 4696).

On the whole, the above-mentioned slogan 'serve the people' (*wéi rénmín fúwù* 为人民服务) would still seem to be very common. The 17 111 occurrences found in the BCC corpus and the 138 157 occurrences found on the *People's Daily* website demonstrate this beyond any doubt. The *People's Daily* occurrences are found for the most part in articles related to the Chinese Communist Party (中国共产党新闻, 49 618 occurrences), but also in the section on 'current politics' (时政, 7304 occurrences), and in the section 'Opinions' (观点, 7230 occurrences). It is worth stressing this renowned expression, 'serve the people' (*wéi rénmín fúwù* 为人民服务), can be also used with a certain ironic distance. This can take the form of a bitter-sweet disenchantment, or a satirical form. And generally speaking, this is also true of the word *rénmín.*

Hence, in current discourse, the expression *wèi rénmín fúwù* 为人民服务 'serve the people' is at times subject to irony. On the one hand, the people have rights, but on the other, they are expected to pay for them. Self-sacrifice in the service of the greater good is transformed into a service that must be paid for. This transforms the State into a service provider anxious to make sure it is not being short-changed. For example, in one cartoon, Lǐ Xiǎoguāi 李小乖 shows the people being asked to pay 'the service cost' (服务费).[34] This is only one example. By recycling the American symbols of empowerment circulating during the first years of Obama's administration, Chinese posters and T-shirts were displayed, in an ironic postmodernist manner, figuring Obama with the slogan 'serve the people'. This shows how international symbols of the global community are recycled and fused with national traditions in the Chinese mindset.

In the provocatively satirical novel by Yán Liánkē 阎连科 (1958–), *Serve the people!* (为人民服务, 2005), the title refers to the way a young woman makes use of the subordinate of her older husband, a high-ranking colonel, for her own sexual requirements. The colonel's young wife not only exploits the subordinate's willingness to serve, but even makes use of a sign in the kitchen on which the slogan 'serve the people' is written to negotiate the times and terms of her extra-marital relations with her eager-to-please lover. She leaves the sign on the table when he is invited to come upstairs to cater to her erotic requirements.

Another amusing example of this ironic use of the expression was found in the imaginary 'daily political dialogue' (*Rìcháng zhèngzhì duìhuà* 日常政治对话) which was written by the essayist Wú Jiàxiáng 吴稼祥 (1955–), known for his thesis on neo-authoritarianism (*xīnquánwēizhǔyì* 新权威主义). This dialogue ironically calls into question the very idea of who belongs to 'the people' and can prove it[35] (Wú 2013).

问：你们不是标榜要"为人民服务"吗，怎么是这个态度？
答：是啊，我是为"人民"服务。请问你是人民吗?
问：我不是人民，但我是人民中的一员。
答：你是人民中的一员？你怎么证明你是人民中的一员？
…你既不能代表人民，也不能证明你是人民中的一员，我能接待你就不错了。我可是只为"人民"服务的啊。

> Question: You advertise that you have to serve the people. Why do you adopt this attitude?
> Answer: Yes, we serve the people. May I ask, are you the people?
> Question: I'm not the people, but I'm a member of the people.
> Answer: You're a member of the people? How can you prove that you are a member of the people? ... As you cannot represent the people, neither prove that you are a member of the people, it's already good of me to receive you.
> Indeed, I am only required to serve the people.

The word *rénmín* can also be called into question, as in the *China in Ten Words*, discussed above, in which Yú Huá writes:

> When everyone united in the urge to make money, the economic surge of the 1990s was the natural outcome. After that, new vocabulary started spouting up every-where – netizens, stock traders, fund holders, celebrity fans, laid off workers, migrant laborers, and so on – slicing into smaller pieces the already faded concept that was 'the people'. (Yu 2013: 6)

Otherwise, among the different usages of the word *rénmín*, it is worth mentioning that the term is included in the title of the artist Cáo Fěi's 曹斐 project *Rénmín chéng zhài* 人民城寨 (lit. 'the 'People's walled city'). This is usually rendered in English as RMB city (RMB being the abbreviation for the Chinese currency), originally a virtual world of Second Life. This project also inspired a theatre performance entitled *Rénmín chéng zhài yàngbǎnxì* 人民城寨样板戏 'Model operas of the People's city' (with an ironic reference to the Cultural Revolution period 'model operas', *yàngbǎnxì* 样板戏, used for political education and propaganda). However, these ironic usages show how significant the word *rénmín* and related expressions are in the contemporary Chinese lexicon.

In general, the word *rénmín* remains a pivotal term in political, official, and institutional discourse. In such discourse, this word itself and the related expressions are not, of course, used ironically, as they are in the cartoons about 'service cost' or the stories of a subordinate soldier catering to the sexual needs of his superior's wife. On the contrary, the connotations of the people in official rhetoric and institutional discourse remain ardently idealistic, and unequivocally positive.

Among the numerous examples of this term used in the slogans and speeches of Chinese political leaders, we can quote, first and foremost, the 'Eight honors and eight shames' (*Bā róng bā chǐ* 八荣八耻), the moral and political guidelines formulated by the former president Hú Jǐntāo 胡锦涛 (1942–):

以服务人民为荣
以背离人民为耻

Honor to those who serve the people,
Shame on those who betray the people.
(translated by Lin 2006, quoted by Zhong 2011)

The 'people' is often used in a palpably patriotic manner. This was the case, for instance, in the speech delivered by Hú Jǐntāo on 1 October 2009 to celebrate the sixtieth anniversary of the founding of the People's Republic of China,[36] where in the first sentence the former president celebrated 'the people of all ethnic groups in China' who 'feels extremely proud of the development and the progress of the great motherland and is fully confident in the bright perspective of the great rejuvenation of the Chinese nation' (全国各族人民都为伟大祖国的发展进步感到无比自豪，都对实现中华民族伟大复兴的光明前景充满信心), as well as 'the revolutionary predecessors and martyrs who have performed immortal feats for the nation's independence and people's liberation, for the country's prosperity and for the happiness of the people' (向一切为民族独立和人民解放、国家富强和人民幸福建立了不朽功勋的革命先辈和烈士们，表示深切的怀念). This speech ends with three 'long live' wishes, for the People's Republic, the Chinese Communist Party, and the Chinese people. The final sentence reads: 'Long live to the great Chinese people!' (伟大的中国人民万岁!).

The word *rénmín* also remains central in the political discourse of the current president Xí Jìnpíng 习近平 (1953–). The speech he gave as the newly elected President on 17 March 2013, at the closing meeting of 1st session of 12th National People's Congress, can be regarded as a fairly representative example of the way he uses this word in his political discourse: *rénmín* was used no less than forty-four times.[37] For instance, in this famous speech, focusing on the ideas of the Chinese rejuvenation and of the Chinese dream, Xí[38] claims that:

中国梦归根到底是人民的梦，必须紧紧依靠人民来实现，必须不断为人民造福。

The Chinese dream, after all, is the dream of the people. We must realize it by closely depending on the people, and we must incessantly bring benefits to the people.³⁹

Hence, the people are affirmed to have a central role in the construction and in the scope of the 'Chinese dream', the key political formula of the actual president. The Chinese dream and the people were once more coupled, when the realization of the Chinese dream was directly correlated to better living conditions for the people (实现中国梦, 创造全体人民更加美好的生活).

In this speech, we also find references to the need of 'listening at all times to the voice of the people, responding to people's expectations, ensuring the right to equal participation and equal development for the people' (随时随刻倾听人民呼声、回应人民期待，保证人民平等参与、平等发展权利), as well as 'developing the fundamental interests of the overwhelming majority of the people' (发展好最广大人民根本利益), a sentence echoing a deeply rooted expression in Chinese political rhetoric, already used by Máo Zédōng and Jiāng Zémín as we saw above.

The political dimension of the word *rénmín* can be seen in the usages of this word in Chinese academic discourse. When we carried out a search for this word on the National Social Science Database (*Guójiā zhéxué shèhuì kēxué xuéshù qīkān shùjùkù* 国家哲学社会科学学术期刊数据库), we found the following results for the 74 715 academic publications containing this word. The word proved most frequent in the section 'Politics and law' (政治法律, 23 682 results), followed by 'Economics and management' (经济管理, 21 237 results), and 'Sociology' (社会学 12 504). It proved far less frequent in such fields as the 'Arts' (艺术) and in 'Literature' (文学), in which 2388 and 2349 results were found respectively. Similarly, the expression 'serve the people' (为人民服务) produced 3386 occurrences, more than a half of which (1802) were found in publications belonging to the field of 'Politics and law' (政治法律). With 570 results related to 'Sociology', it appeared to be far less frequent in that field. The relatively frequent expression 'the interest of the people' (人民利益), produced somewhat similar results: with 1690 results, more than half, 1178 results, were found in political and legal publications (政治法律).

The Google Books Ngram viewer tool, based upon the extensive Google Books corpus, can give us an idea of the presence and trajectory of the word *rénmín* in the written sources of the last decades. Results show that this term became frequent at the end of the 1940s and the beginning of the 1950s (a period coinciding with the foundation of the People's Republic, 1949), and remained frequent till the mid-1970s, with peaks in the years 1957 and 1968) which were characterized by controversial political campaigns. Frequency decreased markedly in the 1970s and 1980s, remaining relatively stable up to 2000.

The frequency diagram (频次图) of the BCC corpus also shows a sharp increase in the usage of this word in 1949 and 1950, followed by peaks in the 1960s. Usage frequency progressively decreased in the 1970s, to become relatively stable in recent years. Our findings lead us to conclude, therefore, that this term proves to be relatively frequent in recent and contemporary sources, even though its frequency has declined somewhat in recent decades.

Concluding Remarks

As we have tried to show in this chapter, the word *rénmín* has a long, rich, and complex history in Chinese sources. It was already being used in the pre-imperial period, even though it was the monosyllabic form *mín* that had designated 'the people' in political rhetoric for centuries that was in use. This form is still present in crystallized idiomatic expressions.

A number of metaphors are associated with the term *mín* and with the people in ancient political rhetoric, like the parenthood metaphor, in which the benevolent ruler is imagined as the parent of the people. Another metaphoric frame posits the people as the root of the country. And this metaphor continues to frame discussions and questions on the role and the rights of the people in contemporary debates.

During the twentieth century, the form *mín* was replaced by the disyllabic word *rénmín*, and the political metaphors and political rhetoric about the people underwent a significant change. The word *rénmín* became inseparably linked to Chinese communist discourse and, most significantly, to Máo Zédōng's political rhetoric.

Who belongs to the people? 'The people' – *rénmín* – can function as an inclusive as well as an exclusive category. Various categories were considered to belong to the people at different periods in history. At the same time, others were excluded and dubbed as 'enemies of the people' or 'non-people' (Schoenhals 1994). The idea of 'the people' was characterized by a strong class character, in which the people were invested with a historical role and a national vocation. These dimensions of the concept of the people, however, gradually began to fade in the period following 1976, as is shown when dictionary entries published in the recent decades are compared.

Nonetheless, the word *rénmín* proves far too fundamental to be shelved or abandoned. Three aspects of usage should be borne in mind. Firstly, it remains unshakably part of Chinese political and institutional discourse, as can be seen in contemporary speeches of China's political leaders. Secondly, *rénmín* remains a keyword in both academic literature and newspapers. And thirdly, the question of who belongs to the people, the people's rights, what they deserve, and how the people should be served are at times the subject of jokes. Such jokes refer to an overarching dominant discourse about the people that remains solid. Perspectives change, but *rénmín* continues to function as a core concept in Chinese today. This is all too clearly demonstrated by the title of successful TV series *In the Name of the People* (*Rénmín de míngyì* 人民的名义), revolving around the attempts made by a prosecutor to get to grips with corruption in an imaginary city in contemporary China. For our study, *rénmín* acts as a doorway into the Chinese cultural mindset. A diversity of feelings and thoughts, convictions, and ambivalent sentiments are all entangled in this complex concept. But it is only by striving to understand the various perspectives and positions taken up regarding the people throughout China's history that we can begin to understand how this 'universal' concept takes on the specific tinges and hues of a nature, unique to the Chinese experience and worldview.

NOTES

1. Chinese text and translation by James Legge of the *Mèngzǐ* 孟子 'The works of Mencius' quoted from the Chinese Text Project database, http://ctext.org/mengzi/jin-xin-ii/zh?en=on
2. For a detailed analysis of the semantic stratifications of *mín* 民 in the formative period of the modern Japanese lexicon, see Burtscher (2012).
3. Djamouri (2011: 985) describes Classical Chinese as the language formed before the establishment of the empire (221 BCE), whose grammatical and stylistic rules were 'ideally' based on the Confucian Classics. Djamouri points out that 'as a living language, it probably ceased to be used before the end of the Han Era (after 220), but until the modernist movements at the beginning of the

4. 20th Century, it remained the principal administrative language and language of literature in China' ('*son emploi en tant que langue vivante cessa vraisemblablement avant la fin des Han (+220) mais il demeura longtemps, jusqu'aux mouvements modernistes du début du XXe, la principale langue administrative et littéraire en Chine*').
4. Five texts, the *Classic of Changes*, the *Classic of Poetry*, the *Classic of Documents*, the *Records of the Rites*, the *Spring and Autumn Annals*, were labelled the 'Five Classics' and constituted the curriculum of the Imperial Academy established in 124 BCE. This canon was to be modified during the following centuries and the number of Classics grew to include thirteen texts. The canon was enlarged by including the Confucian *Analects*, the *Classic of Filial Piety*, the *Ěryǎ dictionary*, two ritual texts, the *Rites of the Zhou* and the *Etiquettes and Rites*, and three commentaries to the *Spring and Autumn Annals* (Gardner 2007: xviii).
5. Chinese text and James Legge's (1815–1897) English translation of the poem 'Nánshān yǒu tái' 南山有臺 'On the hills of the south is the tai plant' (from the 'Xiǎo yǎ' 小雅 'Minor odes of the kingdom', 'Bái huá zhī shí' 白華之什 'Decade of Baihua') quoted from the Chinese Text Project database (中國哲學書電子化計劃), created by D. Sturgeon in 2006: http://ctext.org/book-of-poetry/decade-of-baihua/zh?en=on
6. See note 4 above.
7. By the end of Song dynasty period, four texts, the *Analects*, the *Mencius*, and two chapters of the *Rites*, the 'Great learning' and 'Maintaining the perfect balance', were grouped in a collection, the *Four Books*, which 'displaced Five Classics as the authoritative, central texts within the canon' (Gardner 2007: xxi).
8. Chinese text and James Legge's translation quoted from the Chinese Text Project database http://ctext.org/liji/da-xue/zh?en=on
9. For more on this political metaphor see also Levi (2012: 51–81).
10. This was originally a quotation from the *Xīnxù* 新序 'New Prefaces' (chapter *Záshì yī* 杂事一) by Liú Xiàng 刘向 of the Western Han period (206 BCE – BC 9). The digital version of the *Xīnxù* is available on the Chinese Text Project database: http://ctext.org/xin-xu/za-shi-yi/zh. It has become an idiomatic expression, more specifically a *chéngyǔ* 成语 (a specific form of Chinese phraseology that Nguyen defines as 'a quadrisyllabic phraseologized expression': see Nguyen 2006: 176).
11. Chinese text and English translation by James Legge taken from the

Chinese Text Project database http://ctext.org/shang-shu/songs-of-the-five-sons/zhs?en=on

12. Chinese text and translation by James Legge of the *Mèngzǐ* 孟子 'The works of Mencius' quoted from the Chinese Text Project database, http://ctext.org/mengzi/jin-xin-ii/zh?en=on
13. One of the types of political culture, according to Almond and Verba's (1963) classification.
14. Chinese text and James Legge's English translation quoted from the Chinese Text Project website: http://ctext.org/analects/gong-ye-chang/zh?en=on
15. Cf. Chinese Text Project digital version: http://ctext.org/zhanguo-ce/xian-sheng-wang-dou-zao-men/zh
16. Cf. Chinese Text Project digital version: http://ctext.org/han-shu/shi-huo-zhi-shang/zh
17. Cf. Chinese Text Project digital version: http://ctext.org/han-shu/xing-fa-zhi/zh
18. Cf. Chinese text project digital version: http://ctext.org/han-shu/xing-fa-zhi/zh
19. Booji (2005: 114) defines the affixoids (including prefixoids and suffixoids) as 'morphemes which look like parts of compounds, and … occur as lexemes, but have a specific and more restricted meaning when used as part of a compound'. Novotná (1967; 1968; 1969) uses the term 'affix-like formative' to designate these forms in her study on Chinese word formation.
20. On the polysemy of *quán* see Svarverud (2001: 125–143).
21. Chinese text of this speech entitled, *Mínzúzhǔyì* 民族主義 'Nationalism', www.ctcfl.ox.ac.uk/Lang%20work/HT12/三民主义.doc
22. Chinese text and James Legge's English translation quoted from the Chinese Text Project database: http://ctext.org/book-of-poetry/yi/zh?en=on
23. Chinese text and James Legge's English translation quoted from the Chinese Text Project database: http://ctext.org/mengzi/jin-xin-ii/zh?en=on
24. Chinese text and W. P. Mei's English translation quoted from the Chinese Text Project database: http://ctext.org/mozi/book-9/zh?en=on
25. Chinese text and W. P. Mei's English translation quoted from the Chinese Text Project database: http://ctext.org/mozi/simplicity-in-funerals-iii/zh?en=on

26. An Electronic Repository of Chinese Scientific, Philosophical and Political Terms Coined in the Nineteenth and Early Twentieth Century created by M. Lackner, I. Amelung, and J. Kurtz in 2001 (http://mcst.uni-hd.de/projectdescription/aboutMCST.lasso).
27. English translation from the *Selected Works of Mao Tse-tung*, vol. III, published by Foreign Languages Press, Peking, China, https://www.marxists.org/reference/archive/mao/selected-works/volume-3/mswv3_19.htm
28. English translation from the *Selected Works of Mao Tse-tung*, vol. IV, published by Foreign Languages Press, Peking, China, https://www.marxists.org/reference/archive/mao/selected-works/volume-4/mswv4_65.htm
29. English translation from the *Selected Works of Mao Tse-tung*, vol. IV, published by Foreign Languages Press, Peking, China, https://www.marxists.org/reference/archive/mao/selected-works/volume-5/mswv5_58.htm
30. The expression *niú guǐ shé shén* 牛鬼蛇神 'monsters' (literally, 'cow ghosts and snake spirits') is also considered as a *chéngyǔ* (Link 2013: 59). This expression, deriving from the Tang dynasty (618–907 CE) poems by Lǐ Hè 李贺 and Dù Mù 杜牧 (Lu 2004: 59), became an invective used to demonize and denounce opponents during the Cultural Revolution, especially after it was adopted in a 1966 editorial of the *People's Daily* that incited people to 'Sweep away all demons and monsters' (*Héngsǎo yīqiè niúguǐshéshén* 横扫一切牛鬼蛇神).
31. http://v.youku.com/v_show/id_XMTg1ODYwOTgw.html
32. *Rénmínwǎng* 人民网, People's Daily Online: www.people.com.cn
33. The 'Three Represents' refer to what the Chinese Communist Party stands for, according to the former president Jiāng Zémín's 江泽民 formulation:
中国共产党要始终代表中国先进生产力的发展要求。
中国共产党要始终代表中国先进文化的前进方向。
中国共产党要始终代表中国最广大人民的根本利益。
The Chinese Communist Party represents the development trends of advanced productive forces.
It represents the orientations of an advanced culture.
It represents the fundamental interests of the overwhelming majority of the people of China.
34. Quoted from: http://www.cineresie.info/vignetta-servire-il-popolo/; Lǐ Xiǎoguāi's 李小乖 comic strips, http://blogtd.org/

35. http://wujiaxiang.blog.21ccom.net/?p=55, http://wujiaxiang.blog.21ccom.net/?p=56
36. *Hú Jǐntāo zài qìngzhù Zhōnghuá Rénmín Gònghéguó chénglì 60 zhōunián dàhuì shàng de jiǎnghuà* 胡锦涛在庆祝中华人民共和国成立60周年大会上的讲话, 'Hú Jǐntāo's speech at the celebration of the 60th anniversary of the foundation of the People's Republic of China', text of the speech: http://cpc.people.com.cn/GB/64093/64094/10152026.html
37. *Xí Jìnpíng zài dì shí'èr jiè Quánguó Rénmín Dàibiǎo Dàhuì dì yī cì huìyìshàng de jiǎnghuà* 习近平在第十二届全国人民代表大会第一次会议上的讲话, 'Xí Jìnpíng speech at the 1st session of 12th National People's Congress', text of the speech: http://cpc.people.com.cn/n/2013/0318/c64094-20819130.html
38. *Xí Jìnpíng zài dì shí'èr jiè Quánguó Rénmín Dàibiǎo Dàhuì dì yī cì huìyìshàng de jiǎnghuà* 习近平在第十二届全国人民代表大会第一次会议上的讲话, 'Xí Jìnpíng speech at the 1st session of 12th National People's Congress', text of the speech: http://cpc.people.com.cn/n/2013/0318/c64094-20819130.html
39. The English translation is quoted from the article 'President vows to bring benefits to people in realizing "Chinese dream"', available on the Xinhua website: http://news.xinhuanet.com/english/china/2013-03/17/c_132240052.htm

CHAPTER 2

Citizen

If a man be gracious and courteous to strangers, it shews he is a citizen of the world, and that his heart is no island, cut off from other lands, but a continent, that joins to them. (Francis Bacon, 1597, 'Of Goodness and Goodness of Nature')

Reife Bürger wollen direkte Demokratie'. ('mature citizens want direct democracy', www.nachrichten.at)

As a good global citizen, Scotland has a strong and enduring commitment to securing democracy, the rule of law and fundamental human rights across the world. (Mr Yousaf, representing Scotland, cited in http://www.herald.scotland.com)

现代公民身份被看作欧洲特殊政治文化的产物。(Guō 2013)

Modern citizenship is to be considered the product of the European specific political culture.

"在家做个好孩子、在校做个好学生、在社会上做一位好公民"的三好教育. (Example retrieved from the CCL Corpus of Modern Chinese, originally in the *People's Daily*, 2000)

The education of the three 'goods': 'Be a good boy at home, be a good student in school, be a good citizen in the society'.

INTRODUCTION

Understanding the way a concept like 'citizen' works in the lexicon, and the role it plays in the worldview of a linguistic community will prove difficult for three reasons. Firstly, citizenship involves belonging to a place or a community. Secondly, the nature and the definition of the urban environment associated with citizenship must constantly be redefined throughout history. And thirdly, there is the question of how urban spaces evolve and develop within the sphere of the nation.

We cannot hope to understand what 'citizen' denotes in a wide variety of discourses without understanding that it is conceptually dependent upon a dynamics of interacting spatial metaphors. 'Citizen' presupposes belonging. Belonging to what? In modern usage, to both the city and to the State.

This was not always the case, however. Etymologically speaking, the city and citizen evolve inseparably. As Williams (1985) reminds us, 'city' has existed since the thirteenth century and derives from Old French. But its meaning was initially related to the Latin concept of *civitas*, which did not originally relate to a contained urban environment (*urbs*, in Latin). Rather than a particular type of settlement, *civitas* referred rather to a body of citizens. 'Citizen' derives from *civitas*, and it is from this original meaning of a body of men and women that the modern usages of citizen stem. We speak of a nation of citizens, or of the citizens of Glasgow, using this concept of citizen as 'belonging to', or being 'of' a certain place. A Londoner or a Glaswegian are citizens of those respective cities. This justifies Google Translate's translation into German of 'citizen of Berlin', as '*Berliner*'. And the appropriateness of the translation is borne out whether we consider spoken or written German. The term '*civitas*' was also applied by the Romans to the peoples of Gaul. 'Folk', 'people', 'members of a community', and 'civilians' are all closely related in these usages.

All of these definitions set up container or containment metaphors. Whether we are questioning, defending, or reaffirming the legal rights and obligations of citizens, we are activating container or containment metaphors. There are insiders and outsiders, and even if one container contains another one within it, even if the city is the microcosm of the macrocosm, the State, both containers will inevitably generate 'outsiders' who are excluded from one or the other conceptual space, if not from both. You can be a citizen of Ireland, but, you may see yourself as alien to Dublin, all the more because you are perceived as such, and identified as a rural inhabitant, someone from the country, a 'hick', from some backwater over there, beyond the social, political and cultural 'here', the centre. You can be a citizen of Paris, without being French, with (albeit limited) voting rights and tax obligations. And unless your status as a citizen is formally and legally recognized, whether you belong to the Ancient Greek *polis*, or to contemporary Prague, given the enduring exploitative logic of all cities, you will suffer from a paradoxical form of exclusion. While the market binds you to your abode, as a foreign illegal worker in the tolerated black market, you will benefit from no social or legal protection, nor will you have any right to or access to medical care. Yesterday's *Meteks* – the temporary residents and migrant workers in the Ancient Greek *polis* – are today's Ukrainians working in Prague, or the Colombians working in Barcelona.

The individuals that make up those workforces are very much enrooted within the social fabric of the city, and are vital to its survival. Yet these insiders are not citizens. They remain penned in 'within' the confines of exclusion, deprived of the rights of fully recognized politically empowered residents. In this respect, their status is similar to that of inhabitants living in the ghettos. In India, the slums form an integral part of the economy, though they are hidden away. This makes it absurd to try to conceive of the slums as somehow 'belonging' on the outskirts of the city, or hanging onto the margins. Speaking of them in this way is only a symbolic attempt to keep them hidden away and marginalized. The slums of Indian cities, as Odette Louiset, the Rouen-based anthropological geographer, has argued, are as central as they are fundamental to the functioning of the urban environment with its mode of production and its networks of communication and affiliations (Louiset 2009, 2014, https://webtv.univ-rouen.fr/videos/2014-apprehender-lespace-villes-dici-et-dailleurs/).

Moreover, the nature of the city is of course problematic, in all of the languages we will be investigating or touching upon. The multiplicity of the term's synonyms in English (burg, town, village), and the ambiguous and ill-defined terms for 'suburbs', 'urban sprawl', and 'outlying towns', only goes to show that knowing what we mean by 'going down town' and 'being a resident of the city' is hard to pin down. Predictably, French terms like '*ville*' and '*grande ville*' prove notoriously difficult to transpose into English, since those distinctions do not respect the same dichotomies as 'town' and 'city'. The same can be said of '*Stadt*' and '*Grossstadt*' in German. And *vesnice* and *město* in Czech, which are usually translated into 'village' and 'town' or 'city' respectively, cause translators similar problems.

This cannot be reduced to a simply linguistic hitch. This is a problem of translation because it is a problem of conception. It reminds us that conceptualization takes us not back to universal underlying prototypes, but to historical and cultural contexts. What is considered a 'village' today, would have been considered a 'town' in the sixteenth century. When the French-speaking Flanders historian, Froissart, a scribe of the English Court, spoke of the 'City of London' during the Hundred Years War (1337–1453) it wasn't any bigger than the Carlisle of today. And when the great scientist explorer, Alexander von Humboldt, visited America's capital, Washington, back in 1804, the town had only 70 000 inhabitants.

Thirdly, translating into Chinese spatial dynamics of settlements and cities, citizens and outsiders, deprived of the rights of the insiders, may well prove difficult, since urbanization in China has not developed along the same lines as Western cities, which have moved through the various overlapping stages of the Greek *polis*, the Roman military stronghold, the market town, and the urban industrial, and post-industrial, cities.

This complexity is worth bearing in mind since we will be forced to make careful distinctions between villagers and town-dwellers. American and English conceptions of the citizen vary over time and do not fully coincide with one another. At what point can we declare, here we have a city, and within it, citizens? This introduces questions of settlers and Native Americans, of property rights and reservations. Once the American government declares that 'Indians' are killing 'citizens', we have moved into a conceptual dynamics that has left 'adventurers', 'frontiersmen', and 'settlers' behind. Now we are being conceptually constrained to accept we are dealing with legitimate landowners, living within an established community, an ordered society whose rights have been violated. Violated? By whom? Certainly not by 'fellow citizens'. The American Indians are catalogued as 'natives', 'heathens', or 'savages' according to the discursive strategy.

Citizens clearly take us into history and culturally defined political dynamics. The native Indians and the native Scots will live through different stories with different dynamics. The roles open to them as citizens, actors in history, will not be the same. So as we move onto the question of the etymology and the development of the term 'citizen' throughout our various Englishes, it is best not to forget that the term always constitutes something at stake in an argument that is being staked out. The terms synonyms, antonyms, and the idioms and expressions are already value-loaded. And the ways 'citizen' is used in discourse strategies in literature and newspapers, is rarely innocent. 'Citizen' is always political, always problematic.

SCOPE OF THE CORPUS-BASED STUDY

As we pointed out in our introduction, we found that dictionaries often provided an account of our keywords which was at odds with our impression of the way they function in discourse. Existing corpora proved useful in giving a more balanced view, but even when our personal corpus was used to compensate for shortcomings in the BNC and the COCA, we were still left with an impression that the keyword 'citizen' was underrepresented, and that our findings did not enable us to get a grasp of the phrases and collocations related to citizenship. We had the same impression of the findings furnished by our research into 'individual', the subject of the next chapter.

For this reason, we found it judicious to develop the study-specific corpora (MyEnglishCorpus, MyAmericanCorpus) that would to establish the way 'citizen' and 'individual' are used in various forms of English. This involved incorporating a Scottish Corpus into an extended English corpus, and opening up to a much wider American corpus. Integrating the works of Hobbes, Locke, Hume, Smith, Mill, and James, among others, into these corpora provided us with an enlightening source of information for clarifying when and where 'citizen' and 'individual' are used. This formed the basis of our corpus 'History of Ideas Corpus' (MyHistIdeasCorpus). That corpus also enabled us to establish whether words were used or not. For often, rival synonyms and related terms are used for 'citizen' and 'individual', and the use or absence of these terms is rarely innocent in the discursive strategies adopted.

All in all, our findings are drawn from over 1000 usages of the English term 'citizen', found in dictionaries, and online dictionaries such as the *OED* and *Merriam-Webster*, in encyclopaedias, in dictionaries of quotations, in political and philosophical texts, both online and written, in novels, poems, and songs, in the BNC, the COCA, the Leipzig Corpus, and our own various corpora.

Gathering together our impressions, we aim to provide a deep, insightful, and accurate understanding of the term's usage. As we have already stressed, what we offer are tentative conclusions. Other texts related to citizenship will highlight other facets of this crucial and complex concept. Other cultures at other times are all caught up in their own narratives, so 'citizen' is rarely a static concept: it is invariably dynamic. Our impression of it will inevitably change as a nation goes through various reconfigurations, and as the configuration of Europe changes. International realignments and geopolitical confrontations will inevitably affect the way we think about and feel about 'global' citizenship, in the same way.

As nations explode or implode, notions of citizenships are transformed. French citizenship has become a hot issue since the terrorist attacks of 2015 and 2016. The referendum in Scotland led to heated debates on Scottish citizenship. Brexit has sparked tensions related to borders in Ireland, and what it means for Northern Ireland, as nation within the United Kingdom, and the south, Ireland, as Member State of the European Union (see Cauvet 2016, https://webtv.univ-rouen.fr/videos/philippe-cauvet-universite-de-poitiers-le-brexit-et-lirlande_71526/).

All of these questions will alter the way we speak of 'citizens' in the language of these countries. Nonetheless, the authors feel relatively optimistic that the impressions listed below – drawn from painstaking analysis and synthesis of changing contexts – will contribute to clarifying the core of the concept and the way the contours of this keyword are likely to be retraced over time and in different situations.

CRITERIA FOR CITIZEN IN ENGLISH

Before launching into diverse cultural contexts and complex or paradoxical uses, let's start by establishing some common ground. Despite a wide variety of usages (citizen of the world, Citizens' Advice Bureau, Citizen Band Radio, Citizen Kane, for example), a core concept of 'citizen' does emerge in English, and by that we mean English English, American English, Canadian English, Scottish English and Welsh English, and so forth. The main elements of citizenship can be summarized as follows:

1. A free man (or woman) with rights: first and foremost, the right to the city. This is a political status. The citizen has a voice, and can intervene in the political sphere, of the *polis*, town or city, or State.
2. The citizen has responsibilities as well as rights. He or she must contribute to the safety and well-being of the city, *polis*, or State.
3. The citizen has either been born within the civil society, the city or the State, or has been 'naturalized'. He or she is thereby accorded rights and, at the same time, accepts the obligations of citizenship.

4. Not all of those living in, or working for, the city, can be considered 'citizens'. The social organization of the city sets up spaces and hierarchies which provide exclusion within inclusion. The State functions in a similar manner concerning immigration, work permits, and the black market. Limitations on citizenship may relate to origins, length of residency, race, sex, or age.
5. Citizens of a State, can, of course, live on the land. Nevertheless, citizenship is generally associated with urban residents, and the term is often used in a restricted sense to relate to them alone. For this reason, we often oppose citizens with those living in the country, with villagers or with nomads, or migrant populations, such as Gypsy groups.
6. Citizen is related to civil society, and for this reason soldiers are not considered 'citizens'. They belong to a body apart. This explains the usage of 'civilians', in warfare: 'civilian casualties' are contrasted with soldiers who fall in battle. This proves paradoxical, however, since the requirement of a citizen to fight on the ramparts of the walled city to fend off enemy invaders is crucial to the Greek definition, and this idea persists throughout medieval and early modern definitions.
7. Citizen is invariably positive in meaning. Just as 'urbane' and cosmopolitan tend to mean open-minded, educated, polite, well-mannered or well-bred, citizen enjoys the same aura. Narrow-mindedness is associated with those living on the land, without benefiting from education and the social circles open to 'citizens' living in the city. Being a 'citizen of the world' is paradoxically antithetic to the meaning of belonging to the city, of course, but it is, nonetheless, related. Cities do exist by exchange with other cities. The urban experience invariably keeps us in contact with the wider world. Therefore, we tend to assume that being a citizen of the city will make us more inclined to become a world citizen, or what the French call '*un citoyen du monde*'.

ORIGINS AND EVOLUTION OF THE CONCEPT

'Citizen' first enters English as 'citisein', or 'citizein' in the course of the twelfth century. The online *OED* records an example from around 1330:

Þe citiseins of þat cite Wel often god þonkeden he.

And it makes reference to examples of 'citisains' around the same time. Although 'citizen' is rare in the Bible, examples can be found in the King

James Version of the New Testament (1604), and the *OED* refers us to an example in the 1382 Wycliffite Bible, in Act XXI. 39:

> I am a man, of Tarsus, a citeseyn or burgeys, of a citee not unknown.

And the term is found in Chaucer from around the same time as the Wycliffite Bible was written. 'Citizen' is not common in Shakespeare's plays, and this no doubt reflects the relative rarity of the term in everyday speech during his times, but the *OED* does quote from Act IV in *Henry VIII*:

> Citezens of Cities and Burgeys of boroughes and Townes.

All three examples confirm that various terms were in circulation, competing for the concept in Middle English relating to urban life. In fact, these were not the only ones: others included citisain, citiseyne, citesayne, citezeyn and citizein.

Urban residency is not part of the original definition, however. As Calvert Watkins reminds us in *The American Heritage Dictionary of Indo-European Roots* (2000: 38), 'city', 'civic', and 'civil' are all related to the Latin concept of '*civis*', denoting the member of a 'household'. Houses and members of households were very much symbolic in nature then, however, and remain so. Houses can be seen as teams or groups, or even as regions we belong to. This is difficult to understand for the English-speaker, because the English distinguish between 'house' and 'home': home is more about affections and affinities, while house designates more the physical space, and the architecture of the building. The French and Poles, on the other hand, organize these affinities and associations differently, but have a single complex generic concept (*maison* and *dom*, respectively).

Although our concept of citizenship is associated equally with Greek usages (referring to the city state), and Roman usages (related to the nation, or empire), it is important to bear in mind the idea of a household and a space we belong to when we consider the concept of the citizen: because citizenship and non-citizenship is always about belonging or not belonging. Just as the Houses of Europe (*les Maisons d'Europe* in French) refer to the great dynasties that carved up Europe in the Middle Ages and the Renaissance, citizenship refers to belonging to groups with links or alliances.

Nonetheless, belonging to the nation and belonging to the city at times involve very different conceptions of the term. The opposition between the city and the rural dwellers is obvious in an example from the *OED* from 1508, when 'Cytezyns' are quoted as blaming 'the rurall men agayne'. Other oppositions relate to conflict between the aristocracy and citizens or soldiers and citizens in the *OED* examples. A civilian is not a soldier, but neither is a member of the landed nobility or the gentry considered as a 'citizen'. This leads us into the logic which will posit that a man of trade, a citizen, is not a 'gentleman'. This opposition was made famous by Molière's burlesque ridicule of his *Bourgeois Gentillehomme*, an opposition which works less well in English translation because, though we tend to translate '*bourgeois*' as 'bourgeois', the French word plainly refers to 'man of the city', a member of the rising trading classes, that would make up the middle class citizens that were beginning to take hold of towns and cities, politically speaking.

The *OED*'s examples for 'citizens' of a nation refer us to Hume in the eighteenth century, and Gladstone at the end of the nineteenth. But earlier examples are quoted. From 1538, the *OED* cites, 'The nombur of cytyzyns in every commynalty cyty or cuntrey.' And in 1640, P. Massinger was quoted in the *OED* as arguing in *The Guardian*: 'To save one Citizen is a greater prize, than to have kill'd in War ten Enemies.'

Further examples of the citizen used to denote the national or resident of a country can be traced back to the 1382 Wycliffite Bible. Among the examples quoted by the *OED* from around the end of the eighteenth century, American usages are included. These foreign examples reflect the impact of debates, conflicts, and questions related to the American War of Independence and the impact of the French Revolution. They bear witness to the way international conflicts and crises impinge upon the consciousness of Britons, reshaping the contours of their worldview as it manifests itself in speech and writing.

The *Merriam-Webster* online dictionary provides a broadly similar definition for 'citizen'. The British and American concepts appear to coincide. But as we shall see, this is somewhat misleading. Our dictionaries already point to different nuances and facets of the term being harnessed and highlighted. *Merriam-Webster* for its part, stresses the status of the freeman within the city, and the fact that he does not belong to a separate category, as a servant of the State, notably, a soldier. As synonyms, for 'citizen', *Merriam-Webster* offers 'freeman' and 'national'. And when 'subject' is cited, it appears to refer to the British meanings associated with 'citizen' or to the meanings associated with the colonial period of American history.

Specialist dictionaries such as Gordon Marshall's *Oxford Dictionary of Sociology* (1998: 71–72) complement this shared definition without contradicting it. Marshall's entry for citizen refers to three conceptions of 'citizenship', changing over time:

1. Citizenship in the Greek *polis*, in which relatively little State intervention perturbed the active engagement of free men, defining their own destinies and the destinies of their communities.
2. Citizenship in republican states such as the United States and post-revolutionary France.
3. Citizenship within the welfare state.

Marshall (1998: 71–72) goes on to argue that the active nature of citizenship, involving military service and engagement in battles, in the first phase, is gradually downplayed, as the conception of rights and services emerges more strongly in the final welfare state understanding of the relationship between the individual and the collective. Two schools of thought emerge in the third phase. Certain thinkers see capitalism as alienating people, and depriving them of rights, thereby undermining citizenship. Authors such as Talcott Parsons, on the other hand, see citizenship as part of the project of modernity, believing bourgeois liberalism to bring about expanding freedom, while the rights and benefits of citizenship are enjoyed by an increasing number of people throughout society, irrespective of sex or ethnic origins. These two schools of thought provide opposing conceptions of the way rights are established. The latter school feels they are handed down from a benefactor state. The former school believes citizenship, and the rights that go with it, must be fought for by radical political protest.

This extrapolation will prove useful as a prism for understanding the various usages of 'citizen' that we shall quote from texts and corpora. But from a lexicographer's point of view, neither school of thought outlined above questions the idea of a shared definition. Sociologists are clearly working with the idea of a 'universal' concept that can be applied to US or UK societies, and to other countries around the world. And indeed, up to an extent, the *OED* and *Merriam-Webster*, for their part, provide us with a fairly coherent clear-cut concept that appears to be interchangeable with definitions for analogous terms such as '*Bürger*' in German, or '*občan*' in Czech, in a wide variety of contexts.

For this very reason, however, corpus study proves to be revealing, because it draws us back into discourse and dialogue. If we seek to understand how 'citizen' operates within the culture of a linguistic community, we should consider individual discourse strategies. Only by tracing the ways individuals use the concept of citizenship in their conversations and negotiations can we establish to what extent the various facets of a concept are being mobilized and maintained, and the degree to which a generic abstract concept has any real meaning within the hearts and minds of the members of a linguistic community. At this point, indeed, it often becomes clear that ideals of citizenship, preserved in key texts, laws, and education, are often at odds with the impoverishment of the concept. And at times, this keyword disappears from debates in which we might logically expect to find it.

Linguistic communities often harbour widely different conceptions of 'citizens' and 'citizens' rights'. Various interest groups will harness rights and obligations in order to advance their own ends. Ruling elites will resist claims from subjects and by refusing to consider them 'citizens', or by limiting the number those who can 'legitimately' claim citizenship. Independence movements in America and in Scotland will revise notions of the freedom of citizens. Forms of inclusion and exclusion will be set up in order to impose social hierarchies. And macabre forms of marginalization will, at times, have very real, often horrific, consequences for those not invited into the civil space of the citizens. This proves to be a crucial question for humanity in that it forces us to revise what humane conduct involves, whose dignity must be respected, and who is to be accorded rights. At this point the citizens – so open-minded and tolerant in some respects to their fellow citizens – will prove themselves hostile and brutal when it comes to those they expel from their midst. And these misadventures or nightmares of exclusion will be of very different natures in the histories of the US and the UK, as our corpora should help us understand.

SYNONYMS, ANTONYMS, AND RELATED TERMS

Before entering into conflicts and confrontations, we should, at this point, briefly review our findings in order to establish the way citizen interacts with its rival synonyms, either competing with them or completing them, and the way it opposes other key concepts in dynamic oppositions.

The *OED* quotes compounds and collocations include 'citizen king', 'citizen sovereign', 'citizen prince', 'citizen magistrate', 'citizen life', and 'citizen like'. More significantly, it refers to 'citizen's arrest', an Anglo concept which does not bear much relation to anything in many other legal systems around the world. It also refers to the 'Citizen's Charter', which is the name given to various documents concerning citizens' rights, a British government document produced in 1991, designed to guarantee the efficiency of public services, and provide a means of redress when standards are not upheld.

As we have seen, *Merriam-Webster*, for its part, stresses the status of the freeman within the city, and the fact that he does not belong to a separate category, as a servant of the State, notably, a soldier. As synonyms, *Merriam-Webster* offers 'freeman', 'national', and 'subject', though the last synonym refers to the British meanings or the meanings associated with the colonial period of American history.

As antonyms, *Merriam-Webster* offers 'alien' and 'noncitizen'. 'Foreigner', 'stranger', immigrant', and 'nonnative' are considered as 'near antonyms' by *Merriam-Webster*. And as related terms, it lists 'compatriot', 'countryman', 'inhabitant', 'native', 'nonimmigrant', and 'resident'.

The British and American conceptions of citizenship imply a dynamic opposition between foreigners (non-residents or aliens), and citizens. Citizens are enfranchised inhabitants of a country, residents with rights. The citizen is not a slave, so slaves are not citizens. It remains unclear to what extent 'subjects' are citizens in our British sources, though the opposition becomes crucial for American English. English English dictionaries tended to highlight somewhat the more urbane, cultured, facet of being a citizen. This involves the country–town opposition, though it does assume that city-dwelling citizens are more internationally aware, and more open-minded. This 'city-bred' facet is very much part of the *OED* definition, although similar characteristics might be more likely to be found in an opposition between 'city slickers' and 'hicks' in American English. Citizenship is about taxation and representation for American society as a whole.

CORPUS ANALYSIS

COCA

The Google Ngram viewer tool, based upon the extensive Google Books corpus, shows the term 'citizen' to have a frequency in texts that ranges between 0.00150 per cent and 0.00315 per cent, with a relative high around 1920, but tapering off around the turn of the twentieth century to a level slightly lower than its frequency in 1800. By comparison, 'democracy' proves far less constant, far more volatile, for the same period, varying from 0.000500 per cent to 0.00600 per cent, with a dramatic peak during the 1940s. 'Nation' proves far more commonplace, varying from 0.2 per cent to 0.1 per cent between 1800 and 2000. And, as we shall see, 'individual' proves somewhat more frequent. But what can be said about the British and American usages of 'citizen'?

The first and perhaps most striking difference between the usage of 'citizen' in British English and American English relates to the frequency of the term. While the 100 million word BNC recorded 1352 examples, the 450 million word COCA recorded 11 340. Even given the fact that the latter corpus is a little over four times the size of the former, this does not explain why we have around ten times as many examples in the American corpus. The COCA is composed of texts and televised shows, and so is closer to everyday English. But on closer examination, it becomes clear that it is not in everyday speech, but in bureaucratic, local and state government discourse that the term dominates in British English. From our close observation of British television, radio, and online media, over a period of five years, 'citizen' appeared to be fairly rare in British English: and this seemed to be equally true from what the authors could gather from everyday speech in England. In American discussions in everyday situations and in online media, it appears more likely that 'citizen' will come up more frequently than it does in everyday English in the UK.

In what form is it used in the US? What facets of the definition as we have outlined it above are highlighted? For the most part, when 'citizen' is used, the national definition dominates. A review of the COCA's highly useful search for collocations generated a list of the terms most often linked to citizen. Of the first twelve words, the most prolific were 'American', 'US', and 'every': these obviously pertain the national identity of the citizen. And the words, 'average' (sixth) and 'became' (seventh), both also obviously relate to the national identity.

Nonetheless, the Americans appear to demonstrate a vigorous capacity for negotiating citizens' rights, which is attested to by the fact that, of the top twelve collocates, 'private' (seventh), 'action' (tenth), 'groups' (eleventh), 'participation' (twelfth), clearly relate to the preservation of, or the negotiation over, citizen's rights. Collocates such as 'senior' (senior) and 'public' (fifth) also lead us to believe that the Americans are eager to define and preserve the specific nature of rights for certain groups.

If we can judge from everyday speech and written texts, 'citizen' is a very vigorous concept in the contemporary American worldview. It is at the centre of debates and discussions about rights and responsibilities. While many references related to dual citizenship, for example the nationality of Germans, Turks, Estonians, New Zealanders, Finns, and residents of Hong Kong, a great deal of the entries related to negotiating and defining the rights of migrant workers, immigrants, and criminals. The term also appeared in commentaries on citizen's arrests, and murder within the civilian sphere and within the scope of military interventions.

Businesses are 'considered moral persons', 'corporate citizens'. Local governments appeared to take to heart their obligation to 'take citizens' calls' at the mayor's office. Private citizens were described as 'taking on a democratic role as "citizen journalists" telling the world [of conflicts] and recording history'. In Syria, businessmen, pilots, teachers, and engineers became 'citizen journalists', putting their lives in danger on daily basis, in one example quoted.

What does this imply about the American worldview? A large number of examples suggest that Americans would appear to care about citizens' rights and their right to defend those rights against those that encroach upon them, against predatory big business, and against bloated and corrupt State administration. Such a civic attitude appears in references such as:

- Craig Holman, a lobbyist for the watchdog group Public Citizen.

On the other hand, some significant entries also made it clear that citizenship was a key concept at work in debates on terrorism, torture, and the invasion of foreign countries. Inevitably, those debates involved parties trying to justify their actions and trying to refute the fact that they were themselves infringing upon, or flouting, the human rights or the rights of others, be they foreigners or citizens of the US. Even entries relating to race relations at times proved ominous. One entry made reference to:

> a nationwide publicity campaign to impress upon the Negro citizen of the United States the importance of full and honest cooperation. (1940 US census records, cited by COCA, Domestic News, 2012)

The implication of this 1940s perspective is all too clear: 'Negros' are 'not playing the game'. In rhetoric like this, they are being implicitly indicted for being dishonest, and for refusing to shoulder the responsibility of citizenship. They are being 'invited' to respond to the State's demands to set things straight.

More ominous still was the 'tortured' logic of debates over violations of citizens' rights when 'suspected terrorists' were subjected to torture. The judiciary deprived victims of the right to take their persecutors to court and struggled to justify this infringement on civil liberties. This was clearly the case in the following example in which a crime becomes a question:

> a case examining whether government officials who order the alleged torture of a US citizen on American soil can be sued for violating the citizen's constitutional rights.

And such references were not isolated, as the following example shows:

> abuse in the name of national security, even the brutal torture of an American citizen in an American prison.

Admittedly, such examples recorded legal negotiations over the means of redress. Nonetheless, the fact that citizen has become inextricable from debates about Bush's wars that the Obama administration took on is far from reassuring. And obvious violations of the rights of foreign civilians in countries occupied by US forces, and violations of the rights of US citizens who have been detained without trial and subjected to torture, would appear to corroborate the fact that the neoconservative worldview has carved a new facet onto the face of US citizenship.

BNC

First impressions of 200 of the 1352 references from the British National Corpus give a somewhat unflattering picture of the English usage. The corpus is clearly out of date when it comes to contemporary usage. It is of great use for establishing a common core to the concept, but the examples of this corpus, which ends in the early 1990s, inevitably relate to the Thatcher era. This explains the references to the liberation of South Africa, and the Cold War.

Most significantly, we find only three references to 'European citizen', while a minor revolution has evidently taken place in the political discourse since the 1990s as Eurospeak has gradually asserted itself. Even the American writers and speakers quoted in the COCA provide twice that number, and 'European citizen' is clearly commonplace in the British press today. The Google search engine provides 12.3 million references, for example.

In the first 200 BNC examples, references were not made to British citizens, but to what the French State would do with its Declaration of the Rights of Man, and its republican constitution, if a certain European treaty were adopted. The focus of such discussions was on the harmonization between Member States and Brussels, rather than on the citizens themselves, and British citizens were certainly not central in these examples. But this proved to be misleading. References to British citizens proved commonplace after further investigation, and of the top ten collocates, 'British' came third (while 'American' came fifth).

Although the concept and the reality of citizenship is of course fundamental for the British, the term itself was not particularly commonplace. Perhaps its relative rarity can be partially explained by the fact that 'British national' replaces 'British citizen' in many cases. The BNC statistics appear to confirm this hypothesis: 217 examples of 'British national' were found, as opposed to fifty-two examples for 'British citizen'.

Like many of the COCA examples, the BNC introduced questions of immigration, emigration, dual citizenship, and foreign workers. Citizens' rights were also central to the discussions recorded in the examples studied. These rights related to civil law, disputes between citizens, welfare state rights, and the rights of disabled citizens. References were made to citizen protests, but these tended to be rare. On the whole, the activity of citizens appeared to be less vigorous in the BNC's British English examples than those cited in the COCA. The examples tended to relate to the State according rights to citizens. References were frequently made to 'senior citizens', as was the case in the COCA's more recent corpus.

Is citizenship a party-political question in British English? Thatcher is clearly shown to be antagonistic to the welfare state conception of the citizen in several of the BNC's examples. The following reminder from her is fairly representative of the way she argued we should return to a more 'responsible version' of citizenship.

> Duties and responsibilities are not merely available to a citizen; they are an integral part of being a citizen.

And criminals were reminded by her and her government that they could be deprived of their rights as citizens. Several examples seemed to indicate that this trend was being consolidated: references to 'dutiful citizens', 'model citizens' can be read in this light. All in all, these examples represented the State as a provider, dishing out rights, but expecting responsibilities in return. The media were enlisted as a means of informing citizens of their rights and responsibilities, and an emerging discourse reminded citizens of the way they were supposed to act in society. One example stressed the need to show:

> the citizen the rules by which he is to play and the goal at which he is to aim.

This attitude would tend to coincide with European discourse on citizenship which has emerged in English in the decades following the constitution of the BNC corpus in 1990. This tendency reinforces the idea that the discourse on citizens and citizenship is not so much the rhetoric of the people demanding their rights as the State's discourse. The State and the European Union clearly believe in bourgeois liberal capitalism, and in its capacity to broaden the scope of the citizens' rights, and provide ever increasing numbers of individuals with those rights. By and large, the discourse concerning citizen's rights was neither radical nor critical. It appeared, in contrast to the American examples from COCA, to be rather placid and complacent. The following example is rather representative in this respect:

> Nevertheless, despite the advent of 'contracting out', local authorities still carry out over fifty functions; indeed, the average British citizen probably has more contact with the state through the services provided by local government than through the outputs of any other level of public administration.

More lively references touched upon the War Office, Russia, and antagonism with the USSR, and included the shooting of British citizens in foreign countries. References to Afghanistan and its citizens concerned what the USSR was doing there, and what its soldiers were doing to the local population. The BNC corpus examples of 'citizen' anchors us firmly in 1980s Afghanistan, a far cry from the post-2001 joint British–US invasion. The roles have changed, and the perspective of Afghan citizens has since undergone a major change in the British imagination.

On a more positive note, hostility to foreign citizens was almost imperceptible in the examples found in the BNC. This makes a great change from the discourse of the contemporary British tabloids, and even the more respectable papers, and government discourse, with its phobia of illegal immigrants, and mistrust of migrant labourers. Rare examples of xenophobic outbursts were recorded in the BNC, however. In an English version of the far-right rhetoric that Sarkozy adopted during his term in office: 'Leave France, if you don't like it here!' (*'Si tu n'aimes pas la France, tu la quittes !'*), Norman Tebbit attacked Salman Rushdie, when he dared to criticize British politics. Using his inimitable mixture of outdated invective and backstreet satire, Tebbit upbraided the writer who had been resident in the UK for a quarter of a century as 'an impertinent, whining guest, an outstanding villain'.

Nonetheless, such criticisms of foreign nationals were very scarce among the BNC's examples. And, on the whole, things on the home front appeared quiet. No Scots or Welsh were demanding independent citizenship in the texts from which the BNC was generating its corpus. And conflicts in Northern Ireland, curiously enough, did not crop up in the examples for 'citizen' we surveyed in the BNC. In a further search, of the four references to 'Irish citizens', one referred to 'Irish workers', and though the others referred to the 'Irish Citizen's Army', very little of the reality of the conflict over national boundaries, sovereignty and independence, with its bombings, shootings and hunger strikes, appears to have broken into the examples of 'citizen' listed by the BNC. In contrast to the dynamism of American citizens, the BNC examples depict the passive populations of four nations, living under one flag and one Sovereign. Citizen's Advice Bureau appears to be the most active form of citizen activity in the peaceful land in which the State and the Sovereign graciously accord rights to individuals. And those individuals are as much 'subjects' as 'citizens' it would appear in the examples generated by the BNC.

COMPOUNDS AND COLLOCATIONS

Lexicographers who compile dictionaries do of course have an obligation to take etymology and the history of a term into account. Corpora such as the BNC and the COCA tend to focus attention on contemporary usage. It is therefore not surprising that the compounds and collocations that appear do not coincide in these two very different sources. But in as much as we continue to consult dictionaries in order to ascertain how a term is, or should be, used, it will prove interesting to compare and contrast the compounds and collocations that corpora provide with those listed in the *OED* and *Merriam-Webster*.

As we have already mentioned, the *OED* quotes compounds and collocations including 'citizen king', 'citizen sovereign', 'citizen prince', 'citizen magistrate', 'citizen life', and 'citizen like'. The adjective, 'citizenish', the adverb 'citizenly', the nouns 'citizeness' for female citizens ('*citoyenne*' in French), 'citizenism, and the verb 'citizenize', were also listed. But though 'citizenship', also listed, remains a current form, these former terms seem to have almost entirely disappeared from use. No trace in the BNC could be found for 'citizenish', 'citizeness', 'citizenism, and the verb 'citizenize': and only four examples were found for 'citizenly'. Apart from this, then, the former terms can be considered to be obsolete. *Merriam-Webster* likewise listed 'John citizen' and 'Sunday citizen' in its definition but only one example of each was to be found in the COCA.

What are the current compounds and collocations that our corpora generate then? Among the most common compounds we found: 'corporate citizen', 'dual citizen', 'citizen taxpayers', 'citizen legislators', 'citizen volunteers', 'good business citizen', 'upstanding citizen', 'responsible citizen', 'citizen's inviolable rights'. These would seem to corroborate the idea that citizen can be defined in terms of three criteria: birth and residency, rights, and obligations. And usages in the http://europa.eu website would seem to indicate that these three criteria are likely to be maintained in debate and discussion about citizenship in the coming decades.

As far as collocates go, the BNC linked citizen most closely to 'every', 'British', 'State', and 'individual', and 'American' was commonly linked to citizen. 'Citizen's advice' was a common phrase. And so was 'citizens' rights'. With 4886 examples, 'entitled' was significantly less commonplace, but, notwithstanding, a tenacious phrase. But the fact that there were only 2631 examples of 'citizen' collocating with 'participation' tends to confirm a more passive conception of citizenship. Neither 'active' nor 'participation' make it into the top ten collocates for 'citizen' in the BNC.

In contrast, the COCA examples appeared to present American citizens performing more fully their democratic role, demanding representation, and negotiating rights, with collocates like 'action', 'groups', 'participation', and 'rights' being listed as the tenth, eleventh, twelfth, and thirteenth collocates for 'citizen'.

LIMITS OF CORPUS ANALYSIS FOR 'CITIZEN'

The IT revolution has, of course, transformed our lives. For researchers, this is on the whole a transformation to be embraced. Thirty years ago, academics would have spent months if not years trying to establish whether the concepts of 'freedom' and 'liberty' coincide in the scope of their diverse related meanings. Contrastive studies of the difference between 'subject' and 'citizen' would have entailed endless close textual analysis in order to gain only an approximate impression of how these words operate within our language and our culture. Corpora like the BNC and the COCA have made spectacular progress in the last two decades. The various corpora for international and specific forms of English, the extensive corpora for foreign languages, and the comparative corpora that enable us to compare and contrast 'citizen' with '*citoyen*' in French and '*Bürger*' in German, like the Leipzig Wortschatz corpus are making possible undreamed of comparative studies that would have amazed the great linguists and philologists of the nineteenth and twentieth centuries, like Wilhelm von Humboldt, Ferdinand de Saussure, Roman Jakobson, Edward Sapir, and Émile Benveniste.

Nonetheless, electronic corpora inevitably bring with them disadvantages, and open the door to a multitude of academic sins. Hurried research students can compile wads of undigested material. Students with only a basic grasp on the way a language works can begin reeling off phrases and sections of texts. Those who neither read plays nor visit the theatre can suddenly start comparing wordplay in Shakespeare's plays. This amounts to something akin to plagiarism. But since the Internet itself is generating so much automated data, compiling and compressing information that is truly of great use, it becomes difficult for students and academics born after the IT revolution to distinguish between research that is reliable and what amounts to no more than the hasty conclusions and ill-informed impressions of dilettantes, who neither know nor care about the sources they are quoting. It is, therefore, worth reminding ourselves of the limits of existing online media for assisting linguistic research. Conventional online corpora can lead us into error for at least seven reasons.

1. The wealth of examples can mask the relatively low frequency with which a term in used.
2. The variety of sources can give the false impression that a corpus is balanced.

3. The linguistic criteria used to select the material is not always stressed or understood.
4. The ideological principles guiding the selection of sources is often not clearly stated even if it is understood by the compilers. All periods tend to generate what is considered to be a 'normal' or 'natural' impression of the state of the language. But as we know, every generation sees all too clearly the ideological presuppositions of the generation that precedes it. For this reason, dictionaries and corpora are 'updated' when they begin to appear 'outdated'.
5. Linguistic study and corpus compilers aspire to objectivity and neutrality: for this reason 'radical' texts and speech tend to be avoided. What can be considered 'neutral' and 'radical' remains a question of perspective, however.
6. The fact that certain canonical texts tend to be privileged, obscures more commonplace uses of a term. Literary and religious texts can be given a status in corpora that they do not truly have within the cultural mindset of a people at a given moment in time.
7. Secondary quotes often take on a great importance in corpora that they did not originally have in the works of given authors. Repeatedly quoting a source in both texts and in corpora can mask the way a concept works within an author's work. There is one Adam Smith for the Scottish Enlightenment, and another for twentieth-century American right-wing economists, just as there is one Foucault for the French of the 1960s and another for the Americans of the 1990s.

The BNC and the COCA are no more caught up in these problems than the rest of us. Textual analysis and critical discourse analysis have also been transformed by the IT revolution. Nowadays, we can constitute a corpus of thirty texts in a day using online search engines like Yahoo or Google. Thirty years ago, readers would spend months reading *The Times*, *The Guardian*, or *The Herald Tribune*, in order to establish a corpus of a similar size. This process would have forced the researchers to read articles in context, and that would have given them an entirely different impression of the ways the words and concepts were operating within a given context, and within a given country, over a specific period of time.

Bearing in mind these pitfalls, as authors we have opted for a wide range of sources, and have tried to take into account discussion and debate, in order to avoid, as much as is humanly possible, overlooking essential facets of the concepts we are dealing with. The comparative method has helped us greatly in this endeavour: because the facets highlighted in one language induced us to look for similar uses of citizen in English and Chinese. This forced us to look beyond dictionaries and corpora and even beyond the specific corpora designed for our book. After long discussion and deep reflection, our study of citizen induced us to widen the scope of our sources to include:

- a newly revised MyAmericanCorpus of million words;
- a Scottish corpus of thirty texts related to the Independence movement;
- a new corpus of political and philosophical texts (MyHistIdeasCorpus, $c.9$ million words).
- textual analysis and electronic corpora for French, German, and Czech terms considered equivalent to 'citizen'.

We feel convinced that these innovations have enabled us to form a fuller and more representative impression of the complex ways 'citizen' is acting as a concept in the English speakers' worldview, and the way our specific concept contrasts with those used by the speakers of other languages. This revised corpus should, we trust, help us to outline specific ways in which American and Scottish usages differ from those found in mainstream English. And comparing and contrasting usages should enable us to draw some conclusions about coinciding patterns, patterns which will find literary and political parallels in other languages at other times. And this is ultimately the aim of the present study of our four English keywords. Rather than starting out from the hypothesis that a shared universal concept exists and which takes on various specific forms in different places and times, we are starting out with the hypothesis of a variety of terms which coincide to a greater or lesser degree. We are, therefore, trying to discern the way they oppose one another or converge in parallel logics. Cross-linguistic investigations reveal incommensurable differences, but, as we shall try to demonstrate, they also unveil surprising parallels between usages in English, French, German, Czech, and Chinese.

THE RIGHTS OF MAN, AND EXCLUSION FROM HUMANITY

What did our new extended corpus reveal about the way 'citizen' is used as a concept in debate and in written discourse? From what we were able to judge from our texts and sources throughout the languages we investigated, the Rights of Man are invariably upheld in principle, though rarely in practice. This means that often only lip service is paid to 'citizens'. Indeed, such rhetoric often involves discourse strategies that seek to justify the situations in which 'citizens' rights are upheld, but not everyone is privy to these rights as citizens. In practice, this means that 'undesirable' or unfortunate elements are being excluded from the category of 'legitimate citizens'. And often the arguments used involve excluding them from the human race. The strategies adopted may vary from outright relegation, to mild forms of neglect that involve a rhetoric of objectification and disparagement. In wartime, enemies are regularly transformed into monsters, into barbarians, or into the heathen servants of the forces of evil, infidels in short. Such rhetoric invariably reactivates 'dormant' conceptual metaphors, which though they are not usually felt to reflect the reality of modern times, tap into deep-seated cultural paradigms and prejudices. The religious rhetoric of George W. Bush Jr and Sarah Palin is representative of this kind of discourse. Suddenly, the Biblical rhetoric of infidels takes on a new poignancy in the face of a perceived or portrayed evil or imminent threat. At this stage, marginal prejudice often becomes mainstream propaganda.

Most ruling classes and governments are loath to admit that they are flouting the rights of individuals or persecuting them. Discourse on 'citizenship' fits into this logic in a predictable manner. The question becomes: Upon which criteria can unwanted members of a community be excluded, either physically or legally? As we saw at the opening of this chapter, fully enfranchised citizens can actively participate in the governing of the city or the State. But for centuries, only wealthy landowners were eligible as voters in Britain. The very fact that the House of Commons – traditionally peopled by wealthy citizens and the landed gentry was supposed somehow to represent the 'common people' – reveals all too clearly the way access to rights and political representation has been fettered throughout the centuries in British history.

The fact that it took the fierce radicalism of feminism to force the establishment to endow women with the vote, tells a similar tale of exclusion. The BNC reflects this history of sexual exclusion, by providing 491 entries for 'freeman', but only three for 'freewoman'. A Google search provided more encouraging results: 400 million links between 'women' and 'citizens', as opposed to 309 million links between 'men' and 'citizens'. Perhaps this testifies to the political motivation to empower women in democracies, but our corpora and textual analysis bears witness to historical and enduring prejudices which tend to relegate women to secondary roles and often exclude them from citizenship.

Immigrants and slaves do not share the rights of citizens, and though The Society for the Abolition of the Slave Trade was founded in Britain in 1787, slavery itself was not abolished throughout the British Empire until 1883, eighteen years after the end of the American Civil War. And debates upon whether ex-patriot Britons returning to the British Isles from the colonies still 'possessed' rights over their imported slaves were hotly debated in the second half of the nineteenth century, as James Robertson's novel *Joseph Knight* (2003) movingly portrays.

Political exclusion from citizenship in America follows the European model until the Declaration of Independence, at which point the Rights of Man, declared as the founding principles of the nation, would embroil the State administration in complex strategies of exclusion based upon residency, religion, race, and nationality. Using MyAmericanCorpus, we were able to trace some of the major arguments that shaped the discourse of exclusion from citizenship, something that neither *Merriam-Webster* nor the COCA corpus of contemporary usage revealed.

Native Americans

Texts, films, documentaries, and interviews with indigenous populations revealed a clear-cut strategy to deny Indians any real rights as full US citizens. After the Franco-Anglo wars in Canada displaced many tribes, and encouraged them to take up a nomadic lifestyle, as the Plains Indians, their descendants became labelled as landless nomads. This displacement was crucial, since it deprived them of the right of belonging to a politically defined place. It conveniently excluded these originally sedentary tribes from the 'city' and made them 'non-citizens'. As civilization set itself up, they were considered to belong to Nature. As 'savages', they could hardly be deemed 'citizens'. Paradoxically, the definition of white American newcomers as 'settlers' complicates this opposition. But the temporary status of the new residents does not seem to have troubled the settler-citizens, who were understandably more concerned with defending their families, their homesteads, and their communities, than preserving the rights of local residents or upholding humanitarian rights. .

An underlying logic was still at work, however. The American definition of citizenship often works in relation to religious conceptions of territory. The parish church defines the sphere of the community, and non-believers are conceptually excommunicated from that sphere. Exclusion brings with it inclusion: the expropriation of land rights necessitates putting indigenous native populations elsewhere. From the texts consulted, this clearly seems to have involved confining them within barren lands in what often amounted to concentration camps. The 1968 Indian Civil Rights Bill was designed to provide the citizens of the Indian Nations with broadly similar rights to those of US citizens, but the vagueness of their status remains.

This embroils us in a paradox: Native Americans do not appear to be legally speaking full 'natives' in the sense of 'nationals', US citizens, subject to the rights accorded to, and the responsibilities required of, full American citizens. The confusion was palpable in the references to 'native' found in MyAmericanCorpus. 'Native place' and 'native country' tend to apply to US citizens, while references to 'native Americans', and 'with the aid of natives' tend to refer to the indigenous population considered to stand outside civil society. This meaning is clearly implied by the following passage from Benjamin Brawley's chapter on 'The Indian, the Mulatto, and the Free Negro' in *The Social History of the American Negro* published in 1921 (http://www.gutenberg.org)

> All such legislation, however, was radically changed as a result of Nathaniel Bacon's rebellion of 1676, in which the aid of **the natives** was invoked against the English governor. Henceforth **Indians** taken in war became **the slaves** for life of **their captors**. An elaborate act of 1682 summed up the **new status, and Indians** sold by other **Indians** were to be '**adjudged, deemed, and taken to be slaves**, to all intents and purposes, any law, usage, or custom to the contrary notwithstanding.' (Emphasis added)

Religion excluded heathen non-believers. Firearms were employed to chase off less well-armed populations. And what became landless nomads were excluded from the rights of citizenship which logically apply to residency within a self-governing community. The dictum, 'No taxation without representation', inevitably worked two ways, excluding non-taxpayers. Natives today are still considered to belong to, and to belong on, 'reservations'. They do not appear to be conceived of as belonging to self-governing urban communities, cities with citizens. Cities and citizens are closely linked in the American imagination, and despite the provisional nature of White settlements throughout the nineteenth century, 'citizens' tend to represent themselves defending their townships and communities as fending off 'the natives'. As the frontier expands, penetrating further into new territories, increasing demands are made upon government and on the army, to protect the rights and well-being of citizens against aggressors and trespassers, from illegitimate incursions from non-citizens. Indian rights have undergone great changes since the Civil Rights movements of the 1960s, but the COCA corpus which gives a more up-to-date impression of how words are linked within the American worldview than some of the texts we consulted provides only three links between 'natives' and 'citizens', and only one of those refers to Native Americans, a reference to Minnesota, 'in which two thirds of the citizens are natives'.

Afro-Americans

In *A History of the Negro Problem in the United States*, by Benjamin Brawley (1977, http://www.gutenberg.org/ebooks/12101), we learn that the 'slave had none of the ordinary rights of citizenship'. Nor was the state of the 'free Negro' far removed from slavery. 'Liberty, the boon of every citizen, the free Negro did not possess' we are told by Brawley. Afro-Americans were not even regarded as potential citizens by most Americans prior to the Civil War.

The Rights of Man are at the heart of debates related to the American and French revolutions. And the French Revolution was indirectly to have a great impact on the consciousness of American slaves. In the same work, we are told by Brawley that:

> When the General Assembly in France decreed equality of rights to all citizens, the mulattoes of Santo Domingo made a petition for the enjoyment of the same political privileges as the white people. (1977, http://www.gutenberg.org/ebooks/12101)

This forced some Americans to face up to the question of whether Afro-Americans had to be treated in the same way, as 'all men created equal'. And indeed, the Quakers had long denounced slavery on religious grounds. The Quakers appeared to remain, however, a minority, judging from the references generated from our corpus: throughout the texts we consulted, we found Americans inventing arguments similar to the ones enlisted by colonial powers to deprive individuals and communities, and entire races of peoples, from human rights to which the power in place paid lip service at least.

One further strategy was enlisted in exclusion: criminality. Since poverty and oppression inevitably leads to conflict, and since the oppressors hold the power over what is defined as 'crime', the 'criminals' who revolted against their masters and against the conditions they were subjected to were deprived of the rights of citizens. As 'outlaws', enemies of civil society, they could hardly expect to benefit from the rights of citizens, it was felt. In a cruel irony, in 1711 a group of 'Negros', among which the infamous Sebastian, a 'Spanish Negro', who robbed and plundered the inhabitants of the province, were brought in to Charleston by triumphant Indian bounty hunters after a £50 reward was offered for Sebastian alive or dead.

What is significant for the present study is that Afro-Americans can be slaves, and 'Negros', whereas Native Americans can be 'Indians' or 'Savages', but neither are considered 'to belong', as 'citizens' to the communities in which they settle or to which they are brought by physical force or by force of circumstance. Citizens and non-citizens are thus caught up in legalistic debates in which natives and slaves are rarely represented as the victims of criminal acts perpetrated against them. In the various stories related in texts, and online interviews and documentaries that we consulted, the 'citizens' who were robbed, plundered, raped, or murdered invariably belonged to the White settler class.

COCA offers a more positive image with 134 references to black citizens. These examples refer to protecting black citizens, to their voting rights, to the role of black citizens, and to the debt owed to them. And though the poverty of their social situation remains a concern, and though racism and opinions about the inferiority of blacks is at times expressed, things are clearly changing. When a wider more historical impression of the American worldview is taken into account, however, it remains clear that references to 'good citizens', 'fellow citizens', 'useful citizens', 'common citizens', invariably apply to 'white citizens' and to 'American citizens'. These Americans come together in 'meetings of citizens', but to these meetings Native Americans and Afro-Americans do not seem to be invited for the most part. Further detailed study is clearly required to determine how this situation is changing, and to elucidate the degree to which Native Americans and Blacks are considered to be fully enfranchised citizens by the majority of American citizens. But from what we could gather from our corpus findings, these groups remain subject to marginalization when it comes to citizenship.

SCOTTISH CITIZENS

After the build up to the Scottish Independence Referendum which took place on 18 September 2014, any Internet search engine produced a vast array of articles and references to Scottish citizens and citizenship. Advocates of independence set up a website (http://www.scotreferendum.com) to answer questions like:

> Will a British citizen habitually resident in Scotland on day one of independence be entitled to Scottish Citizenship?
>
> Will a British citizens born in Scotland but living outside of Scotland on day one of independence be entitled to Scottish Citizenship?
>
> Will a Child born in Scotland to at least one parent who has Scottish citizenship or indefinite leave to remain at the time of their birth be entitled to Scottish Citizenship?

The answer to all three questions was an unequivocal 'yes'. But this remained a hot issue. So was the Scottish education policy of refusing to introduce exorbitant student tuition fees. Why? Because throughout Europe, students were flocking to Scotland to profit from a high standard of tuition in English at reasonable rates, while fellow Brits from south of the border were not able to take advantage of the Scottish system. Severin Carrell, *The Guardian*'s correspondent for Scotland, writing on Thursday, 13 January 2011 (http://www.theguardian.com) in an article entitled, 'European student numbers soar at Scotland's free universities', argued that 'Scottish ministers fear[ed] its universities h[ad] become [the] "cheap option" for EU students facing rising fees at home'. This poses the question of Scottish, British, and European citizenship. Can you be all three at once? And what does this mean legally speaking in terms of rights?

Generally speaking, we have worked with the dichotomy that distinguishes between American and British English. But in this instance, our research findings forced us to make a further subdivision between English and Scottish English, since it became clear that Europe and citizenship take on a different meanings in English and Scottish English. The case should not be overstated. In both English English and Scottish English, the frequency with which 'citizen' was used was not particularly striking. And a great deal of uses of 'citizen' converged in Scottish English and English English.

Nonetheless, a marked difference was at times clearly observable. These findings should of course be verified by a study of far greater scope than we were able to carry out, but it is important at this stage to list the distinctions found in use, and to trace the degree to which the working hypotheses we formed were borne out or invalidated. The general impression left by our findings was that Scottish texts generated discussion about citizenship that was:

- more frequent;
- accorded greater importance;
- revealed more open and positive attitudes to immigration, to Europe, and to the world in general.

At the same time, many of the stories in the Scottish press were patently from British newspaper sources: stories about immigration and terrorism for example. That said, questions concerning British citizenship, which never appeared to make front page news in the English or British press, were accorded greater prominence in the Scottish texts.

Furthermore, although Scottish texts found in British sources tended to follow the same logic and rhetoric as the sources they had been borrowed from, the Scottish versions often showed a certain degree of critical distance. Questions were raised, and arguments were questioned. Definitions were discussed.

This was clearly to be seen in the article published online in the http://www.herald.scotland.com on 7 September 2015, entitled 'Cameron reveals British jihadists killed in RAF drone strike'. On the whole, the arguments and rhetoric used in the Scottish texts related to ISIS terrorists coincided with the discourse of their English counterparts. However, in this article, where Cameron portrayed himself as a protector of the people, the question of citizens, and the State's right to eliminate them, was raised. Cameron was quoted, assuring MPs: 'My first duty as Prime Minister is to keep the British people safe; that is what I will always do.'

This was his justification for the 'military strike by a British-controlled drone on August 21 [that] had targeted Reyaad Khan, an Isil terrorist from Cardiff [and his] fellow Isil fighter Ruhul Amin, 27, originally from Aberdeen'. These persons were 'British' in Cameron's discourse. They could be 'nationals': but not 'citizens'? Why?

Because according to the logic of his discursive strategy, Cameron was protecting citizens from terrorists, and these categories appear to be binary opposites, and mutually exclusive in his rhetoric. This enabled Cameron to claim that killing the said terrorists was a 'legitimate' act of 'self-defence'.

But this case also poses the question of the definition of 'soldiers' and 'citizens', because the same article stressed that 'The operation was the first occasion in modern times the UK had used military force in a country where it was not engaged in a war.' If there is no war, there are no soldiers. But the threat made the prospective terrorists 'soldiers' from Cameron's perspective, which explains why the British government excluded Khan and Amin when they assured the public that though '[b]oth men were killed; there were no civilian casualties'. The PM's spokeswoman said: 'This was a threat posed to our country and British citizens.' At home the British citizens were safe, protected from attacks from abroad.

The people and the citizens on the one hand, were protected by the State from enemies and terrorist on the other hand. This reveals to what extent 'citizen', 'national', and 'Briton' are not neutral synonyms, but the stakes employed in discourse strategies. They become the means by which we carve up the debates and create sympathies and antipathies.

The *Herald Scotland* did not allow such rhetoric to stand alone on the stage but invited discordant voices and dissent. Though one of the voices was Scottish, the Scots were not sniping at the English, but rather airing debates on the legitimacy of assassinations in the name of anti-terrorism. And criticisms came from the government's own Tory backbenchers too.

> Senior Tory backbencher David Davis, a former Shadow Home Secretary, argued there should be a formal check on such decisions, suggesting they otherwise amounted to an 'extra-judicial execution'. Brendan O'Hara for the SNP [Scottish National Party] demanded Mr Cameron 'come clean' over his future military plans, saying: 'I fear David Cameron is planning to use this awful humanitarian tragedy as a smokescreen to fulfil his long-held desire to involve UK forces in more military action in Syria.' Kate Hudson, general secretary of the Campaign for Nuclear Disarmament, said: 'That a British citizen was targeted and killed by these strikes - and another killed by mistake - is particularly alarming and sets a dangerous new precedent.' This is extrajudicial killing: A British Prime Minister now claims the right to kill British citizens when they travel abroad. (http://www.herald.scotland.com)

The law, and what the State can lawfully do to its citizens to protect them from one another was what was at stake here. But the term 'citizen' itself – reattributed to 'the terrorists' by Hudson – strikes a discordant note, revealing to what extent the dominant discourse disseminated by the government is asserting itself. Suddenly, it becomes clear that the government is depriving some of 'citizenship' while according it to others. Without this, its self-defence rhetoric becomes tenuous.

In other articles related to immigration and Syrian refugees, the terms and rhetoric of debates largely coincided in English and Scottish English, in our findings. However, the Scottish Parliament clearly has a different attitude to immigration from its counterpart in Westminster, and has repeatedly stressed that Scotland's economy needs its foreign labour force. Anxious to play the good Member State, Scotland's government proudly parades itself as an open society that welcomes foreigners. Scotland has a dynamic young Development Minister named Humza Yousaf, who (the *Herald Scotland* reported on Monday, 24 August 2015) visited Qatar in April in order 'to raise concerns about migrant worker's rights' (http://www.herald.scotland.com).

> Speaking at Dubai International Writers' Centre during the Emirates Literature Festival on April 7, Mr Yousaf called on Arab states to 'comply with international and human rights law, and condemn human rights abuses'. ... 'As **a good global citizen**, Scotland has a strong and enduring commitment to securing democracy, the rule of law and fundamental human rights across the world. We expect all states to comply with international and human rights law, and condemn human rights abuses wherever they occur. Respect for human right and the rule of law are critical to the economic prosperity and stability of all nations and territories. Scotland has its National Action Plan for Human Rights, setting our ambitions to be the most equal and fairest country in the world ...' (http://www.herald.scotland.com; emphasis added)

This is clearly the diplomatic discourse of Scotland promoting itself on the world's stage, but it does highlight the role Scotland would like to be seen playing as a citizen within a global community and within the European Union. The SNP wishes to be seen as a protector of citizens and their rights within the communities to which Scotland belongs. This would at least seem to corroborate the hypothesis that 'citizens' and 'citizenship' figures more highly among the priorities of the Scottish government and the Scottish press than it does in Britain as a whole.

This glowing picture does not fit with all the findings our study provided. 'Citizen' remains fairly rare in Scottish texts when compared to American usages. Nonetheless, the fact that Scotland has a newspaper called *The Evening Citizen* is not irrelevant to our study. Similarly, a case that 'citizen' is a Scottish keyword in politics and civil life would seem to be supported by further stories. For instance, one news story recounted that 'The Citizen Building in Glasgow city centre has been handed a new lease of life after a hospitality company unveiled plans to open a restaurant in the historic building' (http://www.herald.scotland.com).

Scottish references to citizen were not commonplace in the texts we consulted, and when the term came up, it was at times used to refer to 'Citizen Kane' or the Citizen's Advice Bureau in contexts very similar to those found in our English sources. Without wishing to exaggerate the extent of our findings, however, it would seem that 'citizen' remains a significant factor in Scottish politics and media. And given the pro-European vote throughout Scotland at the Brexit elections, perhaps 'citizen' may become a potential player in the future of the Scottish worldview.

COMPARING CITIZENS IN CULTURES

Comparing the representation of 'citizen' in the English, American, and Scottish imaginations should have helped us to perceive the specificities of each of these three traditions that form part of the Anglo worldview. The following short sections will consider the French, German, and Czech conceptions of citizenship and the way the 'equivalent' terms for the English word 'citizen', '*citoyen*', '*Bürger*', and '*občan*', respectively, are used in those languages. It would be absurd to claim that in such a short space we could do justice to the complexities of each of the traditions of those linguistic communities. But comparative linguistic approaches advance by juxtaposing traditions, cultures and languages, in order to observe both the coinciding patterning and the sharp contrasts that comparison brings out.

Translators on a day to day basis make it obvious that people from different linguistic communities can be made to understand one another if language barriers are bridged. In a vast number of instances, in discussions about citizenship of towns and cities, countries and states, 'citizen' coincides with the way the broadly equivalent keywords are used in French, German, and Czech. When we speak of citizens as nationals, as having certain rights, such as the right to vote and the right to residency, and when we speak about obligation to pay taxes, there is little to distinguish the ways the 'equivalent' terms are used. The European Union, its politics, and its legislation have tended to consolidate this converging tendency.

We are all, moreover, encouraged to believe we exist as citizens of equal status within the Member States of the European Union. However, words resonate within the imagination in cultural traditions that have their roots in very different shared experiences. As a linguistic community, France has long been striving towards a strong concept of the nation state while the German *Länder* remained resolutely independent in many ways, and the Swiss state has an infinitely longer tradition in democracy than the French, the Germans, and the Czechs. The Czechs had no nation of their own for several centuries, and the Second World War and the liberation embroiled Czechs and the inhabitants of their lands in fierce struggles related to patriotism and citizenship. These are unique experiences that helped forge a very Czech conception of citizenship.

The aim in these short sections must be limited to making a solid argument for a modest claim: that dictionaries, corpora, films, and textual analysis make it clear that the terms themselves do not coincide fully, that the cultures often invest very different meaning in these supposedly 'equivalent' terms. As a consequence, each of the linguistic communities produces a whole range of expressions and ideas related to citizens that, to all intents and purposes, remain untranslatable – and difficult to transpose from one culture to another. Indeed, attempts to transpose them often require elaborate explanations to clarify the narratives and logics that citizenship evokes in each culture. Without such explanations, the specific nature of those narratives and logics often appear to other cultures to be perversely idiosyncratic, and risk being dismissed as unfathomable absurdities. In order to make this point perfectly clear from the outset, we invite readers to try to grasp the meaning of the following phrases.

J'étais citoyen de la France universelle, bien loin de l'Ile-de-France.
('I was a citizen of Universal France, far from the Paris region', Frantext; emphasis added)

*Wir sind erwachsene **Bürger**, in keiner Weise bevormundet und wollen das auch bleiben!* ('We are mature citizens, in no way to be patronized, and wish to remain so', http://www.tagesanzeiger.ch; emphasis added.)

*čeští (sudetští) Němci stali **občany** Německa.* ('Czech Sudenten Germans became German citizens', unknown source, cited in the Czech corpus of http://corpora.informatik.uni-leipzig.de; emphasis added.)

We trust that these disturbingly enigmatic statements will justify the following short adventures into other worldviews and serve to demonstrate that 'citizen' cannot be deemed a simple universal concept. Considering citizen to be a shared European concept as it is promoted by the European Union and the http://europa.eu website makes sense for a new union of Member States, but it tends to eclipse the diversity of dynamically evolving traditions of the various linguistic communities involved.

Citoyens, Citoyennes

What '*citoyen*' means within the French worldview will also be further discussed in the sections on the philosophical and literary uses of 'citizen', but it should prove worthwhile to make a few fundamental observations here about the nature of the French concept and the way the term '*citoyen*' works within the patterning of the French language. Because France is a republic, the '*sujet*' (subject) is replaced by the '*citoyen*', thereby gaining in status. But this involves a long process of evolution, with much preparation and great resistance. The philosopher, Voltaire, admired Switzerland with its 'equality according to which the citizen is subject to laws alone and which protects the liberty of the weak against the ambition of the stronger' ('*égalité par laquelle le citoyen ne dépend que des lois, et qui maintient la liberté des faibles contre l'ambition du plus fort*' (Voltaire, quoted by Oster 1990: 554). And the Revolution does bring with it the celebration of citizens, which explains why a revolutionary like Louis Antoine de Saint-Just would chastise the majority of the masses who all wished to govern rather than become citizens (Oster 1993: 57), and why he considered the 'civil servant' ('*fonctionnaire*') to be beneath the 'citizen' ('*citoyen*') (Oster 1993: 57).

'*Citoyen*' is, therefore, an ideal. As such, lip service is paid to it down to this day when presidential candidates address French people as

'Citoyennes, citoyens ...' The author of *The Count of Monte Cristo* and *The Three Musketeers*, Dumas (1802–1870), looking back on revolutionary days, certainly uses the term frequently as a form of address in the former novel when he writes about the period following Napoleon's fall from glory. And this usage comes into American and British English through the translation of the novel, though it is clearly perceived as being 'French', and, as such, foreign to the Anglo worldview.

Three points should, however, be made at this point.

- The frequency with which the term appears to be used in French does not undergo a 'revolution' with the Revolution. Though the *Dictionnaire de citations françaises* (Oster 1993) does offer more examples for the nineteenth and twentieth centuries than volume one (which covers the Middle Ages up to the Revolution), the number is rather negligible: nine in the second, as opposed to seven in the first. The Frantext corpus offers a multitude of pre-revolutionary examples of '*citoyen*', and some of its contemporary traits are clearly discernible.
- In a wide range of fields – and in everyday speech in general – *citoyen* is not frequently heard, however much it is used in political rhetoric and in the language and laws of the French State.
- The French Revolution is heralded as a 'civilizing project', a project of the Enlightenment. France is not simply going to liberate its own subjects and elevate them to the status of 'citizens'. France is going to liberate the world. This is the spirit that animates the times, and makes Saint-Just exclaim: '*le people français vote la liberté du monde*' ('The French people vote for the world's liberty', Oster 1993: 57).

This may help us somewhat to begin to understand the concept of 'a universal France', and to apprehend something of what the French invest in their version of '*Les droits de l'Homme*' (human rights). According to this belief, the French were the first to understand the universal Rights of Man and to elevate them into sacrosanct principles in their Revolution. French expansionism in the Napoleonic era would therefore be justified by the French in the name of liberation.

Removing the tyrants from the world is an image adopted by Soviet propaganda that portrayed a giant Lenin astride the earth with a broom in his hands, brushing aside kings and corrupt statesmen. The same logic continues to animate the most idealistic Frenchmen such as Alexis Jenni, who, in his *L'Art français de la guerre*, published in 2011, wrote the perplexing phrase quoted above: '*J'étais citoyen de la France universelle, bien loin de l'Ile-de-France.*' 'I was a citizen of Universal France, far from the Paris region' (Frantext; emphasis added).

How are we to comprehend Jenni's nostalgic anxiety? Jenni is lamenting the gap that divides the ideal France that animates the universalistic ideals of the Republic and its ex-colonies, and the reality of civil society in metropolitan France today. Jenni is not renouncing his ideals, however; he is reaffirming them. This is only one facet of a wider concern for what it means to be a citizen of France. Throughout French history there have been long periods of conflict over the status of citizens, and much debate over who can be considered citizens; whether women are citizens, and what rights and obligations citizens must be considered to have. And this history is feeding into French debates about the nature of European citizenship.

One essential difference that conditions the course of 'citizen' and *citoyen* is that the latter from the outset, and down to this day, covers not only the ideal or legally designated rights and status of inhabitants of towns and countries, but also covers a whole range of more down-to-earth functions and traits in workaday experience. While English-speakers are generally more tempted to speak of 'individuals', 'residents', 'inhabitants', 'dwellers', 'members of society', 'nationals', 'the general public', or quite simply 'people', the French media and administration often speak of *citoyens*. French dictionaries (such as *Le Nouveau Petit Robert* (Rey-Debove and Rey 1993), or Larrousse, http://www.larousse.fr/dictionnaires/francais) tend to define '*citoyen*' as belonging 1. to a political or social unit, '*une cité*', 2. to a town or city, a bourgeois rather than a small landowner ('*paysan*') or farm labourer, 3. to a nation ('*ressortissant*' or '*national*'). But the historical use cited above, of '*citoyen*' used as a form of address during the revolutionary period ('*La citoyenne Tallien*'), is also frequently cited, as in *Le Nouveau Petit Robert* (Rey-Debove and Rey 1993: 384). There is also a curious, but fairly common, pejorative usage of *citoyen*, which parallels a similar usage of *individu, personnage* in French. In this sense, *citoyen* is a familiar expression used to denote a person who looks or acts in a bizarre and ridiculous manner ('*Individu aux allures ou au comportement plus ou moins bizarres*', http://www.larousse.fr). And this usage explains a whole range of rather derogatory terms related to animals (*oiseau, zèbre*, translated respectively as 'bird' and 'zebra') which are sometimes used as synonyms for *citoyen* in common speech. As fairly approximate English translations of such expressions we might suggest 'curious bird' or 'strange duck'. But 'citizen' would certainly evoke none of the implicitly pejorative connotations associated with the French expression.

The CRISCO (Centre de Recherches Inter-langues sur la Signification en Contexte) corpus for synonyms generated by Caen University in Northern France (http://www.crisco.unicaen.fr) gives the order of frequency for the synonyms for *citoyen* shown in Figure 2.1

homme [man]	
individu [individual]	
personne [person]	
type [guy/fellow]	
habitant [inhabitant]	

Figure 2.1 Synonyms for '*citoyen*'

Clearly, the criterion of residency comes after the classification of people as individuals and groups of individuals. And if we consult the top twenty synonyms for this keyword using CRISCO, we find that the moral nature of the *citoyen* as a member of the Republic is important (with synonyms such as *démocrat, égal, enfant, fils, patriote*, and *républicain*). In other words, we consider the citizen to be a child or son of the Republic, who is democratic, patriotic and republican, and sees all other citizens as his equals. Judging from the CRISCO resources, this is not the prototypical core of the concept, but it is an important dimension specific to the French conception. And this dimension becomes all the more obvious if we consider the antonyms for *citoyen* listed in the CRISCO:

- *aristocrate* [aristocrat];
- *barbare* [barbarian];
- *étranger* [foreigner];
- *sujet* [subject].

In this modern usage, using *citoyen* clearly involves taking a political stance, the CRISCO resources indicate. The modern French citizen refuses aristocracy and refutes the idea that he can be considered a 'subject'. He is patriotic. He distinguishes between himself and foreigners, and the latter can be considered to be barbarians at times, while the citizen clearly considers himself to be 'civil' and 'civilized'.

In parallel to English, with its 'civil–civic' distinction, the adjectival forms related to the noun *citoyen* can be divided into *civil* and *civique*, and the two adjectives cover somewhat different domains of experience. Like all dynamically contrasting semantic distinctions, these turn out to be culturally specific in the way they have developed throughout history. *Civil* refers to the entire body of citizens of society, of the State, and of the Revolution. It is used to cover discussions concerning the relations between citizens and their rights and obligations to one another. In this sense, its meaning is extended in legal terms to distinguish between civil and criminal law, as in English. But there is also a usage of *civil* which has passed into English, though it has become somewhat outdated in contemporary French, according to which *civil* means 'affable', 'agreeable', amiable', 'polite', and courteous'.

Civique has preserved the moral dimension of this concept, but the associations are of an entirely different order to the polite good citizen who is supposed to remain courteous in his relations with his fellow citizens. *Civique* implies *vertus civiques* (civil virtues), such as *courage*, and here *courage* is being used in a patriotic post-revolutionary sense to designate the *esprit civique* of the patriotic citizen who assumes his role as a full and loyal citizen. The opposite of such an attitude is called *incivilité*, and one can 'commit an uncivil act' (*commetre une incivilité*). The *Robert-Collins Dictionary* (1998: 464) translates *incivilité* as 'rudeness', and certainly this translation works in a great range of situations. But this hides what is not translated: that *incivilité* is an expression of *incivisme*, and *incivisme* denotes a lack of civic or public spirit. The difference here is that English-speakers generally tend to think in terms of what is 'done' or 'not done' in public and in 'polite society'; French-speakers are thinking of what kind of behaviour the Republic has the right to expect or prescribe. This opens up a whole field in French for a non-dialogue between protesters and hooligans on the one hand who see no legitimacy in the State, and, on the other, the voices of the Establishment who cannot conceive of any legitimate reason for citizens rejecting the State's definition of what is and what is not 'civil' behaviour.

Among the examples of *citoyen* generated by our corpus research, Frantext furnished a great range of examples from sixteenth and seventeenth-century French. These have the advantage of acting as a counterpoint to our post-revolutionary Republican examples. The moral dimension of the concept of *citoyen* is clearly manifest in these examples, as in the following example: '*Les dames disoient qu'il estoit bon frere et vertueux citoyen*' ('The ladies said that he was a good brother and virtuous citizen.') In the same vein, we find a great number of collocations and phrases consolidating the idea of 'the good citizen' (*bon citoyen*) being a virtuous citizen. He is a 'sober' citizen (*'sobre'*, designating 'well-behaved', 'serious' as well as literally 'not drunken'). '*Notable citoyen*' and '*Il ne fut jamais un meilleur citoyen*' (Frantext) partake of the same logic. These sixteenth- and seventeenth-century examples allow us to form the hypothesis that the prototypical good citizen of those times was a law-abiding, god-fearing, male city-dweller who both possessed – and therefore respected – property.

The religious dimension is palpable here. Examples in which moral judgements can clearly be discerned are commonplace. And such judgements become sharper with the Reformation. For with the Reformation, all of the moral and religious conceptions of citizenship will be brought into play. To whom the actual physical right to the city will be accorded or contested becomes based upon religious grounds in conflicts between Protestants and Catholics. Similarly, conflicts over land rights, and property rights, and who has the right to govern towns and cities are all questions that imply the citizen. Who can be considered a 'good' citizen, and which citizens are judging each other becomes a political and religious question.

Frantext did produce some curious examples such as '*citoyen des forests* [*sic*]', and '*citoyen des cieux*', but these references to forests, pastoral life, and residency in the world hereafter tended to be found in literary works. '*Citoyen du monde*', on the other hand, was commonplace in our sixteenth and seventeenth-century sources. This concept of universal citizenship belongs to the tradition leading from the Stoics, through to the Neoplatonists, and down to the Church Fathers who all stressed the importance of universal brotherhood, and a 'cosmopolitan' religion, rather than a 'political' ethics for the '*polis*', the city state governed by citizens.

The concept of national appurtenance proved rare among the sixteenth- and seventeenth-century examples studied, with only a single reference to both France and to Paris found in our selection. References to other cities (such as Geneva, for some reason) were more common, and frequent references to Rome stressed the continuity in terms of government, law, literature and ideals, between French and Latin models of citizenship.

Deutche Bürger

French has influenced English, but what about other European traditions? For other languages, understanding the way keywords are used proves more complicated. This is the certainly the case for *Bürger*. For centuries, the Paris–Versailles tandem managed to maintain itself as the centre of gravity for the French language and for *la francophonie*. But there is no centre to the German language: Swiss German and Austrian German can in no way be considered subservient to a national ideal of the German language, however much *Hochdeutsch* has managed to assert itself. We are required to limit our study, however, so we have chosen to focus on *Hochdeutsch*, and noted any specific distinctions, where we felt them to be significant.

Throughout standard German, at any rate, *Bürger* proves to be an extremely coherent and productive lexeme. In English, 'burgher' has gone out of use, and the only echo of it that still resounds within the imagination is to be heard in the names of towns (Pittsburgh or Edinburgh, for instance). *Bürger*, in contrast, remains a very commonplace term in everyday usage. Searching for 'burgher' in English on http://www.google.com, produces historical references to the burghers of Calais, relating to the Hundred Years War, or to the Afrikaans citizens of the Boer Republic in South Africa. The various corpora studied in German, on the other hand, produced a vast and vibrant selection of usages related to citizens, civil rights, and to political and social life. The unbroken tradition that defines *Bürgers* as the residents of towns and cities with certain rights, privileges, and obligations was clearly reflected in the animated exchanges over the nature of those rights, privileges, and obligations that were in the various corpora and articles studied.

The *Oxford-Duden German Dictionary* (1994: 178) provides three main definitions for '*Bürger*': 1. a citizen of a State, 2. a citizen of a town (*Die Bremer Bürger*), 3. a bourgeois. In the English imagination, 'bourgeois' either sounds both French and intellectual, on the one hand, unlike 'middle-class', or, on the other hand, it sounds political, reminding us of the way Marxists used the word. The German concept, however, is far more widespread and often far more neutral: *Bürger* maintains a logical coherence, linking up semantic spheres and associations that are invariably cordoned off and left without any coordinating core concept in English. The *Bürger* can be an urbane individual who belongs to both the middle class, and the nation. Moreover, as a cultivated or educated member of society, the citizen can be considered a citizen of the world (*Weltbürger*). In its modern usages, a German citizen can, of course, be a man or a woman: *Bürgerin*, covers the same three meanings quoted above according to the *Oxford-Duden* (1994: 178).

What this means is that '*Bürger*' functions as a semantic nexus at which converge the idea of citizenship and the various facets of urban life in modern society. This contrasts starkly with the Anglo concept. Indeed, a whole host of strategies are required to translate into English German words and phrases that are clearly and coherently organized in German thanks to this nexus. The following list of examples selected from the *Oxford-Duden* will suffice to demonstrate this.

- *Bürgeraktion* [public campaign];
- *Bürgerinitiative* [citizen's action];
- *Bürgermeister* [mayor];
- *Bürgerbeauftragte* [ombudsman];
- *Bürgerentscheid* [local referendum];
- *Bürgerforum* [open forum];
- *Bürgerliche Leben* [middle class life];
- *Die Bürgerlichkeit* [middle class or bourgeois way of life];
- *Das Bürgertum* [the bourgeoisie];
- *Bürgersohn* [son of a middle class family];
- *Bürgerliche Küche* [good plain home-cooking];
- *Bürgersteig* [pavement/sidewalk];
- *Der Spanische Bürgerkrieg* [the Spanish Civil War].

Similarly, most of the German dictionaries consulted listed a multitude of references to concepts unconnected with the lexemes 'citizen' in English, and '*citoyen*' in French, respectively.

Our study did not find only positive definitions of the citizen in German. In German, one way of expressing the idea of a narrow-minded way of thinking is to call it '*dieses bürgerlich engstirnige Denken*': narrow-minded middle class thinking. And this is, paradoxically, the antithesis of the urbane educated and enlightened individual characterized in German, French, and English in the expression, 'a citizen of the world'. The bourgeoisie can be the target of criticisms from various quarters. At all levels, public debates, local and national politics, and civic actions involve arguments and conflicts of interests. And *der Spanische Bürgerkrieg*, the Spanish Civil War, inevitably involves violent armed struggle, reminding us that civil war is the ultimate expression of a conflict between the 'citizens' of a single state.

But what is striking about the examples found in the German corpora we studied in the diverse spheres of existence to which the lexeme *Bürger* pertains was the energy of the actors. Citizens appear to be engaged in a dynamic and authentic debate about the nature of modern urban life and the relations that should govern the rights and responsibilities of citizens to one another and to the government. Of course, English and French sources provide examples concerning the civil rights movements and associations such as the Citizen's Advice Bureau. But the degree of democratic negotiation revolving around the '*Bürger*' generated by our research remained remarkable by comparison to the French and English traditions.

Moreover, government was frequently held to be accountable to the '*Bürger*' (citizens). In English, we might be more inclined to think in terms of 'the people' or 'public opinion'. In French, often discourse of this type is often addressed to '*les français*'. It would, therefore, be rash to conclude from this alone that German-speakers are generally more democratic in their thinking and behaviour than the British or the French. Nonetheless, among its German newspaper corpus based on material gathered together up until 2011, based upon 26 142 898 sentences, the Leipzig Wortschatz (http://corpora.uni-leipzig.de) did produce a great number of intriguing examples which resist translation into French or English. Among them, the following are worth noting:

Wir Bürger dürfen uns durchaus artikulieren. ('We citizens should express this clearly', www.goettinger-tageblatt.de)

Was dem Staat zusteht, sollte dem Bürger auch zustehen. ('What the State is entitled to, should also accrue to citizens', www.tagesanzeiger.ch)

Reife Bürger wollen direkte Demokratie. ('Mature citizens want direct democracy', www.nachrichten.at)

Also an alle noch denkenden Bürger ... ('So to all thinking citizens ...', www.bernerzeitung.ch)

It is not by chance that many of the phrases which stress staunch negotiation over rights were found in Swiss German sources. Switzerland has a long history of democratic governance of the citizens by the citizens. But rather than being exceptions, those examples appeared, upon study, to reflect and epitomize an existing dialogue over the democratic rights of citizens that is common to what might be considered the German Worldview. The collocations which translate awkwardly into 'mature citizens' and 'thinking citizens' were part of a rhetoric of indignation faced with a government that seemed to think it could ignore public opinion. But it was also a rhetoric that clearly aimed to cultivate that sentiment of indignation and channel it into the democratic claims for respect and the representation of citizens.

In the same respect, 'public confidence' is expressed in terms of '*Das Vertrauen der Bürger*'. This is a commonplace phrase, but it implies a democratic claim. The German people are expressing their demand to be taken seriously as citizens of a democracy. French-speakers and English-speakers can, of course, make similar claims, but the patterning of the German language would seem to make such claims unnecessary, in the sense that they are already implicitly contained in everyday expressions and modes of thinking and feeling about citizenship. Consequently, a whole range of discussions that would involve 'people' in English, tend to be conducted in terms of '*Bürger*' in German. Germans speak of the '*die Kaufkraft der Bürger*' (the spending power of citizens, Leipzig Wortschatz). '*Bürger*' are protected by new police security measures. '*Bürger*' are invited for vaccinations by local government. '*Bürger*' enjoy firework displays. These appear to us as curiosities, if we try to translate them into English. They clash with the usual patterns of thinking that are organized around the concept of the 'citizen'. And they would appear to testify to the greater depth and coherence of '*Bürger*' as a cultural keyword explored by German-speakers in everyday speech. This is what Humboldt had in mind when he spoke of 'the work of the Mind/Spirit' (*Arbeit des Geistes*), as the way a people appropriates and explores the potential of a word by carving out a complex patterning (*Wechselwirkung*) (Underhill 2009). The Germans appear to have established a very rich and dynamic patterning around the term *Bürger*, thereby making it a great tool of democratic expression.

This remains a hypothesis of ethnolinguistic research. Much greater study would be required to verify the legitimacy of such a hypothesis, but our research so far would appear to confirm that the three meanings of citizen, as a resident of a town or city, a national, and as a free right-bearing individual remain balanced in the German imagination and in public dialogue concerning citizenship. And even when German-speakers express irritation and disgust as citizens, they tend to express that irritation and disgust not in terms of disengagement or alienation, but by adopting the rhetoric of 'we citizens' (*wir Bürger*), something which appears almost ridiculous, or perhaps even unthinkable for many people living in France of Britain today.

Český Občany

The Czech concept of '*občan*' resembles the German concept '*Bürger*' in the respect that it opens up a wide range of related meanings and phrases in everyday speech. The fact that, like its German equivalent – and unlike its French and English counterparts – the adjective (*občanský*) is clearly derived from the noun (*občan*) helps to clarify the way a whole range of issues and debates related to civil and civic rights and privileges pertaining to the citizen are held together within the Czech linguistic worldview.

Dictionary definitions give a concise but elliptic impression of the way the lexeme functions in the language, and the way the concept resonates in the Czech imagination. Poldauf's classic Czech–English dictionary, *Česko-Anglický Slovník*, defines the term as referring to nationals, urban residents and those holding civil rights (1986: 440–441). Poldauf also quotes a diminutive form, *občánek*, a colloquial form used in familiar speech, and his communist dictionary faithfully cites a condescending aristocratic usage of '*občan*' as belonging to the 'low-born'.

But the political and emotive charge of the term can hardly be intuited from the examples Poldauf provides, and this is regrettable, since the various stages of twentieth-century history have greatly shaped and shaded debates on Czech citizenship. Until 1918, there was no Czech Republic, and there were, therefore, no 'Czech citizens'. And the fusion between the Czech and Slovak peoples into Czechoslovakia was not always a straightforward process. The fact that three million German-speakers found themselves transformed into Czechoslovak citizens, was a tender point which became a burning issue with Hitler's rise to power and his policy of *Lebensraum* which meant annexing states to the East under German rule. Both before and after the war, many such citizens were unsure if they were German, Austrian, or Czechoslovak citizens, or all three. The occupation gave a romantic and revolutionary resonance to '*občan*' in the Czech imagination. And with their rise to power in 1948, the communists capitalized on the feeling that the citizens had been liberated, to promote a communist conception of socialism rebuilding the citizen's state. For this reason, in films of the time, the terms, '*občan*', '*občany*', '*občansky*' often make themselves heard. These terms cover pretty much the same affective range of meanings covered by 'comrade' in the post-liberation communist chapter in Czech history.

Like its European counterparts, '*občan*' has undergone a transformation with the Czech Republic's adherence to the European Community.

Despite a certain Euroscepticism that is more manifest among the citizens of the Czech Republic than in their Slovak neighbours, and until recently their Polish neighbours, debates on the rights of Czech workers and citizens throughout the Member States resemble, for the most part, debates being conducted elsewhere throughout Europe. The Český Národní Korpus (https://www.korpus.cz) and the Czech Corpus accessible at Wortschatz Universität Leipzig (http://corpora.informatik.uni-leipzig.de/) – which is curiously longer than the German equivalent (with 31 396 531 million sentences) – both confirm this, as did follow-up research carried out using Internet search engines (such as Google, Yahoo).

In contrast to English and French, a whole range of spheres of life still appear to be considered in terms of citizenship in Czech. The Leipzig Czech Corpus provided various examples, from which the following ones offer us a glimpse of the scope of discussions in which '*občan*' comes into play in Czech:

- Entrepreneurs and business propose services to 'citizens' (*občany*).
- Rest homes are provided not for 'the sick or aged' but for 'underprivileged citizens' (*občany*).
- Bus links are maintained not for the benefit of 'the public' but to 'bind the citizens (*občany*) of neighbouring towns'.

Traces of the communist history of the Czechs can still be found among the examples from the contemporary Czech Leipzig corpus. We are reminded, for instance, that 'practicing believers became second class citizens' under communism (*Aktivní věřící se stali občany druhé kategorie*; emphasis added). But the sources cited inevitably bear the ideological bias of the post-communist Czech worldview. For these days, we are being told a story in which the Czech victims were persecuted by the communists. In this rather fanciful fairy tale, the Czech nationals are the victims of supposedly external forces, the communists: *občany* are preyed upon by *komunisté*:

> *Čeští komunisté i nadále pronásledovali a perzekvovali své odpůrce - občany Československa.* ('Czech communists continued to pursue and persecute their opponents – citizens of Czechoslovakia', http://corpora.informatik.uni-leipzig.de/; emphasis added)

Without in any way wishing to diminish the crimes of the Czechoslovak communist regime, it is important to remember that, unlike the German occupiers of the Nazi period, the communists were Czech citizens too. Here we are clearly stigmatizing communists, and the logic of the argument somewhat perversely implies that the rights and privileges of the victims should not be accrued to those who persecuted them. Like the British terrorists in the example of Cameron's strikes, they are denied citizenship and the rights that go with it.

Political oppression, the lack of free speech during the communist years, but also unemployment at home and career possibilities abroad following the Velvet Revolution, are factors that helped shape debates on what Czech citizens did, where they went, and what they desired. Foreign marriages and a fascination with the West are themes less prominent in the Czech imagination – perhaps since the Czech citizens have always been more comfortable, financially speaking, than their neighbours – but they too have influenced the questions raised and discussed and the problems encountered by Czech citizens.

The French stories do not coincide with the stories we encounter in Czech or in German, and they all contrast with the stories of citizens in Scotland, England, and America. These intriguing digressions certainly do not give more than an overall impression of what citizenship means for each of these cultures. Specialists of Czech, German, and French will inevitably find dozens of phrases, expressions, quotations, and anecdotes coming to mind, as they read our accounts and provisional conclusions. This is in the nature of comparative research. Further studies will help to modify and remould the impressions listed above. But from the sources we have gathered, after careful examination and analysis, we hope to have demonstrated that though the concept of 'citizen' can find counterparts in each of the various European languages we have considered, history, society, and individual imaginations continue to shape and reshape the way we think and feel about the various spheres in the private and public life of citizens. Turning from these culture-specific conceptions of the 'citizen', it is now worth asking in what dimensions of life, being a 'citizen' is considered to be of importance. Is the question of citizenship a religious question? A philosophical question? Does the citizen figure in literature?

Is Citizen a Philosophical Question?

As mentioned above, the Bible does make reference to citizens. But in the King James Version, it is not until we enter the New Testament that we find any reference to them. Luke, in 15: 5, refers to the prodigal son as a citizen of a certain country. And we quoted above an example from the *OED* found in Wycliffite's 1382 Bible, in the Acts of the Apostles.

In Biblical usages, the definition is not precise. In the New Testament, there is a conflation between citizens belonging to cities, nations, and religions. This is not surprising since 'citizen' is an export of Hellenism. The New Testament is translated from Greek. Hebrew seems to generate no equivalent terms for what might be considered as a concept of citizenship. The Old Testament is peopled with families, clans, tribes, kingdoms, and subjects. One thing does link the Old to the New Testament, however. Religious concepts of citizenship are not of that political kind associated with republican ideals of freedom and equality. True, the Book of Nehemiah, in a sense, constitutes the celebration of rebuilding Jerusalem as a walled city state, peopled by, and defended by, soldier-citizens who build the city walls with a brick in one hand and a sword in the other. This is a rare exception however. On the whole, the Bible is no source of inspiration for citizens looking for rights and protection. There seems little reason, therefore, to consider 'citizenship' to be a religious concept. Would it be fairer to regard citizenship as a philosophical concept then?

It would seem tempting to believe so, but it is debatable whether 'citizen' is a philosophical concept. For the great philosopher of space, Henri Lefebvre (2000; see also Deulceux and Hess 2009: 211), the development of philosophy is inseparable from the city, the *polis*, the political locus of free men, deciding their own destinies, and dreaming up their modes of lifestyles and debating their policies. The highly respected online *Stanford Encyclopedia of Philosophy* (http://plato.stanford.edu), offers the following definition: 'A citizen is a member of a political community who enjoys the rights and assumes the duties of membership.' And the *Stanford Encyclopedia* goes on to enlarge on that initial definition as follows:

> The concept of citizenship is composed of three main elements or dimensions (Cohen 1999; Kymlicka and Norman 2000; Carens 2000). The first is citizenship as legal status, defined by civil, political and social rights. Here, the citizen is the legal person free to act according to the law and having the right to claim the law's protection. It need not mean that the citizen takes part in the law's formulation, nor does it require that rights be uniform between citizens. The second considers citizens specifically as political agents, actively participating in a society's political institutions. The third

refers to citizenship as membership in a political community that furnishes a distinct source of identity. (http://plato.stanford.edu/entries/citizenship/)

Yet more compact paperback dictionaries of philosophy such as Antony Flew's *Dictionary of Philosophy* (1979), and J. O. Urmson and Jonathan Rée's *Concise Encyclopedia of Western Philosophy and Philosophers* (1991) find no place for entries for 'citizen'. This is not particular to English. This state of affairs proves to be similar to that of the French concept: '*citoyen*' only appears in the 2042 page *Dictionnaire de la philosophie*, published as part of the *Encyclopædia Universalis* edition, indirectly, listed under other terms. Of course, this tells us more about the narrowing definition of philosophy over the last century or so. Ancient and even nineteenth-century philosophers spread their nets wider than their modern counterparts.

All that is social is 'political' for ancient philosophers like Plato and Aristotle, for 'modern' philosophers, like Hobbes, and for nearcontemporary Marxists, like Henri Lefebvre. Nonetheless, judging from a varied assortment of American and West European dictionaries it appears clear that philosophy has become increasingly concerned with ontology and being, and less concerned with 'being-together' in the social sphere. For this reason, the *Dictionnaire de la Philosophie, Encyclopædia Universalis* lists '*citoyen*' and '*citoyenneté*' under three related references: 'the antique city', 'the social contract', and 'political philosophy'.

The *Dictionnaire de la Philosophie, Encyclopædia Universalis* does remind us of the importance of citizen, but in the interaction between man and his context, it is the 'just city which engenders the just man' in its reading of Plato's *Republic* (2000: 227). In truth, Plato saw neither the man nor the city as the cause, but rather considered both to be inextricable, interacting influences. The Larousse is imposing a modern, deterministic, sociological reading on Plato here. But the *Dictionnaire de la Philosophie, Encyclopædia Universalis* is, nonetheless, right to affirm that, for the Ancient Greeks, the city was a 'collective organism', and that it was constituted of 'citizens united by the same history and cult' (2000: 227). Aristotle maintains that one of the key differences between men and animals is that the former are grouped into city communities. The close bond between the citizen and the city explains the necessity of freedom and autonomy. In order for the city to express the collective will, the will of individual citizens should not be hindered. Citizens must obey the law, of course, but in the ideal or well-governed State, the laws they obey are of their own construction and reflect their interests, desires, and aspirations. Moreover, for Plato and Aristotle, laws concern all dimensions of life and take in the spheres of morality, religion, art, creation, education, and the development of the soul.

Rousseau and Locke both shared the desire for a law which would be engendered by the collective will. In their conceptions, the citizens' rights and well-being would, ideally, be guaranteed by just laws, freely expressing and safeguarding their interests. Rousseau did make allowances for different classes of citizens, but the unanimous expression of the collective will was supposed to guarantee that nobody was oppressed by anyone else, so long as the classes were not allowed to become entrenched, and no one faction was allowed to rule over another. Rousseau also seems to have allowed for the fact that the collective will must not necessarily be unanimous, but can emerge from dynamic interaction (*Dictionnaire de la Philosophie, Encyclopædia Universalis* 2000: 282).

This does indeed advance us in understanding the concept of citizenship. But how do philosophical texts actually use the term? This is the ethnolinguist's question.

It was because 'citizen' proved to be so rare in our three million-word MyEnglishCorpus, specifically developed to be used as a counterpoint to established electronic corpora, that we found ourselves obliged to seek out influential English texts that faithfully represented the way the term is used by the major philosophers. This led us to assemble a nine million word philosophical corpus, MyHistIdeasCorpus. In that corpus, the term certainly figures among the pages of the great political philosophers. But for some reason, it appears not to have taken root in the English-speakers' worldview, as it has done in worldviews engendered in the French, German, and Czech linguistic communities. Unlike the French, German and Czech terms, 'citizen' appears to have difficulty in asserting itself as a nexus for debate on the relationship between individuals and society. The reasons explaining why some words enter into common usage and other words are excluded are always complex, but this situation may perhaps be partially explained by two fundamental reasons.

1. Englishmen have long been considered 'subjects': they may consider themselves 'free Englishmen', but they have always nonetheless been subject to their sovereign (except for the short interval under Cromwell's Commonwealth, 1649–1659).
2. The French Revolution tended to provoke hostility to Republican ideals in England, and set the ruling classes, the media and literature

in general, of a philosophical or literary nature, against expressions of liberation and civic involvement, of a radical political kind.

It is important not to overstate this case. Counter-examples abound. Nonetheless, as we saw in the preceding sections, 'citizen' does not link into such a rich network of meanings as its French, German, and Czech counterparts do.

The various dictionaries of proverbs consulted in French generated examples of '*citoyen*', but only one reference was made to 'citizen' in *The Penguin Dictionary of Proverbs* (Fergusson 1983: 186), and that was to 'citizen of Cork', in Ireland. In English speech, the citizens live elsewhere, it seems. It would appear, then, that there exists something like a rift between the common meaning and the philosophical term. Citizen remains abstract. If we accept this, we might ask what kind of examples of 'citizens' can be found in the works of philosophers?

In his essays, Francis Bacon (1561–1626) uses the term to apply to the citizens of nations and of cities. He also uses it to speak of 'citizens of the world'. As a philosopher of law, he also discusses the rights of the citizens and how they should be protected. Thomas Hobbes (1588–1679), on the other hand, the great political philosopher of the State, uses the term 'citizen' only three times in his *Leviathan* (1651). Two out of the three examples refer to Greece and Rome. And in the third, Hobbes asks us what opinion we have of our 'fellow citizens' when we ride about armed and lock our doors. Clearly, Hobbes places little hope in the 'citizen', and the 'subject' usurps his place, where in other languages speakers might have been inclined might to speak of citizens.

In his *Essay Concerning Human Understanding*, written in 1689,[1] John Locke (1632–1704) discusses the rights and privileges of 'citizens' or 'burghers', and the way those rights are generated and maintained, as we can see in the following example:

> Sometimes the foundation of considering things with reference to one another, is some act whereby any one comes by a moral right, power, or obligation to do something. Thus, a general is one that hath power to command an army, and an army under a general is a collection of armed men obliged to obey one man. **A citizen, or a burgher, is one who has a right to certain privileges in this or that place.** All this sort depending upon men's wills, or agreement in society, I call INSTITUTED, or VOLUNTARY; and may be distinguished from the natural, in that they are most, if

not all of them, some way or other alterable, and separable from the persons to whom they have sometimes belonged, though neither of the substances, so related, be destroyed. (Upper case in original; bold emphasis added)

However, in the writings of many philosophers, the keyword 'citizen' seems to be avoided. We must look to Scotland to see the word assert itself in Adam Smith's *Wealth of Nations*, published in 1776, the year of the American Declaration of Independence. The two following quotes give a fair idea of how the concept operates in his thought:

> **Nobody but a beggar chooses to depend chiefly upon the benevolence of his fellow-citizens.** Even a beggar does not depend upon it entirely. The charity of well-disposed people, indeed, supplies him with the whole fund of his subsistence. (Emphasis added)

> All the improvements in machinery, however, have by no means been the inventions of those who had occasion to use the machines. Many improvements have been made by the ingenuity of the makers of the machines, when to make them became the business of a peculiar trade; and some by that of those who are called philosophers, or men of speculation, whose trade it is not to do any thing, but to observe every thing, and who, upon that account, are often capable of combining together the powers of the most distant and dissimilar objects in the progress of society, philosophy or speculation becomes, like every other employment, **the principal or sole trade and occupation of a particular class of citizens.** Like every other employment, too, it is subdivided into a great number of different branches, each of which affords occupation to a peculiar tribe or class of philosophers; and this subdivision of employment in philosophy, as well as in every other business, improves dexterity, and saves time. Each individual becomes more expert in his own peculiar branch, more work is done upon the whole, and the quantity of science is considerably increased by it. (Emphasis added)

Smith is a pragmatist who sees citizens as working together as 'fellow citizens'. This is already light years away from Hobbes' pessimistic conception of the violent savage creature who must bow himself to a greater power to avoid his own destruction, in a life that is 'nasty, brutish and short', to quote his infamous phrase. Smith has become the darling of the American right today, but any reader who spends the least time with his economic or moral philosophy will be struck by Smith's humanity and lucidity, and the way he describes the needs of groups of people and the way they negotiate with one another in organizing themselves in social endeavours. Citizens have obligations to the State, and are therefore subject to taxation, according to Smith. Smith's references to citizens involve payment, revenues, and investment. But above all, the obligations citizens owe are to one another, and to the collective society in which they live and act as moral and political subjects. Thus, Smith's Scots English transforms the Sovereign's subjects into 'political subjects'.

In *On Liberty* (first published in 1859), John Mill (1806–1873) follows Smith in discussing the way individual citizens must combine in society as 'fellow citizens' in order to create and sustain democracy, but with one important distinction. Smith is writing before the American and French revolutions, Mill is writing after them, in a political environment that is much more hostile to revolution and republicanism. In his time, ceding any rights to the poor or to the middle classes appears like one step towards anarchy, for many of Mill's contemporary compatriots. Consequently, Mill is inevitably fighting an uphill battle. The following example from *On Liberty* is ironic in the light of Thatcher's reactionary nostalgia for Victorian values and her resentment against the abuses of the welfare state. Mill's words appear to be both lucid and forward-thinking, in contrast to her tone. Like her, he stresses the obligations of the family, but does not spare the State when it comes to the essential question of the well-being of the child brought into society at birth:

> Consider, for example, the case of education. Is it not almost a self-evident axiom, that the State should require and compel the education, up to a certain standard, of **every human being who is born its citizen?** Yet who is there that is not afraid to recognise and assert this truth? Hardly any one indeed will deny that it is one of the most sacred duties of the parents (or, as law and usage now stand, the father), after summoning a human being into the world, to give to that being an education fitting him to perform his part well in life towards others and towards himself. But while this is unanimously declared to be the father's duty, scarcely anybody, in this country, will bear to hear of obliging him to perform it. Instead

of his being required to make any exertion or sacrifice for securing education to the child, it is left to his choice to accept it or not when it is provided gratis! It still remains unrecognised, that to bring a child into existence without a fair prospect of being able, not only to provide food for its body, but instruction and training for its mind, is a moral crime, both against the unfortunate offspring and against society; and that if the parent does not fulfil this obligation, the State ought to see it fulfilled, at the charge, as far as possible, of the parent. (Emphasis added)

Today's right invariably chastises individuals for shirking responsibility, but here Mill clearly states that both the family and the State are responsible for creating citizens and generating citizenship. On the whole, our corpora-based research did not reveal a proliferation of the term 'citizen' in the philosophical writings of the English during the eighteenth and nineteenth centuries, in any way that that was comparable with the use of '*citoyen*' in French, or '*Bürger*' in German, during the same period. Kant uses '*Bürger*' and '*Bürgerlich*' where the term 'citizen' in English does not seem to have taken root in philosophical discourse (Flew 1984; Urmson and Rée 1991).

It is true that after Smith and Mill, the questions of democratic rule, voting rights, and citizenship remain central to discussions and debate in English. These debates will be framed within political discourse and legal texts however. The philosophers will, on the whole, either retrace their steps from society into existential questions, or move into questions of logic. Bertrand Russell (1872–1970) does admittedly span the gulf between the two parting paths, with his philosophical writings and his political activism. But Russell is somewhat of a rarity, uncharacteristic of the philosophers who tend to leave the citizen to other thinkers and writers as the nineteenth century draws to a close and the twentieth takes us into the ages of the two world wars, communism, fascism, and the Cold War. Will literary writers take up the word, and with it, the cause of the citizen?

Is 'Citizen' a Literary Concept?

If citizen is not particularly common in everyday English, and if it is often avoided in philosophical treatises, can we expect to find it in our literary heritage? That would perhaps seem a little optimistic. As we have seen, 'citizen' is used in Shakespeare's plays, but not often. It does not figure in the tragedy, *Macbeth*, nor can it be found when the people of the city are revelling in the comedy, *Twelfth Night*. It is found, albeit on rare occasion, in what we call the five Henry Plays (*Henry IV*, parts 1 and 2, *Henry V*, and *Henry VI*, parts 1 and 2). In *Henry V*, for example, mention is made of 'The ciuil Citizens'. And one character in the same play remarks:

> How London doth powre out her Citizens,
> The Maior and all his Brethren in best sort,
> Like to the Senatours of th' antique Rome.

Amusingly, when the great English Conqueror-General Talbott is entrapped by a French countess who believes he has been taken in by her feminine charms, she chastises and threatens him in the following way:

> And I will chain these legs and arms of thine
> That hast by tyranny these many years
> Wasted our country, slain our citizens,
> And sent our sons and husbands captivate.

This is an English play, however, and Talbott has his army hidden. The righteous countess, reviewing the changed situation, changes tactics, and reverts to her seductive charms, thus allowing Talbott to pillage her town and her body. The great general takes obvious relish in this, although, as we can imagine, in many stagings of the play, the lady herself proves not entirely dismayed by the turn of events. French citizens pay tribute to English virility and violence, in this and in other parts of the Henry Plays. Interestingly, though, it is the French who make speeches about citizens. The English, in one of the examples above, only think of Englishmen as citizens when comparing them to Romans.

Elsewhere, when the term 'citizen' is used, as in *Titus Andronicus*, we are clearly situating the drama within the context of Rome. Besides, who uses the term in *Titus*? It is the sly and insipid demagogue, Saturnine, who makes an appeal to the citizens, as the 'defender of his right', as he tries to enflame them with a violent sense of outrage at his judicious and even-tempered brother's claim to power. Titus is humiliated and all but one of his twenty-four sons have sacrificed their lives for the good of the commonwealth of Rome. Yet Saturnine stands by or assists in the persecution of Titus and his family. This should give us a fair impression of how much faith Shakespeare laid in the people and their Senate in democratic societies.

In French, we find a similar situation. Though supposedly a cornerstone concept in republican ideals, 'citizen' proves rare in French literary works. In Corneille's *Cinna*,[2] a character exhorts his fellows to seek revenge ('*Vengeons nos citoyens*', Revenge our citizens!). In *Horace*, Curiace makes a heartfelt speech in which he sees the love of his nation, his city, and his beloved as one intertwining whole that drives him on to bravely taking up their joint defence:

> *Je n'abandonne point l'intérêt de ma ville,*
> *J'aime encor mon honneur en adorant Camille.*
> *Tant qu'a duré la guerre, on m'a vu constamment*
> *Aussi bon citoyen que véritable amant.*
> *D'Albe avec mon amour j'accordois la querelle:*
> *Je soupirois pour vous en combattant pour elle.*

> In no way do I abandon my concern for my city,
> I love my own honour more by loving Camille.
> As long as the war lasted, everyone saw me at all times
> To be as good a citizen as a lover.
> With my honour, D'Albe, I took up the fight
> And breathless, sighed for you, while fighting for her.

But where are these characters taking their stand? Not in France, but in an imagined Rome. In French plays about France, citizens appear to be scarce. Even in Corneille's most famous play, *Le Cid*, set in Spain close by, just beyond the Pyrenees, we speak of '*sujets*' (subjects), not citizens, when the town is defended against the invaders. Citizens do not seem to be welcome into the city in French literature.

A typical member of the up-and-coming bourgeoisie will be ridiculed as an uncouth upstart by Molière in his hilarious *Le Bourgeois gentilhomme*. And various references in French and English texts from the sixteenth to the nineteenth century make reference to the fact that one cannot be a 'citizen' and a 'gentleman'. A 'Gentleman' belongs to the Aristocracy, and the Aristocracy remains enrooted in landed wealth.

In post-revolutionary French, we will find no 'citizen' in Baudelaire's *Fleurs du Mal*. And the French author and *homme de lettres*, Rémy de Gourmont (1858–1915), has nothing but contempt for the citizen:

Le citoyen est une variété de l'homme; variété dégénérée ou primitive, il est à l'homme ce que le chat de goutière est au chat sauvage. (Rémy de Gourmont, quoted in Oster 1993: 521)

The citizen is a variety of man; a degenerate and primitive variety. He is to man what the alley cat is to the wildcat.

Closer to home, Wordsworth has a love of the people, but it remains a love of the 'common people': this is the paternalistic landed gentry's condescending pity for uprooted homesteaders, and the victims of the 1801 Enclosures Act. Blake speaks of the 'citizens of London' (quoted by Whitson and Whittaker 2013: 157), but, otherwise, references prove extremely rare. Byron proves something of a paradox. On the one hand, he is a romantic hero, and a political activist who is willing to go off and risk his life to defend the liberation of the Greeks. But he shows surprisingly little sympathy for the key concept of Greek democracy, citizenship, when it comes to his fellow citizens. The word does not appear in his enormous epic poem, *Don Juan*, for example. All in all, as the nineteenth century progresses, the keyword, citizen, does not appear to take hold within English literature.

Jane Austen's heroines move between the country and London, but there is no mention of citizens in *Pride and Prejudice*. Dicken's *Great Expectations* is a great study of the class structure of the time, of poverty, and the status of criminals and their exportation as slave labour to the colonies, but in the London of *Great Expectations* there are no 'citizens'. Victorian literature offers little scope to citizens, it seems. Oscar Wilde's *The Picture of Dorian Gray* is the work of a broad-minded cultivated author at home in Ireland, London and Paris, but Wilde appears to have little time for citizens. Only 'world citizen' is found in *Dorian Gray*. And is it not possible that this celebration of the cultivated worldly wise individual hides something akin to contempt for the worker and the citizen of the political sphere that Remy de Gourmont and Oscar Wilde seem eager to turn their backs on?

In France, Zola invents protagonists who champion the people and the citizens. But in French literature, we rarely find characters like Étienne, Zola's hero, who asks: '*Est-ce que tous les citoyens n'étaient pas égaux depuis la Révolution?*' ('Haven't all citizens been equal since the Revolution?' Zola *Germinal*, http://www.gutenberg.org)

Such exclamations would seem to be out of place in the English literary tradition, and, from our research, it would seem that we would be more likely to find them in translations than in the well-known literature we associate with the English classics.

The same cannot be said about German literature. Goethe is capable of satirizing citizens just as Molière does, but citizens do figure in his plays, as his *Faust* shows. 'Bürger' has its place in Kant's and Goethe's work, and the term is enrooted in the German language. Indeed, because the word is variously translated into English as 'citizen' and 'city-dweller', or 'bourgeois', literary writers and thinkers can hardly avoid using the term.

The French Revolution appears to determine the degree to which the concepts of 'citizen' and 'citizenship' take root in the worldview of a linguistic community. Nineteenth-century Britain and post-revolutionary France certainly seem to be positioning themselves in terms of the concepts along ideological lines. So what can we expect from the literature of America, a country which has forged itself through its revolution, and its War of Independence? Obviously, each writer will position him- or herself differently in relation to the political sphere, the social world, and the imaginary world peopled by his or her fictitious characters. But generally, just as Obama made fairly authentic appeals to the 'people' as 'citizens', the literature of the United States has a more plentiful stock 'citizens' than either the French or the English literary traditions, which appear to cling to the prejudices of the *Ancien Régime* down to this day.

The fiction texts of our extended American corpus generated a vast number of references to 'citizen'. Not all writers feel an affection for citizens. The term does not appear in the three volumes of Emily Dickinson's collected poems, for example. But unlike his English counterparts, Whitman proves that 'citizen' can be embraced as a romantic ideal, as he demonstrates in the following example, in which he speaks of a free-thinking people affirming its own identity and its right to cultivate that identity and to make that it heard:

> **Where the populace rise at once against the never-ending audacity of elected persons;**
> Where fierce men and women pour forth, as the sea to the whistle of death pours its sweeping and unripped waves;
> Where outside authority enters always after the precedence of inside authority;
> **Where the citizen is always the head and ideal**—and President, Mayor, Governor, and what not, are agents for pay;

Where children are taught to be laws to themselves, and to depend on themselves;
Where equanimity is illustrated in affairs;
Where speculations on the Soul are encouraged;
Where women walk in public processions in the streets, the same as the men. (Emphasis added)

In our research, we found few such celebrations of the activity of citizens. An active organic people celebrating itself in collective actions proved a rarity throughout our French and English texts, especially in literary texts. The final line of Whitman's inspired celebration of the citizen as an ideal develops the concept to take in a notion that briefly became an ideal of the French Revolution, the '*citoyenne*', celebrated by Delacroix's painting of the bare-breasted '*citoyenne*' waving the flag of France during the storming of the Bastille. That Delacroix's incarnation of Liberty, *La Citoyenne*, adorned the 200 frank banknote for decades tells something about the French people and how they like to see themselves, but Oster's two volumes of the *Dictionnaire de citations françaises* (1990 and 1993) tell a very different tale. Of a total of 9052 entries, for the nineteenth and twentieth centuries, there were only nine references to '*citoyen*'. And there was a grand total of zero, for '*citoyenne*'.

Where Can We Find Champions for the Citizen?

The great French historian, Jules Michelet, digs deep into the archives and the collective reality of France to bring back a more balanced picture. Like the Marxist historians, Hobsbawm and E. P. Thompson, Michelet listens to the people, and the negotiations related to them, and reads what is published about them. In Michelet's *Les Femmes et la revolution*, we read of the people's movement that advances in procession, with an old man at its head, surrounded by young women. The women speak of going off with the army, but not simply in order to tend to their comrades wounds, like Florence Nightingales. These women promise to give themselves only to 'citizens':

Elles juraient de n'épouser jamais que de loyaux citoyens, de n'aimer que les vaillants, de n'associer leur vie qu'à ceux qui donnaient la leur à la France. (1855, https://www.gutenberg.org/files/18738/18738-h/18738-h.htm)

They took the sermon to marry only loyal citizens, and to love only the brave, and to link their lives only to those who give themselves and their lives to France.

There is something akin to the spirit of Whitman to be found in these words. It is the spirit of open-minded engagement in civic action. These women believe in France and in those that defend her and her citizens. American politicians and writers still seem capable of tapping into that shared collective reality, the project of a democratic society animated by civic action and lucid and engaged discourse. That is the discourse that Obama taps into when, in his opening address, after his first election, he addressed the people in the following words:

My fellow citizens: I stand here today humbled by the task before us ... (https://www.whitehouse.gov)

This was the discourse of a man at least trying to conceive of political action as a common project, and seeing himself as a partner of the people. There was something of that discourse even in the wealthy Roosevelt's claim that 'Profits should go to the citizens.'

That discourse of the citizen is, however, sadly lacking in the political discourse, the literature of France and Britain, and in the everyday conversation to be heard in pubs, bars, and cafes in those countries. Will the Chinese worldview resemble more the class-based concept of the citizen that dominates in the French and English worldview? Or will it prove closer to the American ideal?

CITIZENS IN CHINESE

Introduction

The reference dictionary for contemporary Mandarin Chinese, the *Xiàndài hànyǔ cídiǎn* 现代汉语词典 *Dictionary of Modern Chinese* (2015, sixth edition) defines the word *gōngmín* 公民 'citizen' as follows:

具有或取得某国国籍，并根据该国宪法和法律规定享有权利和承担义务的人。在我国，公民与国民含义相同。

A person having or obtaining the nationality of a given country, enjoying rights and assuming obligations according to the

Constitution and the laws of that country. In our country, [the words] *gōngmín* 公民 and *guómín* 国民 are similar in meaning.

In this dictionary entry we find a reference to another word for 'citizen', *guómín* 国民. In fact, the words *gōngmín* 公民 and *guómín* 国民 have both been used since the nineteenth century to mean 'citizen'. They have, however, followed different trajectories in modern and contemporary China, and their status and the way they are used have changed noticeably during the twentieth century. In the same dictionary (*Xiàndài hànyǔ cídiǎn*, 2015), the definition of *guómín* is more synthetic than *gōngmín*. It makes reference only to nationality: 'a person having the nationality of a country is a citizen [or a 'national'] of this country' (具有某国国籍的人是这个国家的国民).

However, the definition of 'citizenship' is even more complex, because a third word, *shìmín* 市民, should be taken into account. In 'The Origins of Modern Citizenship in China' (2002), Peter Harris includes this third word, *shìmín* 市民, in his interpretation of the way the notion of citizenship is understood and expressed. He underlines how the etymologies of these three words have had an impact on the way they are used and what they entail:

> The critical questions may well remain the ones raised by those who first introduced the notion of citizenship into Chinese political discourse a century ago, questions embedded in the etymologies of *gongmin*, *guomin* and *shimin*. How, in the end, will ordinary people in the People's Republic come to define themselves? (Harris 2002: 199)

First of all, it is important to retrace the etymologies of these keywords from their first recorded usages, and then compare the way they are used in different contexts. This involves considering the kinds of texts they are used in, and highlighting the connotations related to each of these keywords and the trajectories they follow.

Words for 'Citizen' in Late Qing China

Various words were adopted to designate the notion of 'citizen' in the late Qing period (1644–1911) and in early twentieth century China. And this means we need to take into consideration what can be called 'quasi-synonyms', which can be described as words with similar meanings but which are not interchangeable. Among these quasi-synonyms, the three words mentioned above are still largely used in Mandarin Chinese:

- *guómín* 国民, which can be translated as 'citizen' or 'national' (formed with *guó*, meaning 'country', and *mín* 'the people' or 'one of the people');
- *shìmín* 市民, which can be translated as 'citizen' or 'city dweller/urban resident' (derived from *shì*, meaning 'city, town');
- *gōngmín* 公民 'citizen' (derived from *gōng*, meaning 'public').

As Goldman and Perry (2002: 5) underline, 'these terms ... highlight different aspects of state-society relations: nationalism in the case of *guomin*, public spirit in the case of *gongmin*, and urban rights and responsibilities in the case of *shimin*'.

The words *guómín* 国民 and *gōngmín* 公民 were widely used towards the end of the nineteenth century and the beginning of the twentieth century. Guō Táihuī (2011: 145, 148), quoting Jīn and Liú's statistical data (2008: 495), affirms that it was respectively in 1902 and 1903 that they became particularly frequent. Indeed, they 'reached the apex of usage frequency' (使用次数 ... 达到顶峰) during those years. This coincides with increasing interest in Western socio-political thought at the turn of the century.

The middle of the nineteenth century saw the development of the Westernization movement (洋务运动), which focused first on technical and military knowledge (during the *zìqiáng* 自强 'Self-Strengthening' phase of this movement), and then focused on Western inspired economic theories (in the *fùqiáng* 富强 'Wealth and power' phase). Towards the end of the nineteenth century, an increasing interest in Western political thought and social sciences could be observed (see Coccia 1998: 491–494). This resulted in a massive process of translating Western works related to the social sciences (Tsien 1954: 327). It was in this context that several key terms from Western political thought were introduced to China.

The way the words designating citizenship spread was also marked by Western influence. Guō Zhōnghuá (2013) states that 'modern citizenship is to be considered the product of the European specific political culture' (现代公民身份被看作欧洲特殊政治文化的产物), while P. Zarrow claims that:

> the *mingben*[3] tradition might be considered the prehistory of the idea of popular sovereignty, but thinking precisely and explicitly

in terms of citizenship did not emerge until the late nineteenth century under Western influence. (Zarrow 1997: 3)

The late nineteenth century saw the emergence of the reformist movement in which the role of reformist intellectuals proved crucial in spreading the ideas of the citizen and citizenship. As Keane points out: 'the citizen concept emerged during the dying embers of the imperial period and was championed by the reformer Liang Qichao in the first decade of the century' (Keane 2001: 2).

The reformist intellectual Liáng Qǐchāo 梁启超 (1873–1929), one of main figures of the 1898 Hundred Day Reform Movement, was the author of the influential political essay *Xīnmín shuō* 新民说 (1902). Significantly, he called his Yokohama-based journal *Xīnmín cóngbào* 新民丛报. What does '*Xīnmín*' mean in Liang's vocabulary? *Xīn* can be translated as 'new' or 'to renew', while *mín* is the word for 'the people' (cf. Chapter 1). But *mín* also assumed the meaning of citizen, as we shall see. Hence, the expression *xīnmín* has been interpreted in various ways. De Bary (1998: 110) chooses to translate *xīnmín* as 'Renewing the people'. He underlines the fact that its origin can be traced back to 'Zhu Xi's (1130–1200) formulation of the Three Main Guidelines (*san gangling*) in the *Great Learning*, the first in order of his Four Books'. De Bary also points out that 'Liang's sense of "a people" is one of "a nation" informed by a Western (and a Japanese) sense of nationalism' (De Bary 1998: 111). These associations with *mín* at the turn of the century are confirmed by sources listed in the MCST. In Kwong Ki-chiu's *English and Chinese Dictionary* (1923, first edition 1882), *xīnmín* is regarded as the equivalent of 'to reform a nation' (MCST database).

Tang Xiaobing (1996: 17) translates the title of Liang's essay as 'Discourse on the New Citizen', while Burtscher (2006) translates *xīnmín* as 'new people', and the journal's title as 'New people's gazette', even though he considers that Liáng's pen-name *Zhōngguó zhi xīnmín* 中国之新民 should be translated as 'new citizen of China'.

According to Fairbank (1989: 220–221), the meaning of Liáng's *xīnmín* changed under Japanese influence (during Liáng's exile in Japan), and the meaning of this expression was broadened to encompass the new dimensions of citizenship and citizenship rights.

Polysemy and semantic stratification still play a role in defining the three contemporary keywords that might be considered the equivalents of 'citizen': *gōngmín* 公民, *guómín* 国民, *shìmín* 市民. While the spread in usage of these words used to designate citizens can be traced back to the nineteenth century, these forms were already found in the Chinese lexicon.

Gōngmín 公民 can be found in early sources. It appears in the chapter 'The Five Vermins' (*Wŭ dù* 五蠹) of the *Hán Fēizi* 韩非子 (III BCE), in which we can read:

私安則利之所在，安得勿就？是以公民少而私人眾矣。[4]

> If they can obtain anything so profitable as private security, how can you expect them not to resort to such measures? Hence men who are concerned with public welfare grow fewer, and those who think only of private interests increase in number. (Watson 2003: 116)

In this passage, *gōngmín* 公民 is translated as 'men who are concerned with public welfare', as opposed to *sīrén* 私人 'those who think only of private interests'. Judge (1994: 3) points out the connotations and resonances of the word *gōng* 公 in Classical Chinese, and stresses that the word is closely bound up with the antonym *sī* 私:

> The concept of *gong* is rich in classical resonances and multiple historical meanings. Most often conceived in a dichotomous relationship with *si* (meaning privateness and selfishness, wickedness or injustness [*buzheng*]), definitions of *gong* range from openness and publicness to the ethical principles of moral equality (*pingfen*), justice (*zheng*) and fairness (*gongping*).

Goldman and Perry (2002: 4) also underscore that the word *gōng* 公 'was often counterposed in Confucian discourse to *si*, or private, which implied selfishness', and add that 'the origins of the term *gongmin* lie in the Confucian celebration of the public service'.

The disyllabic word *gōngmín* 公民 is generally considered as a *wàiláicí* 外来词 'word of foreign origin' (see Gāo and Liú 1956: 121). More specifically, it constitutes a 'return graphic loan' (Masini 1993), that is, a form found in Classical Chinese, which was adopted in Japanese to designate a new concept and reintroduced with these new connotations into Chinese. We find numerous such terms and concepts ascribable to Western thought migrating between the end of the nineteenth and the beginning of the twentieth century. In fact, the Japanese language became a medium for introducing Western knowledge into China, and a considerable part of existing scientific terminologies was introduced via Japanese (Masini 1993: 104). Hence, the disyllabic form, *gōngmín* 公民, acquired the new meaning of 'citizen' as a graphic loan from the Japanese word, *kōmin* 公民.

The Chinese keyword, *gōngmín* 公民, was frequent in Chinese reformist writings. For instance, the scholar Kāng Yǒuwéi 康有为 (1858–1927), one of the leaders of the 1898 Hundred Day Reform Movement, adopted it in his essay *Gōngmín zìzhì piān* 公民自治篇 ('On Self-government by the Citizenry'), published in the reformist newspaper *Xīnmín cóngbào* in 1902.

Quoted by Fāng and Wáng (2006: 141), Kāng wrote:

人人有议政之权，人人有忧国之责，故命之曰公民。

Since all the people have the right to participate in assemblies and they all have the responsibility to be concerned about their country, they are called citizens. (Translated by Goldman 2005: 11)

This word was destined to become the main term used to define citizenship in Mandarin Chinese and a key term in the post-1978 debates.

The form *guómín* 国民 (non-simplified form 國民), today meaning 'citizen' or 'national', already existed in Chinese more than 2000 years ago. It was used 'in pre-Qin texts to refer to inhabitants of rival warring states' (Goldman and Perry, 2002: 4). This form was found in the *Chūnqiū Zuǒzhuàn* 春秋左传 'Zuǒ Qiūmíng's 左丘明 Commentaries [to the Spring and Autumns Annals]' (in the section dedicated to the thirteenth year of the duke Zhao; see Liu 1995: 308). In this passage the form *guómín* 国民 was used to designate 'the people of the state', according to J. Legge's translation (1872: 650):

私欲不違，民無怨心，先神命之，國民信之[5]

He has not, to gratify himself, gone against the people. They have no feeling of animosity against him, and the Spirits formerly gave the appointment to him. The people of the State believe in him.

As Liu highlights (1995: 308), *guómín* is also to be considered as a return graphic loan, that is to say, a Chinese form which acquired new meaning in Japanese and was reintroduced with this new meaning in Chinese. The Japanese word *kokumin* 國民 assumed different connotations during the nineteenth century under Western influence. It was used in Japanese to designate the people, the nation, and the citizen, during the Meiji era (Burtscher 2012: 65).

In his essay on the meanings of the form 国民 (or 國民 in non-simplified characters and in Japanese) in Chinese and Japanese, Guō Táihuī 郭台辉 (2011: 137) retraces the process that led to this form becoming one of the main terms used to designate citizens in both languages in the nineteenth and early twentieth centuries:

"国民"作为一个汉语复合词古而有之，但成为使用率极高的现代政治概念，却产生并兴盛于明治日本时代，在辛亥革命10余年前才传入中国。

As a compound form, *guómín* was used early on in Chinese, but as a modern political concept of large diffusion, it emerged and flourished in the Meiji era in Japan and was introduced into China only almost a decade before the *Xinhai* revolution [1911].

In late Qing China, the word *guómín* was progressively used to designate 'citizen', even though the meanings of 'the people', 'people of a nation', and 'nation' were also current throughout the nineteenth and early twentieth centuries, as sources clearly demonstrate (see the MCST database).[6]

As Bastid-Bruguière (1997: 230–231) underlines, this form was used by Liáng Qǐchāo to express J. K. Bluntschli's (1808–1881) notion of '*Volk*' in the essay 'The Doctrine of the Political Scientist Bluntschli' (*Zhèngzhìxué dà jiā Bólúnzhīlǐ zhī xuéshuō* 政治学大家伯伦知理之学说), published in 1903. Liu (1995: 47) points out that this word was used to translate the notion of 'national character', and she quotes two expressions for 'national character' formed with *guómín*: *guómínxìng* 国民性 (*xìng* meaning 'nature' or 'quality') and *guómín de pǐngé* 国民的品格 (*pǐngé* meaning 'moral qualities'). She underlines that Liáng Qǐchāo reflected on the Chinese national character to identify 'the cause of the evils responsible for the deplorable state of the Chinese *guomin* (citizen)' (Liu 1995: 48). This is clear in Liáng's essays *Lùn Zhōngguó guómín zhī pǐngé* 论中国国民之品格 'On the Character of Chinese Citizens', published in 1903 and in *Guómín shí dà yuánqì lùn* 国民十大元气论 'On the Ten Essential Spirits of the Citizen', published in 1899.

This word was strongly associated with a concern for Chinese sovereignty and national rescue, as Goldman and Perry underscore: 'in adopting the term *guomin*, late Qing and Republican-era elites revealed their preoccupation with asserting China's position vis-à-vis the foreign imperialist powers, rather than with ensuring the rights of individuals vis-à-vis the state' (Goldman and Perry 2002: 6).

Hence, the word *guómín* was also used by several publicists of the influential reformist newspapers *Shíbào* 时报 (Judge 1994: 13, 21) and *Sūbào* 苏报 during the first decade of the twentieth century (Guō 2013).

Furthermore, *guómín* 'entered state-sponsored textbooks … around the time of the 1911 revolution' (Goldman and Perry 2002: 4). It also figured in the 1911 constitution (*Xiànfǎ zhòngdà xìntiáo shíjiǔ tiáo* 宪法重大信条十九条) promulgated at the end of the Qing government (Guō 2011: 145). And it also figured in the temporary constitution (*Zhōnghuá mínguó línshí yuēfǎ* 中华民国临时约法) promulgated by the new republican government in 1912 (Guō 2011: 146). It is clear, therefore, that it constituted a keyword in the Chinese political lexicon in this period.

Shìmín 市民, which is used today used to designate 'citizen' or 'urban resident', was also widely used in early Chinese. We find this form in Xún Yuè's 荀悦 (148–209 CE) political treatise *Shēn jiàn* 申鉴 'Extended Reflections' (chapter *Shíshì* 时事 'Current affairs'). According to the etymological dictionary *Cíyuán* 辞源 (1986: 996) such a usage designates 'urban inhabitants' (*chéngshì jūmín* 城市居民).

Like the Japanese *shimin* 市民, the Chinese word *shìmín* 市民 joins the notions of citizenship and city, as its equivalent terms do in various European languages. Nevertheless, this link appears to be foreign to Chinese and East Asian history, because, as Zarrow (1997: 5) underlines: 'at no time did China possess an equivalent of the *polis* which formed the starting point for most Western thinking about citizenship'.

The diffusion of the word *shìmín* 市民 in late imperial China was tied to the emergence of urban communities and urban political activism (Goldman and Perry 2002: 5), and it was destined to be employed widely by political activists in China as well as in Taiwan (Keane 2001: 6).

The references to political and social rights assumed by the word *shìmín* are clear today in its use in *shìmín shèhuì* 市民社会, one of the expressions designating the 'civil society'.[7]

It is worth pointing out that various other forms were used in the nineteenth and early twentieth centuries as equivalents of citizen, but in the course of time these were abandoned. As already mentioned, *mín* was widely used to designate citizen in this period. Besides being used by Liáng Qǐchāo in *Xīnmín shuō* 新民说, as we saw above, we can also quote a translation by W. A. P. Martin (1827–1916). In Martin's

1864 translation of the *Elements of International Law* (written by Henry Wheaton and first published in 1836), which was published under the title of *Wànguó gōngfǎ* 万国公法, the term 'citizen' is rendered by *mín* 民:

> Controversies between two or more States; between a State and citizens of another State; between citizens of different States; between citizens of the same State claiming lands under grants of different States; and between a State, or the citizens thereof, and foreign States, citizens, or subjects. (Wheaton 1866: 55)

> 数邦所有争端，此邦与彼邦之民所有之争端，彼此之民所有之争端，一邦之民凭二邦之权索地基而兴讼者，各邦并各邦之民与他国或他国之民有讼事 (Wheaton 2002: 25)

In other passages, the English word 'citizen' is translated as *rénmín* 人民 (see Chapter 1):

> As to wrongs or injuries done to the government or citizens [*rénmín* 人民] of another State. (Wheaton 1866: 43)

> 他国被害，并他国人民受屈 (quoted by Guō 2014: 56)

The disyllabic word *rénmín* 人民 'the people' can also be used to mean 'citizen' in some nineteenth and twentieth century bilingual dictionaries. In the *Vocabulaire français-chinois des sciences morales et politiques* (Médard 1927), the word *citoyen* is translated as *rénmín*, and the expression *citoyen de la République* as *mínguó rénmín* 民国人民 (MCST database). In the *Deutsch-Englisch-Chinesisches Fachwörterbuch* (Wilhelm 1911), the translation given for *mínguó rénmín* is '*Bürger*', and 'citizen' in German and English, respectively (see the MCST database).

The word *píngmín* 平民 ('common people', 'commons') was given as the equivalent of '*simple citoyen*' in the Médard's (1927) dictionary. *Qímín* 齐民 was competing with it as a term used to mean 'citizen' in Lǐ Guī's 李圭 (1842–1903) *Huán yóu dìqiú xīn lù* 环游地球新录, published in 1876 (MCST database).

The word *chénmín* 臣民 which can be translated as 'subject' was another term used to designate 'citizen': *chén* 臣 means 'subject' or 'minister'. Examples of *chénmín* 臣民 can be found, for example, in Zhāng Chūntáo 张春桃 and Guō Kāiwén's 郭开文 translation of Shimizu Kyoshi's 清水

澄 dictionary of law and economics (*Hàn yì fǎlǜ jīngjì cídiǎn* 汉译法律经济辞典) (see MCST database).

These examples are symptomatic of the semantic changes that took place in the early period of Chinese terminology. They reflect a long process in which equivalences are being negotiated (to use Lackner et al.'s (2001b) words). Liu (1999: 152) speaks of 'negotiating commensurability' between Western-inspired notions and Chinese translations.

The Words for Citizen after the Foundation of the People's Republic of China

In the first chapter of *Democracy and the Rule of Law in China*, Yu Keping (2010: 3) writes:

> Political terminology is, as a general rule, specific to the political era in which it is created. This is especially true of China, where people have witnessed numerous political movements since the founding of the People's Republic of China (PRC) by Mao Zedong in 1949. Previously prevalent political jargon has been replaced by new terminology as one political era has succumbed to the next.

These remarks about the way political terminology changes are especially true of the words used to designate citizens. After playing a crucial role in reformist circles and in the intellectual debates between the end of the nineteenth century and first decades of the twentieth, these words were destined to be overshadowed by new terms in the first years of the People's Republic of China. In those years, the emphasis shifted from the citizen to the people and the masses. As Michael Keane underlines:

> The idea of the citizen has been conspicuously dormant within the lexicon of Chinese Communist Party discourse since the establishment of the People's Republic in 1949. When one takes into account the citizen's 'bourgeois' heritage, its central role in state building in the modern capitalist West, and its connotations of political and civil rights, this is not an altogether surprising disclosure. (Keane 2001: 1)

The concepts of 'citizen' and 'citizenship' evoked negative connotations in the new society because of their Western and bourgeois legacies:

'the citizen ... was viewed as antithetical to the socialist goal of mass mobilization, class struggle and collectivism' (Keane, 2001: 3).

Tang (1986: 276) also underscores that the word *gōngmín* became rare: the word was confined for the most part to legal contexts, and in general the words for citizen became marginal in official and political discourse.

It was between the end of 1970s and the 1980s that a renewed interest in the concept of the citizen emerged, reflecting China's political and social changes. Two years after Máo Zédōng's death in 1976, Dèng Xiǎopíng launched what was to become known as the 'Open door policy', and thereby inaugurated a profound transformation of Chinese society. Unsurprisingly, this resulted in a great deal of lexical changes, and part of that process involved some terms coming back into current usage. As a consequence of this, as Hooper points out, there was a renewed interest in the concept of citizen; so much so that the notion even became central for official discourse:

> The concept of the Chinese citizen, with the rights and obligations attached to citizenship, has been the subject of considerable attention in China during the post-Mao era. Official discourse has shifted from people's collective identity as 'the masses' or 'the people', or individually as 'comrades' contributing to that collective identity, to 'citizens' with individual rights as well as obligations. (Hooper 2005: 6–7)

The Words for Citizen in Recent Decades

In recent decades, the concepts of citizen and citizenship have been subject to much interest, and we can observe a renewed desire to use the words defining citizenship in a wide range of discursive contexts. The above-mentioned words, *guómín* 国民 and *gōngmín* 公民, have known different trajectories, and, as Goldman and Perry (2002: 4) underline:

> Over the course of the twentieth century, the term *gongmin* largely replaced *guomin* in both official and popular parlance as the accepted designation to refer to those persons who are legally recognized as members of a state.

The results of this shift become evident if we compare the frequency diagrams (频次图) of the BCC corpus (compiled by the Beijing Language and Culture University, http://bcc.blcu.edu.cn/hc) for the two words.

The diagram of *gōngmín* shows an increase in the usage of this word since the end of the 1970s, coinciding with the launching of the 'reform and opening up' policy. There are some peaks (for instance, in 1989 and 2002–2003), then frequency becomes stable at a relatively high level as of 2011. Otherwise, the frequency diagram (频次图) of *guómín* shows a strong decrease in the early 1950s (after the foundation of the People's Republic), and frequency gradually falls off as of the 1980s. This corresponds to the increasing use of *gōngmín*.

This shift is also reflected in the definitions and examples listed in the reference dictionaries that have appeared in recent decades. In the 1997 edition of the *Xīnhuá cídiǎn* 新华词典 (hereafter abbreviated as XHCD) *Dictionary of New China*, for example, the entry *gōngmín* 公民 was defined as follows:

具有一定国家的国籍,依据法律规定享有政治权利和承担义务的人。不同社会制度的国家,对公民权利和义务的规定,有本质的不同(*XHCD* 1997: 297).

A person having the nationality of a given country, enjoying political rights and assuming obligations according to the laws. According to the various countries' social systems, the determination of the rights and obligations of the citizen shows substantial differences.

In the same dictionary, reference to the political rights and duties of the citizen is completely absent in the entry for *guómín* 国民, which – according to it – simply designates a 'person having the nationality of a country' (具有一个国家国籍的人, *XHCD* 1997: 329). The 2001 edition of the same dictionary gives a slightly different definition of the entry *gōngmín* 公民. In this definition, no reference is made to the various rights and obligations of the citizen according to different social systems: 'a natural person having the nationality of a country, equally enjoying rights and assuming obligations according to the constitution and its laws' (具有一个国家的国籍,依据宪法和法律平等享有权利和承担义务的自然人, *XHCD* 2001: 326). It is worth noting that in this dictionary, the entry *guómín*, 国民, is contrasted with the word *gōngmín* 公民, the prevalent term used to designate the citizen. Moreover, it is compared with the term's use in Japanese, a language that uses the same characters in its writing system. Thus, the first meaning given for *guómín* 国民 is:

公民。作为法律名词,多数国家用公民,仅少数国家用国民,如日本。(*XHCD* 2001: 361)

Citizen (*gōngmín* 公民). As a legal term, most of the countries use *gōngmín* 公民, only a few countries use *guómín* 国民, like Japan.

The second meaning given is '*běn guó de rénmín*' 本国的人民 'the people of the country', which reminds us of former usages of *guómín*, as we have already seen.

As mentioned, a comparison between the words *gōngmín* and *guómín* could also be found in the 2015 edition of the reference dictionary *Xiàndài hànyǔ cídiǎn* 现代汉语词典 *Dictionary of Modern Chinese*. In this dictionary, the definition of *gōngmín* makes reference to the rights and obligations of the citizen, according to the constitution and the law. And the lemma is followed by the expression *gōngmínquán* 公民权, 'citizen's rights' or 'civic rights', defined as the rights enjoyed by the citizens according to the constitution (公民根据宪法规定所享受的权利).

Moreover, *gōngmín* 公民 is the official term adopted to designate citizenship in the constitution of the People's Republic of China. We can find fifty-one occurrences of this word in the constitution. For instance:

第二章 公民的基本权利和义务
第三十三条 凡具有中华人民共和国国籍的人都是中华人民共和国公民。
中华人民共和国公民在法律面前一律平等。
国家尊重和保障人权。
任何公民享有宪法和法律规定的权利,同时必须履行宪法和法律规定的义务。[8]

Chapter II. The Fundamental Rights and Duties of Citizens
Article 33. All persons holding the nationality of the People's Republic of China are citizens of the People's Republic of China.
All citizens of the People's Republic of China are equal before the law.
Every citizen enjoys the rights and at the same time must perform the duties prescribed by the Constitution and the law.[9]

In contradistinction, the word *guómín* is found only five times. And each time it is used with a different meaning, with no reference being made to citizenship. The expression *guómín jīngjì* 国民经济 'national economy', is an apt example.

Hence, *gōngmín* has become the legal term used to define the citizen. It is central in official and political discourse, but it is also widely used in civil rights discourse, in newspapers, as well as in academic literature, as can be shown by comparing the way the word is used in various contexts.

The word *gōngmín* 公民 is frequently found in the influential Chinese newspaper, *People's Daily* (online version *Rénmín wǎng* 人民网, http://www.people.com.cn/). For our purposes, it proved interesting to analyse the frequency with which the word is used in various fields. Of a total of 597 300 occurrences, the highest percentage of examples (60 828) were related to the Chinese Communist Party (中国共产党新闻 'Chinese Communist Party news'). This was followed by 45 194 occurrences in the section 'International' (*guójì* 国际). There were 34 928 occurrences in the section 'Opinions' (*guāndiǎn* 观点), and 29 875 occurrences related to contemporary political affairs (*shízhèng* 时政).

What are we to conclude from these statistics? It would appear that the frequency with which the word is used in the section related to contemporary political affairs and Communist Party news demonstrates that *gōngmín* can be considered a keyword that is used widely in official political discourse. On the other hand, current debates on the topic of citizenship could explain the high frequency of the occurrences in the section 'Opinions'.

It is interesting to analyse some of the most frequent collocations of *gōngmín* in the *People's Daily*. The following expressions are chosen among the most frequent collocations of the word *gōngmín* in the BCC corpus of Modern Chinese (BCC 现代汉语语料库, http://bcc.blcu.edu.cn/).

In this corpus, we have a total of 51 041 occurrences of *gōngmín*. *Dàodé* 道德 'virtue' or 'morality' appears as the most frequent collocative of *gōngmín*: 3249 occurrences are found for *gōngmín dàodé* 公民道德 'citizens' or civic virtue'.

In the *People's Daily Online* 19 949 occurrences were found for the expression *gōngmín dàodé* 公民道德. This expression is particularly frequent in the section related to the 'Chinese Communist Party news' (4740 occurrences) and 'Current political affairs' (1189 occurrences). Among the examples, we can quote 'promote the strengthening of civic virtue' (推动公民道德建设) and 'promote the innovation of citizens' moral education' (推进公民道德教育创新).

The expression *gōngmín shèhuì* 公民社会, one of the forms used to designate the 'civil society', is also widespread. It is the sixth most frequent collocation in the BCC corpus (478 occurrences) and 11 684 occurrences can be found on the *People's Daily Online*. References are particularly prevalent in the sections on the Chinese Communist Party news (中国共产党新闻, 2604 occurrences), 'Opinions' (观点, 1108 occurrences) and 'International' (国际, 732 occurrences).

In the CCL corpus of Modern Chinese, compiled by the Centre for Chinese Linguistics of Peking University, only 164 occurrences were found for the expression *gōngmín shèhuì* 公民社会 'civil society'. These included examples such as

- "公民社会"是改革开放后引入的对的新译名
  'civil society [*gōngmín shèhuì*] is a neologism, a translation of "civil society" [in English in the text] introduced in China after the "Reform and Opening up" policy';
- 在十多年前的中国，"公民社会"还是一个十分敏感的话题
  'in the China of the last ten years, "civil society" has still been a very sensitive topic';
- 改革开放后,一个相对独立的公民社会已经在中国迅速崛起
  'After the 1978 reforms, a relatively independent civil society has been rapidly rising in China';
- 中国公民社会的发展也面临着许多困境
  'the development of civil society in China is also facing many difficulties'.

Among the various collocations of *gōngmín*, it is worth stressing the widespread use of *gōngmín sùzhì* 公民素质, an expression that can be translated as 'citizen's quality'. The word *sùzhì* 素质, which has more than thirty different translations and is usually rendered by 'quality', appears to be asserting itself as a new keyword (Kipnis 2006). Indeed, post-Mao China has seen the emergence of a '*suzhi* discourse'. Kipnis (2006: 295) claims that:

> The word *suzhi* has become central to contemporary China governance and society. Reference to *suzhi* justifies social and political hierarchies of all sorts, with those of 'high' *suzhi* being seen as deserving more income, power and status than those of 'low' *suzhi*.

Among the examples found in the *People's Daily Online* (*Rénmínwǎng* 人民网) we can read of 'improving citizens' quality' (*tíshēng gōngmín sùzhì*

提升公民素质); 'the overall improvement of citizens' quality and the degree of social civilisation' (*gōngmín sùzhì hé shèhuì wénmíng chéngdù quánmiàn tíshēng* 公民素质和社会文明程度全面提升). The highest percentage of a total 5200 occurrences can be found in the section devoted to the Chinese Communist Party news (中国共产党新闻, 976 occurrences). This seems to confirm its relevance in official discourse.

The word *gōngmín* is also used in expressions related to 'socialist citizens' and 'good citizens'. 'Good citizens' become 'a frequent topic of public discourse' as Hooper points out (2005: 3). This expression is attested to in all the corpora we consulted, but it is not extremely frequent: 302 occurrences of the expression *hǎo gōngmín* 好公民 ('good citizen') are listed in the BCC corpus; 1324 in the *People's Daily Online*. Only ninety-seven occurrences of the expression *hǎo gōngmín* are found in the CCL corpus. This represents only a small percentage of the 20 273 total number of occurrences of *gōngmín* found in the CCL corpus. Among the examples from this corpus, for instance, we can find the following:

- 'cultivate socialist citizens with ideals, moral qualities, culture and discipline' (培养有理想、有道德、有文化、有纪律的社会主义公民);
- 'a good party member and a good citizen' (好党员好公民);
- 'to be a good kid, a good student, then a good citizen, a good employer, a good parent and so on' (好孩子、好学生，然后是好公民、好的就业者、好父母等);
- 'the education of the "three good": "Be a good boy at home, be a good student in school, be a good citizen in the society" ("在家做个好孩子、在校做个好学生、在社会上做一位好公民"的三好教育).

Otherwise, the word *gōngmín* is associated with the idea of 'civil rights', or citizens' rights in Chinese *gōngmín quánlì* 公民权利 or *gōngmínquán* 公民权. In the BCC corpus 2359 occurrences of the expression *gōngmínquán* 公民权 are found. We can find examples like 'violate citizens' rights' (侵犯公民权), 'safeguard citizen's rights' (维护公民权), 'protect citizens' rights' (保护公民权), 'guarantee citizens' rights' (保障公民权), and 'exercise citizen's rights' (行使公民权).

A total of 942 occurrences of the expression *gōngmínquán* 公民权 'citizen's rights' or 'civil rights' are also found in the *People's Daily* and 932 in the CCL corpus.

The word *gōngmín* seems to be central in civil rights discourse and figures highly in political activism in mainland China. For instance, it has been adopted as a keyword and insignia by the civil right activists of the New Citizen's Movement (*Xīn gōngmín yùndòng* 新公民运动). In the writings of the main exponent of this movement, Xǔ Zhìyǒng 许志永, we can find expressions like 'new citizen's spirit' (*Xīn gōngmín jīngshén* 新公民精) and 'free citizens' (*zìyóu gōngmín* 自由公民).

Furthermore, the political scientist Liú Jūnníng 刘军宁, one of the signatories of the 'Charter 08 petition' (08宪章), contrasts the notions of the people and citizenship, claiming that

> the state and government must be given back to the citizens. In the past, China only had the people, not citizens, in the future China must have only citizens, not the people (必须把国家与政府还给公民 ....。以前的中国只要人民，没有公民，未来的中国应该只有公民，没有人民。) (Quoted by Wú 2013)

It is also highly significant that the word *gōngmín* 公民 recurred almost thirty times in the three-page petition Charter 08.

Wú Jiàxiáng 吴稼祥 compares the words *gōngmín* 公民 and *guómín* 国民, underlining a 'crucial difference' (关键的差别) between the two: *guómín* is necessarily and etymologically bound to a specific country and nation ("国民"不能脱离具体的国家和民族而存在), while *gōngmín* can be understood without having to refer to a given country. Consequently, the idea of 'world citizen' can be only conveyed by *gōngmín* and translated as *shìjiè gōngmín* 世界公民 (where *shìjiè* 世界 means 'world'; 公民可以是世界公民，但没有世界国民, Wú 2013).

It is also worthwhile considering the usage of the word *gōngmín* and what it entails from the point of view of news events that have high coverage in the media and social media. The Chinese media researcher Zhao Yuezhi (2008: 256) analyses the use of the word *gōngmín* in the Sūn Zhìgāng 孙志刚 affair, the case of a university student beaten to death by Chongqing police. Zhao Yuezhi concludes that:

> Sun Zhigang became a symbol for the more generalized category of 'citizen' (*gongmin*) in an emerging liberal citizen rights discourse. This eventually became the dominant framework of media and internet discourse around him.

She also points out that 'of the 251,000 items that contained "Sun Zhigang" in a Google search, the term "citizen" appeared 71,000 times, the term "university student" appeared 64,700 times' (Zhao 2008: 256).

We chose not take into account the occurrences of the word *guómín*, because of its polysemy. *Guómín* means 'citizen' or 'national' ('a person having the nationality of a country'), but it can also correspond to the English adjective 'national' (for instance in the expressions *guómín jīngjì* 国民经济 'national economy' and *guómín shōurù* 国民收入 'national income') or 'nationalist' (like in the name of the *Guómíndǎng* 国民党 'Nationalist Party' or 'Kuomintang'). These last two meanings are unrelated to the meaning of citizen.

The third word for citizen, *shìmín* 市民, proves far more frequent than *gōngmín* in both the *People's Daily Online* (with 1 958 478 occurrences) and BCC corpus (with 71 538 occurrences). In the *People's Daily Online*, the word *shìmín* is generally present in local news and social news. The most represented sections are 'Society' (社会 88 732) and the local editions like 'Hainan window' (海南视窗, 84 760 items), 'Shaanxi' (陕西频道, 74 660) and 'Shandong' editions (山东频道, 61 387), followed by the section 'Chinese Communist Party news' (中国共产党新闻, 65 771 occurrences). In the section 'Local' (地方), 57 166 occurrences are found.

Among the frequent collocations listed in the BCC corpus, we can mention *shìmín shèhuì* 市民社会, meaning 'civil society' (the first in rank, with 955 occurrences) and *shìmín sùzhì* 市民素质 'citizen's quality' (the third most frequent collocation, with 782 occurrences). These data confirm how significant 'civil society' and 'citizens' quality' are in contemporary debates.

In the CCL corpus we found 26 548 occurrences for the word *shìmín* 市民. There were 166 occurrences of the expression *shìmín sushi* 市民素质 'citizen's quality', most of which (136) in combination with the word *tígāo* 提高 'to improve' or 'improvement' (for instance, 提高市民素质 'to improve the citizen's quality', and 市民素质的提高 'improvement of the citizen's quality').

It also worth stressing that among the 149 results found for the expression *shìmín shèhuì* 市民社会 'civil society', several examples refer to Marxist and Gramscian notions of civil society. The Marxist examples included:

- 'what Marx called the "civil society"' (马克思所称的'市民社会");
- 'Marx emphasized the economic importance of civil society' (马克思强调市民社会的经济意义);

- 'Marx's theory of civil society' (马克思关于市民社会的理论);
- 'the starting point of Marx's analysis of civil society' (马克思分析市民社会的出发).

The Gramscian examples included:

- 'Gramsci also strongly emphasized the role of civil society' (葛兰西也特别强调市民社会的作用);
- 'Gramsci did not stress the economic significance of civil society, but its social and cultural significance' (葛兰西强调的不是市民社会的经济意义,而是其社会文化意义).

Despite its relative rarity in this source, *shìmín shèhuì* 市民社会 'civil society' does occur in other contexts, as in the following examples: 'the relationship between political party and government, political party and civil society' (政党与政府、政党与市民社会的关系), and 'Chinese civil society' (中国的市民社会).

Among the expressions containing the word *shìmín* 市民 'citizen' or 'urban resident', *xiǎo shìmín* 小市民 (which translates literally as 'small citizen') deserves to be mentioned. We encountered 940 occurrences of this expression in the BCC corpus and 305 in the CCL corpus. The expression *xiǎo shìmín* 小市民 originally designated petty merchants, artisans, or those belonging generally to the lower social strata of urban residents. However, it is used as a pejorative expression in everyday language to refer to narrow-minded, short-sighted 'common' people. Among the examples we found were 'the prejudices of small citizens' (小市民的偏见) and 'small clerks, small citizens' (小职员、小市民). Other examples included, 'the heaviness of small citizens' lives' (小市民生活的沉重), and 'proto-typical small woman citizen' (典型的小市民女人).

The expression *xiǎo shìmín* 小市民 'small citizen' can be opposed to *dà gōngmín* 大公民, which translates literally as 'great citizen'. For instance, we can quote some examples of the 'small citizen'–'great citizen' distinction in blogs and forums. On the question and answer website Zhihu (*Zhī hū* 知乎 'Do you know that?')[10] in February 2014, the following comment was posted in reaction to the topic of debate, 'Is Shanghai a cultural desert?' (上海是文化沙漠吗？):

上海绝不会输给香港，小市民也会成长为大公民。

Shanghai will not be inferior to Hong Kong, small citizens (*xiǎo shìmín*) will become great citizens (*dà gōngmín*).

Once more, in the social media *Rén rén wǎng* 人人网,[11] one blogger writes:

我一定不再是北京的小市民，我要成为北京的大公民，为这个目标奋斗。

I will no longer be a small Beijing citizen (*xiǎo shìmín*), I will become a great Beijing citizen (*dà gōngmín*), struggling for this goal.

It is important to stress that in these examples the distinction is marked not only by the opposition between the adjectives 'small' and 'great' (*xiǎo* 小 and *dà* 大), but also by the opposition between the words *shìmín* and *gōngmín*. These examples bear witness to the highly positive connotations associated with the word *gōngmín* in contemporary Chinese.

In order to get an idea of the usage of the words for citizen in Chinese academic discourse, we consulted the National Social Sciences Database (http://www.nssd.org/). It is important first to state that the results for *guómín* 国民 have not been taken into account, being controversial because of the polysemy of this word.[12]

Of the other two words, with 10 385 results, *gōngmín* 公民 is far more frequent than *shìmín* 市民, with only 4766 results. *Gōngmín* can be found in academic publications in the fields of politics and law (政治法律: 6179 such articles were found); 1719 publications were related to the economy and management (经济管理); and 1145 to sociology (社会学).

Broadly speaking, the word *gōngmín* 公 is used in writings related to:

- 'civil society', *gōngmín shèhuì* 公民社会, 962 papers;
- 'citizens' rights', *gōngmín quánlì* 公民权利, 904 papers;
- 'citizens' education' or 'civic education', *gōngmín jiàoyù* 公民教育, 520 papers;
- 'citizens' participation' or 'civic participation' (*gōngmín cānyù* 公民参与) is also a widely researched topic: 595 publications contain this keyword. To these, we should add 118 articles referring to 'citizens' political participation' (*gōngmín zhèngzhì cānyù* 公民政治参与), and 122 ascribable to the more general topic of 'political participation' (*zhèngzhì cānyù* 政治参与).

Among the main topics containing this word we can also quote the following:

- 'citizens' awareness' or 'civic awareness' (*gōngmín yìshí* 公民意识, 429 papers);
- 'citizens' morality' or 'civic morality' (*gōngmín dàodé* 公民道德 954 papers).

The 4766 papers mentioning the word *shìmín* 市民 were found in the fields of economics and management (经济管理 with 1664 articles), politics and law (政治法律, with 1145 articles), and sociology (社会学, with 1043 articles).

A considerable number of publications – no less than 1257 – concerned 'civil society' (*shìmín shèhuì* 市民社会). This number confirms that this topic is very relevant and that the expression *shìmín shèhuì* 市民社会 is in widespread use.

CONCLUDING REMARKS

How should we sum up our findings for the concept of citizenship in Chinese culture and the keywords used? The contemporary words for citizen, even though they can be found early in Chinese, began to take on their present meaning in the late Qing period, under Japanese and Western influences (Guō 2013; Guō 2011; Zarrow 1997: 3; Liu 1995: 25). The spread of these words was linked to the massive process of the introduction and translation of Western socio-political thought that was taking place at the turn of the century, a period in which China experienced a deep political, economic, and social crisis. During this period of transition, new disciplines and theories were introduced as tools to be used in an attempt to rescue the country (Hsü 1970).

In this context, it was *guómín*, with its explicit reference to the country and its nationalist appeal, that appears to have become the dominant term used to define the citizens, and this explains why it was adopted in early twentieth-century constitutions (Guō 2011). With the establishment of People's Republic of China, the focus shifted from individual citizens to the people and to the masses. In this context, the notion of the citizen and the related terms came to be overshadowed by these terms in political and official discourse (Keane 2001; Tang 1986).

However, in the post-Mao era, the notions of citizen and citizenship are stressed more and more. Most of all, it is the keyword *gōngmín* that has become central in debates in recent decades, even though the words *guómín* and *shìmín* also appear to be making a comeback. The term for 'citizen' (*gōngmín*) was adopted in the Constitution of the People's Republic of China, and we found it to be characterized by very positive connotations in all the wide range of sources consulted, from newspapers to blogs, and from social media to academic writings. The word *gōngmín* is widely used today. Not only is it frequently used in official discourse, it is also commonly used throughout academic papers and newspapers and it proves to be a keyword in civil rights discourse.

This is a very different story from the European story. But there is one thing the two traditions share: although citizen may seem to be a fundamental concept of potentially universal importance, the status of citizens in politics and social life fluctuates. At times, citizens are held up as the actors of the city's destiny or as the guardians and protectors of the State. At other times, it is the rights of citizens that political parties and states claim to protect. The rights of citizens in Europe's Member States are discussed at great length in the European Parliament and enshrined in its legislation.

Citizenship is invariably linked to space, and the ultimate question is: What is the social body to which the citizen belongs? To the town or city? To the Nation? To the union of states or nations, as in the United Kingdom, or the United States of America, or the European Union? Multiple forms of citizenship are not mutually exclusive categories. There is no reason why a person cannot be a citizen of Glasgow, of Scotland, of Great Britain, and – up until 2016 – a citizen of Europe, just as someone can claim to be Bréton first, then French, and European all at once. These are not exclusive identities.

But inevitably, these various levels of citizenship are different in nature, and the obligations and rights they involve vary. The feeling of belonging that is essential to active citizenship may differ greatly in degree from level to level. Indeed, many people today like to regard themselves as 'world citizens', which implies a certain disregard for the other levels of citizenship related to cities and states.

In general, liberal democracies tend to extol citizens and citizenship. Radical parties and revolutionary movements, on the other hand, often celebrate the people and attribute to the people a nationalist role. The rise of nationalism in England and France shows this all too clearly, and judging from the recent elections in Germany, the Czech Republic, and Poland, this is a general European-wide trend. Populist movements often rally groups with calls to the people to defend the country against foreign influence and above all against immigrants.

The people and citizens need not be perceived as being in opposition. At the end of the Second World War, many of the resistance freedom fighters in Poland, Slovakia, the Czech Republic and France, were communist patriots who believed in the people and fought for the freedom of their fellow citizens. Likewise, individuals and institutions in the US extol both the American people and celebrate the citizens and their rights. In doing this, they act very much like the French during the first decades after the French Revolution, who celebrated active citizens fighting for the freedom, equality, and fraternity of the French people. Historical circumstances may dictate that one form of belonging dominates while others are marginalized. This explains why *guómín*, with its patriotic appeal for celebrating the nation, became a keyword at the beginning of twentieth century in China, and why the Communist Revolution in China shifted the emphasis from citizens to the people, from groups of individuals to the collective masses.

Of course, it is obvious that all democratic political parties need the citizens to vote for them at election time, and this inevitably means that politicians try to win over the people by addressing them as citizens. How far we can take the promises and engagements announced by politicians during elections is questionable. Nonetheless, citizenship remains a key question, and in most European languages at most times, a similar concept appears to be indispensable. The governments of the USA, of Britain after Brexit, and the individual Member States of Europe must all negotiate the rights and responsibilities of the individuals that belong within designated physical and political boundaries. And citizens and citizenship will remain a key factor in the politics of any system, as long as the members of groups belonging together in one place protect themselves against attacks from without and from exploitation from rival forces within the society they belong to.

NOTES

1. All quotes from MyHistIdeasCorpus, including the examples above from Hobbes http://www.gutenberg.org/ebooks/3207, Bacon http://www.gutenberg.org/ebooks/575, and all of the following examples from the philosophers quoted hereafter are taken from the electronic versions provided by http://www.gutenberg.org.
2. Unless otherwise stated, the literary references are taken from MyFrenchCorpus, a three million word corpus of texts downloaded from http://www.gutenberg.org.
3. 'The people as the root': see Chapter 1.

4. Chinese text retrieved from the Chinese Text Project database http://ctext.org/hanfeizi/wu-du/zh
5. Available on the Chinese Text Project database: http://ctext.org/chun-qiu-zuo-zhuan/zhao-gong-shi-san-nian/zh
6. For instance, *guómín* was considered as an equivalent of 'the people', in the 1907 legal and economic dictionary *Hàn yì fǎlǜ jīngjì cídiǎn* 汉译法律经济辞典 by Shimizu Kyoshi 清水澄, translated by Zhāng Chūntáo 张春涛 and Guō Kāiwén 郭开文 (MCST database). The word *guómín* is also used to mean the 'people of the nation' in the famous *Hǎi guó tú zhì* 海国图志 'Illustrated Treatise of the Countries Overseas' by Wèi Yuán 魏源. It is used as an equivalent of 'nation' in the *Tetsugaku jii* 哲学字汇 *Dictionary of Philosophy* (1884) by Inoue Tetsujirô and Ariga Hisao.
7. The other frequent forms are *gōngmín shèhuì* 公民社会 (lit. 'citizens' society') and *mínjiān shèhuì* 民间社会, where *mínjiān* 民间 (lit. 'among the people') means 'non-official', or 'non-governmental'.
8. Chinese text: http://www.people.com.cn/GB/shehui/1060/2391834.html
9. English translation from http://www.china.org.cn/english/features/89012.htm
10. https://www.zhihu.com/question/20088942
11. http://blog.renren.com/share/276054113/9923104235
12. As already mentioned, this word means 'citizen', but also 'national' and 'nationalistic'. That is why it is used in reference to the 'national economy' (*guómín jīngjì* 国民经济), the 'national income' (*guómín shōurù* 国民收入), and the 'Nationalist Party' (Kuomintang, *Guómíndǎng* 国民党), with no reference to the meaning of citizen.

CHAPTER 3

Individual

- '37% of all Europeans expect that, in years to come, more importance will be given to individualism than to solidarity'. (http://europa.eu)
- '*France, tu seras heureuse lorsque tu seras guérie enfin des individus*' ('France, you shall be happy once you have been cured of individuals') (Anacharsis Cloots, in Oster 1993: 10)
- 社会是个人集成的。除去个人,便没有社会;所以个人的意志和快乐,是应该尊重的。(Chén Dúxiù, quoted by Lǐ 2008: 109)
  'Society is formed by individuals. Without individuals, there can be no society. Consequently, the will and happiness of the individual deserve to be respected.'
- 我這個"小我"不是獨立存在的,是和無量數小我有直接或間接的交互關係;是和社會的全體和世界的全體都有互為影響的關係的。[…]"大我"是永遠不滅的。"小我"是有死的,"大我"是永遠不死的。(Hú 2013: 60)
  'I—this "lesser self" (xiaowo)—do not exist independently. I am in direct or indirect relationship with myriads of lesser selves, with the whole of society and with the entire world, influencing one another. … the 'greater self' lives on eternally, flowing inexorably like running water. The lesser self will disappear, the greater self will not.' (Translated by Fung 2010: 154–155)

DICTIONARY DEFINITIONS

If we consult dictionaries in English, 'individual' can generally be taken to refer to one of the following three meanings:

- relating to, or existing as, just one member or part of a larger group;
- having a special and unusual quality that is easily seen;
- intended or designed for one person.

This has the merit of keeping things clear and simple. But of course, as we shall see, things are much more complicated. The *Merriam-Webster* definition clearly carves out four distinct meanings, but the fact that the first is given as 'obsolete' indicates that the lexeme covers different meanings at different times:

1 *obsolete*: inseparable
2 a: of, relating to, or distinctively associated with an individual <an *individual* effort>
  b: being an individual or existing as an indivisible whole
  c: intended for one person <an *individual* serving>
3 existing as a distinct entity: separate
4 having marked individuality <an *individual* style>. (http://www.merriam-webster.com/dictionary/individual)

Unlike many lexemes which are ordered alphabetically in dictionaries in separate entries, such as 'strong' and 'strength', the noun and the adjectival forms are held together here. *Merriam-Webster* has therefore respected the fact that they are semantically and lexically indissociable from one another, forming one complex concept or notion with a series of facets that may be activated or highlighted in different fields or discourse strategies. The multiple translations of the lexeme 'individual' will take us on a tour through linguistic patterning, revealing how the concept is often carved up in surprising ways. At a grammatical and morphological level, it is, nonetheless, clear for us in English that the adjective 'individual' is related to both the nouns 'individual' and 'individualism'.

The lexeme 'individual' derives from medieval Latin (*individuum*). By 1600, it was being used to refer to a 'single object or thing', and the colloquial use of 'individual' for 'person' is attested in 1742, though the use of 'individual' for 'an individual member of a species' goes back to the fifteenth century (http://www.etymonline.com/index.php?term=individual).

The French word *'indidividu'*, which has influenced our conception of the 'individual', and which stems from the same Latin root, proves somewhat more prolific in the French lexis than its English equivalent. And for this reason, French entries for *'individu'* are frequently more detailed in standard dictionaries than their English equivalents. *Le Petit Robert* (Rey-Debove and Rey 2000), the standard French equivalent of the *OED*, offers (appropriately enough) individual entries for: *individu, individualisation, individualiser, individualisme, individualiste, individualité, individuation, individuel/elle*, and *individuellement*.

The *OED* online (http://www.oed.com) also affirms that 'individualism', in English, is derived from both Latin and French. But the *OED* defines it as:

- Self-centred feeling or conduct as a principle; a mode of life in which the individual pursues his own ends or follows out his own ideas; free and independent individual action or thought; egoism.

The *OED* quotes L. T. Rede, *Road, to Stage*, from 1827, in which the author begs his readers to believe him when he 'disclaims' that certain persons related to certain establishments should be tainted with 'any individualism'. The other references to individualism from nineteenth-century authors tend to confirm the pejorative connotations associated with individualism.

Neutral objective definitions of the 'individual', as the particular member of a group or society, are soon abandoned as moralistic stances assert themselves in regard to individualism. In religion, and in most social groups, individuals will be censured if they fail to take into account the desires and feelings of others. This stands somewhat at odds with the ways individuals are represented in the media, though. And here it is important to both distinguish between the media of Anglo cultures, and the degree to which American media dominates them.

Are the Americans more prone to individualism? Judging from the seemingly unstoppable production of Hollywood films featuring resolute individuals played by actors from John Wayne and Charles Bronson, down to Michael Douglas and Brad Pitt, who stand up against those around them, and lay down the law, it would certainly seem so. Hollywood still seems to juxtapose the Wild West in some films with the nightmarish inner city in others. At home, citizens are represented as facing the threat of Black crime, and the fear of Latino invasion. Meanwhile, abroad, American citizens are shown facing threats of terrorist attacks. One of the recurrent themes throughout these films is the impotence of the law, its institutions, and its executive in protecting American citizens. And this paves the way for the Saviour who steps in. Sheriffs in the Wild West, and priest-like policemen in downtown

LA and New York, combat corruption among their colleagues and wage their own personal wars against the organized crime that threatens to engulf them all. CIA agents work undercover in the shadows of faithless regimes or fanatical totalitarian theocracies, flirting with the dark side to win moral battles in struggles between Good and Evil, in the murky waters that lie in between.

These are familiar scenarios, and they are the states of chaos upon which the individual will impose his will and bring about a violent but necessary moral renewal. This individual is the father that is 'hard but fair'. Even the cosmos is conceived in terms of a 'Final Frontier', and USS *Enterprise* Star Trek commanders boldly set out to sort out the aberrations of the universe. This is the cause of a whole nation, a culture of hope. And that culture invites us to consider it as the whole of humanity. But the expanding sphere of the nation depends upon the actions of individuals to impose its collective will in such narratives. Human societies and humanity itself depend upon individuals, capable of standing up, and standing above the community and the masses in these stories.

This element of American society is often observed and criticized by Europeans, but the counterbalances on individualism are less clearly perceived. The churches of America have various checks and balances to limit and condemn what is perceived as 'excessive individualism'. Faith, morality, but also civic duty and community service all form part of these checks and balances. However, the vast array of pro-individualistic scenarios and stories promoted and recycled by American media reflects a faith in the individual will that should help to explain why American dictionaries do not highlight 'individualism' as a form of 'selfishness'.

Judging from their principal dictionary, the Americans invest heavily in a worldview that hopes for individual solutions to shared social problems. *Merriam-Webster* online therefore gives a fairly positive definition of 'individualism':

- a doctrine that the interests of the individual are or ought to be ethically paramount;
- the conception that all values, rights, and duties originate in individuals;
- a theory maintaining the political and economic independence of the individual and stressing individual initiative, action, and interests. (http://www.merriam-webster.com)

The organization of terms in regard to antonyms proves interesting here. When *Merriam-Webster* gives 'conformity' as the antonym of 'individualism', does this not tend to assert that it is individualism that is being promoted? 'Rule-abiding' and 'upright' may have positive associations, but it is hard to see conformity in a positive light, from the perspective of individualism. It would seem that adapting to social trends and collective interests is being denigrated here as a lack of individual personality and initiative, or even moral courage, while an intrepid spirit of the frontiersman appears to be implicitly promoted in the opposition, individualism versus conformity.

But this would be going too far: it would mean putting to one side three manifest characteristics of the American spirit that continue to strike foreigners who visit the US or people who meet Americans abroad:

1. the fundamental generosity of American people, and their manifest friendliness;
2. the efficiency of the various American churches as community organizers;
3. the strong philosophical tradition of enlightened pragmatic individualism to which William James (1842–1910) and John Dewey (1859–1952) belong, thinkers who stressed both the role of society in shaping the individual and the vocation of the individual for furthering the moral well-being of society and for invigorating its culture.

Inevitably, in idealizing a certain form of individualism, it would appear that Americans have invested values in this concept that have not been highlighted by other English-speaking or European cultures. And when Americans are criticized for 'their' individualism, it is perhaps an impoverished form of individualism that critics have in mind, one that does not do justice to the ideals and realities of American society.

The *OED* online gives a far more exhaustive definition of individualism but one which coincides largely with the definitions already discussed. The following fundamental characteristics that emerge from the definitions, distinctions, and examples provided by the *OED* can be summarized as follows. To speak of something as 'individual', using the adjective, is to speak of the single or peculiar quality of something. 'Individual' is also used early on in the history of the English language to refer to a single individual entity, substance, or essence. This is what Milton meant when he spoke of dividing 'the individuall Catholicke Church into severall Republicks' (1641, Milton quoted in *OED*). The same usage was in play when the 'indyuyduall Trynyte' was spoken of as early as 1425 (*OED*).

As an adjective, the 'individual' could be contrasted with, or set in opposition to, 'the collective', as J. S. Mill used it in *On Liberty*, when he argued: 'There is a limit to the legitimate interference of collective opinion with individual independence' (*OED*).

When the *OED* defines 'individual' as a noun, it lists the following definitions and qualities:

1. A single member of a species; a single specimen of an animal or plant. In the *Origin of the Species*, in 1859, Darwin speaks of 'individuals of the same species [that] are cast in the very same mould'.
2. A single human being, as opposed to Society, the Family, etc.
   a. This can be a neutral definition in which one individual is set against another arbitrarily.
   b. But it can also be used in a value-loaded sense to stress
      i. As a form or praise used to stress the noteworthy or remarkable characteristics of an individual.
      ii. As a derogatory phrase used to imply the undignified or untrustworthy nature of a person.

This cluster of meanings and usages is worth stressing, as it reflects some dimensions of concepts found in various languages. At the same time, it reveals some associations which are probably specific to the English-speakers' worldview. And this is important for comparative linguistic studies. Ethnolinguistics seeks

1. to gain an overall impression of the worldviews of language-cultures;
2. to grasp the keywords of their worldviews;
3. to understand the internal dynamics of those conflicting and converging mindsets which animate worldviews.

This lexical overview of 'individual' should enable us to do two things in comparing concepts in different languages:

1. to discern common (though probably not universal) attributes associated with the lexeme, 'individual';
2. to understand the conceptual, social, political, and moral tensions involved in the English-speakers' concept of the 'individual', and the

way it resonates within the mindset of a given group within the Anglo language-culture.

This sets up a much more refined model of comparative linguistics that involves considering the way individuals situate themselves within mindsets, and the way mindsets are situated within the context of the language-culture. This is, admittedly, a more complex model, but it is one that should prevent us from falling into schematic representations of the way individuals think and feel, and the way worldviews frame their thoughts and feelings. We cannot content ourselves with setting up French against English, or German against American English. It would be naïve to 'ascribe' meanings, arguments, and values to other cultures. The terms of debates are often value-loaded, but their meanings are debated, discussed, and often criticized and rejected. Linguistic worldviews are never simple, static, and uniform: they are always complex. They are made up of multiple fluctuating perspectives that compete with one another in lively debate and discussion. When individuals interact, they argue over the meanings and definitions of the concepts they share in their communities and subcultures. Sharing these fundamental concepts is a prerequisite of debate and discussion. Cultural mindsets make politics, polemics, debate, and dissent between individuals and between communities possible, because the various actors and subcultures all play a, role in defining and maintaining the complexity of a single shared multifaceted linguistic community.

Individuals and individualism are keywords that reveal this all too clearly, because they are at the centre of the tensions that tug the language towards one or another cultural mindset. Some mindsets champion the community and the people, regarding the individual as a part of the collective group. Other mindsets represent individual will as the source of real faith, as the motor force of historical change, or as the solution to social inertia and conformity.

This explains why the individual and individualism are often what is at stake when nations define themselves and their ideals in terms of other cultures. French mainstream media often satirizes the overt individualism of Americans. One classic contemporary example is the use that is made of a puppet of Sylvester Stallone in the French comedy series, *Les Guignols* (http://www.dailymotion.com/video/x3uonpu) who portrays the 'ambassador' of the American hawks, suggesting absurd militaristic solutions to complex international crises. This satire is, however, undermined by a long-standing French tradition that champions the great revolutionary George Jacques Danton (1859–1894) and his rousing slogan '... *de l'audace, encore de l'audace, toujours de l'audace*' (Danton cited by Oster 1993: 19). The prejudice is palpable. The French media and political leaders still cherish '*audacité*' as a keyword of their own, which explains why presidential candidates such Ségolène Royale and Emmanuel Macron, for example, activate '*audacité*' and '*audacieux*' as buzzwords in the run-up to elections. Audacity in Americans is frequently portrayed as foolhardiness and simple-mindedness in the French media, however.

The French media also tend to portray neoliberalism and the individualism that goes with it hand in hand as an American threat penetrating the shared culture of France. But as far as we can tell from Rey and Debove-Rey's definition, given in France's most prestigious dictionary, *Le Petit Robert* (Rey-Debove and Rey 2000), by 2000, individualism was already being hyped in France. A decade after the crisis of the USSR and the breakaway of the satellite nations, the French worldview was already well-rooted in the same spirit of 'Conquering Capitalism' that inspired Francis Fukuyama's claim that we had reached the 'End of History'. After the fall of the Berlin Wall, France seemed to have espoused an idea very similar to the one Fukuyama was promoting, that is to say that liberal democratic capitalism was the logical, natural, and inevitable destiny of all peoples of the world (see Fukuyama 1992). Of all the definitions of individualism consulted, the French authors provided the most strikingly individualistic stance. By playing down the antisocial, potentially selfish connotations often associated with individualism, their entry provides a somewhat curiously unabashed affirmation of the ego as the cornerstone of culture. Moreover, their entry presents itself as a reasonable, straightforward definition, not a polemical stance. And this was very different from the contentious way the neoconservatives were moving into a new form of discourse legitimizing individualism in the US. French individualism appeared to be being advanced as a perfectly 'natural' phenomenon.

Fukuyama's (1992) book, *The End of History, and the Last Man*, was met with a mixture of jubilation, scorn, and criticism in America and elsewhere, however. And this seems to suggest that the legitimizing of individualism remained a question of hot debate, before Fukuyama's deterministic neo-Hegelian conception of the march of history began to take hold of mainstream political rhetoric, with the end of the Clinton administration and with Bush Junior's two administrations. True, our research leads us to believe that individualism seems to be gaining ground in most sectors of the US media, but this would appear to be a general trend in Western countries: the same rhetoric seems to be gaining ground in Europe judging by the European Union website (https://europa.eu/european-union/index_en).

It would, at any rate, appear wholly unfounded to present individualism as an American export. And ethnolinguistic studies should at all costs avoid anti-Americanism or any other form of uninformed prejudice that risks obscuring the way we perceive meanings migrating and transforming themselves. In this endeavour, it is, therefore, worth quoting the *Columbia Dictionary of Modern Literary and Cultural Criticism* (Childers and Hentzi 1995: 153) to avoid oversimplifying the complex dynamics of the American tradition of individualism celebrating independent action within society, politics, and religion. As the editors of the *Columbia Dictionary*, Childers and Hentzi, point out:

> During much of its history, individualism has been attacked from both the right and the left – in the first case, for undervaluing the wisdom of the traditions represented by established social forms, and in the second, for underestimating the extent to which the individual is shaped by the social relationships into which he or she is born.

For both the right and the left in the US, the legitimacy of individualism remains a central question in political debate and civic upheavals such as the Occupy Wall Street movement of 2011–2012.

The Ngram resource generated by Google Books certainly affirms 'individual' as a commonly used keyword in English sources. In fact, usage steadily grows from 1800 (at around 50 per cent) until it peaks in the 1970s (at around 250 per cent) before starting to taper off very slightly and stabilize in the 1980s (at around 225 per cent, as of 30 June 2018).

As with our other three concepts (the people, citizen, Europe), a selection of around 700 usages was initially drawn from online corpora, our own corpora, texts, and videos. This proved unsatisfactory, because in many of the texts consulted examples proved rather scarce. This seemed at odds with our impression of the frequency with which the lexeme is used in everyday speech, and in the media. We considered that our original corpus relied too heavily on literary sources in which 'individual' was less likely to occur. For this reason, we made use of the same extended nine million word corpus of sociological, political, and philosophical texts and online resources that we were using for our study of citizen. This gave us a more representative impression of the way the term 'individual' is used by the great authors such as Thomas Hobbes, Adam Smith and John Dewey, in the Anglo-American history of ideas. This helped to supplement the findings derived from corpus analysis. Before we discuss these findings, it may be a good idea to consider the way we can organize the 'individual' as a concept into various emerging trends.

THE INDIVIDUAL AS A CONCEPTUAL PROBLEM

Let's quickly try to organize, provisionally at least, the meanings and values attributed to the term 'individualism', into two broad overarching categories: individualism as a virtue and ideal, and individualism as a vice condemned on moral grounds.

Individualism is a Modern Ideal, a European Characteristic

> ... in an open society that values individualism and entrepreneurship against the horrors of censorship. (Peter Mandelson on 'Europe's Challenge, (https://europa.eu/european-union/index_en)

> 37% of all Europeans expect that, in years to come, more importance will be given to individualism than to solidarity. (http://europa.eu)

> The 'construction of Europe' is a construction of 'spiritual liberty'; the European project is a project of 'decorporialization.' The new Europe completes the modern democratic project only by simplifying it, by robbing it of one of its essential parts: instead of the duality, sometimes the tension, between the individual and the citizen, one gets the unilateral affirmation of the rights and the opportunities of the individual. It is impossible, Manent suggests, for human beings to live fully without belonging to a political body that requires their allegiance, for such a political body is the instrument and product of their common action. Human beings can not live simply in a civilizational space as economic and moral agents, in a territorially ambiguous and politically undetermined and perhaps undeterminable entity. (Damjan de Krnjevic-Miskovic,

Pierre Manent and the New First Philosophy of Politics, quoted in Perspectives on Political Science, Summer 2002, in COCA)

Individualism is a Form of Selfishness That Runs Counter to Religion, Morality and Socialism

Socialism as long as it attacks the existing individualism, is easily triumphant. (Mill, 1851, quoted in *OED* online)

On his return he would sit ... with that pride of individualism that is half the fascination of sin, and smiling with secret pleasure at the misshapen shadow that had to bear the burden that should have been his own. (Oscar Wilde, 1890, *The Picture of Dorian Gray*, http://www.gutenberg.org/files/174/174-h/174-h.htm)

CORPORA

The three online corpora consulted, the Liepzig Wortschatz, the COCA and the BNC, enabled us to verify the degree to which each of these two broad meanings imposed themselves in the various usages of the lexeme.

Leipzig

Among its 219 individual language corpora, the English corpus of the Leipzig Wortschatz with its 49 628 893 sentences drawn primarily from American and British sources gives a very clear idea of the way 'individual' is situated at the centre of a series of discourses. 'Individual' tends to appear in English discourse related to 'individual needs' and 'individual requirements'. Conversely, products should 'suit' individual needs and requirements. A second semantic field shows 'individual' coming up as part of the discourse of groups and members. For this reason, 'group' and 'each' are the terms associated with 'individuals'. 'Needs' and 'requirements' come up again and again. Among the right-hand neighbours in collocations, we find 'your individual' as in 'your individual needs or requirements', and as left-hand neighbours in collocations we find 'circumstances', as in 'your individual circumstances'.

What is immediately clear from this – but what remained unclear in dictionary definitions – is that we are dealing primarily with the adjectival form in these examples. The individual has requirements, but it is those requirements and needs that are inquired about and catered to. This puts 'individual' primarily in a commercial or civic context. Examples included, 'individual game scores', 'to order individual copies of the CD', and 'provide individual heated accommodation'.

Individuals were at times addressed. Consumers were assured, for example: 'Under no circumstances will your details be passed on to any other individual or organisation.' But it is worth noting that the nominal form – much rarer than the adjectival form – entailed a passivized subject–object: individuals do not tend to do much, as the following examples indicate:

The **individual** is posited as outside of and prior to history, only later becoming ensnared in externally imposed chains. (a-r-c.gold.ac.uk; emphasis added)

Habitual Sadness is focused more on each **individual** character. (a-r-c.gold.ac.uk; emphasis added)

Like this straight-jacketed **individual**, he is at the point of his struggle before he finally accepts his fate. (a-r-c.gold.ac.uk; emphasis added)

These are not the inspired and enlightened individuals that fought for the French Revolution. This is neither the tone of Danton declaring the need for audacious individuals to conquer oppression, nor the tone of Fukuyama's conquering individualism. The individuals referred to here are not the aspiring bourgeois characters made famous in the works of Balzac, Stendhal, Dostoyevsky, Dickens, and Whitman. Edmond Burke (1729–1797), the philosopher and politician, was quoted for speaking of great aristocrats as 'great oaks' with 'great ambitions'. But individuals as active subjects proved rare in the examples studied in the Leipzig corpus. When real individuals were cited, they were passive, or their actions were narrowly circumscribed. For example, they risked 'missing their chances', or they had to worry about 'how long their pensions would last' if they lived too long after retirement.

And many individuals were not of the human species. A certain number of the entries concerned species of plants and animals. But 'individual molecules' and 'individual galaxies' were also to be found. In short, 'individuals' can be great or small. Their scale is not limited. However, they remain more objects than subjects. And it is more their individual characteristics that are of interest rather than their actions that are at stake. How do these findings compare to our specific American and English corpora?

COCA

Curiously, the COCA provided some very different examples. The individual was often subjected to actions or portrayed as the receiver, beneficiary, or object of actions. This involves a certain 'passivization', it is true. The nominal form was, nonetheless, clearly asserted. Examples included the 'individual's goals', the 'individual's preferences', and the 'individual's name'. There were 'individual students' attending 'individual schools'. But the positions of individuals were held to be significant. The 'individual's motivation' was taken into account.

When individuals were spoken about in the COCA examples, the questions raised were posed in terms of rights and obligations. The individual was posited as an actor. He or she was defined in terms of the citizen, the socialized individual who could exercise his or her free will. The individual was considered from the following three perspectives:

- myself as an individual, directly reported;
- perspective of the individual, reported by a third party;
- bureaucratic perspective: accommodations must be made on an individual case-by-case basis.

These active forms of the lexeme remained, on the whole, rather rare though. Only sixty-nine phrases containing the lexemes 'individual' and 'citizen' were found in the COCA's 450 million word corpus. Much more common were instances of the 'individual' used as the object of discussion. This broadly confirms the findings derived from the Leipzig Worschatz. Examples such as the following give a fair idea of this usage:

- in the name of the individual;
- a particular individual;
- one individual;
- each individual;
- rights of the individual;
- to malign the other individual;
- a very liberal individual.

These usages merged with the adjectival uses, to objectify the 'individual' as the element protected by, or provided for by, the State, as in the example, 'to provide individual protection for each citizen'. In a somewhat excessive form, individuals were treated not only as objects but as problems. As the following examples show: 'treating individuals' was a recurrent theme in the examples found in the COCA examples consulted:

- treating sexual perversion;
- treating drug users using the same equipment with sexual partners;
- treating individuals struggling with pornographic addiction.

Health and well-being were recurrent themes in the examples. One example found was 'the new Age of Psychology promotes and emphasizes the development and self-fulfilment of the individual'. But as the above examples show, this concern for health began with sickness and distress. In a prophetic article on the homeless and the hungry from ABC *Nightline* back in 1990, a speaker satirized policies on the homeless that sought 'to break people down into different categories and into little square pegs, so that they could keep the attention focused on rehabilitating the individual to fit back into society'. In other words, explanations were being generated to consolidate arguments that homelessness was more a problem of individual responsibility than a symptom of crises, precarious employment, and inefficient State action.

Most remarkable was a tendency to negate forms of individual action: when the power of the individual was mentioned, it was often immediately annulled or curtailed, as in the following examples, affirming the impotence of the individual:

- The individual can't control the stock market.
- The individual can't control unemployment.

Though these examples were not particularly common, they did make up a certain number of the nominal forms of the total 68 586 examples of 'individual' found in the COCA corpus.

When 'individual' was used in its adjectival form, it was found in phrases immediately preceding the following words:

- standpoint, perspective;
- investor, taxpayer;

- person, every single, businessperson;
- income;
- rights, privacy, liberties;
- clubs, hotels;
- nations.

The collocates for 'individual' found in the COCA, listed in order of importance, reveals the narratives and stories individuals are perceived to be involved in: 'rights', 'needs', 'collective', 'freedom', 'responsibility', 'investors', 'factors', 'characteristics', 'mandate', 'achievement', 'basis', 'identity', 'liberty'. This gives a fair idea about how Americans speak about and think about individuals. But how do these findings compare with the way people think and speak about individuals in British English or in other languages?

BNC

It would be hasty to make assertions about 18 804 examples based on an inevitably finite set of samples. Nonetheless, on most points, the overall impression of the 200 references to 'individual' consulted on the British Nation Corpus website confirmed what was found in the COCA corpus of contemporary spoken American English.

- **The adjectival form dominated**: generating individual hotels, individual guests, individual products, individual tickets, individual kitchens, individual hospitals, individual requirements, individual rights, individual liberty, and so forth.
- **In both the adjectival forms and nominal forms active agency was rare**. Examples were often drawn from the commercial sector: individuals were targets of advertising that claimed to anticipate and respond to their basic requirements and specific tastes. Individual rights were being 'provided' in a similar manner: they were not being demanded. They were not 'hard won', nor were they even being denied. The political examples belonged, on the whole, to the politics of bureaucracy, not to political dissent. Nor were they traditionally accepted forms of negotiation such as labour movement actions or street protests of the kind seen in Occupy Wall Street.
- **Celebration of the specific nature of individual style persisted, but did not dominate**. Jazz styles were compared. But even when poets spoke of individuality in the examples found, it was often for

commercial purposes: potential customers were invited to come and meet Sylvia Kantaris, 'on an individual basis', in one advert. The *Gay Times* celebrated individuality, in one BNC entry: 'Julian Clary hosts this glittering contest to find Brighton's most alternative individual.' But once again, the celebration of the original outsider had clearly been assimilated into the market-oriented discourse celebrating the identity that Brighton wished to cultivate, promote, and profit from.
- **Individual agency of active subjects was extremely rare**, with only one reference out of 200 to individual protestors. 'Individuals' in the plural form generated 7914 examples, but those individuals were frequently passive: they were 'addressed', 'asked', 'sponsored', 'drawn from …', 'constituted', 'targeted'.
- **Negation of the individual was extremely rare**, and in the single example found, the noun was not implicitly pejorative; it was modified by the negative adjectives when the speaker claimed a man was 'the most selfish, egotistical individual I have ever met'.

Generally speaking, the examples of 'individualism' the BNC offered did leave us to conclude that the subject was open to discussion and often contested as a principle of liberal democracies. On the one side, there were the advocates who spoke of 'the virtues of individualism', 'rugged individualism', 'the cult of individualism', 'new individualism', and of 'freedom and individualism'. Discussions seemed to be related to Thatcher's transformation of the British Society: 'eighties-style individualism', seemed to refer to 'recent generations [who] prized individualism' and 'economic individualism'. And this conception appeared to be considered to be both a compatible and a legitimate form of 'freedom and individualism'. Indeed, in the Anglo worldview, despite his reserves, individualism finds legitimacy in writers such Mill who might be considered as favouring a tradition that produces examples from the BNC that valorize the tradition of 'utilitarianism, paternalism, and individualism'.

On the other side, detractors expressed doubts about, or condemned, 'blatant individualism' and 'self-indulgent individualism'. They denounced all that fostered 'isolation and individualism', and regretted the lack – or the loss – of 'informed individualism'.

The celebrators of individualism tended to dominate in approximately a third of the total number of examples consulted: those who had 'a strong sense of individualism', a 'competitive individualism', who spoke of 'boldness and individualism' seemed to be appropriating individualism for their camp. Indeed, that camp even countered those who feared 'rampant individualism' by speaking of dangerous forces that could be responsible for 'the subversion of individualism into collectivism'. The BNC examples go up to 1993. What has happened since, as these predominantly 1980s examples tend to indicate, the moral and social forces opposing individualism were taking a beating? We will return to this question when we consider whether 'individual' is a sociological category or a philosophical question. But at this stage it is worth considering how other European linguistic communities apprehend the individual and integrate it into their traditions. This should go some way to stressing the diversity of cultures and the tensions involved in converging towards one single shared model of the 'individual' in European policy and discourse.

European Individuals

Ludvik's story

Ludvik, the hero-anti-hero of *The Joke*, the novel that was to make Milan Kundera's reputation in the Czechoslovakia of the 1960s, comes from that lower middle class from which the revolutionary Czechoslovak Communist Party was to draw its support. His generation and his class would transform the worldview of the country in the post-war era. Liberated from the Nazi occupation by Stalin's troops, the Czechs and Slovaks looked East, and it was with a feeling of shared 'brotherhood' with their Russian comrades, and hopes for a better future for society as a whole, that many young Czechs and Slovaks turned their backs on 'Western bourgeois liberalism'. In doing so, they celebrated collective ideals. The Czech films of the 1950s and 1960s revisit fairy tales in which the king turns against his corrupt, self-serving ministers, and sides with the people. Kings, queens, and most of all princesses, dance with commoners in fairy tales, and in communist films of that period. And a vast array of communist films adapted Czech, French, and English novels of the nineteenth century that all too vividly displayed the sufferings of workers, the humiliation of the servile classes, and the bloated narcissism of the moneyed classes, and their manifest contempt for all who served them.

Times have changed, and Luvik's generation has helped to change them when our story opens in the early 1960s. But Ludvik, like many others of his generation, has been socialized within the values of bourgeois individualism, and he has difficulty in shaking off his resolutely individual nature. That attitude leads him to adopt a sardonic, mocking stance as his friends and colleagues dance in rings and sing their songs of solidarity. Most of Kundera's main characters have a lyrical dimension to them, but theirs is the lyricism of the Romantics, the individual looking back, looking on, yearning to join in with others. Something, somehow, always holds his protagonists back. As individuals, they are unable to mingle with others and fit in. The ego holds them back, refusing to melt into the mood, or go with the flow of the zeitgeist. Even when Kundera's protagonists do join in, they are painfully self-aware, as though they observe themselves going through the motions of merging with the group: pretending.

Ludvik's story is the story of an ironical man who is caught in palpably 'unironic' times, times when joking about Stalin does not go down well. Ludvik is a sardonic youth who is sent to a Correction Camp, after sending a jealous message to his girlfriend who prefers to devote a week of her summer holidays to a political instruction seminar rather than giving herself up to a week of love and lust with her boyfriend, Ludvik. As the message is sent on a postcard, the private becomes political (something that was to become the hallmark of all of Kundera's Czech novels). The title of the novel, *Žert*, means 'the joke' in Czech, and in a sense not only is Ludvik a 'joker', but his whole life comes to symbolize the cruel irony of unironic times. The 'joke' is on him: but nobody is laughing, when Ludvik writes:

Zdravý duch páchne blbostí! *Ať žije Trockij!*

Optimism is the opium of the people. A healthy spirit stinks of idiocy. Long live Trotsky!

The consequences are absurd, but brutally unstoppable. The sardonic youth is gradually ground down and transformed into an embittered cynical middle-aged man. By the time, we meet up with him again, fifteen years later, his main ambition is to seduce the wife of the 'comrade' from the early years of communism who, after promising to help Ludvik in his difficulties, prefers to give a prize performance in moralizing. He preaches to the converted tribunal, in denouncing his 'friend'. This is another ironic nail in the coffin of Ludvik's sense of self, for both the orator and Ludvik are above all 'individuals'. Some individuals, however, know how to play to the times and advance their careers better than others. Ludvik is 'individualistic' but he is not enough of a careerist to know better. And this serves to distinguish between the self-seeking go-getter individual, and the authentic individual celebrated by bourgeois liberal free thinking. Kundera is subtle and sardonic, but his sympathies are clearly drawn to the latter.

What are we as Europeans at the beginning of the twenty-first century to make of this tale? Perhaps the essential thing for us to understand today is simply that, as far as Ludvik's politically engaged generation was concerned, 'individualism' had become a social evil. When Ludvik's well-meaning friends criticize him for 'individualism', Ludvik does not resent it: he defends himself against the charge. How do you know, he asks? In what way does my individualism manifest itself? The answers are uncertain, equivocal: something in his eyes, in the way he talks.

Crucially, nobody questions that individualism is a grave impediment to the projects of the times and an affront to the moral values that are taking hold of the new ruling class. But this 'truth' is something that Ludvik has failed to grasp. For education purposes, the Czech dictionaries, encyclopaedias, and textbooks of the time were consolidating the same antagonism to individualism. In the *Stručný Slovník Politický* (Fingl et al. 1962: 105–106), for example, published by the State Publishing House for Literature in Prague, the authors give a short but unequivocal definition of *Individualismus*:

> Individualismus – the elevation of the interests of the individual [*jednotlivec*, from *jeden:* the one] above the interests of the collective or of those of society as a whole: the opposite of *collectivism*.

The authors go on to state that *individualismus* is characteristic of bourgeois morality and ideology, and they suggest that *individualismus* reduces all history to acts of 'exceptional individuals' and 'personalities' (*osobností*, that is, 'personalities' (Fingl et al. 1962: 106)).

Whatever political stand we take, the communist and socialist rhetoric and arguments of the times have an undeniable coherence. Individualism and collectivism are clearly opposed to one another in their extreme or polarized forms. Even those who abhor collectivism and denounce socialism would not deny that. The great Russian exiled writer, Vladimir Nabakov (1899–1977), knew the two were incompatible all too well when he declared:

> A work of art has no importance whatsoever to society. It is only important to the individual, and only the individual reader is important to me. (*Strong Opinions*, 1973, quoted in the *ODQ* 1992: 489).

Nabakov was from a different country, and a different generation to Kundera. He was rejecting the Soviet revolution of Lenin, Trotsky, and Stalin. Emigré writers like Nabakov were holding onto their dispossessed tradition of bourgeois liberalism in Mother Russia. Closer to the *fin de siècle* Chekov, in spirit, they embraced, albeit half-heartedly, the liberalism of Western Europe and the US.

The philosopher–novelist Aym Rand (1905–1982, born Alissa Zinovievna Rosenbaum, *Алиса Зиновьевна Розенбаум*, in Saint Petersburg) was to become a controversial figure of the 1950s and 1960s in America for similar reasons. Arguably less talented than Nabakov, but certainly more virulently pro-liberal, Rand has become a great inspiration to the Radical Right in the US. For this reason, it was not particularly surprising that Donald Trump quoted her as he was running for election, although Aym Rand admirers saw a great gap between Rand's objectivism and Trump's opportunism (https://www.youtube.com/watch?v=nfSbZjMj_hU).

For our purposes, it is important to understand that Rand denounced what she claimed were perverted forms of altruism, and espoused a form of 'healthy Epicureanism', which she perceived American ideals as reflecting and communism as thwarting.

Rand's novel, *Anthem* (which can be read or listened to on http://www.loyalbooks.com/book/anthem-by-ayn-rand), first published on the eve of the Second World War, in 1938, after two decades of Bolshevism, for example, opens with the following words from a member of a regime condemned for solitary individualistic expression and free thinking:

> It is a sin to write this. It is a sin to think words no others think and to put them down upon a paper no others are to see. It is base and evil. It is as if we were speaking alone to no ears but our own. And we know well that there is no transgression blacker than to do or think alone. We have broken the laws. The laws say that men may not write unless the Council of Vocations bid them so. May we be forgiven!
>
> But this is not the only sin upon us. We have committed a greater crime, and for this crime there is no name. What punishment awaits us if it be discovered we know not, for no such crime has come in the memory of men and there are no laws to provide for it.

Rand perfects an eerie mixture of the familiar and the oppressively foreign in her dystopia. Here, the oppressive homespun American

Calvinist religious rhetoric and syntax combines with the mechanistic bureaucratic anti-individualistic style of Marxism–Leninism, or Stalinism, at least. Such a style continues to generate American dystopia fiction right down to the recent blockbuster film, *The Hunger Games* (2012). If Western Cold War rhetoric often lacks the coherence of socialist discourse, it was certainly more subtle in the uses it put writers such as Rand and Nabokov to in denouncing communist claims to egalitarianism and in promoting Western individualism. They served the State, and served it well, by formulating the various shades and forms of covert propaganda. Promoting both native and foreign writers is rarely innocent: if Rand and Nabokov were promoted alongside Alexander Solzhenitsyn and George Orwell, it was in part because all four writers were supposed to serve as warnings about the dangers of regimes promising social equality. Their dark dystopias, and the stories of individuals escaping oppressive systems served to refute the claims for Utopias.

Kundera was all the more instrumental in this process of negating the Communist Bloc and its ideals, having himself been a communist. He was the Cold War's equivalent to the 'Lost Sheep', the deluded idealist, punished for his integrity as an individual. The fact that, like Nabokov, Kundera was undisputedly a major writer of great talent, could only facilitate the task of indirectly denouncing alternative forms of government, and rival ideologies. The East had good writers, it was implied, but it didn't appreciate them. It suffocated the talents of the free spirit, while Western writers were free to breathe the fresh air of democracy. Most of all, the West opened its arms to the dissidents of the East who craved to breathe that air and tell their truths to eager ears.

In the context of present debates about 'empowerment of individual citizens', and 'the rights of individuals', it seemed to us important to remind ourselves of various traditions in which individualism has been considered a pernicious influence undermining society. Traces of such traditions can still be found in the major European languages, but the fact that they are often no more than traces seems to suggest that the final battle of a war between individualism and rival philosophies is being waged. Individualism no longer seems to be under attack or forced to fight for its existence. Increasingly, it would seem, individualism has become 'normalized'. And perhaps soon it will become very difficult to question it, as it has been questioned over the centuries, since the time of the Greeks. What the examples of Nabokov, Rand, and Kundera indicate, is that the foreign is imported, either as a representation or as an in-house discourse that consolidates the representations and oppositions that underpin dominant discourses and rhetorical strategies in the Anglo worldview.

German Einzelpersonen

We should of course be wary of reducing cultures and linguistic worldviews to individual perspectives. Ludvik's story is revealing but a wealth of pro-individualism can be found in the discourse of the Czech press, politics, and everyday life today. Similarly, the German corpus of the Leipzig Wortschatz provides a wide variety of examples of the German term for 'individual', '*Einzelperson*': *Einzelperson* is found in neutral examples related to family, friends, and groups. However, cultures show a greater or lesser predilection towards individualism, and this tends to change over time. There is a strong Judaic tradition in German that reminds us of the ills of excessive individualism which can prevent the individual from entering into any authentic form of relationship with others. This is the religious perspective that is espoused by Martin Buber (1878–1965) who puts that danger in the following terms:

> How discordant the I of the individual! It may stir great compassion if it comes from lips compressed in the tragedy of concealed self-contradiction. It may rouse horror if it comes chaotically from lips that wildly, heedlessly, unsuspectingly, show forth the contradiction. If it comes idly and glibly it is painful or disagreeable. He who speaks the separated *I*, with the emphasis on the capital, lays bare the shame of the worldspirit which has been degraded into spirituality. (Buber 1996: 88–89)

> Wie mißtönig ist das Ich des Eigenmenschen! Es kann zu dem großen Mitleiden bewegen, wenn es aus einem tragischen, vom Verschweigen eines Selbst-Widerspruchs gepreßten Munde kommt. Es kann zum Grauen bewegen, wenn es aus einem chaotischen, den Widerspruch wild, sorg-und ahnungslos darstellenden Munde kommt. Wenn es aus einem eitlen und verglättenden kommt, ist es peinlich oder widerwärtig. Wer das abgetrennte Ich mit großem Anfangsbuchstaben spricht, deckt die Schande des Weltgeistes auf, der zur Geistigkeit erniedrigt wordern ist. (Buber 1995: 64)

These words might be welcomed by Muslims and Christians alike. As Buber goes on to argue, this form of lonely individual existence is a form of inauthentic isolation: it is not the calm of the person who is capable of relating to others but who stands back from relating to contemplate life, in a religious retreat. For the religious man, making an individual stance in relation to others, to life, and to God is important. For this reason, most of the advocates of the major monotheistic religions stress the importance of the individual's capacity for reason and free will. This is held to be the basis of faith. And that explains the significance of an authentic form of individualism for religious writers. Buber, for example, affirms:

> Every real relation in the world rests on individuation, this is its joy – for only in this way is mutual knowledge of different beings won ... (Buber 1996: 128)

> Jeder wirkliche Beziehung in der Welt ruht auf der Individuation, dies ist ihre Wonne, den nur so ist Einanderkennen der Verschiedenen gewährt ... (Buber 1995: 95)

Individualism is not the problem, then, for religious thinkers or believers. The question is: What kind of individualism corresponds to faith and life in a moral and religious community? This question obviously transcends national borders, and the worldviews of linguistic communities, but the German tradition does pose the question in a vibrant and gripping way.

Spanish Individuals

As in Czech or German, Spanish provides us with a rich variety of perspectives of the 'individual' as a keyword. If we consult the 100 million word Spanish corpus, *Coprus del Español* provided by Mark Davis, on the BYC website (www.corpusdelesanol.org), and compare it with the BNC corpus of the same size, we find some interesting results, with converging and diverging patterns. This can be seen all too clearly if we compare the words 'individual' in English and Spanish collocate them in order of frequency (Table 3.1).

What comparable trends appear to be emerging here? The English examples insist upon the single status of individuals, with 'each' as the primary collocate. The fact that *'iniciativa'* (initiative) comes sixth in the list of collocates in Spanish indicates a similar stress on personal responsibility. However, *'libertad'* (personal or individual freedom) appears to be the main concern when it comes to Spanish.

Table 3.1 Comparing Spanish and English collocations for 'individual'

1	*Libertad*	Each
2	*Colectiva*	Needs
3	*Forma*	Rights
4	*Propiedad*	Behaviour
5	*Social*	Responsibility
6	*Iniciativa*	Freedom
7	*Seguridad*	Differences
8	*Derecho*	Collective
9	*Consciencia*	Projects
10	*Colectivo*	Autonomy

Source: Our compared findings are drawn from http://www.corpusdelesanol.org, and the BNC corpus online at https://corpus.byu.edu/bnc

Both languages reveal that the speakers of their linguistic communities are concerned with rights and responsibilities ('conscience' comes ninth in the Spanish list). But the nature of those rights and responsibilities would appear to be somewhat more social and collective in the Spanish worldview, judging from this list: 'collective' comes only eighth in English, while in Spanish it comes both second and tenth in its feminine and masculine gendered forms, respectively. And 'social' comes fifth in Spanish, though it doesn't make it into the top ten collocates in English.

The English collocates stress that 'individual needs', 'individual rights', and 'individual responsibilities' are central to the concept, at least in mainstream media. But English makes no room for religion or morality, above the moralizing of bureaucratic discourse concerning the dispensing of rights and demands concerning individual responsibilities. In Spain, a country in which the Catholic Church maintains a strong foothold, the concept of 'individual conscience' came in as the ninth collocate. And individual conscience and collective and social actions appeared to form part of the same debates. This suggests something about the way different Member States will understand and face up to the neoliberalism of the European Union. Age-old moral debates, fundamental to the concept of individualism, seem to be affecting the ways people act and think together in society, in politics, in the market, and even in the home, alone with their own consciences.

When it came to individualism in Spanish, the individualist (*individualista*) was invariably linked to forms of excess (too individualistic, *demasiado individualista*, totally individualistic, *totalmente individualista*, ferociously individualistic, *ferozmente individualista*). And the West was denounced as being 'too individualistic' (*el exceso individualista del Occidente*). Debates on individualism clearly concern the relationship between Spain and the world, and between Spain and the other cultures and nations that make up 'the West'. These debates also proved culturally specific in terms of gender. The individualism of men and women was discussed in relation to the family and the collective society. This raises a very fundamental problem: Can we consider men and women as individuals irrespective of their sex, or does individualism tend to attach itself to one of the genders in the worldview of a linguistic community? Dialogues such as the following one are hard to imagine, at any rate, in either English or American English.

> Your wife doesn't see things like you. Is she not entitled to think otherwise? Do you think you're entitled to sacrifice her for your ideal?
> Yes.
> - That's sacrificing a person against their will. Why do you have to force her to think and act like you? You, who love freedom so much?
> Yes, that's true. But freedom cannot be individual, it must equally be collective, for all people. When a people is free, all citizens are free. And everyone is required to make an effort, because the fate of all is at stake. People who are not fully aware of their dignity can have no self-esteem.

> - *Tu mujer piensa de manera distinta a ti. ¿Es que ella no tiene derecho a pensar de otra forma? ¿Tú crees que tienes derecho a sacrificarla a ella por tu ideal? - Sí. - Eso es sacrificar a una persona en contra de su voluntad. ¿Por qué la tienes que obligar a ella a opinar y actuar como tú? Tú, que tanto amas la libertad ... - Sí, es cierto. Pero la libertad no puede ser individual, sino es, al mismo tiempo, colectiva, de todo el pueblo. Cuando un pueblo es libre, todos los ciudadanos lo son. Y ese es un esfuerzo exigible a todos, porque es el destino de todos. La gente que no tiene conciencia plena de su dignidad no tiene autoestima.* (Patricio Chamizo's short story, *Paredes, un campesino extremeño*, http://www.cervantesvirtual.com/FichaObra.html?Ref=4797, quoted in http://www.corpusdelespanol.org)

Are freedoms individual freedoms, or is our collective freedom dependent upon the sacrifice of individual freedom? Are women and men accorded the same freedoms? And who decides and dictates the terms of those freedoms? These are ideological questions, which vary from culture to culture and which are discussed and debated within cultures. But grasping the concepts and the keywords, the way they work within cultural mindsets, and the way they are interpreted in discourse strategies proves difficult.

Les Individus à la Française

Like most nations, the French celebrate their own heroes, but they are particularly good at promoting around the world their individual heroes, from Joan of Arc to Napoléon, and from Hugo to Baudelaire. Arguably all four are 'great individuals'. They have entered 'world history' and films are made and books are written about their lives, inviting people from far-off nations to enter into their struggles and ambitions, their hopes and dreams. For that reason, it is worth juxtaposing two opposite views on the individual that animates debates on individualism within the French cultural mindset. For the French Romantic poet, François-René de Chateaubriand (1768–1848), history is impossible without individuals: individuals form history just as they are formed by it.

> *Annuler totalement l'individu, ne lui donner que la position d'un chiffre, lequel vient dans la série d'un nombre, c'est lui contester la valeur absolue qu'il possède, indépendamment de sa valeur relative. De même qu'un siècle influe sur un homme, un homme influe sur un siècle.*
> (Chateaubriand, quoted by Oster 1993: 66)
>
> To totally annul the individual and to accord to him the mere position of a number in a series of numbers, amounts to contesting the absolute value he possesses, independent of his relative value. Just as a century influences a man, a man influences his century.

On the other hand, French revolutionaries were not alone in seeing individualism as a plague on their nation. For this reason Anacharsis Cloots (1755–1794) declared: '*France, tu seras heureuse lorsque tu seras guérie enfin des individus*' ('France, you shall be happy once you have been cured of individuals', quoted by Oster 1993: 10). In many walks of life, the individual's rights are staunchly defended, judging from the examples we considered. And this coincides with the fact that of the three French constitutional values, '*Liberté, Egalité, Fraternité*', it is brotherhood that tends to be neglected in many discourses. It remains unclear how many French people actually aspire to a project for social or financial egality. But egality resists as an ideal, and arguably the ideal of '*solidarité*' consolidates the desire for '*fraternité*' in introducing a more modern social or trade union dimension to the concept.

Liberty, in contrast, resonates as an unquestioned ideal, an aspiration, and an unalienable right for a vast variety of people from all classes and all generations, and both sexes in France, judging from the results of our corpus research. In a fundamental sense, 'I'm allowed to', 'I have the right to' (both translated as '*j'ai le droit de* ...'), and 'free to', ('*libre de* ...') are crucial phrases. They coincide in a cluster of discourse strategies that are bound up together and invariably staunchly defended as uncompromising positions in everyday spoken French. What the individual has the right to do – his or her constitutional freedoms – are already taught at *l'école maternelle* (primary school). Socialization and the politics of individualism are therefore political and social questions from the beginning of education, and the entry of the individual child into the social sphere. This takes us into the politics of everyday life. Is the individual a social or a sociological category?

Individual: A Sociological Category?

In general, sociology dictionaries and textbooks (Marshall 1998: 304, for example) stress that individualism is often contrasted with collectivism, as Clément argues below in the section on the individual as a philosophical question. This opposition between individualism and collectivism was clearly in evidence in the polarized rhetoric of the Cold War. In such rhetoric, the West played the defender of bourgeois liberal ideas, ideals and interests, while the USSR and the Eastern European satellite States played the defenders of the greater good of the collective will, often at the expense of free speech and individual interests. But polarized positions rarely stand up to analysis, and Marshall (1998: 304) suggests that in the 1980s, groups of American sociologists gathered around Robert N. Bellah (the author of *Habits of the Heart* 1985) were already arguing against the destructive forces working within bourgeois liberalism. According to Marshall, Bellah and his colleagues believed that American individualism had become so aggressive that it risked destroying the moral integrity of society, an argument that many Marxists would have found perfectly plausible. Indeed, such an argument would have eased the minds of those sending outspoken individualists like Ludvik to correction camps.

This concern for the moral well-being of the society as a whole, expressed by various political groups and academic disciplines in the West, concords with the various misgivings expressed by all the major religions about exalting the interests of the individual above the group, parish, community, town, or nation. Nonetheless, in Britain and America the relation between religion and individualism proves paradoxical.

As Marshall reminds us, one unique form of individualism was enshrined within the underlying tenets of America's main religion: Protestant individualism. In contrast to Buber's Jewish dialogic philosophy of religion as an encounter between the 'I' and the 'you' (quoted above), Protestant individualism emphasizes the direct and personal relationship between believers and their God. Unmediated by the church and its hierarchy, individuals were invited to enter into direct communion with the divine. Here we have a more democratic, immediate relation with the Godhead, but one that isolates the individual and leaves him with an unstructured relationship. Individuals must grope their way to God alone, and stand before Him, alone, unaided by the advice and fellowship of the church as an institution.

Buber had already expressed grave doubts about this. And he did not hesitate to take on the thinkers who were held up as exponents of this individualistic Protestantism. His critique of the Copenhagen philosopher, Kierkegaard (1813–1855), portrayed him as a tortured person incapable of relating to others in an authentic manner as either a man or as a philosopher. For Buber (1973: 60–108), Kierkegaard failed as a believer, when he retreated into his own conception of God, and declared: 'Everyone ... should speak only with God and with himself' (Buber 1973: 208). Such a retreat runs contrary to Jewish religion. But it also expressly contradicts John's indictment expressed in the *First Epistle*:

> If a man say, I love God, and hateth his brother, he is a liar: for he that loveth not his brother whom he hath seen, how can he love God whom he hath not seen? (1 John 4: 20, https://www.kingjamesbibleonline.org/1-John-4-20/)

Individualism is clearly a moral and a social question, at any rate, and the important thing to grasp here is the way religions entail selective readings: church dogma and dominant trends both involve motivated interpretations of Scripture. Capitalism grows out of a certain form of Christianity. Weber's (2012) study of the concomitant destinies of the

Protestant Church and the rise of modern capitalism was first published in German between 1904 and 1905, and has now become a Western classic whose influence has gone far beyond the confines of sociology. This in itself is revealing. Faith, economics, and individual aspirations are all at stake in the tensions and dynamics generated in the cultural mindset that is emerging in the modern Anglo worldview with the rise of liberal capitalism.

It is not just in society and in politics, then, that the individual proves central. In sociology itself, the 'individual' also proves to be a problem of methodology and conception: there remains an underlying tension in sociology concerning agency and the structure of society. And this is the crux of many debates on the nature and the role of the individual in society. This tension tends to divide sociologists in methodological terms, into

- those who believe we can understand society without focusing upon the individual and
- those who believe we must work from individual experience back towards an overview of the whole.

Durkheim tended to side with the first camp. Like Durkheim in sociology, the great German-American ethnolinguist, Edward Sapir (1884–1939), believed that each social and linguistic entity has a totality that is distinct and cannot be reduced to the sum of its individual components. He argued as a result that we could find something of the whole of society's culture in the individual consciousness and in his or her language, but not all of it. However we approach the problem, interpreting the individual certainly seems to introduce us into spheres and relations which cannot be defined, studied, and understood conceptually or pragmatically in the individual logic of any given person, isolated from society as a whole.

The online *Stanford Encyclopedia of Philosophy* reflects the difficulty of opposing the individual and the collective, notably in its section on 'Shared Agency'. As its authors argue: 'shared activity and intention is of interest for a variety of disciplines, including politics, social science, economics, ethics, law, epistemology (especially testimony and social epistemology), and psychology' (http://plato.stanford.edu/entries/shared-agency). However, the authors admit that the question of what it means 'to act together' is somewhat controversial and has received sustained discussion in contemporary debates on the philosophy of action.

These central concerns relate to how the individual cooperates with others, and with groups or society as a whole.

In these debates on the ontology of intention, the opposition between the individual and the collective is implicitly questioned by the use of concepts such as 'shared activity', and 'joint' or 'collective action'. Such terms stand in stark contrast to the silhouette of the Lone Ranger in the Wild West, who comes as the social Saviour to sort things out 'individually'. Between sociology and Hollywood, there is a gaping gulf. Perhaps our corpora will help to bridge the gap. By studying everyday language in our corpora and texts, however, we hope we have revealed something about how English-speakers in America and Britain understand the concept of the 'individual', and the way they negotiate its various forms and facets in defending their own 'individual' discourse strategies.

The Individual: A Philosophical Question?

How we define an individual is clearly a political and a social question, and to say that it is a personal question of conscience would appear patently self-evident. But at what stage, exactly, does the individual become a preoccupation of philosophy? When do philosophers start to take an interest in what individuals do, or are allowed to do? We know that historically speaking, even in literary prose, 'individual' is hard to find.

Despite a few examples in the *OED*, the lexeme 'individual' proves rare before Shakespeare's day, though we find it in the fifteenth century, and we have seen Milton using it in the seventeenth century. Seventeenth century references from Spencer tend to confirm it was a religious question, one that Thomas Aquinas had discussed (in Latin of course), and religion and philosophy were clearly inseparable at that time. The early *OED* examples confirm the religious interest in the 'individual'. Religious debates on the status of the individual relate to Creation and to the single nature of things, as a whole, created by God however. Consequently, the relation between the individual and the species, and between the species and the genus become questions of spiritual import. These are inevitably perceived as religious questions within the prism of the Christian worldview, in as much as everything that exists has been created, by God, the Creator. How things relate to one another and how they are to be distinguished from one another are questions of Christian dogma. And this is true as much for the German philosopher, Leibniz

(1646–1716) writing in Latin or French, as it is for Aquinas (1225–1274) or Bonaventure (1217–1274), writing in Latin.

Western philosophy has its roots in Greek, of course, but judging from the absence of the lexeme in the King James Version of the New and Old Testaments, Hebrew, Greek, and Latin do not appear to generate religious concepts of the 'individual'. Nonetheless, the 'individual' is very much a philosophical question, and this remains true down to this day. This is significant for our study, since it will be clear that none of our other concepts (Europe, the citizen, the people) would be generally accepted today as philosophical problems.

Philosophy dictionaries constantly make reference to the Classical philosophers, Plato and Aristotle, in approaching the question of the individual. If we seek an etymological definition in Ancient Greek, however, we will be put off to find the term being translated is *'atomos'*. This proves disconcerting for two reasons. Firstly, we can see we are dealing with different lexemes. Consequently, philosophers and the compilers of encyclopaedias find themselves engaged in a circus act of hopping from one to the other while trying to preserve intact a single unitary, definable term or concept. Secondly, *'atomos'* literally means 'indivisible'. And the whole nuclear age will take us into a new dimension with that crucial moment at which point in time the 'indivisible atom' was divided, with the horrific consequences we know only too well.

This etymology does, however, help to explain why the term 'individual' – which is supposed to inherit the meaning of *'atomos'* – is so often used in the biological sense, as the smallest indivisible member of a community or greater whole. It is tempting today to consider this definition in modern, materialistic terms, but this proves an error. Plato was no materialist, and Aristotle would be used in very non-materialistic terms by the Neoplatonists that inspired Christian dogma. Leibniz's smallest indivisible units of existence, the *'monads'*, are not material in nature, they are concentrates of spiritual essence, the building blocks of a very metaphysical Creation. In some people's minds, the post-Darwinian world of modern science seems to reduce all that exists to an empirically observable manifestation of matter, but Darwin, for his part, was certainly no materialist. Darwin was enamoured of the Christian design of the universe and his books regularly sing the praises of that Divine Order in something that echoes the Protestant hymns that invite us to contemplate all things bright and beautiful. Darwin loved all that was tiny and transcendental, as if he understood the religious precept that God is in the detail.

French philosophers are faced with the same difficulty of trying to tie the tradition of the '*individu*' to that '*atomos*'. Catherine Clément, the author of the entry for '*individualité*' in the *Dictionnaire de la philosophie, Encyclopædia Universalis* (2000: 863), rightly points out that 'individual' cannot be defined by the etymological strategy usually adopted by philosophers. Nor can it be defined in terms of axiomatic reasoning from accepted principles. Clément, like many other authors, stresses the social and the biological definitions of the concept of the '*individu*', but she makes three essential points:

1. Whenever the concept of the 'individual' [*individu*] is invoked, it is used in opposition to another term.
2. The concept of the 'individual' appears to belong to various distinct fields of semantics, without there being any obvious link between the various uses of the concept.
3. Paradoxically, though the word derives etymologically from the non-divided, the concept of the individual never exists in any form other than that divided. (*Dictionnaire de la Philosophie, Encyclopædia Universalis* 2000: 863)

Conceptually speaking, at least, we may deny the existence of the individual, cut off from its context, or we may consider it to be no more than a useful fiction, but our representation proves highly resistant, and we invariably do conceive of the individual in isolation. The very fact that we set it in opposition to other terms would seem to confirm this. Clément summarizes these opposition-relations which define the individual in various semantic fields as follows:

1. The individual as opposed to the total or the whole (the biological definition)
2. The individual as opposed to the universal (stressing the specific nature of an individual)
3. The individual as opposed to the collective, the social, sociological, and political definition of the individual.
(*Dictionnaire de la Philosophie, Encyclopædia Universalis* 2000: 863)

Whatever the case may be, one thing is certain, the individual is not only a philosophical question, it remains something of a philosophical conundrum.

Individuals and the History of Ideas

As in our study of 'citizen', the lexeme 'individual' proved challenging for our research project. Three things tend to cloud our understanding of the trajectory of this lexeme as it emerges, evolves, and encrusts itself in everyday debates. Firstly, philosophical and religious debates, from Classical times down through the Middle Ages and into the Renaissance, tend to conflate 'individual' with other terms related to the part, the separate entity, or element. This situation is aggravated by translations from Latin. Secondly, dictionaries give the impression that the term is more widespread than it would appear to be, if our samples of texts can be trusted. And thirdly, the omnipresence of the lexeme 'individual' in twentieth century philosophy, and the social sciences, and bureaucratic and political rhetoric today tends to assume that what we conceive of as the 'individual' can be found in earlier texts. These impressions did not, however, coincide with our initial research findings.

Our original three million word corpus proved insufficient in the number of occurrences it provided: or at least we intuitively felt that these findings were misleading in that they did not correspond to our persisting impression that 'individual' is a historically crucial keyword in the Anglo culture. We decided, therefore, to make use of the same extended corpus used for the study of 'citizen', a nine million word corpus of texts from thinkers and philosophers. Furthermore, as our corpora findings indicated that 'individual' was more current in modern American than in British English, the works of the American philosophers of the turn of century, William James and John Dewey, were added to the existing history of ideas corpus. This revised and extended corpus provided more satisfying results.

In British English, 'individual' starts to take root in the seventeenth century, as the *OED* and *Merriam-Webster* confirm. The English philosopher Francis Bacon uses 'individual', 'particular individuals', and the adjectival form 'individual life' in his *Essays* (1597, http://www.gutenberg.org/ebooks/575). In his *Leviathan* (1651), the sixteenth-century philosopher Hobbes contrasts the 'universall' with 'the individuall' (https://www.gutenberg.org/files/3207/3207-h/3207-h.htm). His use of the double 'll' initially defied our corpus analysis search for 'individual', but the concept certainly does appear, in both noun and adjectival form. However – unlike Bacon who was writing a generation or two before him – Hobbes follows the French syntax (popular in his times but not obligatory) in making the adjective follow the noun:

Hobbes speaks of the 'constitution individuall', and the 'world universall' (1651, https://www.gutenberg.org/files/3207/3207-h/3207-h.htm). It is perhaps Hobbes' concern for the judiciary that inclines him to Latinate syntax: at any rate, the examples in which he uses 'individuall', often concern 'Injurie', 'Injustice', and 'any individuall person injured', and 'care applyed to Individualls', which all relate to the civil rights of individuals. Hobbes' examples relate to the relationship between the Human Law of the Commonwealth, and 'Naturall Law'. On the whole, Hobbes tends to read 'individual' into the texts that inspire him. As we have seen, the Bible does not know 'individual' any more than Adam and Eve know sin; but Hobbes does not hesitate to speak of Adam and Eve as sinning in Eden 'in their individuall persons'. Consequently, when he quotes the Scripture, Hobbes quotes 'man', but when he comments upon 'men', he translates the concepts into the emerging socio-legalistic concept of his times, as the 'individuall'. This should be clear in the following example:

> And though there be many places that affirm Everlasting Fire, and Torments (into which men may be cast successively one after another for ever;) yet I find none that affirm there shall bee an Eternall Life therein of **any individuall person**; but on the contrary, an Everlasting Death, which is the Second Death: (Apoc. 20. 13,14.) 'For after Death, and the Grave shall have delivered up the dead which were in them, and **every man** be judged according to his works; Death and the Grave shall also be cast into the Lake of Fire. This is the Second Death.' Whereby it is evident, that there is to bee a Second Death of every one that shall bee condemned at the day of Judgement, after which hee shall die no more. (1651, https://www.gutenberg.org/files/3207/3207-h/3207-h.htm)

This is an important contrast in two respects. Firstly, it indicates that the concept of the individual is emerging within the sphere of a Christian worldview. Secondly, it suggests that that worldview is going through a process of transition in which the fundamental concept of individuality is being integrated and revised. This is crucial: but it should not be overstated for all that. For in fact Hobbes uses 'man' and 'woman' and 'person' far more often than he uses 'individuall'.

And Locke, writing at the beginning of the eighteenth century, uses the lexeme 'individual' only seventeen times, in his work on human understanding. Is it possible today to imagine a work on human understanding and consciousness – a work on cognition, psychology or social rights – that would use 'individual' less than half a dozen times per page? How are we to explain this? In the seventeenth and eighteenth centuries, 'self' and 'soul' are still competing for the turf that 'individual' will come to dominate in the modern social sciences. Consequently, the relative rarity of 'individual' is a general phenomenon. In oral English, it would appear to be rare, considering the language of the English folk that comes down to us in written down reported speech, prose, and verse. It is also significant that the *Penguin Dictionary of Idioms* has only one reference to 'individual', suggesting it is as rare in speech as it is in the literature of our and former times. This tends to be confirmed by the fact that the philosophers that use the term appear to be introducing it rather than reaffirming an established key concept of modern thought and everyday life.

It is possible that 'individual' encounters some resistance. A certain number of instances seem to imply that the term 'individuall' is negative for the less than optimistic Hobbes, who is more concerned with 'everlasting fire' and damnation than with everlasting life. When he speaks of dissent, he uses individuals, and his definition of the church depends upon a distinction between a group of individuals and the body of the church. In his words, the excommunicated are 'no more a Church, but a dissolute number of individuall persons'. This posits the 'individuall' as fundamentally 'individualistic', as if it is somehow 'anti-religious'.

Later uses among eighteenth-century thinkers do not appear to carry any particular negative connotations, on the other hand. They rather imply a neutral, would-be-objective usage. For the Scottish Enlightenment philosopher, David Hume (1711–1776), for example, 'the individual':

> is a principle generally received in philosophy that everything in nature is individual, and that it is utterly absurd to suppose a triangle really existent, which has no precise proportion of sides and angles.
>
> Abstract ideas are therefore in themselves individual, however they may become general in their representation.
>
> The word raises up an individual idea, along with a certain custom; and that custom produces any other individual one, for which we may have occasion.
>
> (Examples quoted from *An Inquiry into Human Understanding*, 1748, cited in http://www.gutenberg.org/ebooks/9662)

Neutral usages become more widespread in Hume's times, it would appear. Phrases such as 'one individual', 'individuals', and 'individual ideas' and 'individuality' are gradually taking hold in Scottish philosophical debates towards the end of the eighteenth century. Hume expresses something that appears to him as self-evident when he says that 'individuals are collected together, ... placed under a general term with a view to that resemblance, which they bear to each other' (1748, http://www.gutenberg.org/ebooks/9662). And Hume discussed the mind and the imagination in terms of 'the individual'.

From Hume and the Romantics onwards, definitions of understanding, creativity, and speculation would become dependent upon such conceptions of the individual imagination. And right down to T. S. Eliot's and George Orwell's defence of individual creativity, it was the creativity and the truth of the individual perspective that was at stake. During the Cold War, condemnations of socialist conceptions of shared class consciousness and censorship were shaped in terms of the defence of individual free speech. It was the individual's writings as a form of free expression that was championed. His or her 'individuality' was seen to be almost sacrosanct. This is the 'individuality' that T. S. Eliot, the free verse modernist poet and theoretician, was defending when he wrote 'Art and the Individual Talent' (an essay written in 1920; see Eliot 1998). This short essay was to become a framework for thinking about aesthetics in the post-war period, and though he converted to Anglican Catholicism in 1928, Eliot saw no reason to revise his conviction that the individual was of paramount importance: individuality was not individualism for him; individual conscience was part of Christian faith, and the choice, or leap, that faith requires.

The seventeenth-century Scottish philosopher of economics and ethics, Adam Smith, was using 'individual' in a very 'pragmatic' way, around the same time as his compatriot, Hume. The following example is characteristic of his usage of the concept, and it is easy to see from it why Smith would become such an inspiration to American pragmatism in the late nineteenth and early twentieth centuries.

> ... every individual who is able to work is more or less employed in useful labour, and endeavours to provide, as well as he can, the necessaries and conveniencies [sic] of life, for himself, and such of his family or tribe as are either too old, or too young, or too infirm, to go a-hunting and fishing. (Smith, *Wealth of Nations*, 1776, http://www.gutenberg.org/ebooks/3300)

There is one essential distinction, however, in Smith's usage of the term. While the American post-war right-wing exalts the individual and sees him as a champion towering above his fellow men, and society as a whole, when Adam Smith uses the term 'individual' it is invariably connected to others. The individual exists for the good of society as a whole throughout Smith's moral and economic philosophy. For Smith, if the individual must be respected, it is because he is constantly working for and with society, aiding it in its overall shared well-being as a shared social project. This is the ethical Scottish Enlightenment conception of the 'individual'. And as a paradigm it will connect words and concepts in a way that differs from the way they are harnessed in the contemporary Anglo worldview. When Smith speaks of 'wealthy individuals' he is not concerned with 'tax havens' and the protection of property, but about taxation and sharing riches. He is concerned with the 'conduct of individuals' and their 'misconduct': their liberties, rights, and obligations, on the one hand, and the punishment of those who do not fulfil their obligations to their fellow citizens on the other.

Smith even conceives of laws and regulations as abstract but necessary forms of social links that meaningfully bind individuals together as such, though they do not know one another, and can hardly fathom how they are in fact bound to one another for their mutual well-being. This becomes clear in the following example:

> A regulation which obliges all those of the same trade in a particular town to enter their names and places of abode in a public register, facilitates such assemblies. It connects individuals who might never otherwise be known to one another, and gives every man of the trade a direction where to find every other man of it. (1776, http://www.gutenberg.org/ebooks/3300)

This certainly places the individual at the heart of society at any rate. Similarly, when John Stuart Mill begins writing his famous *On Liberty*, the individual has really begun to assert itself as a fundamental concept, and it appears to be becoming the key principle upon which bourgeois liberalism is based. True, the lexeme 'individual' is used much more rarely by Mill than by contemporary political and philosophical writers, but the concept can, nonetheless, be seen to be crucial from the fact that *On Liberty* opens with the concept in its very first sentence.

> The subject of this Essay is not the so-called Liberty of the Will, so unfortunately opposed to the misnamed doctrine of Philosophical Necessity; but Civil, or Social Liberty: the nature and limits of the power which can be legitimately exercised by society over the individual. (1859, https://www.gutenberg.org/files/34901/34901-h/34901-h.htm)

Mill is championing the rights of the individual in the face of three forces, the continuing monarchy, the interests of capital and the bourgeoisie, and the emerging State.

If we turn to America, we see America turning back to the Old Continent, Europe. The James brothers are symptomatic of this inclination. Like his brother, the famous novelist Henry James (1843–1916) who spent much of his life between Europe and the US, the great American thinker and psychologist, William James, remained very 'European'. William James was the author of a highly influential text, *Pragmatism: A New Name for Some Old Ways of Thinking*, first published in 1907, a work that was to have lasting influence upon the American worldview. James dedicated that book to 'the Memory of John Stuart Mill from whom I first learned the pragmatic openness of mind and whom my fancy likes to picture as our leader were he alive to-day' (James, *Pragmatism*, 1907, http://www.gutenberg.org/ebooks/5116).

The idealistic conception of the individual running through the works of Mill and James is palpable: throughout his works, James defended philosophy as a personal expression of individual existence:

> For the philosophy which is so important in each of us is not a technical matter; it is our more or less dumb sense of what life honestly and deeply means. It is only partly got from books; it is **our individual way of just seeing and feeling** the total push and pressure of the cosmos. (James, *Pragmatism*, 1907, http://www.gutenberg.org/ebooks/5116; emphasis added)

James was concerned with the way reason, feeling and faith converge to help us gain a balanced and accurate impression of experience:

> Rationalism usually considers itself more religious than empiricism ... It is a true claim when **the individual rationalist** is what is called a man of feeling, and when **the individual empiricist**

prides himself on being hard-headed. (James, *Pragmatism*, 1907, http://www.gutenberg.org/ebooks/5116; emphasis added)

But James himself lectured on religious experience, and recorded those lectures in his famous work published in 1902 that remains a classic today, *The Varieties of Religious Experience* (http://www.gutenberg.org/ebooks/621). He did not consider himself 'hard-headed'. His pragmatic individualism was concerned with the way men of feeling empirically feel and think their way towards reality, and the way they reach out beyond it.

His pragmatism did not turn its back on culture. His is not the empiricism of the here and now that fails to appreciate culture, dreams and aspirations. Tradition and creativity converge in the individual who makes something new from something old and enduring. The individual both reaffirms and reanimates tradition:

> The observable process which Schiller and Dewey particularly singled out for generalization is the familiar one by which any individual settles into new opinions. The process here is always the same. **The individual** has a stock of old opinions already, but he meets a new experience that puts them to a strain. (James, *Pragmatism*, 1907, http://www.gutenberg.org/ebooks/5116; emphasis added)

The individual both contains and transforms culture. This is very different from a kind of objectifying individualism that was taking hold of thinkers of his times. James was fundamentally hostile to the kind of determinism that would emerge from the post-Hegelian Marxists who portrayed the individual as a mere expression of social forces at work. Society may act upon men and women, but it does not 'produce' them as an unthinking objects. James grasped that men and women mould society as much as they are moulded by it. This explains why he celebrated individuals and denounced all those who denigrated them or diminished them:

> Determinists, who deny it, who say that **individual men** originate nothing, but merely transmit to the future the whole push of the past cosmos of which they are so small an expression, diminish man. (James, *Pragmatism*, 1907, http://www.gutenberg.org/ebooks/5116; emphasis added)

John Dewey was part of the same Pragmatist movement as James, who was his senior by seventeen years. Dewey employed the psychology that he was developing in his New School system, and he remains a major reference in pedagogy throughout the world today for his innovative and humanistic form of liberalism. Seeing education not as a means of getting individuals to fit into society as conformist workers, but as a means of ensuring they would develop as individual human beings, Dewey was closer in spirit to Wilhelm von Humboldt who founded the Berlin University based on the conception of education as *Bildung*, the development of individual feeling and understanding, the cultivation of both the senses and the mind. Creating creative human beings is a thread which links Kant, Humboldt, Mill, James, and Dewey in a vibrant idealistic but pragmatic project for human beings and society. And individualism is inseparable from that idealistic project that was to be put in practice.

Rather than seeing the individual child as a *tabula rasa* upon which to project a preconceived instruction, Dewey stressed the need for educators to understand where the individual student came from:

> We look for an account of social antecedents; a description of early surroundings, of the conditions and occupation of the family; of the chief episodes in the development of character; of signal struggles and achievements; of **the individual's hopes, tastes, joys and sufferings**. (Dewey, *Democracy and Education*, 1916, http://www.gutenberg.org/files/852/852-h/852-h.htm; emphasis added)

Dewey considered individuals as the individual 'elements' or 'units' of culture, and he was not putting them above culture, he was putting them in context when he suggested:

> **Each individual, each unit** who is the carrier of the life-experience of his group, in time passes away. Yet the life of the group goes on. (Dewey, *Democracy and Education*, 1916, http://www.gutenberg.org/files/852/852-h/852-h.htm; emphasis added)

The idealism of James and Dewey was not naïve. And as a pragmatist, Dewey realized that people often 'use' one another. As he put it:

> **Individuals use one another so as to get desired results**, without reference to the emotional and intellectual disposition and

consent of those used. (Dewey, *Democracy and Education*, 1916, http://www.gutenberg.org/files/852/852-h/852-h.htm; emphasis added)

For Dewey, however, education must never be about using people or forcing things upon them. Besides being immoral, Dewey believed this was ultimately counterproductive. We cannot force ideas and attitudes upon people. We must understand where they are coming from to guide them to where they are going. This enlightened individualism takes us beyond the nature–nurture debate. For Dewey, we exist within society as society exists within us. In order to cultivate individuals, we must understand how they see things, how they feel, and why they behave in a given way. We must seek to understand their values and the way they seek approval in other peoples' eyes. Once we have done this, we will know how to guide them and influence not only their actions but their deeper desires and convictions.

> The required beliefs cannot be hammered in; the needed attitudes cannot be plastered on. But the particular medium in which an **individual** exists leads him to see and feel one thing rather than another; it leads him to have certain plans in order that he may act successfully with others; it strengthens some beliefs and weakens others as a condition of winning the approval of others. Thus it gradually produces in him a certain system of behavior, a certain disposition of action. The words 'environment,' 'medium' denote something more than surroundings which encompass an **individual**. (Dewey, *Democracy and Education*, 1916, http://www.gutenberg.org/files/852/852-h/852-h.htm; emphasis added)

These words are light years away from Hobbes' tentative and sceptical uses of 'indivduall'. Indeed, they take us far beyond Mill's conception of individual human liberties with his concomitant doubts about individualism. Here we have a fully fledged programme for society and for both the men and women who people it, and the children who recreate it with each generation. James and Dewey share an enthusiasm for individualism that is far more convincing and appealing than the versions their British fellow philosophers and thinkers offer us.

Provisional Conclusions

James and Dewey represent the high point in American enlightened individualism. For our purposes, in this study of how keywords are used, and how frequently, they offer us impressive results. They both use 'individual' frequently. Dewey often uses the word several times on a single page, but this is not so remarkable. In this, he is perfectly consistent with the discourse of his contemporaries working in the social sciences. For both James and Dewey, the individual is the cornerstone of modern psychology, philosophy, and education.

In this respect, both James and Dewey are very American. The English, from Shakespeare's times to the Brexit crisis, tend to invest heavily in tradition, and time-worn solutions. But this is not the frontier spirit. This is not the spirit of a nation creating itself from 'nothing'. James and Dewey are concerned with how we create individuals, cultivate and educate them, on the one hand, and way individuals sustain society, on the other. They see education as a means of moulding children, but not manipulating them. These thinkers do not 'target' individuals as modern publicity does. Nor are they concerned with simply ascribing individuals social rights as passive recipients: this is arguably what the European Parliament or the individual Member States do, judging from the way the word is used on the European Union website (https://europa.eu/european-union/index_en).

James and Dewey are interested in individuals as actors. Their pragmatism, their explanations, and their objectives are all very American, but they are also very moral and very much in tune with the school and the university as institutions of the Enlightenment. Their concept of individualism is perfectly in tune with Kant's conviction that individual freedom is the necessary prerequisite of all worthwhile thinking and creativity.

This is a far cry from many of the demands for individual freedom that come from the market today. The various forms of rampant individualism that are denounced in our Spanish, Czech, and German sources would not be considered tenable demands in the eyes of James and Dewey. Their convictions are of an entirely different nature. They were interested in the development of the individual and the development of society as a social project sustained by the interaction of groups of individuals.

In this chapter, up till now, we have been going through sociology, philosophy, and religion to try to understand better how the various words and phrases related to the individual work. This has involved considering how the individual is enrooted in various periods, various cultures. And it has led us to explore different philosophies of the relationship between the part and the whole in society. As we can see, a great diversity of usages of the individual come into play. Fundamental oppositions underpin our conceptions of the role of the individual in society.

These dynamic oppositions change over time, just as they change from linguistic community to linguistic community. Some essential traits seem to prevail throughout the West, however. The term 'individual' becomes increasingly common in the modern era, especially towards the end of the nineteenth century. The individual is a vibrant concept in the twentieth century. The communists may condemn individualism, but they certainly sustain 'individualism' and the 'individual', as key concepts, in contrast to which they erect their own collective ideals. This partly explains why, since the breakdown of the Soviet Union, individualism has had fewer and fewer critics. The church put the brakes on individualism in Mill's times back in the nineteenth century. But the failing influence of the church in the West has tended to mean critiques of 'individualistic behaviour' have become less voluble.

Our sources show the concept of individuality to be subject to change. The individual is the object of much contention and debate. This inevitably makes it difficult to pin 'individual' down as a keyword. It adapts and reinvents itself as the cultural context changes. Our study leaves us with a complex, dynamic, and paradoxical concept. This may be disconcerting, but the impression of 'individuality' that has emerged should at least have achieved two things. It should help us to avoid setting up individualism as a Western ideal. And it should make us wary of falling into the Cold War clichés which present the West as the defender of individualism and human rights. Individualism may be a contemporary value espoused by European Member States, but both Europe and individualism have very complex traditions.

For this reason, trying to grasp how another culture understands European individualism should prove interesting. Such a project would take us far beyond the scope of this book, but investigating the way the concept of the individual migrates from Europe and takes on new meanings in China should enable us both to understand something of China's experience, and something about the concept of individualism itself. As we saw, the Czech communists and Mill, the champion of liberalism, and the church, all share doubts about individualism. As we consider what forms of individualism were adopted in China, we must leave behind the Cold War propaganda of a West championing individual freedoms and rights, and an East enclosed in oppressive mechanisms oppressing individuals. Investigating the way the concept of the 'individual' has emerged in the Chinese worldview may even reveal something about Europeans and the values they cherish.

WORDS FOR INDIVIDUAL AND INDIVIDUALISM IN CHINESE[1]

In the 'Marginal Notes to: Friedrich Paulsen, A System of Ethics' (*"Lúnlǐxué yuánlǐ" pīzhù* 《伦理学原理》批注) written between 1917 and 1918 (according to Wǔ and Jiāng 1996: 69), Máo Zédōng 毛泽东 claimed that:

> 事固先有个人而后有团体，个人离团体固不能独存，然团体无意思，其有意思仍系集合个人之意思也。… 且团体者乃个人，乃大个人也。人一身乃集许多小个体而成，社会乃集许多个人而成 … (quoted by Wǔ & Jiāng 1996: 69)

> It is a fact that there are individuals before there is a group, and that individuals cannot exist alone apart from the group, but the group in itself has no meaning, it only has meaning as a collectivity of individuals. ... Furthermore the group is an individual, a greater individual. The human body is constructed of the aggregation of a number of individual parts, and society is constructed of aggregation of a number of individual persons. (Mao 1992: 208)

In these lines from Máo, the relationship between the individual, the group, and society is stressed. Máo adopted two words:

- the word *gèrén* 个人, that was destined to become the most widely used term for 'individual';
- the expression *dà gèrén* 大个人 ('a greater individual'), also found in early twentieth-century writings on the individual and individualism.

In the same essay Máo affirmed that 'society is created by individuals not individuals by society' (社会为个人而设，非个人为社会而设也). Moreover, he claimed that 'all values depend on individuals' (百般之价值依个人而存). We also find the expression 'spiritual individualism' (in

Chinese *jīngshén zhī gèrénzhǔyì* 精神之个人主义): 'this is an individualism of the spirit and may be called spiritual individualism' (此个人主义乃为精神的，可谓之精神之个人主义). According to Huang (2007: 3), Máo's spiritual individualism 'was the result of a hybridization of the traditional Confucianism with the newly imported German idealism and nationalism, emphasizing individual development and fulfilment as the foundation of the Chinese nation-building project'. Once more we find that concepts are migrating from Europe, but not necessarily from French or English. And the concept will be radically redefined within the Chinese worldview as it undergoes transformation in the revolutionary era.

This merging of Western and Chinese intellectual traditions within the Chinese worldview can be regarded as an essential element of the early twentieth-century Chinese discourse on the individual and individualism. This discourse was also characterized by the link that was forged to fuse this affirmation of the individual with an ideology promoting national liberation, on the one hand, and a transformation of society, on the other.

The words *gèrén* and *gèrénzhǔyì* have a complex and controversial history in modern and contemporary China. They have been celebrated, exalted, and demonized. They have been overshadowed, marginalized, and rehabilitated. And they have been debated again and again. For instance, in the 1907 essay *On the Misorientation of Culture* (*Wénhuà piānzhì lùn* 文化偏至论, quoted by Jī 2008: 155), the father of modern Chinese literature, Lǔ Xùn 鲁迅 (1881–1936), affirmed the need to investigate the real meaning (夷考其实) of the word *gèrén* (个人一语). According to Lǔ, the word *gèrén* was already subject to misunderstanding only a few years after its introduction into China (入中国未三四年). Lǔ claimed it was wrongly associated with 'self-centeredness at the expense of others' (迷误为害人利己之义, English translated by Liu 1996: 12).

In this section, it is important to gain an overview of this keyword's history and the semantic trajectories that the individual and individualism have followed. This should enable us to begin to grasp connotations that become associated with the terms used and the way each term is used within different periods. That's why we shall begin by comparing and contrasting the various synonyms that were adopted to designate these concepts in the late Qing period, when a massive process of translation was taking place that entailed accommodating foreign words and concepts (Lackner et al. 2001; Liu 1995: 26).

It is not our intention in this chapter to analyse issues related to the pertinence of the individual, the self, and individualism, or the place they hold within the Chinese language and culture. That would be a daunting endeavour that would take us far beyond the purposes of the present chapter. Besides, these questions have been discussed in detail in other contexts in recent decades (for instance by Hansen 1983, 1985; Brindley 2010).

According to Shun (2004: 184), the questions 'about the applicability of these Western notions to Confucian thought' are to be regarded as a 'terminological issue'. According to him, the answer 'depends in part on how we construe the notions under consideration'. Lydia Liu, for her part, moreover, underlines that questions about the 'correspondence' or 'equivalence' between terms and notions in Western and Chinese traditions are 'rather dubious because they overlook the fact that the 'trope of equivalence' between English and Chinese words 'has been established only recently in the process of translation and fixed by means of modern bilingual dictionaries' (Liu 1995: 7–8). 'Trope of equivalence' is a key concept for Liu (1995: 7–8) and it proves to be a fundamental for understanding our migrating meanings. Lui defines this concept in the following terms:

> ... when knowledge passes from the guest language to the host language, it inevitably takes on new meanings in its new historico-linguistic environment; the translation remains connected with the original idea and, perhaps no less, than a *trope of equivalence*. Everything else must be determined by the users of the host language. (Liu 1995: 60)

The following paragraphs will therefore focus on various synonyms for individual and individualism found in the translations, essays, and multilingual dictionaries that appeared in the late Qing period. According to Lackner et al. (2001b), this period shows a process of 'negotiating equivalences' between Western inspired notions (and Western words) and Chinese reconceptualization. This process was already well underway in the late Ming and early Qing periods.

Terms for Individual and Individualism in the Late Qing Period

In the Chinese translation of J. S. Mills' *On Liberty*, which was first published in 1903, Yán Fù 严复 (1854–1921) rendered the English term 'individual' as *xiǎojǐ* 小己. This word can be translated literally as 'small self': *xiǎo* 小 means 'small' and *jǐ* 己 is a word widely used in Classical Chinese to define 'oneself as contrasted to others' (Shun 2004: 187). In this sense, it refers 'to the self in a reflexive and emphatic manner as well as to one's actual person' (Brindley 2010: xxviii). In Yán's translation, this word is also used in the expression *xiǎojǐ zhī zìyáo* 小己之自繇, to translate 'individual independence'. The title of the chapter 'Of the Limits to the Authority of Society over the Individual' is rendered by Yán as *Lùn guóqún xiǎojǐ quán xiàn zhī fēnjiè* 论国群小己权限之分界. In this title, the word 'society' is translated as *guóqún* 国群 (a word formed from binding together *guó*, 'country', and *qún*, 'group'). Individual is rendered as *xiǎojǐ* (lit. 'small self'). Otherwise, the title of Mills' work, *On Liberty*, has been translated as *Qún jǐ quán jiè lùn* 群己权界论, that is, 'On the boundary between the rights of society and the rights of the individual' (according to Wright's translation, 2001: 236). Here the above-mentioned form *jǐ* (lit. 'self, oneself') is used to designate the individual.

As Liu (1995: 82) underlines, the words *jǐ* and *xiǎojǐ*, which are used to translate both 'individual' and 'self', are derived from Classical Chinese philosophy, 'although with a radical and important shift of meaning'. Huáng (2004: 45, 47) also stresses the Confucian echo of these words, affirming that Yán Fù had shifted the focus to stress the relation between society and the individual (嚴復卻把焦點轉移到群己關係), thereby conceiving of the concept of individual in a Confucian manner (嚴復對個人的肯定是一種儒家式的). Huáng explains Yán Fù's choice of the term *xiǎojǐ* as follows:

> 「小己」源於《史記》，其實與日本人所譯的「個人」類似，但嚴復不採「個人」而用「小己」，主要是因為「小己」一詞隱含了由小到大、由己到群的意涵。(Huáng 2004: 46)

The [expression] *xiǎojǐ* came from the *Records of an Historian*:[3] it was similar to the word *gèrén* used in Japanese translations, but Yán Fù preferred using *xiǎojǐ* instead of *gèrén*, chiefly because it implies the connotation of a shift from the small to the big, from the self to the group.

This translation for 'individual' clearly highlights the social and political dimension of the concept. The 'individual' is conceived in terms of his or her relationship with the group, the society, or the country.

The term *xiǎojǐ* was later to be dropped, and is no longer in current use today. Nevertheless, it made a great impact during in late Qing and early republican periods. For instance, this term was adopted by Gāo Yīhán 高一涵 in the essay *Zìzhì yǔ zìyóu* 自治與自由 (1916). Gāo distinguished between *xiǎojǐ* 小己 (lit. 'small or lesser self'), that is, the individual, and *dàjǐ* 大己 (lit. 'great or greater self') 'visualizing the self in society at large' (Svarverud 2010: 216).

The relationship between the individual and the society was expressed by various oppositions and series of words. Among these were the antonymic adjectives 'small' and 'great' (Liu 1995: 92). Besides *xiǎojǐ* 小己 and *dàjǐ* 大己, this relationship was expressed by the pair *xiǎowǒ* 小我 and *dàwǒ* 大我. These words can be literally translated as 'small or smaller self' and 'great or greater self', as *wǒ* 我 is the currently used word for 'I' or 'me'. These words were adopted by the writer Hú Shì 胡适 (1891–1962) in the essay *Bùxiǔ - wǒ de zōngjiào* 不朽——我的宗教 'Immortality-my religion' (1919), in which we can read:

> 我這個"小我"不是獨立存在的，是和無量數小我有直接或間接的交互關係；是和社會的全體和世界的全體都有互為影響的關係的。[...]"大我"是永遠不滅的。"小我"是有死的，"大我"是永遠不死的。(Hú 2013: 60)

> I—this 'lesser self' (*xiaowo*)—do not exist independently. I am in direct or indirect relationship with myriads of lesser selves, with the whole of society and with the entire world, influencing one another. ... the 'greater self' lives on eternally, flowing inexorably like running water. The lesser self will disappear, the greater self will not. (Translated by Fung 2010: 154–155)

The notion of 'greater self' or 'greater individual' was also expressed by the form *dà gèrén* 大个人, as in the above-mentioned essay by Máo Zédōng ('the group is an individual, a greater individual', Mao 1992: 208).

The terms currently used for 'individual', *gèrén* 个人 (traditional characters 個人) and *gètǐ* 个体 (traditional characters 個體) were widely used in late nineteenth-century dictionaries and translations. In these sources, we can also find the derived word *gèrénzhǔyì* 个人主义 'individualism', formed by adding the suffixoid *-zhǔyì*, corresponding to the English suffix '-ism'.

For instance, the word *gèrén* 个人 'individual' and *gèrénzhǔyì* 个人主义 'individualism' are both listed in the *Xīn ěryǎ* 新尔雅 dictionary[4] by Wāng Róngbǎo 汪荣宝 and Yè Lán 叶澜, which was published in Shanghai in 1903. Both terms were also listed in *A Dictionary of Philosophical Terms: Chiefly from the Japanese* (Richard and MacGillivray 1913). The intermediary role that the Japanese language played in the way the word *gèrénzhǔyì* spread to Chinese has been underlined by Liu (1995: 83): 'This neologism, like many others, was invented by Meiji intellectuals in Japan, to translate Western liberal and nationalist theories of individualism (*kojin shuji*)'.

The word *gèrén* was adopted by reformist intellectuals between the end of the nineteenth and the early twentieth centuries. For instance, Liáng Qǐchāo, one of the leading figures of the Hundred Day Reform Movement, adopted this word in the essay *Xīnmínshuō* 新民说 (see Chapters 1 and 2), underlying the importance of individual responsibility, which should precede group responsibility (勿徒以之責望諸團體，而先以之責望諸個人; quoted by Yáng 2004: 32).

In the essay *Jìnshì dì yī dà zhé Kāngdé zhī xuéshuō* 近世第一大哲康德之学说 'The Theories of the Greatest Philosopher of the Modern World, Kant' (1903), Liáng emphasized the individual's responsibility in relation to the State (個人對於國家之責). In this essay, we also find the expression *gèrén zhī zìyóu* 個人之自由 'individual freedom' or 'freedom of individuals'. Yáng (2004: 27) points out that Liáng Qǐchāo tried to legitimize and explain the importance of individual autonomy and freedom in the context of a search for national salvation and self-strengthening (梁啟超則是在追求富國強兵的考慮下，反過來就所擬建置國家政治的性質與結構，考慮如何正當化 (legitimize) 和說明個人自由與自治的內涵和重要性。). As Liu (1995: 88) stresses, in Liáng's writings the interests of the state predominate over the individual, and the liberty of the people and nation over the individual freedom, because 'the violence of the encounter with the West forces nationhood upon selfhood' (Liu 1995: 10). The political dimension of the notion of the individual in Liáng Qǐchāo's writings is also highlighted by Zarrow (2012: 87) who affirms that: 'the individual naturally represented a private realm, which thus was not a residual category--left over after the public sphere is defined--but an essential part of the late Qing reconceptualization of the political'.

The other current form, *gètǐ* 个体 (個體), was already listed with the meaning of 'individual' in the *Tetsugaku jii* (*Dictionary of Philosophy*) by Inoue Tetsujirô and Ariga Hisao, published in Tokyo in 1884. The form *gètǐlùn* 个体论 for 'individualism' was listed in the *Chinese New Terms and Expressions, with English Translations* by Morgan and Evan, published in Shanghai in 1913 (MCST). This derived word was formed by fusing the word *gètǐ* 个体 with *lùn* 论, which means 'theory' or 'doctrine', and was used as a suffixoid corresponding to the English '-ism'.

As already underlined, the words *gètǐ* and *gèrén*, which today are the main words used as corresponding concepts for 'individual', were not the only terms used during late Qing China. Numerous synonyms were widespread in the late Qing period, but they were dropped in the following decades. Among the alternative Chinese concepts for individual we find the following:

- *gèzì* 各自, which translates literally as 'each and all of you', or 'each for yourselves' (MCST) in Inoue Tetsujirô and Ariga Hisao's *Tetsugaku jii* (*Dictionary of Philosophy*, 1884),
- *rén* 人 (lit. 'man, human being'), was listed in Kwong Ki-chiu's *English and Chinese Dictionary*, whose first edition dates from 1882,
- *dú* 独 (lit. 'alone', 'independent'), was found in the same source, as was,
- *dān* 单 (lit. 'single member', 'individual single person'),
- *sī* 私 (lit. 'private') (MCST).

According to the MCST, *dú* 独 'usually has no nuances of loneliness, but can sometimes come to connote an intense feeling of personal uniqueness'. The word *dān* 单 is described as the antonym of *qún* 群 'group', 'in a group', and 'has no emotional nuances and simply refers to the single member of a set' (MCST).

Sī 私 is a word in Classical Chinese that covers various meanings and connotations, both positive and negative. In the MCST, *sī* 私 is defined as 'the dominant current word for privacy', being a term that 'focuses on the aspect of discreetness in secrecy' as opposed to *gōng* 公, which indicates openness. It is also 'the standard word for selfishness in classical Chinese' (MCST). Moreover, 'the word designates everything that falls outside the responsibility of public administration'. As we saw in Chapter 2, *sī* 私 is the antonym of *gōng* 公, signifying 'public' (MCST).

The form *zìwǒ* 自我 'self', on the other hand, was also used to translate the notion of the individual (Liu 1995: 82). *Zìwǒ* 自我 can also mean 'ego' in the *Zhéxué gàilùn* 哲学概论 'An Outline of Philosophy' published in 1902, which is Wáng Guówéi's 王国维 Chinese translation of Kuwaki Genyoku's 桑木嚴翼 work. In *A Dictionary of Philosophical Terms: Chiefly from the Japanese* (Richard and MacGillivray 1913), this term is considered an equivalent of the English term, 'self'. Individuality is clearly a slippery notion: and for this reason, Liu introduces 'slippage' to explain the way it is reconceptualized. According to Liu (1995: 83), 'the slippage of *ziwo, wo, geren, gewei, geti* and *ji* not only inherits the slippage of words between self and individual in the English original, but reflects the complex scenario of translingual practice and its politics in the Chinese context'.

It should be clear by now, that we are not simply translating European terms here. In order to begin to grasp the way notions take root and grow in Chinese, we must consider the traditions and currents of thought that condition and transform the Chinese worldview. The concepts of *zìwǒ, wǒ, gèrén, gèwèi, gètǐ*, and *jǐ* are not various partially satisfactory equivalents for 'individuality' in English, French, German, or Japanese. They are rich conceptual plants which cannot be understood by violently uprooting them from the linguistic, literary, cultural, and political contexts in which they live. Only by accepting that European paradigms must be left behind can we hope to intuit the real scope of such terms and the subtle networks of meanings they evoke.

The process of lexical formation, and the vast number of terms borrowed from Europe and from (or via) Japan are part of the great transformation the Chinese language was undergoing during the Qing period. Translating 'individual' reveals this state of affairs all too clearly. The ambivalence of Chinese terms related to individuality, and their semantic instability, are characteristic of the transformation of the Chinese lexicon that was taking place in late imperial and early republican periods. The so-called 'equivalences' between the Western words for 'self', 'individual', 'individualism', and the corresponding Chinese translations were established during the nineteenth century and in the first years of the twentieth century using neologisms, loans, and return graphic loans.[4] Moreover, after the end of the imperial period, the words for individual and individualism became central in debates and writings, and they 'achieved enormous popularity in the New Culture movement' (Liu 1995: 80).

Individual and Individualism in the First Decades of the Twentieth Century: Terms and Concepts

Numerous essays published during the first decades of the twentieth century prove how central the words *gèrén* and *gèrénzhǔyì* were to debates of those times. Among them Yán and Wáng (2011: 23) give the following examples:

- *Gèrén shuō* 个人说 'On the Individual' (Anonymous, 1906);
- *Lùn gèrén zhī zìyóu* 论个人之自由 'On the Freedom of the Individual' by Mèng Yáng 孟扬 (1913);
- *Gèrén zhī gǎigé* 个人之改革 'The Reform of the Individual' by Dù Yàquán 杜亚泉 (1914);
- *Gèrén yǔ guójiā zhī jiè shuō* 个人与国家之界说 'Definitions of the Individual and the State' also by Dù Yàquán (1917);
- *Gèrénzhǔyì yǔ guójiāzhǔyì* 个人主义与国家主义 'Individualism and Nationalism' by Liáng Qǐxūn 梁启勋 (1915);
- *Gèxìngzhǔyì yǔ gèrénzhǔyì* 个性主义与个人主义 'Individuality and Individualism' by Jiǎng Mènglín 蒋梦麟 (1920);
- *Gèrénzhǔyì yóulái jí qí yǐngxiǎng* 个人主义由来及其影响 'The Origins and the Development of Individualism' by Hú Shì 胡适 (1920);
- *Xūwú de gèrénzhǔyì jí rènzìránzhǔyì* 虚无的个人主义及任自然主义 'Nihilistic Individualism and *laissez-faire* Theory' by Chén Dúxiù 陈独秀 (1920).

These titles demonstrate the way the words *gèrén* and *gèrénzhǔyì* were gradually taking hold of the shared lexicon used in discussing political and social questions. But the discourse on individualism was not limited to these titles, as individualism is patently obvious in some synonyms which were to be abandoned in later years. One such example was the form *gèwèizhǔyì* 个位主义, used as the title of an essay by Jiā Yì 家义 that appeared in *Dōngfāng zázhì* 东方杂志 'Eastern Miscellany' in 1916. Furthermore, the topic of individualism was discussed in essays that do not themselves include the word 'individualism' in the title. The above-mentioned article, 'On the Misorientation of Culture' by Lǔ Xùn, is one such example.

The notions of the individual and individualism were central throughout the first decades of the twentieth century, a period that saw three key events: the end of the millennial Chinese empire (1911), the proclamation of the Republic, and the May Fourth Movement in 1919. Wang Hui (1996) insists on the historical context of the May Fourth Movement's claim for a renewal of Chinese society by explaining the interest in personal emancipation and individual affirmation. He claims that 'after the revolution of 1911, and particularly in the context of the anti-traditionalist May Fourth Cultural Movement, the concept of the individual was interpreted within the ideological framework of tradition and modernity, old and new' (Wang Hui 1996). He also points out that concepts such as 'individual' and 'individuality' came to be even more important than 'state', 'society', and 'family', because 'the liberation of the individual [was seen] as a prerequisite for the liberation of the collective, society and the state'.

In his history of modern Chinese thought, Lǐ Zéhòu 李泽厚 (2008: 11) argues that the affirmation of the individual resulted in strong criticism of the ideal of *xiào* 孝 'filial piety' (要变易 "家族本位主义", 否定传统纲常，首先便是反 "孝"), which was the core notion of the Confucian socio-political vision (Lǐ 2008: 10). Lǐ (2008: 10) underlines the two dimensions of this process:

当时这些知识者抨击"孝"有这两方面的论证:一是启蒙性，即追求个体从大家庭中冲决解放出来，以取得自由、平等、独立的权利和地位。一是政治性的，即揭露"孝"是"忠"的基础。

In this period, these intellectuals' criticisms against 'filial piety" were characterized by two aspects: one was enlightening, that is the pursuit of individual emancipation from the clan and the family, in order to obtain freedom, equality, independent rights and status; one was political, as the 'filial piety' is the basis of the 'loyalty' [to the superiors and to the ruler].

Lǐ Dàzhāo 李大钊 (1888–1927), one of the founders of the Chinese Communist Party, in the essay *Yóu jīngjì shàng jiěshì Zhōngguó jìndài sīxiǎng biàndòng de yuányīn* 由经济上解释中国近代思想变动的原因 (1920), published in the influential *New Youth* (*Xīn qīngnián* 新青年) magazine, claimed that:

孔子所谓修身，不是使人完成他的个性，乃是使人牺牲他的个性。牺牲个性的第一步就是尽"孝"。(Lǐ 1920)

Confucian self-cultivation does not aim to the accomplishment of individuality; it results in the sacrifice of individuality. The first step of this sacrifice is respect for 'filial piety'.

In this passage, we find another keyword related to the notions of the individual and individualism, *gèxìng* which can also be translated as 'individuality', as 'individual character', but also as 'personality'. This word is still in use. In Lǐ's quotation, we can observe the contrast between the two expressions containing the word *gèxìng*: *wánchéng*

... *gèxìng* 完成 ... 个性 'to accomplish' or 'to fulfil individuality' and *xīshēng gèxìng* 牺牲个性 'to sacrifice individuality'.

The word *gèxìng* was also used by Yù Dáfū 郁达夫 (1896–1945), one of the main modern Chinese writers, who claimed that since the May Fourth Movement, the development of modern prose could be attributed to the liberation of the individual(ity) (自五四以来，现代的散文是因个性的解放而滋长了; quoted in Yán and Wáng 2011). In this sentence, Yù adopted the expression *gèxìng de jiěfàng* 个性的解放, which can be translated as 'liberation of the individual' or the 'liberation of the individuality'. Yù also considered the 'expression of individuality' (*suǒ biǎoxiàn de gèxìng* 所表现的个性, lit. 'the individuality that is expressed') as the main feature of 'the new prose' (现代的散文之最大特征，是每一个作家的每一篇散文里所表现的个性).

In other contexts, the English word 'individuality' was also translated as *gèxìngzhǔyì* 个性主义 (formed by adding the affix-like formative –*zhǔyì*, '-ism'); this was the case in the essay 'Individuality and individualism' published by Jiǎng Mènglín 蒋梦麟 in 1920. Jiǎng explained the words individuality and individualism in the following terms:

何谓个性主义？　Individuality　曰以个人固有之特性而发展之……。
何谓个人主义？Individualism曰使个人享有自由平等之机会，而不为社会个人家庭所抑制也。(quoted in Gěng 2015: 5)

What is individuality [*gèxìngzhǔyì*]? *Individuality* [in English in the text] means developing the inherent characteristics of the individual [*gèrén*] ...
What is individualism [*gèrénzhǔyì*]? *Individualism* [in English in the text] means allowing individuals to enjoy freedom and equality of opportunity, without being inhibited by society and families.

According to Lǐ Zéhòu (2008: 11), it was another of the co-founders of the Chinese Communist Party, Chén Dúxiù 陈独秀 (1879–1942), who played a key role in promoting the Western-inspired notions of the individual and individualism instead of 'familism'[5] (以西方的个人主义来取代中国传统的集体主义). Chén Dúxiù clearly advocated individualism in his essay *Dōng xī mínzú gēnběn sīxiǎng zhī chāyì* 东西民族根本思想之差异, 'The fundamental difference between the intellectual tradition of Eastern and Western peoples', published in December 1915 in *New Youth*. At the time, that publication was called *Youth magazine*, and

Chén Dúxiù was its editor. In that essay, Chén identified the Western focus on individuals as one of the reasons for the West's strength, while the Eastern tendency to value the family and the clan was regarded as a source of weakness. Chén advocated 'replacing familism with individualism' (*yǐ gèrénběnwèizhǔyì yì jiāzúběnwèizhǔyì* 以个人本位主义易家族本位主义; quoted by Lǐ 2008: 12). In this sentence, Chen adopted the expression *gèrénběnwèizhǔyì*, literally 'theory centred on the individual' or 'individualcentrism'. In the same essay, we can also find the term *gèrénzhǔyì* for individualism, as in the expression *chúncuì gèrénzhǔyì zhī dà jīngshén* 纯粹个人主义之大精神 'the great spirit of the pure individualism'.

Chén Dúxiù also adopted the word *gèrén* in his writings on the individual in his essay *Rénshēng zhēn yì* 人生真义 'The true meaning of human life'. He affirmed that 'society is formed by individuals [*gèrén*]. Without individuals [*gèrén*], there can be no society. Consequently, the will and happiness of the individual [*gèrén*] deserve to be respected' (社会是个人集成的。除去个人，便没有社会；所以个人的意志和快乐，是应该尊重的; quoted by Lǐ 2008: 109).

Individualism (*gèrénzhǔyì*) was also advocated by the Chinese writer Zhōu Zuòrén 周作人, Lǔ Xùn's brother, in an essay entitled *Rén de wénxué* 人的文学 'A humane literature'. Zhōu called for 'a kind of individualistic humanism' (*yī zhǒng gèrénzhǔyì de rénjiānběnwèizhǔyì* 一种个人主义的人间本位主义, quoted by Yán and Wáng 2011). He believed that 'in order to reform society [*gǎizào shèhuì*], it is necessary to start by reforming the individual [*gǎizào gèrén*]' (改造社会，还要从改造个人做起, quoted by Fāng 2004).

Zhōu's vision of individualism has to be understood within the framework of his interest in the 'New village movement' and new forms of communal rural organization (Fāng 2004). This was strongly criticized by Hú Shì 胡适, one of the leading figures of New Culture movement. In his essay 'The new life which is not individualism' (*Fēi gèrénzhǔyì de xīn shēnghuó* 非个人主义的新生活), Hú criticized what he called *dúshàn de gèrénzhǔyì* 独善的个人主义, 'detached individualism' (Fung 2010: 154). According to Hú ([1920] 2015, this kind of individualism concerned people who were disappointed by society, and unable to cope with it, people who simply desired to escape and pursue an ideal life outside society (不满意于现社会，却又无可如何，只想跳出这个社会去寻一种超出现社会的理想生活). In the same essay, Hú Shì made reference to John Dewey, the American champion of enlightened American individualism we discussed above. Hú Shì, for his part, distinguished between 'false individualism' (*jiǎ de gèrénzhǔyì* 假的个人主义), which he considered to be equivalent to 'egoism' (*wèiwǒzhǔyì* 为我主义), and 'true individualism' *(zhēn de gèrén zhǔyì* 真的个人主义). According to Hú, 'true individualism' is characterized by 'independent thought' and involves an individual assuming 'full responsibility for the results or consequences of his own ideas and beliefs' (独立思想 ⋯ 二是个人对于自己思想信仰的结果要负完全责任).

Hú analysed the place of the individual and individualism in his other writings, such as those already mentioned: 'Immortality-my religion', 'Ibsenism' (*Yìbǔshēngzhǔyì* 易卜生主义, 1918), and 'Individual liberty and social progress: one more discussion on the May Fourth Movement' (*Gèrén zìyóu yǔ shèhuì jìnbù: zài tán wǔ sì yùndòng* 个人自由与社会进步：再谈五四运动, published in 1935).

More generally, during the first decades of the twentieth century there was much debate as to the place of individualism in Chinese society. For instance, the Chinese intellectual, Jiā Yì 家义 wrote an essay entitled *Gèwèizhǔyì* 个位主义 (a word for 'individualism' that was to be abandoned later) in the *Eastern Miscellany*. In that essay, he claimed that individualism was alien to the Chinese mind. Ironically, the British philosopher Bertrand Russell took up a position which is novel, but difficult to understand today. In the *Problem of China* (1922), Russell claimed that: 'Individualism has perished in the West, but in China it survives, for good as well as for evil' (quoted by Liu 1995: 83). Meanwhile, although various Chinese scholars were claiming that individualism had the potential to radically reform society, this does not necessarily imply that the source of inspiration for that reform was Western individualism. In his article entitled *Gèrén zhī gǎigé* 'The reform of the individual' (1914), Dù Yàquán 杜亚泉 affirmed that genuine reform must come from the individual, an idea that stems from the Confucian legacy of self-improvement. On the other hand, he also established a link between individual reform and the socialist perspective. According to Svarverud (2010: 215), in Dù's view, 'socialism must be envisaged on the basis of individualism': the idea being that only after the individual had been liberated, as the first stage, could society move on towards socialism.

However, the 1920s saw a great wave of publications hostile to the notion of individualism. Among them was Chén Dúxiù's essay *Xūwú de gèrénzhǔyì jí rènzìránzhǔyì* 虚无的个人主义及任自然主义 'Nihilistic individualism and *laissez-faire* theory'. This work deserves to be mentioned because it symbolized Chén's radical change in perspective, or

'Chen Duxiu's about-face on individualism' to put it in Lydia Liu's words (1995: 97).

In his 1920 essay, Chén Dúxiù retraced the origins of nihilistic individualism in Taoist philosophy and attacked individualism as a socially irresponsible, nihilistic idea. A similar position was adopted by Dèng Fēihuáng 邓飞黄 in his article, *Gèrénzhǔyì yóulái jí qí yǐngxiǎng* 个人主义由来及其影响 'The origin of individualism and its impact', published in 1922 in the *Eastern Miscellany*. Dèng considered individualism to be a bourgeois ideology that was destined to be replaced by socialism. Moreover, in 1928, Qián Xìngcūn 钱杏邨 proclaimed the death of individualism and of petit bourgeois liberal ideas. This bears witness to the way rhetoric about individualism was undergoing a major change (Liu 1995: 98).

A pattern is emerging here. After years marked by individualist aspirations, the terms for the individual and individualism had gradually begun to take on negative connotations, while socialist and communist ideas in China were increasingly being endorsed. This discourse was expressed in striking rhetoric with startling metaphors. Individualism was compared to 'a stubborn skin disease which rushes back after having been removed' (Townsend's 1969: 182 translation) in the *People's Daily* (*Rénmín rìbào* 人民日报) on 9 October 1958 (个人主义 … 像顽固的皮肤病，今天你把它消除了，明天它又冲了回来). Individualism was succinctly condemned as the 'source of all evils' in a 1966 speech (quoted by Bowie and Fairbank 1971: 586) (个人主义是万恶之源).⁶

These metaphors highlight the changing perception of the individual and individualism in the first decades after the People's Republic of China was founded. Nonetheless, the case should not be overstated. Chen (2007: 8) relativizes the impact of communist ideas, and resists the idea that they overshadowed individuals and individualism. He underlines that the discourse on individualism in China was closely bound up in the discourse on national salvation, instead of being a 'theme of full-scale individualist enlightenment'. Chen does recognize that 'the collectivist ways in which the Communists carried out their revolution worked against individualism', but he considers that 'the Communists did not smother or kill an already existing May Fourth theme of full-scale Western individualist enlightenment that would celebrate the individual's independence from the nation-state', because, in his opinion, 'such a theme never took root to begin with during the May Fourth movement' (2007: 8).

Words for Individual and Individualism in Contemporary Chinese

The reference dictionary *Xiàndài hànyǔ cídiǎn* 现代汉语词典 *Dictionary of Modern Chinese* (2015, sixth edition) gives as first meaning of the word *gèrén*, 'one person', 'single person' (*yīgè rén* 一个人), as opposed to 'collective, collectivity' (跟集体相对).[7] The illustrative examples focus on the relationship between the 'individual' and the 'collective' (*jítǐ* 集体): the first concerns the subordination of individual interests to collective interests (个人利益服从集体利益), and the second concerns the combination of collective leadership and individual responsibility (集体领导同个人负责相结合). Hence, the notion of 'individual' seems to be perceived in terms of the role it played in collective society.

This coincides with the findings of Fumian's (2014) study of the expression *gèrén fèndòu* 个人奋斗 'individual struggle'. The author analyses the way the individual dimension of the struggle has been redeemed since the 1980s, by focusing on the writings of Xià Wěidōng 夏伟东. Xià (quoted in Fumian 2014: 365) distinguishes between individuals' struggle for themselves and their interests (*wèi gèrén de gèrén fèndòu* 为个人的个人奋斗), which he regarded as negative, and the individual struggle for the benefit of society (*wèi shèhuì de gèrén fèndòu* 为社会的个人奋斗), which he felt deserved admiration. This emphasis on 'individual struggle' and 'individual interests' (even though subordinated to the interests of society), must be understood in the historical context in which Dèng Xiǎopíng was reforming Chinese society. Dèng Xiǎopíng was relying upon individuals and the private economy as the motor forces of development to relaunch the Chinese economy.

This change in the way individualism is now perceived can be observed in various fields. For instance, in their research on moral education in China, Cheung and Pan (2006) have identified these changes of perspective, which seem to indicate a move from an ideology of traditional collectivism to an ideology of 'regulated individualism'.

Nevertheless, the word *gèrén* can also be considered part and parcel of the rhetoric hostile to the collective good and the national dimension. For instance, in a speech entitled *Zhōngguó mèng zài zhěngtǐ yǔ gètǐ zhī jiān* 中国梦在整体与个体之间, 'The Chinese Dream: Balancing the Nation and the Individual',[8] professor Chén Xīxǐ 陈锡喜 points out the differences between Obama's 'American dream' and the 'Chinese dream' (*Zhōngguó mèng* 中国梦). This has become a key expression for the Chinese president Xí Jìnpíng 习近平. Chén states that 'the American

Dream is a dream for the individual [*gèrén mèng*] and the Chinese Dream is a dream for the nation as a whole [*guójiā mèng*]' (美国梦是个人梦，中国梦是国家梦).

This tells us something about the political and social climate of contemporary China. But how is individualism faring in the other spheres of Chinese life? In contrast to the criticism of individualism we have just considered, the word *gèrén* and its derived and compound forms generally appear to be associated with positive connotations in the fields of literature, literary criticism, and the arts. For instance, we can quote the literary critic Chén (2013), who, in the preface of a book on Chinese avant-garde poetry, points out that 'poets search for an individualized language' (詩人尋求個人化的語言), and 'an individualized writing' (個人化的書寫). He speaks of the ways they transform common words into 'new words of individual discovery' (lit. 'individual discovery-like neologisms' 個人"發明"般的新詞), 'as if they were drawing from the deep well of an "individual [personal] etymology"' (像是極於"個人詞源"的深井). The word *gèrén* is used by Chén in the expression *gèrén cíyuán* (translatable as 'individual etymology'). It is also used in 'new words discovered by the individual' (*gèrén 'fāmíng' bān de xīncí*). The derived form *gèrénhuà* (constituted by adding the suffixoid -*huà* meaning '-ization', '-ized') is also used in the expressions *gèrénhuà de yǔyán* 'individualized language' and *gèrénhuà de shūxiě* 'individualized writing'.

In her essay on the individual in contemporary Chinese literature, Wedell-Wedellsborg (2010: 174) mentions another expression containing the word *gèrénhuà*, that is, the label of *gèrénhuà xiězuò* 个人化写作, also translatable as 'individualized writing'. This expression was widely taken up by literary critics in the 1990s and early 2000s to designate different literary trends, from 'body-writing' (*shēntǐ xiězuò* 身体写作) and 'privacy writing' (*sīrénhuà xiězuò* 私人化写作), to 'alternative writing' (*lìnglèi xiězuò* 另类写作) and 'babe-fiction' (*bǎobèi xiǎoshuō* 宝贝小说). Wedell-Wedellsborg (2010: 167) also points out that many novel titles include words like 'private' (*sīrén* 私人), 'individual' (*gèrén* 个人), and 'alone' (*yīgè rén* 一个人[9]). This is considered as a sign of 'a change of priority as the literary representation of the individual … most often tending towards the private and personal, away from the grand narratives of nation and politics' (even though simultaneously 'a distinctly nationalist upsurge in the popular cultural climate' has to be underlined) (Wedell-Wedellsborg 2010: 167).

The examples found in the Corpus of Modern Chinese (*Xiàndài hànyǔ yǔliàokù* 现代汉语语料库, http://www.cncorpus.org/CCindex.

aspx) also indicate the trajectory this word has taken within the Chinese worldview. This corpus includes sources for *gèrén* from the 1930s onward. It is important to stress here that some of the 2580 occurrences listed referring to the 'individual' as 个人 relate to the combination of the classifier *gè* plus the noun *rén* ('one person', 'a person'). Among the results for *gèrén* used to signify 'individual', it proves revealing to compare the sources from the 1950s and 1960s with those from the 1980s. If we focus on 1950's and 1960's sources, we find *gèrén* used in different examples in which the individual is perceived from the perspective of national and collective interests. We read of 'developing the revolutionary spirit, moving from individual/personal love to class love' (发挥革命的精神，从个人的爱扩大到阶级的爱), and 'developing the social spirit and social capacity of the individuals' (发展个人的社会精神与社会能力). Other significant examples include 'the overall interests of the state and society are consistent with the personal interests of citizens' (国家和社会的整体利益是与公民的个人利益相一致的).

Among the examples from 1980's sources, on the other hand, we find: 'individual (or personal) development perspective' (个人发展前途). We find affirmations like: 'the development of the national economy will result in an improvement of individual lives' (国民经济上去了，个人生活才能更美好, 1980). Further examples include: 'to harmonize the relation between the interests of the state, the collectivity and the individual' (协调着国家、集体和个人三者利益关系, 1984), and 'individual needs' (个人需求, 1987). The final example we will quote sums up a trend which was asserting itself in the zeitgeist: 'today's people consider individual needs first' (现代人首先考虑的是个人的需要, 1989).

The word *gètǐ* 个体 has 1103 occurrences. This word is mainly found in sources published since the 1980s (with a few exceptions). Often the word is used to refer to the economy or labour organization. For instance, we can quote the following key expressions:

- 'individual interest and freedom of behavior' (个体利益和行为自由);
- 'the role of private economy' (个体私营经济的作用);
- 'an economy of individual (self-employed) workers' (个体劳动者经济).

In the above-mentioned the 2015 edition of the *Dictionary of Modern Chinese* (*Xiàndài hànyǔ cídiǎn* 现代汉语词典), the first meaning given for the word *gètǐ* 个体 is 'single person or living being' (单个儿的人或生物, 泛指单个儿事物). The second meaning makes reference to the 'self-employed labourer', and to 'privately owned small enterprise' (指个体户). Furthermore, the lemma is followed by examples of compound words or expressions. These include:

- *gètǐhù* 个体户 'self-employed labourer';
- *gètǐ jīngjì* 个体经济 'individual economy';
- *gètǐ suǒyǒuzhì* 个体所有制 'private ownership of the means of production'.

As our translations show, 'self', 'individual', and 'private' are all used in the compound adjectives to translate *gètǐ*.

The National Social Science Database (*Guójiā zhéxué shèhuì kēxué xuéshù qíkān shùjùkù* 国家哲学社会科学学术期刊数据库), a database of academic writings (http://www.nssd.org/) gives 9457 results for the form *gètǐ*. Among them, 867 papers relate to the topic of the 'individual economy' (个体经济), 646 relate to 'individual and private economy' (个体私营经济), 322 relate to 'individual industrial and commercial households' (个体工商户), and 289 relate to 'self-employed workers' or 'small private businessmen' (个体户). These results would seem to prove conclusively that *gètǐ* is used primarily as a term related to labour and the economy.

Gèrén seems to be a more broadly used 'equivalent' for 'individual'. In this database, we find numerous results for the word *gèrén* (19 543), the main fields being: economics and management (经济管理, 7235 articles), political sciences and law (政治法律, 3607 articles), and sociology (社会学, 3202 articles).

Among the topics (主题) these publications were arranged into, 1397 relate to 'individualism' (*gèrénzhǔyì* 个人主义), 466 relate to 'workers' (劳动者), 460 relate to 'personal income tax' (个人所得税), 283 relate to 'collectivism' (集体主义), and 276 relate to 'individual rights' (*gèrén quánlì* 个人权利).

A search for the word *gèrénzhǔyì* ('individualism') in this database furnished us with a total of 2160 publications. These were mainly derived from the fields of philosophy and religion (哲学宗教, 540 articles), sociology (社会学, 498 articles), and political sciences and law (政治法律, 453 articles). These figures provide us with an overall impression of the main fields in which research involving the notion of individualism is being carried out. But what overall impression do we get it if we use corpora of a more general nature? The results proved somewhat surprising. An extremely limited number of occurrences of this word – a mere seventy-five – can be found in the above-mentioned Corpus of Modern Chinese (现代汉语语料库). The examples found in sources from the 1950s onward often carry negative connotations. For instance, we can read of 'individualism, vanity, arrogance and complaisance' (个人主义，虚荣心，骄傲自满情绪, 1955). Other examples included:

- 'to overcome bourgeois individualism and sectarianism' (克服资产阶级个人主义和宗派主义, 1974);
- 'to be opposed to bourgeois individualism and to anarchism' (反对资产阶级个人主义、无政府主义, 1979);
- 'to advocate collectivism and to oppose individualism' (提倡集体主义、反对个人主义, 1982);
- 'to oppose an individualistic value orientation' (反对个人主义的价值导向, 1991).

Even though the number of occurrences remains somewhat limited, *gèrénzhǔyì* appears be the only form used to refer to individualism in this corpus. At any rate, the form *gètǐzhǔyì* 个体主义 (formed by *gètǐzhǔyì* 个体 plus the affixoid -*zhǔyì* 主义) was not found.

In the Center for Chinese Linguistics of Peking University (CCL) monolingual corpus of Modern Chinese we find only twenty-six occurrences of *gètǐzhǔyì*. In contrast, 1428 results can be found for *gèrénzhǔyì*. This form therefore clearly appears to be the most frequently used term for 'individualism' in Mandarin Chinese. Furthermore, in the bilingual (Chinese–English) CCL corpus, the English word 'individualism' generally corresponds to the Chinese *gèrénzhǔyì*, with thirty-one occurrences, and only one occurrence for the form *gèxìngzhǔyì* 个性主义. These results would appear to be conclusive. In the same corpus the majority of the 656 occurrences of the word 'individual' corresponded to the Chinese word *gèrén*. This was true of 249 examples, whereas only eighty corresponded to *gètǐ*.

On the other hand, the word *gèrénzhǔyì* is listed as an independent entry in various monolingual dictionaries. For instance, in the reference dictionary *Xiàndài hànyǔ cídiǎn* 现代汉语词典 *Dictionary of Modern Chinese* (2015, sixth edition), this word is defined as:

资产阶级世界观的核心概念，主张把个人的独立、自由、平等等价值及权利放在第一位。个人主义是资产阶级反对封建主义的思想武器。只顾自己、不顾他人的极端个人主义，是与集体主义道德原则相违背的。

A core notion of the bourgeois worldview, which gives priority to values and rights like individual autonomy, freedom, and equality. Individualism was a bourgeois intellectual weapon to combat feudalism. Extreme individualism, selfish and non-altruistic behaviour, runs counter collectivist moral principles.

We might be inclined to see a parallel between the Czech communist condemnation of individualism and the one above. But that would perhaps be a hasty conclusion. Since only the extreme forms of individualism are being condemned here, as opposed to collective values, it would seem that, in and of itself, individualism is not seen in a negative light. This will appear all the more evident if we compare this definition with the definitions given in previous dictionaries. For instance, the 1997 edition of the *Dictionary of New China* (*Xīnhuá cídiǎn* 新华词典) gave a far more negative definition of this word:

指自私自利，以个人为中心，一切从个人出发的思想和行为。是资产阶级世界观的核心和资产阶级道德的基本原则，也是一切剥削阶级共同的意识形态。

Indicates selfishness, a way of thinking and behavior centered on the individual. Central to the bourgeois worldview and a basic principle of bourgeois morality, it is also the common ideology of the exploiting classes.

The 2001 edition of the *Dictionary of New China* (*Xīnhuá cídiǎn* 新华词典) only mentions the focus on the individual and the central role it plays in the bourgeois worldview. We find the phrase: 'a way of thinking and behavior centered on the individual. Central to the bourgeois worldview and a basic principle of bourgeois morality' (以个人为中心，一切从个人出发的思想和行为。是资产阶级世界观的核心和资产阶级道德的基本原则). The essential thing here is that no mention is made of the ideology of the exploiting classes. The definitions appear to be gradually losing their ideological connotations, and the word seems to be perceived in a slightly more positive light.

Nevertheless, examples of individualism with very negative connotations can be found in more recent sources. For instance, we can quote the article by Yáng Yùwén 杨玉文 published in the *People's Daily* on 11 September 2013, entitled 'Against the "four winds", we must eradicate individualism' (*Fǎn "sì fēng" bìxū chǎnchú gèrénzhǔyì* 反"四风"必须

铲除个人主义[10]). This article refers to 'four winds'; these are the four negative tendencies:

- formalism (形式主义);
- bureaucratism (官僚主义);
- hedonism (享乐主义);
- extravagant wastefulness (奢靡).

These 'four winds' are clearly understood to form part of the cult of individualism (重要原因是个人主义在作祟). Yáng affirms that the 'self' is 'the biggest enemy' in the struggle against the 'four winds' (反"四风"最大的敌人是自己) and that 'the key to eradicating individualism is self-reliance' (铲除个人主义关键靠自己).

In their dialogue on individualism which bore the appropriate title of 'The ups and downs of individualism in China' (*Gèrénzhǔyì zài Zhōngguó de chénfú* 个人主义在中国的沉浮), the Chinese scholars, Liú Zàifù 刘再复 and Lǐ Zéhòu 李泽厚 (2010) describe 'individualism' as 'an extremely sensitive issue in China, that has been criticized for decades' (在中国非常敏感的、遭到批判几十年的个人主义). Lǐ Zéhòu underlines that the notion of individualism comes from the West (个人主义这个概念来自西方). According to this argument, the Chinese tradition lacks individualism (我认为在中国的传统里，是缺少个人主义的). According to Lǐ, examples of 'Chinese style individualism' (*Zhōngguó shì de gèrénzhǔyì*), for instance in Taoism, arose in the attempt to escape from reality (道家有些中国式的个人主义，这是逃避现实). Liú Zàifù also stresses the gap between this kind of individualism and Western individualism. He compares the Chinese type to a form of hedonism (道家式的个人主义，不是西方式的个人主义。道家与其说是个人主义，还不如说是享乐主义更确切一些). Liú also affirms that individualism has often been confused with a doctrine of 'not respecting the traffic light', that is, a doctrine for disdaining everything and sweeping everything to one side (个人主义并不就是闯红灯的主义，并不是蔑视一切、横扫一切的主义). And the two authors go on to stress the link between individualism, and 'citizen consciousness' (*gōngmín yìshí* 公民意识), and speak of the 'citizens' sense of responsibility' (*gōngmín zérèngǎn* 公民责任感).

What are we to conclude from these various perspectives? More than a century after the introduction of the word *gèrénzhǔyì* into Chinese, the way this word is perceived oscillates between criticism and praise. The individual and individualism trigger contradictory associations, and rival modes of reasoning.

Searching for combinations of the words 'individualism' and 'China' or 'Chinese' on Google in August 2016, we found 168 000 results for *Zhōngguó de gèrénzhǔyì* 中国的个人主义 'Chinese individualism'. We can add a further 4490 occurrences for *Zhōngguó gèrénzhǔyì* (also translatable as 'Chinese individualism', without the particle *de* as genitive marker), and 3240 for the expression, 'Chinese-style individualism' (中国式个人主义). We can therefore conclude that these expressions seem to be subject to wide discussion on the Chinese web.

Some key expressions deserve to be mentioned. Among these is the expression, *wǎngluòhuà de gèrénzhǔyì* 网络化的个人主义, corresponding to 'networked individualism'. The Chinese form is widespread today. A Google search in August 2016 provided us with 28 400 results, more than 22 500 results than those for the English term 'networked individualism'. This is somewhat ironic since English is the language in which the expression was coined. Yan (2010: 11) considers 'Internet individualism and activism' as 'an important feature of the rise of the individual in Chinese society', through social networks, forums, and blogs. Blogs are regarded as means of self-expression, in a country counting tens of millions bloggers. Sima and Pugsley (2010) also consider the spread of blogs to be a crucial aspect in the rise of a 'me culture' in China. Yan (2010) emphasizes the political implications of this use of the new media: 'through discussion boards, forums and personal blogs, Chinese netizens have formed a force of public opinion, which ... can have a significant impact on the real world'.

Nevertheless, in the same volume on the rise of the individual in contemporary China, Beck and Beck-Gernshein (2010: xix) emphasize the political implications and limits of individual affirmation in modern China, specifying that: 'this process of liberation is supposed to remain within clear limits. In particular, it is supposed to be confined to the sphere of economic activities and private lifestyles'. The authors (Beck and Beck-Gernshein 2010: xvi) adopt the expression 'truncated institutionalized individualization' to define Chinese modernity and underline that 'a practice of tolerated, even enforced, individualization is occurring, coupled with an official ideological stigmatization of this same individualization' (ibid.: xix). The authors go on to argue that there is 'a kind of limited, state sanctioned individualization in which individuals are condemned to take their own initiatives, while the social safety nets for Chinese state socialism have disappeared' (ibid.: xviii).

Concluding Remarks

What can we conclude, then, about the place of the individual and individualism in contemporary Chinese lexicon? What status does individualism have in the Chinese worldview? Judging from our findings, this question appears to remain central to the most deeply political and personal spheres of life for Chinese speakers. Our research leads us to conclude that the relation between the individual and the group remains a crucial question throughout the histories of each of the languages we have investigated. And the texts and corpora that we have studied corroborate the fact that individualism and collectivism in modern Chinese society are subjects that are as widely and fervently discussed today as they were throughout the twentieth century.

The current words used for individual and individualism started being used in late Qing China, a period of great political and social change, and marked by enormous foreign influence. But we have stressed again and again that it would be misleading to see individualism and the individual as notions that are 'imported' from Europe. Not only does adopting foreign concepts entail transforming them to enroot them within the traditions of the Chinese language and culture, the various words used, and the forms used to construct them, already had long-standing traditions in Chinese, with their own connotations and implications. And it is these connotations and implications that will prove essential in the way political debates choose to highlight the facets of the various words that come into play, be they negative or positive, Chinese or foreign.

Individualism emerges in the contemporary Chinese worldview as a controversial keyword with multiple and paradoxical meanings. The individual appears to be perceived with a certain ambivalence, depending on who uses the word, in which sphere of society, and at what period of China's political tradition. Our study of individualism in Chinese takes us beyond the simple opposition between the East and the West. The multiplicity of terms used for the individual and for individualism reveals the flexibility and the fragile nature of the words that are introduced, debated, and often abandoned. The 'overlexicalization' of the terms for individual bears witness to the semantic instability of this key period in which the modern Chinese terminologies are being formed.

But that is not all. The complexity of the context in which keywords for individual and individualism are emerging cannot be understood without bearing in mind the political and ideological implications of these terms in the context of late Qing and early republican China. The different terms for individual and individualism were already central in intellectual debates and literary writings during the first decades of the twentieth century. They were associated with reformist, anti-traditionalist movements and campaigns, calling for national salvation and China's modernization.

As our various sources indicate, the keywords used to denote individual and individualism have never been neutral. The words were clearly perceived in negative terms for decades, especially after the foundation of the People's Republic. But a considerable change occurred after 1978. A new emerging narrative of the individual and individualism in Chinese contemporary society can be traced from this time. Citizens are discussing the nature of individuals and individual interests in various sectors of society. And the State is attempting to harness those debates with a political agenda, promoting certain types of individual pursuits, and discouraging or disparaging others. The various connotations and implications of the words we have discussed in no way allow us to consider them as simple neutral terms. Nor can we assert that the terms we have discussed have anything more than broadly similar meanings as their European 'equivalents'.

However, we do not consider that a problem. It was never our intention to search for Chinese equivalents that dovetail perfectly with keywords in other cultures. Cultural difference – we would like to believe – makes comparing languages all the more exciting. These keywords can be considered to be the keys to understanding the relationship between the one and the whole in the Chinese worldview to some extent. They do indeed help us to understand the contrasting perceptions of the various ways this relationship has been conceptualized in contemporary China. But this adventure demands a certain amount of conceptual effort for non-native speakers. In order to begin to understand the complexity of the Chinese terms and their instability, the way they are constantly being fought over, European readers will first have to accept the controversial and contradictory nature of their own terms. Once they realize the complexity of their own conceptions of individualism and the oppositions they are bound up in, they will be better equipped for apprehending the way the creative forces of the Chinese experience are forging their own concepts in a very different context with very different individual aspirations.

NOTES

1. A previous and somewhat different Italian version of this chapter was presented during the *Giornate di linguistica cinese* in Milan, in November 2015, and published with the collected papers under the title 'Da *xiǎojǐ* 小己 a *gèrén* 个人: alcune riflessioni sui termini per individuo e individualismo in cinese' (Gianninoto 2016a).
2. *Shǐjì* 史记 by Sīmǎ Qiān 司马迁 (145–87 BCE). The expression *xiǎojǐ* can be found in the section 'Biography of Sima Xiangru' (司马相如列传), see the Chinese Text Project digital library: http://ctext.org/shiji/si-ma-xiang-ru-lie-zhuan
3. Literally 'The New *Erya*', from the title of one of the oldest Chinese monolingual dictionaries.
4. Forms found in Classical Chinese, which have been adopted in Japanese to designate new concepts and are reintroduced with these new connotations in Chinese (see Masini 1993).
5. Family feeling, a kind of social structure that holds the family's needs as a group and traditional collectivism to be paramount, and the individual's needs to be secondary.
6. http://cpc.people.com.cn/GB/69112/163446/163451/9891660.html
7. The second meaning indicated in this dictionary is the use of *gèrén* to replace the first person pronominal form in formal speeches: 自称, 我 (在正式场合发表意见时用).
8. Presented at the conference *Zhōngguó mèng de shìjiè duìhuà* 中国梦的世界对话 (International Dialogue on the Chinese Dream), Shanghai, 7–8 December 2013, http://news.china.com.cn/zhuanti/zgm/2013-12/05/content_30809990.htm
9. *yīgè rén* 一个人 literally means 'one person'. The numeral *yī* 'one' is followed by the classifier *gè*, plus the noun *rén* 'man, human being'.
10. http://paper.people.com.cn/rmrb/html/2013-09/11/nw.D110000renmrb_20130911_2-04.htm

CHAPTER 4

Europe

Business carried on as usual during alterations on the map of Europe. (Winston Churchill, Speech at Guildhall, 9 November 1914, cited in the *ODQ*, 1992: 202)

... nous disons à la France, à l'Angleterre, à la Prusse, à l'Autriche, à l'Espagne, à l'Italie, à la Russie, nous leur disons: Un jour viendra où les armes vous tomberont des mains, à vous aussi ! Un jour viendra où la guerre paraîtra aussi absurde et sera aussi impossible entre Paris et Londres, entre Pétersbourg et Berlin, entre Vienne et Turin, qu'elle serait impossible et qu'elle paraîtrait absurde aujourd'hui entre Rouen et Amiens, entre Boston et Philadelphie. Un jour viendra où la France, vous Russie, vous Italie, vous Angleterre, vous Allemagne, vous toutes, nations du continent, sans perdre vos qualités distinctes et votre glorieuse individualité, vous vous fondrez étroitement dans une unité supérieure, et vous constituerez la fraternité européenne, absolument comme la Normandie, la Bretagne, la Bourgogne, la Lorraine, l'Alsace, toutes nos provinces, se sont fondues dans la France. Un jour viendra où il n'y aura plus d'autres champs de bataille que les marchés s'ouvrant au commerce et les esprits s'ouvrant aux idées. - Un jour viendra où les boulets et les bombes seront remplacés par les votes, par le suffrage universel des peuples, par le vénérable arbitrage d'un grand Sénat souverain qui sera à l'Europe ce que le parlement est à l'Angleterre, ce que la Diète est à l'Allemagne, ce que l'Assemblée législative est à la France ! (*Victor Hugo au Congrès de la Paix de 1849.* (http://www.taurillon.org/Victor-Hugo-au-Congres-de-la-Paix-de-1849-son-discours,02448)

We say to France, to England, to Prussia, to Austria, to Spain, to Italy, to Russia, we say to them: a day will come when the weapons will fall from your own hands too! A day will come when war between Paris and London, between Saint Petersburg and Berlin, between Vienna and Torino, will come to seem just as absurd and impossible as it would be today between Rouen and Amiens, between Boston and Philadelphia. A day will come when France, when you Russia, you Italy, you England, you Germany, all you nations of the continent will fully melt into a greater unity without losing your distinct qualities or your glorious individuality, and you will create a European fraternity in absolutely the same way that Normandy, Brittany, Burgundy, Lorraine, Alsace, all of our provinces have melted into France. A day will come when there will be no more battlefields, but markets open for trade and minds open to ideas. A day will come when the cannonballs and bombs will be replaced by votes, universal suffrage for the peoples, by the venerable arbitration of a great sovereign Senate that will mean the same thing that Parliament means for England, and the Bundestag means for Germany, and the Legislative Assembly means for France. (Victor Hugo at the 1849 Peace Conference)

所谓泛欧文化认同或"欧洲文化"的基石充其量也只是属于精英文化或高雅文化的范畴，这种"大传统"对于欧洲普通民众的影响毕竟有限。(Yán and Shí 2012: 8)

The cornerstone of the so called 'pan-European cultural identity' or the 'European culture' pertains primarily to the 'elite culture' or 'high culture', while this 'great tradition' has only a limited impact on the 'common' European people. (Yán and Shí 2012: 8)

China and EU are not conventional nation-states, but very large and diverse, multiethnic and multinational political entities that strive to behave like nation-states. (Wong 2013: 171)

The American Dream puts an emphasis on economic growth, personal wealth, and independence. The new European Dream puts emphasis more on sustainable development, quality of life, and interdependence. ... The American Dream is assimilationist. We associate success with shedding our former cultural ties, and becoming free agents in the great American melting pot. The

European Dream, by contrast, is based on preserving one's cultural identity and living in a multicultural world. (Jeremy Rifkin, contemporary American sociologist, 2005)

EUROPE IN ENGLISH AND OTHER LANGUAGES

In our opening quotations, Winston Churchill – the imperturbable leader of the British nation and fierce defender of the British Empire – ironically underlines the stoic pragmatism of the British who continue to get on with life as Europe is torn up and drawn up at the outbreak of hostilities in 1914. This turned out to be a naïve misconception, not only in the following four years, but also with the Second World War. Churchill himself would grow great by facing up to the consequences of the Versailles Treaty, the rise of fascism in Germany, and the outbreak of the Second World War. In contrast, Victor Hugo seems to live up to his own ideal of the poet as the seer that rises above the chaos and confusion of particular existences and looks into the future to see it unfolding. He may seem to have been mistaken, as Germany invaded France in the Franco-Prussian war of 1870–1871, mistaken again, with the trench warfare of the First World War, and mistaken once more with the Second World War and the advent of the Cold War and the nuclear threat of the Earth's destruction. Today Hugo, nevertheless, appears something like a visionary. Despite the various crises that Europe has recently been faced with – the breakaway Brexit referendum, the migrant crisis, and the rise in Eurosceptic populism, on other levels, in its management and legislation, the European Union continues to consolidate itself day after day. And as proof of this, the idea of war between Berlin and Paris, and between Rome and London has come to appear absurd, impossible, and economically ill-advised to most political and economic analysts and even to most citizens.

Hugo's quotation is apt for us, the authors of this book on four European concepts, because Hugo clearly defines Europe as a continent of peoples each with their specific individualities. As citizens, how can the individuals of those specific peoples form a federation together? A United States of Europe?

Both Hugo's and Churchill's quotations are apt in that they reveal attitudes to Europe that are characteristic not only of their authors but of the peoples they belong to. In many ways, there are many 'Europes'. Of course, at a geographical level, Europe can be considered a simple affair, the most simple of our four concepts. The online *Merriam-Webster*

Dictionary defines it as a 'continent of the eastern hemisphere between Asia and the Atlantic area 3,997,929 square miles (10,354,636 square kilometers)'. However, the dictionary goes on to stress the ambiguous nature of Britain's relationship to the Continent in its second entry for 'Europe': 'the European continent exclusive of the British Isles' (http://www.merriam-webster.com/dictionary/Europe). Is Britain a part of Europe, or an 'island-outsider'? The question of belonging is crucial for all the Member States, because it is the relationship that nations have to Europe that leads to different definitions of Europe. Europe's history, its vocation, and its objectives are perceived in various ways depending upon the relationship to Europe. The narratives that each nation gets tied up in as the Member States negotiate with one another, are inseparable from the way each state perceives its place 'in' Europe (or 'outside' it).

In this sense, external perspectives are simpler, more clear-cut; yet they can prove surprisingly insightful. Europe can look a mess, but from the outside, Europe is still seen as perfectly capable of asserting itself and staunchly defending its own interests. This is the paradox. Curiously, the European media does not seem concerned with promoting the narrative of Europe as a global powerhouse: within Europe, the newspapers of most of the Member States recount stories of a Europe lurching from crisis to crisis. Does the truth lie between the two perspectives?

Interestingly, from the philological perspective, English is very much part of Europe, as the lingua franca of most discussions. The preponderance of Britain's political and economic weight is unquestioned at a global level, and the enlargement of Europe has tended to consolidate the status of English among new Members of the European Parliament who do not speak French. But the English linguistic community overflows Europe, and the American texts will generate other perceptions and narratives of Europe: external critical perspectives.

There is a Europe that celebrates itself and sees itself as a community with high ideals, and a great power to influence the course of the world in a positive manner. This is 'the Enlightenment narrative'. There is a Europe that celebrates pulling down the Berlin Wall and breaking down barriers (Underhill 2016a). And there is 'Fortress Europe', with the Euro-wide xenophobic reaction to migrants, and discreetly signed contracts with partners in Morocco, Turkey, and Libya to stem the flow of Africans into the EU by setting up buffer zones that filter and police migration with the construction of barriers, walls, and defences outside Europe's official borders.

This is one of the hidden narratives of Europe, but it is one that has been studied in detail by anthropologists outside Europe such as Ruben Andersson (2014) in his book on the ways Europe's increasingly powerful border regime targets and controls migrants. And this story is well known to human rights organizations and activists such as Human Rights Watch Executive Director, Kenneth Roth, who argued in a letter to EU heads of state that the European Union's proposed deal with Turkey on a 'mass-return deal' concerning migrants that was announced on 8 March 2016 represents 'a disturbing disregard for international law covering the rights of refugees, asylum seekers, and migrants' (https://www.hrw.org).

The symbolic language used to explain and understand Europe is not innocent either. Predictably, Europe turns out to be a spatial construct. But should we see Europe as a fixed entity, an actor, with which countries do trade (as China, India, Russia, or the US perceive it)? Or is it an invading space that threatens to engulf the nation state? Or an exclusive private club that keeps other states out, or that treats some Member States as first class, and others as second class citizens? Should we consider it as a 'container' with a cocktail of cultures that sometimes proves 'explosive'? Or a well-oiled machine that can break down? Does it have a clear past, a definite future, or a vocation? Is Europe going somewhere, and taking us somewhere? If so, upon what trajectory do we project Europe? Is it a part of us? Are we a part of it? These questions should make us more aware of the symbolic complexity of the narratives of Europe. To 'think' Europe, we have to understand the conceptual metaphors that form our idea of Europe and the stories we are entangled in as Europeans.

Our study largely followed the same methodology as that adopted for our other three concepts: it took on board the usual corpora (BNC and COCA), and used the Leipzig Wortschatz, and books of quotations in English, French, and German to complete and counterbalance the findings drawn from them. The texts compiled from http://www.gutenberg.org in MyEnglishCorups, MyAmericanCorpus, and MyFrenchCorpus were studied. So were articles, read in paper form, and online, in the press in English, American English, French, and German, using search engines such as https://www.google.fr and the specific newspaper research engines such as http://www.theguardian.com/uk, http://www.nytimes.com, http://www.lemonde.fr, and www.spiegel.de. In addition, a large quantity of texts on the EU website (http://europa.eu/index_fr.htm) in English, French, German, and other languages were consulted and compared. Initially, aiming to compile around 1000 usages for the English term, 'Europe', we soon found that the media continued to bombard us with further usages. Consequently, our overall impression of the way we conceive of Europe was no doubt formed from a total of around double that number.

If we consider the various online media and written press of the world, we can identify at least five relations with Europe that will generate different perceptions, definitions, and narratives.

1. Europe as the federal body to which the Member States are subject (the German, Polish, or Slovak perception).
2. Europe as the expanding project with a universal vocation and at whose centre lies France (the traditional French perspective).
3. Europe as the Continent to which we do and do not belong (British ambivalence, but ambivalence shared by some Eurosceptics such as the former President of the Czech Republic, Vaclav Klaus).
4. Europe as a political force and economic power perceived from without (the US, the Russian, and the Chinese perception).
5. Europe as the powerful neighbouring federation with whom we must do business and find agreements (the Moroccan or Turkish perspective).

Each country debates the activities of Europe, but however diverse the arguments advanced, and however complicated the negotiations prove to be, there are invariably underlying narratives at work shaping those negotiations. And those narratives differ greatly from culture to culture. Often the stories we tell about Europe are so different that the interests and ideals of other Member States seem absurd and incomprehensible. This question will be taken up in the section on the metaphors of Europe, but first we must plunge into the English corpora to trace the kinds of debates that go on in Europe and the questions at stake.

ENGLISH CORPORA

BNC

In the 17 543 references cited in the BNC, a corpus of texts assembled up until the early 1990s, Europe is above all a continent, a space, a container. Not yet a zone – that was to come later – the Europe of the

1980s was a trading area, a place to live, a place to visit as tourists. This is reflected in the collocations that Europe generated in the BNC. Only two out of the top ten – 'America', and 'united' – were not spatial or geographical terms. In order of frequency, those top ten collocates were: Eastern, Western, America, Central, throughout, across, states, North, united, Northern. The top thirty collocates (including China, Russia, and India) strengthen the impression that when the British speak of Europe they are dealing with a geopolitical zone, a trading partner. This would explain, for example, collocates such as 'cooperation'. Judging from the 400 BNC references consulted, other European neighbours are seen as benchmarks against which Britons can compare their own standard of living, rights, working conditions, wages, and even their attitudes to animal welfare.

With almost twice as many references to 'Eastern Europe' as to 'Western Europe', it is clear that the end of the communist era and the division of Europe by what the West liked to call 'the iron curtain' was one of the major issues at stake in the late 1980s and early 1990s. Examples often involved discussions about penetrating and opening up Eastern European markets. Both the Conservatives in office and the Labour opposition party were anxious to stress their commitment to Europe and to helping Eastern Europe find its place within that changing Europe. Those debates were often violent. During one crisis in Europe, Lord Norman Tebbit led rebel backbenchers in an anti-Europe crusade, a venomous attack on the Maastricht Treaty, arguing it would be 'reckless, perverse and bizarre' to allow foreigners to decide Britain's future' (BNC). In what the *Daily Mirror* claimed was 'the most vicious confrontation in the party's history', Norman Tebbit 'hijacked the Tory conference' and 'humiliated Premier John Major with a withering and sneering condemnation of his policies on Europe and the economy. Mr Major seethed with rage as the former Tory chairman challenged his authority'. But Major was able to count on the support of Labour members of parliament in quelling the government's internal rebellion. In another BNC entry, 'Former Labour deputy leader Roy Hattersley warned the party not to do a U-turn on Europe ... He blasted MPs like Bryan Gould calling for a vote with Tory rebels against Maastricht.'

At home in Britain in the early 1990s, British cities appeared to be preparing for increasing trade with the common market. This was the era that saw the coining of the neologism the 'Eurohub'. Soon Birmingham was selling itself as a 'Eurohub' as we can see in the following BNC entry:

There are many other conference centres and hotels with conference suites throughout the city. Birmingham's popularity with meeting planners owes much to its ease of access from all parts of the UK and Europe. Birmingham is at the hub of the motorway and railway networks of Britain. Its excellent airport voted 'Best Overall UK Airport' by the Consumers' Association, now offers even more direct flights to all parts of Europe from its new terminal 'Eurohub'. With over 34,000 hotel beds within a 30 mile radius of Birmingham, the city can accommodate even the largest international events. Birmingham Convention and Visitor Bureau offers a hotel reservation service for groups and individuals both before you arrive or on the day. (BNC)

Britain did not always fare well in comparisons with other European cities. One quote generated by the BNC was: 'European Commission report showed that British workers do the longest hours in Europe.' And the *Belfast Telegraph* reported that Ulster had the lowest rates of breast-feeding in Europe.

The tabloid press and the press in general appeared to glory in disputes and confrontations. The same Euroscepticism that animates the British media today could be felt in the BNC references which spoke of Europe crises, skirmishes over the devaluation of currencies in Europe, Cabinet splits, and governments 'convulsed by troubles over Europe'. Britain was at times portrayed as the victim of Europe, and this generated a 'serves them right', *Schadenfreude* reaction, when European partnerships wore thin. This sentiment was palpable in examples such as the following one:

> While the pound was suffering, the French gloated at our humiliation. Then France's President Mitterrand and Germany's Chancellor Kohl met to sort out their own version of the future of Europe. Now the French franc is under pressure. That may teach them a lesson for kowtowing to the Germans and it should warn us to be wary of both countries. (*Daily Mirror*, cited by BNC)

In the 400 examples studied, Britain was never portrayed as lying at the centre of Europe, or even of unequivocally supporting Europe as a project. Nonetheless, Britain sometimes bought into the French idealism over Europe. And in one example, it was Mitterrand's pro-euro stance that won him praise among the leaders of the world, even if he was being praised as a great man by default.

> In Russia, whatever big Boris Yeltsin may be -- and you only have to look at him to know more about that than you want to -- he is no Gorbachev. So can we look to China for a real world leader? Only if we like geriatric killers. Is Helmut Kohl, the Chancellor of mighty Germany, the man to restore our faith in world leadership? Not when he has botched reunification and his country's interest rates cripple home-owners and industries far beyond his own borders. In Europe, only French President Francois Mitterrand gets anywhere near to the status of political giant. Yet with two huge provisos. He is unpopular. And a Socialist who presides over three million unemployed deserves to be. (*Daily Mirror*, cited by BNC)

Mostly, however, the tabloids spoke of football. Europe was the European Cup, and strikers and defenders, contracts and salaries, were the main concerns. Otherwise, Europe was advertised and consumed as a range of tourist destinations. Palma Nova in Northern Italy was celebrated for its 'glitzy' and 'smart' cocktail bars such as Stadium and Lord Byron's, and its 'crazy golf course called Fantasy Golf, the biggest and best in Europe complete with waterfalls'. Potential tourists were told in adverts: 'It's open till midnight so you can spend many a fun hour here.' Likewise, Spain was beckoning the British working classes in search of sea, sex, and sun: 'So, come to this part of Spain and by the time you leave you'll understand why this area has become the most popular and cosmopolitan playground of Europe for young people.'

COCA

The Obama administration may well constitute a turning point in Euro–US relations. Obama found time to attend Nelson Mandela's funeral in South Africa on 15 December 2013, but not to attend the twentieth anniversary of the fall of the Berlin Wall in 2009. It was as if a message was being sent that Europe no longer constitutes the frontier of American influence, the place that matters. And at the end of his second administration, Obama was admonishing his European allies, calling them 'free riders' of the global order and of American might (10 March 2016, http://www.nytimes.com). Natalie Nougayrède, responding in a *Guardian* article entitled 'Obama's right. Europe's "free riders" need to take the initiative on Syria', found much to agree with in Obama's estimation of the situation. She gave a favourable hearing to Obama's claims 'about David Cameron having been "distracted" away from the focus Libya deserved, post-intervention' and she approved his reprimand concerning 'Nicolas Sarkozy wanting to "trumpet" French military action over the skies of Benghazi in 2011' (www.theguardian.com). Nougayrède went onto argue:

> The president describes his European allies as powers unable or unwilling to match fine words with resources; prone to asking the US to act but incapable of committing themselves to the efforts required for a sustainable outcome. The lesson is clear: an era has passed, and Europe must now become an effective autonomous actor on major security issues if it is to survive as a stable, liberal, democratic, rules-based entity.
>
> That is not to say that the US role within Nato [sic], as a security guarantor to Europe, will altogether disappear. Obama has never wanted that and neither, one suspects, would his successor. But a page has been turned and the US can no longer be relied upon to address the chaos that is spilling out of the Arab world, and weakening the central tenets of Europe's liberal order. (www.theguardian.com)

These are antagonistic stances. And they certainly do not give the full picture. The 51 355 references to 'Europe' in the COCA bear witness to a rich and complex relationship between the US and Europe. The US is engaged in negotiating with Europe on trade, pollution, and world rights. Often Europe is the ally that the US counts on in negotiations with the world on Iraq and Afghanistan. NATO is a transatlantic enterprise. And the 300 COCA examples studied tended to confirm the idea of a shared political worldview in the West that included both the US and Europe. This could be felt in examples such as: 'Obviously, the rise of China concerns both Europe and the US, centrally. China's rise is unsettling' (COCA).

Sometimes Europe was chastised for being a fair-weather friend though. And Britain was at times taken to task. In one reference related to the first war in Iraq in 1990, the compatibility between the British Army's engagement and its equipment was contrasted with the lack of support from Europe as a whole:

> But for Whitehall, the new force will express the strength of political support for Washington and Mrs. Thatcher's irritation that, as she sees it, much of Europe has failed in its practical support for

George Bush. In Parliament, there is broad cross-party support for government policy, no wavering from the consensus that Britain must lead from the front. Opinion polls show three-quarters of the British population support policy here on the gulf, but there is apprehension at what Britain has now committed itself to in the long term. (Nick Gowing, Independent Television News, cited in COCA)

When it came to a trial of strength between East and West, one American commentator stated: 'The only entity in the world that could stop the Russians are us. Europe is not going to do it' (COCA). In another reference, one American commentator complained about the fickleness of Europe's relationship to the US: 'Europe wants us to help them, we show up and they turn us away.'

And yet, at times the COCA recorded examples in which the Americans were not 'the good guys'. In one such example, an author weighed up the Western guilt, apportioning equal shares to the US and to Europe. One Syrian correspondent was quoted as affirming: 'The crisis has been made worse by economic sanctions imposed by the US and Europe, says Shaaban.' This was one of the rare instances in which Europe and the US were perceived as partners in global disorder.

Judging from the examples, the North Americans sometimes appear to see the US at odds with Europe and the world in struggling to defend its interests. Of course, this appears somewhat absurd to Europeans, since they invariably conceive of the US as one great powerhouse. Nonetheless, in one COCA reference, Philip Dow, managing director of Equity Strategy, was quoted as affirming: 'We need to quantify how much Europe can hurt us.' Far from playing the superpower, the US sometimes perceives Europe as a serious rival strength.

In general, though, the interests of the US and Europe are bound up together, judging from the examples that we studied from the COCA. This is a long-standing tradition. The US still identifies with Europe, and it is significant that, on the whole, the COCA seems to provide more historical references to Europe than the BNC. References to the Renaissance, to eighteenth-century European history and the French Revolution were to be found among our COCA samples.

This can be explained by a wide variety of factors. Many Americans consider they 'come from' Europe. And they 'return' to Europe. They value the arts of Europe, and they show concern for both Southern and Eastern Europe. Influencing that European culture remains a concern:

Radio Free Europe was set up in Prague in 1949 and, continuing to this day, broadcasts in twenty-three countries (http://www.rferl.org/info/faq/777.html). Certain Americans expressed this 'benevolent' relationship with a refreshing irony, laughing at what good consumers the Europeans proved to be when it came to products of dubious quality and repute: 'when you think of all the shit Europe does buy from us: Church's Chicken, ZZ Top tours, Internet porn' (COCA).

America naturally follows with interest '(o)ur companies expanding in Europe'. But it is concerned by 'European restrictions on imports'. And European agriculture, health, and diseases were significant among the sample of examples we studied.

In order of frequency, the first twelve collocates for 'Europe' in the COCA were: Eastern, Western, States, United, America, Asia, Central, North, Japan, East, Countries, throughout. Russia was seventeenth, Union came eighteenth, and Germany came twenty-first in the COCA's collocates. This gives a fairly good overall impression of Europe as a trading partner, an economic zone, and a sphere of negotiation. Compared to the 30 726 references to China in the COCA, the 51 355 references to Europe should make it plain that Europe still counts for the US. Examples like the following one bear witness to a genuine interest in Europe among Americans: 'Now, what's its like to live in Europe today?' And Europe remains a reference against which the US can compare its inhabitants' state of health. Honestly, one entry affirmed: 'Cocaine consumption is rising faster in Europe, but the US still has the highest rate of cocaine use anywhere.' The American way of life may not be being celebrated here, but it is still being compared to the lifestyles of Europe.

Leipzig Wortschatz

The Leipzig Wortschatz corpus provides a vast number of usages of 'Europe' in its German corpus. The English word tends to be used in German in connection with firms alongside Gmbh ('Ltd' in German). But the English word has also become commonplace as a borrowed word used in the spheres of tourism, sports, and international awards. Usages of 'Europe' in German also relate to music, though, especially music awards, and to ecology, networks, mining, international business schools, sales, and banks.

In its English corpus based on material from 2002, including 49 628 893 sentences, the most common co-occurrences were spatial in nature. In order of frequency, those were: in, UK, America, Eastern, European.

The spatial dimension of Europe was confirmed by left co-occurrences: phrases such as in Europe, Eastern Europe, across Europe, throughout Europe, Western Europe were cited. The first five examples offered give a fairly good idea of the way Europe is being used in both British and American English according to the Leipzig Wortschatz.

The regions, cultures and qualities of Europe are compared:

> Cornwall remains one of the poorest regions in Northern Europe.

> The Thames Valley ranks within the top 40 regions of Europe in terms of standard of living and is among the wealthiest in the UK.

Trade and commerce figured highly:

> Within Europe, each book is available direct from Rainbow Books. (3lib.ukonline.co.uk/)

> It has close connections with ACW re-enactors in the USA and across Europe. (4th-texas.org.uk/)

References were made to the military's activities in Europe:

> Royal Naval Air Station at Culdrose, the largest helicopter base in Europe ...

The commercial connotations for Europe were clearly felt in the right occurrences for it. 'Ltd' was fourth and 'Limited' was eleventh, while most of the right occurrences were grammatical (punctuation marks '.', ',' 'and', or '?'. In fact, 'Ltd' came up as a co-occurrence around twenty times more than 'convention' and sixty times more than 'statistics', suggesting that both politics and lifestyle comparisons came a long way after commercial concerns. To this extent, the following examples about money and making money together were representative of the samples consulted:

> Experiments in Central Europe and elsewhere in transferring government debt to quasi-private banks may now be investigated.

> Lois Hay Culture and its implications on budgetary practice: the case of Europe's Airbus Industry.

But references were frequently made in the samples studied to international conferences, concerts, and cultural events. International artists reflected upon their national identity and the place to where they belonged:

> When I am in Europe or in the United States I may eventually be led to think of myself as a 'Latin-American artist'.

Culture did figure in the examples studied:

> Balkans as a specific part of Europe where people live in the past and are rooted in mythology.

And the historical development of European culture figured in some examples:

> 'Hazard' was a game introduced to Europe from Arabia.
> Smoking was introduced to Europe in the 1550s by sailors returning from the New World.

Nevertheless, on the whole, business made up the bulk of the Leipzig Wortschatz's examples, with copious discussion of accounting, along with references to European and international journalism, education, technological developments and the spread of ideas, and debates about health and genetically modified food.

The Leipzig Corpus gives a more up-to-date impression of British English and American English than the BNC's 1980s resources. And to the extent that both British English and American English are perceived in pretty much the same way in Europe and around the world, as Global English, the Leipzig Corpus counterbalances the specific perspectives highlighted by both the COCA and the BNC. It can therefore be said to give a fairly accurate impression of the way English conceptions of Europe are being assimilated throughout the world. This should not prevent us from studying the way 'Europe' is used within the specific traditions of English – as we shall now do as we consult dictionaries of quotations – but it should act as a counterpoint or a contrast for those specific uses by providing a backdrop of more widely accepted usages.

Quotations

Although international books of quotations exist, there are no European books of quotations. Books of quotations tend to celebrate national cultures, heritages that are felt should be preserved. To that extent, quotation dictionaries are not particularly 'Euro-friendly'. Nonetheless, it should prove interesting to consider which language-cultures mention 'Europe' as a concept in their cultural heritages, and what they say about it, if they have anything to say.

The *ODQ* (1992) confirms the impression that Europe does not figure highly in the imagination of the British people. Europe is not held up as an ideal, as Victor Hugo holds it to be. The English authors cited do quote Europe, but only rarely, and when they do, it is often only in order to celebrate their own country. The English poet, Joseph Addison (1672–1719), considers the Thames to be 'the noblest river in Europe', for example (*ODQ* 1992: 4). Europeans were indirectly attributed a kind of urbane and cosmopolitan sophistication. The English author, Ada Leverson (1865–1936), spoke of Oscar Wilde as having the easy charm 'of the last gentleman in Europe' (*ODQ* 1992: 419). The great poet, Byron, sought inspiration in Europe and espoused the Greek cause for independence. But Matthew Arnold (1822–1888), the poet-translator and essayist, satirized both Byron and Europe for making 'his woe her own' (*ODQ* 1992: 28), when Byron died tragically young. In this way, the insular Britons tend to scorn the European aspirations of their own countrymen.

At times, geopolitical strife and military developments forced Britons to take up a position on Europe. So we see Herbert Asquith, 1st Earl of Oxford (1852–1928), affirming at the outbreak of the First World War:

> We shall never sheath the sword which we have not lightly drawn until Belgium recovers in full measure all and more that all that she has sacrificed, until France is adequately secured against the menace of aggression, until the rights of the smaller nationalities of Europe are placed upon an unassailable foundation, and until the military domination of Prussia is wholly and finally destroyed. (*ODQ* 1992: 31)

And William Pitt (1759–1806), the British Tory Minister from 1804 to 1806, gave a speech in 1805 in which he declared that: 'England has saved herself by her exertions and, I trust, saved Europe by her example'

(*ODQ* 1992: 515). But apart from leading Europe, and saving Europe, there are precious few examples of Britons seeing Britain as a part of the Continent. Lord Salisbury (1830–1903) was, therefore, going against the grain when he affirmed in a speech in 1888 that: 'We are part of the community of Europe and must do our duty as such' (*ODQ* 1992: 554).

Developments in Europe rarely fire the English imagination from what can be made of the choice of expressions put together by the compilers of the *ODQ*. There is certainly nothing to compare to the French ideal of Europe as a world-determining force, even though the *ODQ* did quote such examples from de Gaulle (1890–1970): '*c'est l'Europe, c'est toute l'Europe qui décidera du déstin du monde*' ('It is Europe, the whole of Europe that will decide the destiny of the world', *ODQ* 1992: 235). Edmund Burke, the Irish-born Whig Englishman lamented the French Revolution, and believed in a much less idealistic tradition, concluding that with the Revolution a world of chivalry had died 'and the glory of Europe is extinguished for ever', only to leave in its stead the petty concerns of 'sophisters, economists and calculators' (*ODQ* 1992: 158).

More pithy and positive images of Europe were quoted, but they were frequently derived from French sources (Chamford, Hugo, and Rimbaud). Coco Chanel, for example, whose real name was Gabrielle Bonheur (1883–1971), scornfully disparaged unaudacious feelings about Europe, and declared that being 'contented' was not enough for Europeans: 'that's for the cows', she retorted (*ODQ* 1992: 190).

The English prove themselves capable of self-deprecation in certain examples quoted in the *ODQ*. The eighteenth-century poet Charles Churchill (1731–1764) found time in his short life to laugh at the charlatan idealism that would fuel the ideology of European imperialism in the colonies. As he put it:

Happy, thrice happy the savage race,
Since Europe took their gold, and gave them grace!
Pastors she sends to help them in their need,
Some who can't write, with others who can't read. (*ODQ* 1992: 201)

Meanwhile, the Americans quoted by the *ODQ* often revealed an ambivalent relationship to England and Europe. Although Americans tend to celebrate England as a part of Europe and celebrate both as part of their own heritage, that did not prevent American authors from satirizing both England and America. Comparing England and America

John Updike (1932–2009) suggested that 'America is a land whose centre is nowhere, England one whose centre is everywhere' (*ODQ* 1992: 707). No doubt, what he meant was that England identifies itself with its Empire, the great project of Great Britain, the Empire on which the sun never sets. But bringing those aspirations down with a bang and scathing bathos, Updike characterized contemporary Britain as a 'soggy little island huffing and puffing to keep up with Western Europe' (*ODQ* 1992: 707) Another American novelist, Mary McCarthy (1912–1989), analysed things in a less flippant manner when she considered America as the realization of a European cultural tradition. She explained the cultural dominance of the US by this argument. As she put it: 'The immense popularity of American movies abroad demonstrates that Europe is the unfinished negative of which America is the proof' (*ODQ* 1992: 436).

This reasoning makes America the logical consequence of Europe and its ultimate end. This forms part of a tenacious 'Western' narrative. Europeans, of course, see things differently. But if Europe is a value, where are we to find idealism for Europe? Not in England, it would seem, judging from the quotations in the *ODQ*, compilers have selected for Europe. Shall we find 'euro-idealism' in Germany? We might be tempted to look for it there. After all, the Franco-German alliance was the motor force behind Europe in the post-war years. The photo of the massive Helmut Kohl and midget François Mitterrand holding hands, looking towards a happier future made an almost absurdly comic image,[1] but that was part of a profoundly heartfelt expression of cooperation, based on a shared experience of war. Those statesmen were creating a very real symbol of hope with their union and promoting a post-war ideal for a Europe that was leaving a past of bloody wars behind it.

Does this story fit in with German narratives about Europe? This is far from certain. Judging from Eberhard Puntsch's *Das neue Zitatenhandbuch* (2007), Europe does not figure highly in the German imagination. '*Europa*' was included in the index. But of the 9000 entries, only one reference to '*Europa*' was to be found. And that reference quoted the Franco-Swiss thinker, Denis de Rougemont (1906–1985), famous for his defence of the federalism of Europe as a means of promoting a grass-roots individualism that allows the personality to develop freely in an enlightened manner.

It is clear from the post-war press that Europe was at the heart of French policy in the second half of the twentieth century, on the other hand. The very prose of Brussels and Strasbourg bears the imprint of French syntax in whatever language it is in. The French *Cours des comptes*, in Luxembourg, becomes *The European Court of Auditors*. English-speakers talk of 'pooling resources' and 'seed capital', but it is the language of French centralization that has carved out concepts such as *European treasury centralization*.

Until around the end of the twentieth century, the French appeared to believe that Europe was very much a French project. However, celebrations of Europe in French are rarer than might be expected. If we look at reliable books of French quotations, it is the French culture rather than the European aspirations of French thinkers that is celebrated. In the two volumes of the *Dictionnaire de citations françaises* (Oster 1990, 1993), Europe does not appear to figure much more than in the *ODQ*. This is significant in itself. And the fact that the first volume ends with the man of letters, Antoine de Rivarol (1953–1801), and Louis XVI (1754-93), while the second takes us from the French Revolution and through the nineteenth and twentieth centurie, enables us to gain some insight into the ways attitudes to Europe changed with the tumultuous events related to the French Revolution that shook European history. At any rate, it should enable us to understand that a series of key events and narratives shape the French conception of Europe that has acted as the animating force of the European adventure. Certainly nothing of the sort could be found in the *ODQ*.

Although Europe seems not to exist as a project for the French during the sixteenth and seventeenth centuries, by the eighteenth it is already more than an ideal. For le Baron de Montesquieu, Europe is a necessity. The individual nations need one another, and all that fail to understand this fact will bring about their own ruin according to Montesquieu:

L'Europe n'est plus qu'une Nation composée de plusieurs, la France et l'Angleterre ont besoin de l'opulence de la Pologne et la Moscovie, comme une de leurs Provinces a besoin des autres: et l'État qui croit augmenter sa puissance, par le ruine de celui qui le touche s'affaiblit ordinairement avec lui. (Oster 1990: 520)

Europe is no longer more than one nation composed of others. France and England need the opulence of Poland, and Moscow, as one province needs the others: and the State that believes it will increase its strength in ruining the strength of its neighbouring states invariably weakens itself with them.

Montesquieu was envisaging Europe in Christian and humanitarian terms. The good of the nation should be considered in terms of the good of Europe, and the good of Europe in terms of the good of humanity. Contrary to contemporary Eurosceptics, Montesquieu saw no contradiction in the multiple obligations that this entails. Unity and the greater good would prevail and the part would serve the whole, he believed. Not all French thinkers were so optimistic. Rousseau thought less highly of the Europeans. '*J'ai remarqué qu'il y a que l'Europe seule où on vende l'hospitalité. Dans toute l'Asie on vous loge gratuitement ... je suis homme reçu chez des humains*' (Oster 1990: 617; 'I have noticed that it is in Europe alone that we sell hospitality. Throughout Asia, they welcome you in freely for the night ... I am a man welcomed by human beings'). Rousseau did prophetically anticipate the arrival of the great Corsican conqueror-legislator Napoléon, however, claiming that Corsica was the only state still capable of legislation, and musing, '*J'ai le pressentiment qu'un jour cette petite île étonnera l'Europe*' (Oster 1990: 605; 'I have the feeling that one day that little island will astonish Europe').

But by 1814, Saint Simone, the great influential thinker that inspired the discipline of sociology later in the century, was affirming that the nation states of Europe should subject themselves to a higher sovereign European Parliament:

> *L'Europe aurait la meilleure organisation possible si toutes les nations qu'elle renferme ... reconnaissaient la suprématie d'un parlement général placé au-dessus de tous les gouvernements nationaux et investi du pouvoir de juger leurs différends.* (Saint Simone, cited by Oster 1993: 26)

> Europe would have the best possible organization if all the nations that it contains ... recognized the supremacy of a general parliament placed above all national governments and invested with the power to judge their discords.

The Romantics were on the side of Europe. For Chateaubriand, the Old Europe had failed to see that Napoléon was a force not only for France but also for all of Europe, for the Enlightenment, and for the future:

> *Cette vieille Europe pensait ne combattre que la France; elle ne s'apercevait pas qu'un siècle nouveau marchait sur elle.* (Oster 1993: 79)

The old Europe thought it was fighting France alone: it had not yet apprehended that a New Century was marching against it.

The French Revolution, the conquering of Europe, and French colonialism would all be caught up in this spirit. The French imagination was fired by the idea that France was enlightened and would light the way for Europe and for the world, taking them both marching into the unfolding future. It was in the same spirit that Louis Antoine de Saint-Juste (1767–1794) had declared that '*Le peuple français vote la liberté du monde*' (Oster 1993: 57; 'the French people vote the freedom of the world'). For Napoléon, the Corsican, the army was the nation ('*l'armée, c'est la nation*', Oster 1993: 93) and the nation had made France and was remaking Europe. In this spirit, Hugo would rewrite history. All those who contributed to forging a new Europe were given a halo of greatness. Charlemagne the Frankish king who, by the time he died in 814, had united much of the territory occupied today by France, Switzerland, and Germany, became a precursor of Napoleon, a great agent of unification. Hugo marvelled at his works:

Ah ! C'est un beau spectacle à ravir la pensée. Que l'Europe ainsi faite et comme il l'a laissée! (Oster 1993: 243)

Ah! It is a wonderful spectacle to ravish the mind, the Europe that he made and left behind him!

These quotations entail complex spatial metaphors regarding the unification of parts into a whole, the trajectories of the people, the nation, Europe, and the world. History lies ahead of us, but inspiration can be found behind us. And at the centre of it all, lies France: the France that has understood the universal destiny of all mankind. The peoples of Europe must unite. Then Europe would be strong, just, and robust. The late Romantic poet Alfred de Vigny (1797–1863) was already proclaiming it to be so:

La loi de l'Europe est lourde, impassible et robuste, mais son cercle est divin, car au centre est le Juste. (Oster 1993: 178)

The law of Europe is heavy, impassable and robust, but its circle is divine, because at its centre lies the Just.

The *poètes maudits* who followed the Romantics would be less enthusiastic about Europe, focusing more on Paris and exoticism. But the poet, Valéry Larboud (1881–1957), was still celebrating Europe at the beginning of the twentieth century as 'one great city full of provisions and all the urbane pleasures' (Oster 1993: 618). The modern poet, Paul Valéry, could be ironic. Like Updike who denigrated England, Valéry satirized France as a little peninsula on the Asian continent (*'un petit cap du continent asiatique'*, Oster 1993: 581). And the modernist Camus, born in Mondovi in Algeria in 1913, described Europe as 'a desert' without roots (Oster 1993: 848).

These are unkind words for Europe, but these modernist musings bear little in common with the great events of the twentieth century. In the twentieth century, the European question is framed in other terms: Europe is a problem. The solution is not clear, but the great European politicians engaged in building it appear to see it more as a problem that is being solved, through striving against adversity and getting to grips with the practical realities of unification. Mitterrand argued that the *détracteurs* ('detractors') of Europe were thinking in terms of an abstract Europe, a geometrical form. For him, '*Le véritable Europe a besoin des parties comme un corps vivant de chair et de sang*' (Oster 1993: 860; the 'real Europe needs its parts as a living body of flesh and blood'). And the author and politician, André Malraux (1901–1976) implicitly acknowledged the organic metaphor of Europe in stressing that it should guard against illness. Malroux asserted that whether or not Europe was *mourrant* ('dying'), it was indeed *menacée* ('threatened'; Oster 1993: 771). And for him, only freedom would ensure the sound health of Europe: the new Europe should therefore determine to what extent freedom rather than destiny should be its guiding principle. In those words, there was a call for a renewal of the ideals animating the European project.

The Swiss writer, Denis de Rougemont, is significant for this book, because he brings all our four concepts together in his concept of Europe: the people, the individual, and the citizen are at the heart of Europe. Rougemont celebrates the small within the great, advocating that politics should always be about people. In his 'personalist' politics, the family should be allowed to play its role within the municipality, and the municipality within the State, and the State within Europe. No greater institution should intervene where a smaller one will enable individuals to resolve their own problems and thereby feel fully engaged in the social project. Clearly, Rougemont's Europe is a Europe of free and enlightened individuals, not of individualists who have lost sight of the greater good. Those individuals understand that it is only in partaking in the greater good that they can continue to enjoy their rights and fulfil their duties as individuals belonging to families, municipalities, States, and to Europe. This Europe involves a Federalism that unites persons and peoples, but ensures that unification does not entail uniformization. It is a bottom-up not a top-down form of organic federalism. Rougemont's ideal for Europe ensures the defence of persons freely following their own development as free agents within the smallest possible unit, family, school, region, and the State (see Ackerman 1996, and https://www.youtube.com/watch?v=-ZLc-mC6DgQ).

PERSONAL CORPORA

The three million word corpora for English, French, and American English gathering together texts available online on the http://www.gutenberg.org site, for example – texts with which the authors are very familiar – were studied in order to verify to what degree the quotations above could be relied upon to give an accurate overall impression of attitudes to Europe in the three cultures.

MyEnglishCorpus

MyEnglishCorpus confirmed a general disinterest for Europe among the various British writers and philosophers included. Exceptions such as Byron and Joyce stand out all the more given the rarity of references to 'Europe'. But even this hardly contradicts the English disinterest, since it must be remembered that Byron was half-Scottish. And Joyce, like Wilde, was Irish. In many respects, Byron was 'anti-English', if by that we mean he resisted the imperialist and royalist rhetoric of his times. Byron had only biting irony for the celebration of Wellington and the Old Order that had crushed Napoleon. He saw this English 'saviour of Europe' more as the enslaver of the people

> Call'd 'Saviour of the Nations'--not yet saved,
> And 'Europe's Liberator'--still enslaved. (Byron 1824, *Don Juan*)

The famished people, retorted Byron, found little to rejoice in when Wellington 'freed fallen Europe from the unity of tyrants'. Joyce for his part, saw in the Irish activist, Collins, a proto-socialist who he believed was the first man in Europe to preach 'Freedom and denounce priestcraft' (*Portrait of an Artist*). For both authors, England was no longer the England of free yeomen, the England that stood in opposition to French tyranny of the Absolutist French kings of the seventeenth and eighteenth centuries. It was logical for Byron and Joyce that Europe offered a forum in which freedom and a radical social upheaval could be debated. At home in Ireland and in England there was famine, poverty and little freedom.

Elsewhere in British English, Europe proves rare. France is a major actor in Shakespeare's plays, and although rare references to Europe can be found in the various plays making up the trilogy of *Henry IV, V*, and *VI*, Europe does not exist in either *Macbeth* or in *Twelfth Night*. Padua exists in *The Taming of the Shrew*, just as Verona exists in *Romeo and Juliet*, and Rome exists in *Julius Caesar*, but on Shakespeare's stage, Europe plays a minor role. In fairness, this does not reflect the spirit of the times accurately. The man of letters, Francis Bacon, Shakespeare's contemporary, does speak about Europe, and considers it in relation to the State, war, and trade. And there persists in Bacon the idea of Europe as Christendom, the Christian Europe that fends off the Turks and the Ottomans, and that expels the Moors from Spain.

Around a century later, the philosopher, John Locke, speaks of 'European philosophers'. And if we can take Wordsworth and Byron as examples, the English Romantics appear to reflect a mood among some people in England that is more open to Europe: Coleridge and Mary Shelley both seek inspiration on the Continent. But the English nineteenth century novel seems uninspired by Europe on the whole. Jane Austen's characters navigate between the parish, the provinces, and London. Charles Dickens characters live in London or round about: they are aware of the expanding greatness of the British Empire under Queen Victoria, but Australia is more real than Europe to them. Dickens' *The Tale of Two Cities* is somewhat of an exception in this respect, in taking Paris and London as its settings. European novels are read, but when British characters seek adventure in the books of Robert Louis Stevenson it is invariably in the squalid quarters of London, in the Highlands, or on distant exotic islands where Long John Silver hobbles along, not in Europe.

MyFrenchCorpus

While the nineteenth century sees England expanding throughout the world and strengthening its grip on its United Kingdom, France focuses more on Europe from what can be made from MyFrenchCorpus. In contrast to the English corpus, the French writers and thinkers regularly make reference to Europe. The man of letters, La Bruyère, mentions Europe frequently. In the *Maxims* of La Rochefoucault, the politics of nations is bound up in the Houses of Europe, families, and dynasties. This is the Europe that Napoléon takes by storm: the conqueror speaks of '*Europe étonnée*', and the French people becoming the '*maîtres de toute l'Europe*' after vanquishing '*les tyrans d'Europe*' (1821, http://www.gutenberg.org/files/12230/12230-h/12230-h.htm). Napoléon would be vanquished by the Anglo-Prussian alliance, but although he brought war, he declared himself to be a force bringing peace, enlightenment and progress:

> *Vous voulez la paix, les Français combattent pour elle: nous ne passons sur votre territoire que pour obliger la cour de Vienne de se rendre au voeu de l'Europe désolée, et d'entendre les cris de ses peuples. Nous ne venons pas ici pour nous agrandir, la nature a tracé nos limites au Rhin et aux Alpes, dans le même temps qu'elle a posé au Tyrol les limites de la maison d'Autriche.*

Do you want peace? The French are fighting for it [her]. We are only passing through your territory in order to force the Viennese Court to submit itself to the desire of desperate Europe, and to listen to the cries of its peoples. We are not coming here to make ourselves greater. Nature traced the limits of our land with the Rhine and the Alps, when it set the Tyrolean Mountains as the limits of the Austrian House.

Something of that sentiment is echoed in Byron's satire of Wellington above. French success would be success for the peoples of Europe. By overthrowing the Houses of Europe, self-interested monarchies used to negotiating the fate of Europe like oligarchs, the French would free the peoples of Europe and allow them to realize their goals.

MyAmericanCorpus

In contrast to the English corpus, MyAmericanCorpus proves a treasure house for references to Europe. American authors appear fascinated by the languages of Europe, and by the inventions of Europe. The immigration of Europeans and the importation of European technology and know-how are considered of paramount importance. Travelling throughout Europe is felt to be fascinating, because it means Americans can return to the roots of American culture. Walt Whitman (1819–1892) and William Carlos Williams (1883–1963) will stand up against this tradition, striking their roots into their own American soil. But the Modernists – who are primarily Americans – from the poets, Pound, Eliot, HD, to the novelists, Henry James, Hemmingway and F. Scott Fitzgerald, will all seek their destiny in Europe. The philosophers and writers of Europe are references for them and for the generations that precede them.

The European powers exert a fascination over the Americans, and those powers are very much seen as 'European': they are considered to form part of one whole unified culture, however much that culture is torn apart by European wars. Long before the Great War and the Second World War, the Americans follow closely the fate of Europe as a whole and the parts that make it up, judging from the authors included in the three million word MyAmericanCorpus.

Europe is linked to religious questions. Europe remains the religious centre for American Catholics who owe allegiance to Rome. But most of all, it is the departure of the settlers looking for a new religious freedom that is fundamental for the American identity. And even when Americans break with Europe, the break they make defines them as a nation. This becomes a pervasive mode of self-definition. Even the most American of poets, Walt Whitman, uses Europe to help define what it means to be American. By opposing Europe, America realizes itself. It is in this spirit that he declares in *Years of the Unperformed*:

> I see the frontiers and boundaries of the old aristocracies broken;
> I see the landmarks of European kings removed. (1865, https://www.gutenberg.org/files/1322/1322-h/1322-h.htm)

In the twentieth century, after initially hesitating and debating the benefits of isolationism, America joined its European allies in combat in the First and Second World Wars. Fighting and winning the First World

War helped to launch a narrative of America as the saviour of Europe, a narrative that would be consolidated with F. D. Roosevelt's declaration of war in 1941. This has proven a very tenacious narrative, and it runs from Roosevelt to Rumsfeld in the second Iraq war (2003). War as a vocation is implicit to US foreign policy and the American imagination. While anti-war activists in 2003 were considering the war in terms of Vietnam (see Underhill 2003, 2012), Rumsfeld was harkening back to images of American soldiers planting the Stars and Stripes on the Reichstag in Berlin in 1945. This narrative has an indisputable force. Roosevelt knew only too well how relieved Churchill and his nation were to finally find America at their side, and that gives an undeniable gravity to his words:

> There is a direct connection between the bonds you have bought and the stream of men and equipment now rushing over the English Channel for the liberation of Europe. There is a direct connection between your bonds and every part of this global war today. (F. D. Roosevelt, 23 June 1944, http://www.presidency.ucsb.edu/ws/?pid=16522)

America was providing a shared narrative for a shared experience. In many ways, throughout Hollywood's representation of the war effort, that narrative asserted itself. But in parallel, especially after the economic crisis of the 1970s and the flagging faith in the American dream, a new narrative began to emerge. Doubts about the idea that anyone could succeed in America with sufficient hard work and tenacity and talent, began to give rise to comparisons with the social and economic model emerging with the European Union. And in those comparisons, Europe fairs well. Jeremy Rifkin's *European Dream*, cited in the opening quotes of this chapter represents the culmination of this logic that leads to a longing for a European model more in tune with today's world. Despite a patriotic love of American ideals and the dream of the resourceful frontiersman, Rifkin concludes that contemporary capitalism, the environment, and human beings in general require another kind of dream than individualism, self-sufficiency, and the capacity to defend against attacks. Rifkin stresses the need to work in networks, find shared solutions to global problems of an economic, social, and ecological order. That kind of world, he believes, requires of us that we cultivate diplomacy and dialogue, tolerance of difference, and creative solutions for promoting well-being. These are not American ideals, but they are, he believes, qualities we require to thrive in the modern world. With great elegance, Rifkin sets the two dreams side by side in the opening chapter of his book whose subtitle reads: 'How Europe's vision of the future is eclipsing the American Dream'.

> For us [Americans], freedom has long been associated with autonomy. ... The more wealth one amasses, the more independent one is in the world. One is free by becoming self-reliant and an island unto onseself. With wealth, comes exclusivity, and with exclusivity comes security.
> The New European Dream, however, is based on a different set of assumptions about what constitutes freedom and security. For Europeans, freedom is not found in autonomy but in embeddedness. To be free is to have access to a myriad of interdependent relationships with others. The more communities one has access to, the more options one has, for living a full and meaningful life. With relationships, comes inclusivity, and with inclusivity, comes security.
> The American Dream puts an emphasis on economic growth, personal wealth, and independence. The new European Dream focuses more on sustainable development, quality of life, and interdependence. The American Dream pays homage to the work ethic. The European Dream is more attuned to leisure and deep play. The American Dream is inseparable from the country's religious heritage and deep spiritual faith. The European Dream is secular to the core. The American Dream is assimilationist. We associate success with shedding former cultural ties and becoming free agents in the great American melting pot. The European, by contrast, is based on preserving one's cultural identity and living in a multicultural world. The American Dream is wedded to love of country and patriotism. The European Dream is more cosmopolitan and less territorial. The Americans are more willing to employ military force in the world, if necessary, to protect what we feel to be our vital self-interests. Europeans are more reluctant to use military force and, instead, favor diplomacy, economic assistance, and aid to avert conflict, and prefer peacekeeping operations to maintain order. The Americans tend to think locally ... The European Dream is more expansive, and systemic in nature and, therefore, more bound to the welfare of the planet. (Rifkin 2005: Chapter 1)

In terms of diplomacy and richness of lifestyle, Europe is celebrated by Rifkin and it would be difficult to find a European who could so clearly define the ideals of the new emerging Europe. Without denigrating his own culture, and its ideals, Rifkin systematically contrasts the different ways Americans and Europeans understand wealth, work, security, geopolitical conflicts, and environmental threats. He is not turning his back on the American dream, but he is affirming that the future needs another kind of dream, and he is dreaming of Europe.

DOES THE PRESS MISREPRESENT EUROPE?

Judging from the press throughout European countries, a problem seems to have been growing over the past decade. France had long been the defender of the European project. But by 1 January 2016, there was nothing particularly surprising about the title in *Libération* 'From crisis to crisis, Europe is heading towards the brink of the abyss' (*Crise après crise, l'Europe fonce vers l'abîme*)

> *L'Union européenne passera-t-elle l'année 2016? Jamais depuis le début de la construction communautaire, dans les années 50, elle n'a encaissé une telle succession de chocs. « Je perçois pour la première fois un danger sérieux de désagrégation de l'UE », a solennellement averti, cette semaine, l'Allemand Günther Oettinger, le commissaire européen chargé du numérique. Jean-Claude Juncker, le président de l'exécutif européen, lui, s'est dit « sans illusion » sur l'année qui commence et, en plaisantant, s'est jugé encore « trop jeune » pour dire si 2015 avait été l'année la plus difficile de toute l'histoire de l'Union ...*

> Will the European Union survive 2016? Never, since the very beginning of the construction of the community, back in the 50s, has Europe suffered such a series of shocks. 'For the very first time, I perceive a serious danger of disintegration for the EU', the European Commissioner, responsible for new technologies, Günther Oettinger warned. Jean-Claude Juncker, the President of the European Executive, for his part, said he 'had no illusions' regarding the year to come, and joked that he considered himself 'too young' to tell if 2015 had been the most difficult year in the history of the Union. (http://www.liberation.fr)

French optimism has certainly seemed to wane in recent years. And with it, enthusiasm for Europe throughout the Union has waned.

Euroscepticism has never been rare. Opportunistic politicians have often relied on resentful feelings towards European legislation and norms to present themselves as defenders of the nation and the people's heroes. The ex-President, Jacques Chirac, considers himself a friend to Europe. But back in the 1970s, when he was angling for the leadership of the party in a stand-off with the pro-European Valéry Giscard d'Estaing, Chirac could be heard ranting that his France would not be *'open like a sieve to all the crises of Europe'*, or subjugated to Germano-American interests that produced unemployment (https://www.youtube.com). Ambitious and adaptable, Chirac was a professional politician. And the conclusion voiced in India's *The Statesman*, on 13 March 2007 (and recorded in the *OED* under the entry 'European', http://public.oed.com) is probably a fair account of Chirac's varying positions on Europe: 'During his pre-presidential political career, Mr Chirac was, at various times, a fierce Eurosceptic and a convinced European.'

Such opportunism is not rare in the politics of the Member States, but, formerly, Europe seemed more resilient and better equipped for fending off criticism. Things have taken a turn for the worse since the 1970s though. By 2016, *Libération* was referring to the 2007 economic crisis, the Greek economic crisis, the destabilization of North Africa, causing the influx of immigrants, and Britain's vote on exiting the Eurozone.

The French were not alone in spelling out their fears of a pending disaster. Catastrophic titles can be found in the Spanish press. On 21 March 2016, *El País* online published an article entitled *'Crisis Refugiados Europa'*: we could read that *'20 países ofrecen funcionarios para aplicar la expulsión de refugiados'* (http://elpais.com; '20 countries offer officials to implement the expulsion of refugees'): the countries were, of course, European countries. And on Christmas Day in 2015, Germany's *Der Spiegel* online lamented the state of Europe in an article entitled, *'Krise der EU: Ach Europe'* (http://www.spiegel.de; 'The EU Crisis: Oh Dear Europe').

Im Flüchtlingsdrama ist keine Einigung in Sicht, die Eurokrise schwelt weiter, Rechtspopulisten gewinnen Wahlen, Großbritannien droht auszusteigen. Ist die EU zum Scheitern verurteilt?

There is no agreement is in sight for the 'refugee drama', the Euro crisis continues to smoulder, right-wing populist parties are winning elections, and Britain is threatening to opt out. Is the EU doomed?

The *Daily Mail* in Britain rejoices in alarmist reports and revelled in titles like 'Helpless French police are over-run as hundreds more migrants storm Channel Tunnel declaring "it's England or death"' (http://www.dailymail.co.uk). And calls to send in the military to deal with the immigrants have been widespread in the British press. In Britain, Nigel Farage, in France, Marine Le Pen, and in Germany, Alternative für Deutschland, were all whipping up anti-European sentiment in 2015 and 2016 among those suffering from unemployment or precarious employment, and among those fearing they would have to foot the bill for immigrants while being asked to bear up to austerity measures imposed by the EU. Similar alarmist titles can be found in Czech, Slovak, and Polish. And even among the Danes and the Swedes the far-right Eurosceptic parties appeared to be gaining ground.

Yet in contrast to these headlines and front page news, the more moderate Czech press, like *Lidové Noviny* (http://www.lidovky.cz/), continued to discuss the shared future of European citizens in a whole host of articles relating to various spheres of life in Europe. Unlike its English counterparts, the Scottish press, *The Scotsman* (http://www.scotsman.com) and *The Herald* (http://www.heraldscotland.com), do have front page news that refers to developments and innovations in EU policy. This contrasts with the general doom and gloom or alarmist rhetoric of both the tabloids and the 'quality papers' in England.

Europe certainly seems to have problems, nonetheless. And the fact that the French press has slipped into Eurosceptic mode is significant, because French idealism worked as a counterweight to scepticism. The erosion of French idealism has left a vacuum. In one sense, it may seem surprising how much the other nations of Europe used to rely upon France's unflinching faith in Europe and in itself as Europe's motor. Indeed, it is strange that so many bought into the logic of the French universalistic European narrative. For that narrative is underpinned by a precarious spatial delusion. Just as France is conceptually constructed on the myth that Paris and Versailles are at the centre (rather than in the North), France used to see itself not so much as being in the West of Europe, as being at the very centre of Europe. However absurd this may seem, if we look at a map, the idea of France – and Paris – at the centre of Europe is a principle that is difficult to dislodge in the French imagination. This inevitably situates Prague and Warsaw on the fringes of Europe to the East, although those cities were very much at the heart of conquests and conflicts over Europe in the eighteenth and nineteenth centuries. The danger is symbolic. If Euro-enthusiasm was withering in this symbolic 'heart' of Europe, then Euroscepticism could develop unhindered. With the implosion of French confidence, Europe appeared to need to find a new leader to inspire it. This explains the attraction that a fair part of the French electorate felt for Emmanuel Macron, and his popularity among pro-Europeans like the German chancellor, Angela Merkel, and her government.

Is it fair though to consider the front page declarations of crises and breakdowns as representative of the public opinions of the Member States on the future of the European Union? Or are Farage and Le Pen only the voices of frustrated petty politicians riding on waves of resentment, as Chirac once sought to do in his bid for presidency? We need to go beyond those antagonistic titles if we want to see more clearly how the discourse on Europe is constructed in the British press. And this will take us into conceptual metaphors and narratives that are framing the debates on Europe's role and future.

METAPHORS FOR EUROPE

Whether Europe is perceived to be 'in crisis' or 'in good health', it is conceived of in metaphoric terms. Metaphor theory in recent years has become a rigorous field of study (see Lakoff and Johnson 1980, 1999; Fauconnier and Turner 2003; Goatly 2007; Underhill 2011; http://www.metaphorik.de). Metaphoric reasoning has long been understood to be a valid form of exploring ideas and expression. And metaphoric thinking differs among cultures. There is nothing deterministic in this though. And we are not the prisoners of the patterning of language. Figurative or symbolic language does not enclose us in a conceptual prison house that forces, constricts, and limits creative or innovative thought. We can choose our metaphors. We can choose to reject metaphors in use, or we can adapt them. Hugo can lift the ideal of Europe up, and hold it to be a 'superior unity' (*'unité supérieure'*). Chirac, on the other hand, can refuse the Europe he denigrates as a mere 'sieve' (*'passoire'*) that lets in all forms of unemployment and interests running counter to the French people. Likewise, English-speakers can creatively resist the metaphors that other peoples use to construct Europe as an ideal or a workaday reality. Whether it is considered to be an 'edifice under construction', a 'household falling apart', an 'adventure', a 'journey', or a 'dead-end', the metaphoric patterning, with its spatial logic, its trajectories, its origins and destinations, can all be espoused, critiqued, or creatively resisted and inverted. Poets, pranksters, and satirists have always played with metaphor. And today it is widely recognized by many linguists that creative thought is inseparable from metaphoric thinking.

Nonetheless, patterning does differ from language to language, and although a massive process of homogenization has taken place with the construction of Europe, and the writing of European laws and guidelines for the twenty-seven Member States, the metaphoric scenarios being played out over the past few decades are neither innocent nor neutral. They have their origins in the traditions of the nation states that produced them and the linguistic communities that developed them. Even at a fundamental level, the rhetoric of Europe has been cultivated to different degrees. Personification and animation intervene to varying degrees, for example in English and French. In the English tradition, Europe is more often than not a space. It is rarely an actor.

Its demise does, admittedly, suppose it once was an actor: so when Burke lamented that the 'glory of Europe is extinguished for ever' as quoted above, he both animates and kills Europe. Declarations that Europe shall speak with one voice are rare in the English tradition however. Consequently, de Gaulle's words that 'all of Europe will decide the destiny of the world' (*'c'est l'Europe, c'est toute l'Europe qui décidera du déstin du monde'* (*ODQ* 1992: 235), strike English-speakers as strange – inspiring perhaps – but curiously novel.

A cursory glance at the press confirms that Europe is remoulded in metaphoric terms. *The Sun* online (http://www.thesun.co.uk) immediately offered the following titles that can serve as examples:

> John Major accuses Brexit campaign of 'fantasy' and says vote to leave will poison Europe.

> Europe's in the bag: next goal is Champs League.

In the first, Europe is animated: as an animal or person, it can be poisoned by the campaign to leave it. In the second, Europe is reduced to the European Cup and, as a trophy, that Europe can be 'bagged'. In other terms, Europe is objectified and recuperated. This reflects a soft version of that kind of barbarian incursion mentality of English football supporters. The logic of 'conquering' or 'pillaging' Europe reaches its logical conclusion in the hooligan culture at times exported by Britain (as well as Holland and Germany, and increasingly Russia). In the example above, the fusion of football rules and the club's strategy, conceived of in terms of 'goals', is a familiar metaphor that proves all too apt here.

Throughout Europe, some conceptual metaphors related to vehicles and houses appear to be widespread. Conceptual metaphors are those fundamental structuring paradigms around which extensions and innovative metaphors converge. Europe can be an animal or a man: a sick man, or a sick animal. Curiously, Europe is rarely feminized as 'liberty' is (even in English idealized personifications). This lack of feminization may appear logical in German in which '*Europa*' is neuter, but in French, '*Europe*' and in Czech, '*Evropa*' are both feminine. And yet no archetypal 'feminine characteristic' – matriarchal, seductive, or otherwise – appears to be projected onto the concept of Europe in either French or Czech.

Europe can be a machine that runs smoothly or breaks down. Or it can be a vehicle that moves forwards, stalls or, once more, breaks down. Europe can be a house, and at times, that house is considered in terms of a household, a home; that is to say, Europeans are invited to see themselves as a 'family'. But this often spells havoc more than harmony. In recent negative usages, the concept of 'divorce' has been used in relation to Europe in various languages. This is not the place to pursue a comparative metaphoric study of Europe, but it is worth tracing some of the main outlines of metaphors and their trajectories in English because recent scholarship has produced some highly impressive studies.

Michael Kimmel, from the University of Vienna, produced just such a study in 'Metaphors of the EU Constitutional Debate – Ways of Charting Discourse Coherence in a Complex Metaphor Field' (2009). Kimmel was not working in a vacuum. His work emerged out of a tradition in metaphor theory that had already explored metaphoric paradigms for Europe (see Chilton and Ilyin 1993; Schäffner 1993; Musolff 2004; Bärtsch 2004; Reining 2005). That wide range of scholars had already demonstrated that the EU is commonly seen in terms of a body, a house, a family, or a journey, and other things besides. However, Kimmel went on to transform their research by investigating not only the ways metaphoric logic can be countered, but also the way fundamentally incompatible conceptual metaphors – for example, metaphors which conceive of Europe as a vehicle, a destination, or a static object, an edifice – can be harnessed together in order to consolidate a greater picture. Although this produced mixed metaphors, those mixed metaphors nevertheless prove effective in eliciting an emotional reaction and in winning over readers to a given perspective. Kimmel's study of the discourse coherence in the complex metaphor field of 'Europe' focused on a corpus drawn from articles related to the 2005 first round of the referendum about the EU's constitutional treaty. In the minds of those backing the treaty, it was supposed to create a stronger basis for Europe by making it more manageable during the ongoing enlargement process. It was also designed to make Europe stronger. But as we all remember, that was not to be.

The treaty was rejected in both the Netherlands and France in May 2005, and this triggered a major EU crisis. As could be expected, the Eurosceptic British press made much of the No vote, all the more so because it came from countries that were perceived in Britain as 'Eurofriendly'. The Tory opposition turned it into an attack on Blair's Yes campaign, and Rupert Murdoch's anti-European media empire had a field day. But Kimmel did not limit his study to the 'tabloids', or what is commonly referred to as the 'gutter press': he was careful to compare and contrast articles drawn from both *The Guardian*, and its Sunday supplement, *The Observer*, as well as *The Sun*. Kimmel found *The Guardian*'s articles to be more eloquent in their arguments. But he found *The Sun* made up for the shortness of its articles with highly dense metaphor packages. Indeed, Kimmel found almost twice as many metaphors per word count in *The Sun* as he did in *The Guardian*.

Among the most fertile conceptual metaphors were the metaphors of Europe understood as 'a journey', 'an edifice', 'a machine', and 'a container'. Kimmel also explored the metaphoric paradigms of 'the centre and the periphery', 'dynamic interaction', 'a body', 'a person', 'a creature', and 'a social group' (Kimmel 2009: 57–61). As a space, Britain could be 'engulfed' or 'left outside', and 'excluded' (p. 61). It could join in the 'club', when Europe was understood as an elite social group. As a dynamic interaction, it could be 'pulled together' or 'pulled apart' (pp. 58–59).

Katharina Leonhardt provided a comparative study of French and German metaphors for Europe conceived as 'a body' or 'a family', with 'adoptive children'. In her study, entitled 'Dem europäischen Körper eine europäische Seele. Körperkonzepte einer europäischen Identität' (2012), Leonhardt demonstrated the compatibility of metaphoric frameworks found in her bilingual French and German corpus. Interestingly, however, it appears that German is translating French ideals and French frameworks of understanding. Thus, even when Leonhardt quoted the German press, French translations could be seen to be shaping the debate in German over the identity and 'spirit' of Europe. The following example from *Die Welt* reveals this all too clearly:

Saarbrücken „Am Ende seiner Amtszeit äußerte er [scil. Jacques Delors] den Wunsch, dem europäischen Körper eine europäische Seele einzuhauchen. (*Welt* 8 October 2004, quoted by Leonhardt 2012: 66)

At the end of his tenure, he [Jacques Delors] expressed his desire that the European body breathe with a European soul.

These metaphoric paradigms take us to the heart of the comparative linguistic project. It is fundamental for understanding the way cultures apprehend concepts and install them into their own culture-specific traditions of understanding. And this introduces the crucial question of how cultures apprehend other culutures' metaphoric frameworks, and how they translate and assimilate them into their own worldviews. For this chapter on Europe though, we cannot afford to give metaphor theory the scope it deserves, and we must content ourselves with a couple of examples of the way metaphors are harnessed in discursive strategies. The edifice and the machine conceptual metaphors, quoted below extensively, should give us an idea of the insights that Kimmel's approach offers us by systematically analysing the ways metaphoric extensions are built upon a central organizing paradigm.

The EU as edifice
THE EU IS AN EDIFICE is a powerful central mapping that engenders different scenarios and variants. A first set of metaphors highlights the EU's political soundness (or not), its institutional permanence (or not), and its underlying vision or plan. The generally very EU-skeptic Sun emphasizes that the EU is not well put-together, welcoming the 'trumpets of doom [that] are sounding across the European Union' and speaking of 'the first wholesale rebuilding of the EU for 50 years' as well as 'the crumbling walls of jerry-built Europe'. Accordingly, the anti-EU front should 'wreck the EU' or 'scupper the blueprint in a [UK] referendum'. In all of these metaphors, the EU's structural integrity is destroyed through force. The Guardian employs the same scenario with a more varied emphasis. It sees the EU as an 'edifice' that needs to be 'constructed'/'built', an 'institutional pillar of the post-war world', although it is also characterized as 'rickety', prone to 'collapse', or being 'wrecked'. It has 'architecture' and 'architects', it 'has to go back to the drawing board' to revise its 'blueprint' or rearrange its

'institutional furniture'. Second, a wholly different line of reasoning concerns the EU enlargement. In this scenario, the EU can 'open its doors' or become a 'fortress', be 'fortified', 'buttressed', build up a 'wall', or 'pull up its Drawbridge'.

The EU as machinery
THE EU IS A MACHINE is deployed mainly with the intent of focusing on the EU's internal preconditions of functioning. In the Guardian (N=24), metaphors depict the EU as an 'engine', 'machinery' or 'motor of integration' that is 'working' or not. Important states are characterized as the 'engine room'. The constitution's purpose is to ensure its 'smooth running', to 'prevent(s) the motor's stalling', to 'oil its machinery', 'keep it going for decades' and to prevent 'gridlock'. The voters' rejection of the constitution 'put[s] a spanner in the EU works', 'dismantle[s]' it or 'send[s] it back to the drawing board'. Two metaphors in the Sun (N=2) emphasize the EU's complex internal structure and complementary mechanic parts in stating that the EU 'works like a ratchet' and describing a country as a 'cog in the massive EU wheel'. (Kimmel 2009: 57)

Metaphors do allow us to think both coherently and imaginatively, even though the metaphors used often prove incompatible. Their logics do not fit perhaps. But as Kimmel argues, competing conceptual metaphors can combine to form what he calls a kind of 'conceptual glue' that enables them to function together as 'a metaphoric cluster' (p. 51). The house, the machine, and the family can all 'fall apart'. We can be cast out of circles, families, and clubs. Buildings must be strong and stable, and ships must be sleek and swift. But buildings falling down and ships being scuttled amounts to much the same thing: they are destroyed, broken up, they go down to their doom, whether they fall or sink.

These would seem to be the metaphors that are being used to represent – and often to denigrate – the actors of Europe and their project. The architects of Europe are often disparaged: Thatcher's 'blueprint' for a union was questioned by *The Guardian*. And 'as the principal architect', Giscard d'Estaing, was 'forced back to the drawing board' (Kimmel 2009: 69).

These metaphors may appear strange to cultures that do not shape the narrative of the Europe story in the way the British press does. One of the fascinating parts of comparing concepts, though, is trying to understand the ways peoples find it virtually inconceivable that such metaphoric patterning makes sense to other linguistic communities. Europe shares metaphors, as Leonhardt's examples suggest, but the logic of some of Europe's metaphoric narratives often proves entirely alien, if not absurd, to those whose languages frame Europe in different metaphoric narratives. What this proves is that learning foreign languages is not simply about learning foreign words, it is about learning to project ourselves into the foreign culture's concepts and into the narratives that those concepts are bound up in. The examples above only touch the tip of the iceberg, but they should outline some of the main narratives that Europe is being written into. This reveals something about the undeniable diversity of Europe. But as we shall see, however diverse they may be, they remain European scenarios, and the scenarios that characterize the Chinese perception of Europe and its activities will be very different.

EUROPE IN EUROPA

Official accounts of Europe give a different impression from the disaster scenarios presented in the popular press of the various Member States. As might be expected, the multilingual EU website tells the story of Europe in very different terms from the ones used in the British press and in Kimmel's study of the 2005 referendum. Of course, Europa is concerned with the promotion of the European project. It spreads information regarding its laws and the difficulties the European Parliament sees itself facing and the solutions it proposes for them. But however biased the website might seem, the sheer scope of the issues handled and the details indicating the methods and modes by which the citizens of the Member States should go about their everyday lives bears witness to the overarching power of Europe. The language of Europe is now everywhere in Europe.

On the Bulgarian page we are invited to consult webpages on 'life, work, and travel in the EU' (*Живот, работа, пътуване в ЕС*, http://europa.eu/eu-life/index_bg.htm). The same pages can be found on the Czech section of the website (http://europa.eu/eu-life/index_cs.htm). In a user-friendly tone, under the heading 'My life in the EU' ('*Můj život v EU*'), Czech European Internet readers are given 'Information and legal advice on your rights to live, work, study and travel abroad' ('*Informace a právní poradenství ohledně vašich práv týkajících se pobytu, zaměstnání, studia a cestování v zahraničí*'). Elsewhere on the website, Czechs can find a wealth of data on the history of the EU and how it works. These are presented neutrally as 'facts'. And indeed, they are not fiction. Workers rights, permits, pensions, and pension payments are all part of our everyday life now in Europe. And they determine who stays where they are, and who goes where they want to. The French may express doubts about whether Europe is working for them, but the French Erasmus programme that sends students off on European grants to study abroad has never once failed in the thirty years it has been working.

In Poland, many people have voiced concern over the hold on parliament and the presidency of the New Right-wing conservative Law and Justice Party (PiS), led by Jaroslaw Kaczynski, who took office in November 2015. And this scared many Europeans and Poles alike given the Eurosceptic alignment of the party. Some Poles satirized the precarious ambivalence of their government, claiming that the PiS government continued to fly the European flag, since sooner or later Poland would run out of money and go running to Brussels for a handout. Euroscepticism finds friends within the State, but the Polish State continues to think of the EU as a piggy bank that can be used to pay compensation for wrongs done to Poland in its history (http://wyborcza.pl/1,75968,19247276,flage-ue-wyprowadzic.html?disableRedirects=true). This is not the place to go into the narratives and myths of national pride and victimization, but the Polish case is not an exception, and parallels can be drawn. England, Scotland, France, Corsica, and the various Spanish states, the Basques and the Catalans are all capable of propagating narratives to defend their own interests and generate a feeling of a shared community of victims. The shared enemy can be Europe, or it can be the nation state (Spain for the Basques; Britain for the Scots). According to the interests being defended, Europe can become the target of attacks or it can be set up as the ally in an independence movement.

On the other hand, Eurosceptic narratives are often contradicted by concurrent narratives. While the PiS government fuels Eurosceptic feeling, the Polish Europa web portal (http://europa.eu/pol/ener/index_pl.htm) continues to explain the way the Poles, as part of Europe, are resolving ongoing economic issues as part of Europe. In one article for example, Poles could read that Europe was dealing with 'a growing demand for energy and struggling with problems of price volatility and supply disruptions' (*Europa stoi w obliczu rosnącego zapotrzebowania na energię i boryka się z problemami zmienności cen i zakłóceń dostaw*').

These everyday examples should not distract us from the enormous problems facing Europe within and without its borders. Europe's borders have unquestionably changed since Brexit. Britain is now facing an economic crisis with loans to be returned to the European Bank, and the consequences of that could prove painful for Europe, since the EU will continue to rely on Britain as a major trading partner. Migrant problems continue to upset citizens and leave communities feeling uncertain as to whether their statesmen at a national and European level are protecting them. This explains the rise in popularity of populist demagogues like Farage in England, and Le Pen in France. It contributes to explaining the loss of faith in the Socialist Party in France that was routed in the presidential elections and the legislative elections of 2017. It partly explains the rise of an angry anti-European left led by Melenchon in the same French elections.

A feeling of fear has taken hold of many European citizens, and this has led to a retreat from Europe. As we saw in the chapter on the people, even the newly elected pro-Brussels President of France, Emanuel Macron, was forced to acknowledge that a fear of the future had fused with a fear of Europe when he claimed on the night of the first round of elections that he had heard 'the fears of the French people' ('*les peurs du peuple de France*', (https://www.youtube.com/watch?v=oTuJud-kgR4). These fears may be deeply felt. Nonetheless, the stories of European negotiations discussed on the Europa website should demonstrate that in terms of trade, energy, laws, work, travel, and education and benefits, Europe is finding solutions to many of its most pressing problems. In this light, the alarmist press of many of the Member States appears somewhat disingenuous. As Europe continues to solidify its foundations and rebuild the way we live together today, it is possible that disaster scenarios reveal a spirit of *Schadenfreude* fuelled by frustration. The more Europe binds us together, the more certain people celebrate pulling Europe apart.

This spirit does have a certain creative enthusiasm, it must be admitted. The *Daily Mail* (http://www.dailymail.co.uk, 22 March 2016) posted the article entitled 'The unlikely anthem for Brexit', about a song written by 'the distinguished actress', Sarah Miles, to encourage people to vote for Britain to leave the Eurozone. The week before, the centre-left weekly, *Le Nouvel Observateur*, in France (http://tempsreel.nouvelobs.com, 17 March 2016) had posted an article entitled, 'What remains of Schengen? Visit Europe in a state of total disintegration'

('*Que reste-t-il de Schengen? Voyage dans une Europe en pleine désintégration*'). The journalist went onto argue:

Contrôles rétablis entre les pays, clôtures, peuples à nouveau séparés ... La crise migratoire est en train de mettre fin à cette expérience unique d'un monde sans frontière. De la Suède à la Grèce, tour d'Europe d'une utopie à bout de souffle.

Control checks reinstated between countries, fences, separating peoples once again ... The migrant crisis is putting an end to this unique experience of a world without borders. From Sweden to Greece, welcome to a European tour of a utopia that is at its last gasp.

Compared to the Europa website, this catastrophic rhetoric may be considered a curious form of schizophrenia. On the one hand, Europe appears poised on the brink of the abyss. And yet it never actually falls. It must hold itself there for decades on the brink, with a sense of vertigo adding to the anguish. Meanwhile, European peoples live a relatively comfortable, prosperous and peaceful existence, in a Europe whose laws and liberties are daily constrained or consolidated by mutual consent according to the democratic process that goes on almost unnoticed by the national press.

PROVISIONAL FINDINGS

If we can understand the translation we have given for the French article on Schengen, it is because a pervasive Euroscepticsim has taken hold of much of the discourse circulating on Europe in the press and in many other publications besides. But there is one stumbling block, the central metaphor of a world without borders: a wall-less world. This is a French metaphor, enshrined in the name of the French humanitarian organization *Médecins sans frontiers*, which translates clumsily into 'Doctors without borders'. France did see itself breaking down the barriers between classes in its French Revolution, and in its expansionist campaigns to 'liberate' Europe. France has continued to preach its universal vocation as a rational force for freedom and *les droits de l'homme* (which does not translate exactly into 'human rights'). In this scenario, France would break down barriers and enlighten the world. Europe took up the torch after France failed to conquer all in its path, and after the two world wars.

The crowning moment of breaking down walls was the fall of the Berlin Wall in 1989, a central narrative of fraternity, unity, and shared vision. That vision was promoted and celebrated within Europe as part of the neoliberal discourse on deregulating markets. And to a large extent, that paradigm was exported and welcomed throughout the liberal capitalist states of the world. But it depended upon the fairy tale narrative of an 'Open Europe' that welcomed everyone into it: a borderless Europe. Throughout the 1980s, Europe had been consolidating its control on immigration across its borders, through the accords it set up with states that acted as filters to stem the flow of migrants.

It may well be that terrorist attacks, the destabilization of North Africa and Syria, and the migrant crisis are combining to force Europeans to rewrite their central narratives (Underhill 2015). Can Europe pretend today that it is opening its arms to all the citizens of the Member States and to the world as a whole? Or does Europe have to face up to the fact that its insiders demand rights and respect, the privileges of citizenship as voters, workers, and natives of Europe? Will Europeans be prepared to accord to 'outsiders' the right to those Euro-specific rights? Whatever the case may be, we have been able to trace some of the major facets of the European concept as it has renewed itself through the dramatic chain of events that have shaped its narrative.

Europe is more than a concept. More than an ideal. Europe is real. And it is transforming the reality of our everyday lives in a vast range of fields. But it is couched in complex, often contradictory metaphors. It is a destination, not yet reached. It is a ship that might sink or be scuttled. It is a machine that can break down. It is a family whose members can file for divorce.

The Americans dream of Europe. The English disparage it. The Scots – both those in favour and those against independence – look to Europe as the new field of exercise for their efforts and their endeavours, cultural, commercial and political. The French are perhaps still going through a period of disenchantment, but they voted for a pro-European president in Emanuel Macron, they still see themselves at the centre of Europe, and they continue to see the Poles and the Portuguese on the fringes. The British press fuels prejudices and fantasies. But the lobbies against Brexit exerted a powerful influence on the June 2017 elections called by Theresa May that led to a disastrous hung Parliament and expressed a lack of confidence in the Conservative Party that was promising to 'get Brexit right'. As it is becoming increasingly obvious, economically, politically and culturally, Britain is very much attached and tied to Europe. The rebellious belligerent British bulldog stance is something of an anachronism that depends upon an idealized 'outsider' perspective. Ultimately, that bears little in common with the actual ways in which British life is organized within the European Union. Recent examples of this fear-fed neurosis tend to rely on ignorance of how Europe actually works. To that extent, Euroscepticism manifests itself as a culturally specific form of indifference for Europe that is quintessentially and traditionally English, rather than Scottish or Irish judging from our corpora study.

The narratives about Europe would appear to be changing. In the wall-less world scenario, Europeans tended to congratulate themselves on being warm and welcoming. They tore down the hateful Iron Curtain when they broke down the Berlin Wall and reunited friends and families in Germany. This narrative sets up Europe as a moral guide, preaching to other nations about universal human rights. As Rousseau had remarked though, Europe is not particularly welcoming; and what was true of the eighteenth century, appears true of the twenty-first. Judging from articles on the migrant crisis in the European press, Europe wants its walls to protect itself from those outside. Increasingly inward-looking today, Europeans no longer aspire to become the world citizens who export the universal ideals of the French Revolution. Neither do Europeans appear to be animated by the pragmatic expansionism of British Imperialism. Today, Europeans appear to be worried about their futures, their job security, and the future of their children.

This means the metaphors of conquering and expansion have given way to metaphors of homes and houses, walls and protection, families, clubs, and partnerships. The disadvantage with such metaphoric scenarios is that they tend to sacrifice the spirit of fraternity to those who are more interested in building a European Fortress. And can Europeans build a community without a spirit of fraternity? Nightmare scenarios seem to have tightened their grip on the imagination of the media throughout Europe, and – paradoxically – dreams of Europe seem to be more cherished outside the European Union than within.

A major shift in symbolism can be observed. Back in 2005, before the economic crises of 2007 and 2008, before the migrant crisis, before the depression in Greece and before Brexit, Jeremy Rifkin was dreaming of an inclusive idealism that respected difference and promoted networking and shared solutions for the economy, for society, and for the planet. He sought inspiration in Europe. Whether we will look back at Rifkin's words, like we do to Hugo's, and see them as insightful remains to be seen, but certainly, many Europeans seem curiously incapable of generating such a generous account of their shared project as a community as the one Rifkin espouses. As he put it: 'My sense is that a European Dream is now beginning to take shape and form. It's still at the birthing stage, but its contours are already becoming clear' (Rifkin 2005: Chapter 1). Sceptics are not hard to find in Europe, but Rifkin insisted that the question was not whether the Europeans were living up to their dream. As he reminded readers, the Americans rarely lived up to theirs. But he insisted that 'Europe has articulated a new vision for the future' (ibid.). And in that future world, Rifkin argues, it is important to try to understand 'why the European Dream might be better positioned to accommodate the many forces that are leading us to a more connected and interdependent globalized society' (ibid.).

INTRODUCING EUROPE TO CHINA, OR CHINA TO EUROPE?[2]

In his history of Chinese linguistics, the Chinese scholar Hé Jiǔyíng 何九盈 included the word *ōuhuà* 欧化 ('to 'Europeanize' or 'Europeanization') among the 'keywords' (*guānjiàncí* 关键词) in modern Chinese knowledge. And he made the following claim:

> 请看中国现代学术史有哪些关键词: 欧化 (西化), 全盘西化, 西学东渐, 反传统, 国学(国粹)。关键词当然不止这些, 而这些应是最重要的, 其中最重要的只有下面这个词: 欧化。欧化, 导致古今学术大别。(Hé 1995: 761)

> Let's consider the key-words in modern Chinese academic history: Europeanization (Westernization), total Westernization, the spread of Western Learning to the East, anti-traditionalism, national studies (national essence). The keywords are not limited to these, of course, but these are the most important of them, and among all of them 'Europeanization' is the most significant. Europeanization led to the distinction between ancient and modern knowledge.

This is truly perplexing for Europeans, since the word *ōuhuà* 'Europeanization' or 'to Europeanize' both refers to their shared culture, but does not refer to a concept that is particularly familiar in any of the European languages. At times, 'Europeanization' can be considered as a quasi-synonym of 'Westernization'. Nonetheless, the use of this term, and the relevance it is attributed when Hé Jiǔyíng claims that of them all 'Europeanization is the most important', reflects the strong impact European culture had on Chinese culture between the eighteenth and the early twentieth centuries. And Hé Jiǔyíng (who describes 'Europeanization' as 一把锐利的双刃剑 'a sharp, double-edged sword', see Hé 2008: 758) belongs to those who question the nature of that influence, which remains a subject of great controversy until today. This brings us to the heart of our concerns relating to the Chinese language and European worldviews: the question of the way the modern Chinese culture bore up to the influence of the European (and more generally Western) ideas, categories, paradigms and disciplines, that it was coming into contact with. For instance, Joël Thoraval analysing this process for 'philosophy' and 'religion', affirmed that:

> *des catégories étrangères comme « religion » ou « philosophie » ont été introduites dans les langues et les pensées extrême—orientales, il y a à peine plus d'un siècle, en raison de la seule hégémonie de la culture européenne* (Thoraval 2005: 91)

> foreign categories like 'religion' and 'philosophy' were introduced into Far Eastern languages and their ways of thinking, barely more than a century ago, as a result of the sole hegemony of the European culture.

What were the repercussions of this transformation for the Chinese lexicon? This is our question. And we are especially eager to understand the impact on the academic lexicon. Jean François Billeter stressed the importance of this influence when he wrote:

> *la plus grande partie des termes utilisés aujourd'hui en matière économique, sociale, politique, en philosophie et dans les sciences humaines sont des néologismes calqués sur des termes européens.* (Billeter 2000: 78)

> most of the terms today used in economic, social, political fields, in philosophy and in the humanities are neologisms modelled on European terms.

Hence, the word *ōuhuà* 欧化 in Hé Jiǔyíng's quotation above must be understood in two ways. On the one hand, it can be considered as a keyword designating Europe's influence on China in recent centuries; on the other hand, from the linguistic point of view, it can be seen as a relevant example of the way contemporary Mandarin Chinese uses and adapts European words and concepts.

And as we shall see, the impact of Europe on China has been highly significant: its words and its worldviews have made themselves felt on China again and again throughout the past two centuries. But, once again, in this chapter, we shall try to grasp the cultural traditions and the conceptual narratives that frame the ways in which European words and worldviews, debates and discourse strategies have been adopted and adapted. The great diversity of China's own culture and the complexities of the social and political upheaval it has undergone over the last couple of centuries make it senseless to speak naïvely about 'borrowings', as if China simply had to absorb European models like a passive sponge. It would be absurd to speak of a simple one-way process of 'Europeanization'. Such a model works with dubious mechanical metaphors involving unthinking forces imposing themselves on inert masses. But these are of little explicative value in understanding the way languages borrow words and meanings migrate. Even in the most bloody military invasions and occupations, the way meanings migrate is always subtle, complex, and difficult to discern. Even the metaphor of 'cultural exchanges' itself soon breaks down as a means of explaining the various forms of fusion, confusion, irony, creative rejection, and reconceptualization that make themselves felt. If we make the effort to try to step outside Europe and see our continent as the Chinese appear to perceive us, we soon discern that the Chinese response is always creative. And that creativity cultivates new forms of thinking and feeling as Europe begins to encroach on the Chinese worldview. This, ultimately, will be the challenging part of this chapter for European readers, just as investigating the migration of European meanings proved challenging for us as the authors.

Given the complexity of the process of cultural renewal, it would be wise to keep certain questions in mind:

- When did European words begin to enter into the Chinese worldview?
- How productive are the words *Ōuzhōu* 欧洲 ('Europe') and the related abridged form *ōu-*?
- How do these words form compound words and expressions?
- How frequently are they used, and how can we determine their frequency by using the corpora at our disposal?
- How do the results of corpus research compare to textual analysis of books and academic articles?
- And how do tensions in Sino-European history, with both the colonial projects of the European nations and the present-day defence of

European interests and policies affect the way Chinese people feel about Europe? And how does their ambivalence impact upon the way they formulate expressions and metaphors used to portray Europe and explain the behaviour of European actors?

The word *Ōuzhōu* 欧洲 'Europe', as well as the abridged form *ōu-* 欧, are relatively productive in Mandarin Chinese. They form a whole series of derived words, which are all used in different contexts with different connotations. Among them, we can find two terms signifying 'Europeanization'. Depending on the context, these can also be translated as 'to Europeanize' or 'Europeanized':

- *ōuzhōuhuà* 欧洲化 is formed from the word 'Europe' with the suffixoid *-huà* 化 added, corresponding to the English suffix '-ization';
- *ōuhuà* 欧化, which, as we have already seen, is an abridged form for Europe *ōu-* 欧, with *-huà* 化 added.

It is also important to mention two further words:

- *ōushì* 欧式 which covers various meanings: 'European style', 'in European style', or 'in a European way'. The suffix *-shì* 式 means 'style', 'way' or 'manner';
- *ōuzhōuxìng* 欧洲性 designating 'Europeanness' or the 'European character', in which *-xìng* 性 means 'character' or 'nature'.

There are also different words formed with the suffixoid *-zhǔyì* 主义 (corresponding to the English suffix '-ism'). These include:

- *ōuzhōuzhǔyì* 欧洲主义 'Europeanism';
- *ōuzhōuzhōngxīnzhǔyì* 欧洲中心主义, 'Eurocentrism', which is formed by combining the words *Ōuzhōu* 'Europe' and *zhōngxīn* 'centre' and adding the suffixoid *-zhǔyì* 主义 '-ism';
- *fàn'ōuzhōuzhǔyì* 泛欧洲主义 which means 'pan-Europeanism';
- *fàn'ōuzhǔyì* 泛欧主义 which covers a similar range of meanings as *fànōuzhōuzhǔyì* (*fàn-* being the prefix equivalent to 'pan-').

It is also important not to forget two words which mean 'Euroscepticism':

- *ōuzhōuhuáiyízhǔyì* 欧洲怀疑主义, formed by the word 'Europe', *huáiyí* 怀疑 'to doubt' or 'doubt', and the suffixoid *-zhǔyì* 主义 '-ism';

- *yí'ōuzhǔyì* 疑欧主义, formed by combining *yí* 疑, meaning 'to doubt' or 'doubt', by the abridged form for 'Europe' *ōu* 欧 and the suffix '-ism'.

We can also find a long list of compound words and expressions related to news concerning the European Union and its recent history. These include:

- *ōuyuán* 欧元 'euro';
- *Ōuzhài wéijī* 欧债危机 'European debt crisis';
- *Ōuzhōu bǎolěi* 欧洲堡垒 'fortress Europe';
- *Ōuzhōu gōngmínquán* 欧洲公民权 'European citizenship';
- *Ōuzhōu jiànshè* 欧洲建设 'European construction';
- *Ōuzhōu móshì* 欧洲模式 'European model';
- *Ōuzhōu qíngyǔbiǎo* 欧洲晴雨表 'Eurobarometer';
- *Ōuzhōu yītǐhuà* 欧洲一体化 'European integration';
- *Ōuzhōu wéijī* 欧洲危机 'European crisis'.

These are concepts, but they are certainly not neutral terms. How do the Chinese feel about them? These are the Lublin ethnolinguistic questions. How are keywords entrenched in culture-specific values? How are cultural relations negotiated in discourse strategies and how are keywords enlisted in those strategies?

In the expressions related to Europe in contemporary Chinese, we have a range of keywords and expressions that reflect the ambivalence of China's relation to Europe and to its own European cultural and linguistic inheritance. Side by side, we find positive and negative terms, and often the words and expressions can be adapted to embrace or reject the West as a whole and Europe along with it. Among the positive or neutral keywords, we can list the following:

- *ōushì* 欧式 'in the European way';
- *ōuzhōuxìng* 欧洲性 'Europeanness'.

Among the pejorative words and expressions we can list the following:

- *ōuzhōuzhōngxīnzhǔyì* 欧洲中心主义 'Eurocentrism';
- *Ōuzhōu bǎolěi* 欧洲堡垒 'fortress Europe';
- *ōuhuà* 欧化 'Europeanization' which carries negative connotations in expressions such as *mángmù ōuhuà* 盲目欧化 'blind Europeanization'.

In the following paragraphs, we will begin to trace the courses that these keywords and expressions have taken throughout history. How have some words and phrases, concepts and ideas, tastes and attitudes migrated from Europe? How do they migrate from one sphere of society to another in China? And what new meanings do theses expressions take on? In what dimensions of the Chinese worldview do they begin to take on a powerful or pervasive meaning? We will begin tracing these trajectories, to try to understand the place of 'Europe' in China, and the connotations the word 'Europe' holds for Chinese people. We shall try to determine the impact on derived words, and understand related words within the scope of the language as a whole and within culture, perceiving both language and culture as dynamic interactive systems.

This is a great task, one that has no clearly defined limits. But all projects must define and limit their scope. And for this reason, we have chosen to limit this first study to the Chinese words and expressions formed with the word 'Europe', *Ōuzhōu*, including in our study the rival synonyms used up until the early twentieth century, and expressions formed using the abridged form *ōu-* 欧 'Europe'.

In order to retrace these trajectories and identify the semantic stratifications involved in structuring the integration of keywords into the lexicon, we will first present some of the earliest occurrences and different usages of these words. We will then contextualize them within the framework of Sino-European relations. The history of those relations cannot be explained here, of course, but we cannot begin to explain Europe without taking those relations into account. Finally, we will analyse the presence of our keywords in contemporary sources. These sources include media and social media, general corpora and academic writing. These sources should enable us to understand the stories and narratives these keywords get caught up in. They should also help us to demonstrate what current usage of such words and phrases reveals about the image of Europe and Europeans in the contemporary Chinese worldview.

Europe in Chinese History

For two millennia, encounters between China and Europe were sporadic and indirect (Masini 2001: 567). The first direct encounters occurred back in the Mongol period of the Yuan dynasty (1271–1368), when merchants and Franciscan missionaries travelled to the East (see Bertuccioli and Masini 1996; Staiger 2004). It is in this period that

Europe gains its first-hand information about China (see Harbsmeier 1998: 8–9; Gianninoto and Casacchia 2017). In the subsequent centuries, the missionaries played a pivotal role in the exchanges between China and Europe. First of all, they introduced several elements of Western knowledge to China, and they were responsible for introducing Western disciplines, from geometry to philosophy, and from astronomy to grammar. In this first phase, the Jesuit missionaries played a major role thanks to their excellent knowledge of the Chinese language and culture. Indeed, it can be argued that they made an essential contribution to Chinese culture through their translations, and they were responsible for transposing European learning to China. This was a period of dialogue, for the Jesuits also established good contacts with the Chinese literati circles and Chinese élite.

As Von Racknitz underlines (2013: 12): 'among Chinese elites, Europe, or rather an imagination thereof, was during the late Ming [dynasty, 1368–1644] and mid-to high-Qing [dynasty 1644–1911] rather represented by Catholic missionaries'. On the other hand, the translations of Chinese works and writings about China compiled by Catholic missionaries, primarily the Jesuits, greatly contributed to broadening the Western conception of China and forged the European idea of China during those centuries. This stimulated a profound interest in China among Europeans, which reached fruition in the '*chinoiseries*' fashion. This culminated in the compilation of numerous European works on China and on the Chinese language (see Chappell and Peyraube 2014; Gianninoto 2014a; Gianninoto and Casacchia 2017).

It was during the nineteenth century that radical changes in the relations between China and the European nations took place. In that period, China became the object of Western economic interests, and a target for its military might (Staiger 2004). After the British Empire lined up its gunboats in a concerted attack on China and defeated it in the Opium Wars (1838–1842 and 1856–1860), China was obliged to accept intolerable bargaining conditions. These involved the imposition of the Unequal Treaties.

As a result, the end of the Qing dynasty was a period of political and social unrest in China, a period in which traditional knowledge and society were being called into question. Among the Chinese elites, this critical national context forced the Chinese to reappraise the stability and the ideals of their civilization. The elites began to question the time-honoured traditional Chinese knowledge and the very foundations of its society and its political structures. This explains why they began looking for answers to the political and intellectual crisis (Hsü 1970: 9–10). This soul-searching and this cultural upheaval encouraged many thinkers to claim that China's modernization was not an option but a necessity.

How did China react then? In a complex manner. It did not seek to ape Europe, but it sought to understand what it could gain from getting to know Europe better. The second half of the nineteenth century saw the development of the *Yángwù yùndòng* 洋务运动 (lit. 'Western affairs movement') usually translated as 'Westernization movement'. This was neither a submission to European culture nor a halfway-house compromise. It was an attempt to learn selectively from the West. The motto of this movement was *Zhōngxué wèi tǐ, xīxué wèi yòng* 中学为体西学为用 'Chinese learning as substance, Western learning as a tool'. Arguably, a better translation would be 'Chinese learning for the essential principles, Western knowledge for practical application'. This motto was emblematic of the strong Western influence in a period in which European countries, mainly France and United Kingdom, were regarded with an ambivalent attitude. The relationship with Europe was neither inconsistent nor paradoxical, but rather the result of a painful period of reappraisal, in which the Chinese elites tried to learn some lessons from their military defeat. European nations were simultaneously regarded as both imperialistic powers and as models of development.

Throughout the nineteenth century and the first half of the twentieth century, the impact of Europe and the West in general involved an enormous wave of translation which introduced many European works into the Chinese culture. How did this affect the language? From a linguistic point of view, this wave of translating resulted in a huge process of transformation involving the transposition of key terms and concepts to the Chinese worldview. This wave was something of a tsunami, in that it washed away or at least considerably shook up established learning, and modes of thinking and feeling. And 'in the climactic decades around 1900, the Chinese scientific and political lexicons were almost completely displaced by new terms, many of which denoted entirely or partly novel ideas', according to Lackner et al. (2001: 2). So, all in all, the influence of European and other 'Western' countries towards the end of the Qing dynasty greatly affected numerous domains, contributing to major institutional changes. The depth and scope of this transformation of the cultural sphere should not be underestimated.

In this period, various Chinese terms designating Europe were used. The phonemic loan *Ōuluóbā* 欧罗巴, 'Europe', as well as the hybrid form *Ōuluóbāzhōu* 欧罗巴洲 were among the terms used in Qing sources to indicate 'Europe' and 'the European continent', as Masini points out (1993: 39). *Ōuluóbāzhōu* 欧罗巴洲 is formed by a phonetic transcription *Ōuluóbā* 欧罗巴, plus the suffixoid *-zhōu*, meaning 'state, province, continent'. Both terms can be found in the 'Ming History' (*Míngshǐ* 明史) presented to the Qing throne in 1736.³

According to the MCST database, the phonemic loan *Ōuluóbā* 欧罗巴 was used a century later in the *Yínghuán zhìlüè* 瀛环志略 'A Brief Account of the Maritime Circuit' written by Xú Jìyú 徐继畬, and published in 1848. The hybrid word *Ōuluóbāzhōu* 欧罗巴洲 was used in the famous *Hǎiguó túzhì* 海国图志 'Illustrated Treatise of Countries Overseas' written by Wèi Yuán 魏源, and published in 1852.

The current word for Europe, *Ōuzhōu* 欧洲, is formed by *ōu-* 欧, the abridged form of the phonemic loan *Ōuluóbā*, plus the suffixoid *-zhōu* 'continent' (*Xīnhuá cídiǎn* 2001), and it was used in the chapter *Lìxué* 力学 'Mechanics' of the *Xīxué guānjiàn* 西学关键 *The Essentials of Western Learning*. It can also be found in the *Wùlǐxué xīn shū* 物理学新书 *New Book of Physics* of the *Biānyì pǔtōng jiàoyù bǎikē quánshū* 编译普通教育百科全书 *Encyclopedia of General Education*. Both of these were published in 1903 (see MCST).

The word *Ōuzhōu* 欧洲 can also be found in literature of the late Qing dynasty. For instance, the novel *Lǎocán yóujì* 老残游记 *The Travels of Lao Can* written by Liú È 刘鹗 between 1903 and 1907, contains the following passage:

然后由欧洲新文明进而复我三皇五帝旧文明骎骎进于大同之世矣。⁴

Then the introduction of the new civilization from Europe will renew the old civilization of the Three Sovereigns and Five Emperors to move swiftly into the era of the Great Unity.

The forms *Ōuzhōu* and *Ōuluóbā* were both used some years later in the *Qīngshǐgǎo* 清史稿 (*Draft History of Qing*), an official history of the last Chinese dynasty published during the Republican era that followed the fall of the empire in 1911. The word *Ōuzhōu* is used in reference to European countries and to their inventions and products. The following examples are characteristic of this usage:

European countries [*Ōuzhōu zhū guó* 欧洲诸国] forced their way into China (欧洲诸国闯入中国边界腹地)

in the fifth year of the *Tongzhi* period, the production of steamships, imitating European [*Ōuzhōu*] military steamships, started in the Fujian province (同治五年，始仿欧洲兵轮船式，于福建省开厂制造轮船。) (*Gǔdài hànyǔ yǔliàokù*)

The phonemic loan *Ōuluóbā* 欧罗巴 can be found in reference to Europe as a geographical entity: 'Portugal is situated at the extreme West of Europe [*Ōuluóbā jí xī*]' (葡萄牙在欧罗巴极西). The current word for Europe, *Ōuzhōu* 欧洲, could already be found during the Qing dynasty, although various rival synonyms also came into use during this period.

Among these rival terms, we can mention: *Xīguó* 西国 (*xī* 西 means 'West' and *guó* 国, 'country'). This term was listed in a Dutch–Chinese dictionary published in 1886.[5] Also found was *Tàixī* 泰西, which literally translates as the 'Extreme West', the counterpart of the 'Far East' for English-speakers.[6] These examples bear witness to the instability of these terms during the formative period of the modern Chinese lexicon.

The word *ōuhuà* 欧化 'to Europeanize' or 'Europeanization' was in use in the early twentieth century, as we can see in the *English-Chinese Dictionary of the Standard Chinese Spoken Language and Handbook for Translators, including Scientific, Technical, Modern and Documentary Terms* by K. E. G. Hemeling, published in 1910 (MCST).

In the above-mentioned *Draft History of Qing*, we can also find the expression *ōufēng* 欧风 to indicate European style or European influence, a term which translates literally as 'European wind'. For instance, we can read the following words:

At the end of the Qing dynasty, the European influence moved eastward [*Ōufēng dōng jiān* 欧风东渐], the sciences blossomed (清之末叶，欧风东渐，科学日昌). (*Gǔdài hànyǔ yǔliàokù*)

In the nineteenth century and in the first half of the twentieth century, Chinese history was marked by European and Western influence. In this period, at least, the modernization of the country was often associated with the notions of 'Westernization' and 'Europeanization'. According to Staiger (2004: 1), after the fall of the empire, Western influence remained strong throughout the Nationalist government. Despite the defence of traditional Confucian values, the Nationalist Party (*Guómíndǎng* 国民党) proposed a modernization programme largely based on Western models and 'under the Nationalist Government the impact of Western culture was so far the biggest in China' (Staiger 2004: 1).

This influence was destined to decline, however, in the decades following the foundation of People's Republic of China (1949). What influences were to take their place? First, it was the Soviet influence that began to make its impact felt. But this period was short-lived, and soon it was the almost complete isolation of China that was to assert itself. This period was to reach its climax with the Cultural Revolution.

Exchange with foreign partners and with Western countries would be resumed in later decades, thanks to Dèng Xiǎopíng's 邓小平 'reform and opening up' policy (*gǎigé kāifàng* 改革开放), which came into effect as of 1978. This followed the EU's recognition of China in 1975 (Wong 2013: 165). Contacts between China and European countries have developed since then, and relations between Chinese and European institutions have gradually broadened in scope in recent decades.

'Europe' and Related Words in Contemporary Mandarin Chinese

The *Dictionary of Modern Chinese* (*Xiàndài hànyǔ cídiǎn* 现代汉语词典, 2015, sixth edition), includes various entries related to Europe:

- the character *ōu* 欧, abridged form for *Ōuzhōu* 欧洲: the examples given are *Xī'ōu* 西欧 'Western Europe' and *Ōuhuà* 欧化 'Europeanization';
- *Ōuzhōu gòngtóngtǐ* 欧洲共同体 'European community' and the abridged form *ōugòngtǐ* 欧共体 'EC';
- *Ōuhuà* 欧化 'Europeanization';
- *Ōuluóbā rénzhǒng* 欧罗巴人种 lit. 'Caucasian race';
- *Ōuzhōu liánméng* 欧洲联盟 'European Union' and the abridged form, *ōuméng* 欧盟 'EU';
- *ōuyuán* 欧元 'euro'.

Relatively detailed definitions are dedicated to four of these entries, *Ōuzhōu gòngtóngtǐ*, *Ōuluóbā rénzhǒng*, *ōuyuán*, and *Ōuzhōu liánméng*, the others being defined by quasi-synonyms or as abridged forms. For instance, the definition of *Ōuzhōu liánméng* 'European Union' reads as follows:

> 由欧洲共同体发展而来，以建立欧洲经济货币联盟和欧洲政治联盟为目标、在世界上具有重要影响的区域一体化组织。1993年11月成立,总部在布鲁塞尔。截止到2011年底,共有成员国27个。简称欧盟。

Developed on the basis of the European Community, an organization of regional integration having an important influence in the world, and the goal of establishing the European economic and monetary union and the European political union. Established in November 1993 with its headquarters in Brussels. By the end of 2011, the EU consisted of a total of twenty-seven Member States. Abridged form *ōuméng* [EU].

The 'encyclopaedic' entries for European Community and European Union were added only recently, and do not figure in the fifth edition of the same dictionary, published in 2005. This one contains only four entries related to the word Europe (the character *ōu* 欧, as abridged form for Europe, *Ōuhuà* 欧化 'Europeanization', *Ōuluóbā rénzhǒng* 欧罗巴人种 'Caucasian race', and *ōuyuán* 欧元 'euro'). The previous 2001 edition did not, of course, mention the euro currency, but it included the form *Ōuxī* (formed by combining *ōu* 'Europe' and *xī* 'West') as an ancient form for Europe (旧时指欧洲).

What conclusions are we to draw from the introduction of these words and from these lexical changes? If we compare the various editions of this reference dictionary, we can gain insight into the changing attitudes towards Europeans, their cultures and their institutions, and the various impressions Chinese people formed about Europe. The differences in the various dictionaries reveal a growing interest in words related to Europe. The increase in the number of the entries formed with *ōu-* 欧 and *Ōuzhōu* in the recent 2015 edition clearly demonstrates the extent of this interest.

The word 'Europe' is often used in the influential Chinese newspaper, the *People's Daily* (*Rénmín rìbào* 人民日报). How does corpus research compare with the findings given above? In our search for the word 'Europe' (*Ōuzhōu* 欧洲) in the online version (*Rénmín wǎng* 人民网), carried out, 11 August 2016, we found a total of 1 042 282 examples. These were divided up into various sections according to different fields. The highest number of examples (116 578) can be found listed in the section 'International' (国际). The second greatest number, with 80 501 examples, was found under 'Finance and economics' (财经). There were 59 527 examples in the section 'Sport' (体育), 38 949 in the section 'Chinese Communist Party news' (中国共产党新闻), and 36 605 in the section 'Cars' (人民网汽车). This can probably be explained by the fact that European and Western cars are seen as status symbols by Chinese consumers. But what do these findings enable us to conclude? Over all, it would appear that economic, geopolitical, and political issues are the fields of interest most widely covered when it comes to Europe in this newspaper.

This interest in the fields of international politics and economics seems to confirm the findings of a study carried out a few years ago by Dai and Zhang (2007) on the way the EU was perceived in China. Their study was based on newspapers, television news, and interviews with members of political, economic and social élites (Dai and Zhang 2007: 58). Dai and Zhang underlined that it was the image of Europe as an economic and political power that prevailed throughout Chinese perceptions of Europe. This was, of course, before the 2008 crisis which modified the image of Europe that was represented in the Chinese media. But prior to that, the authors clearly stated that 'the EU as an economic power was the dominant frame in the print media outlets (with 44%), in the television news media, the EU as a political power led the framing, accounting for 61% of all EU news stories' (Dai and Zhang 2007: 49). It is the role of Europe as actor in the international arena that emerges in this survey. However, the results of the interviews show that the EU is regarded as 'one great power among many in the multi-polar world', 'but not necessarily as a leader in the global political arena' (Dai and Zhang 2007: 58).

Among the topics related to the European economy, the European debt crisis has been discussed widely in the Chinese media and on social media. In our search for the Chinese expression for 'European debt crisis' *ōu zhài wéijī* 欧债危机 (abridged form of *Ōuzhōu zhǔquán zhàiwù wéijī* 欧洲主权债务危机 'European sovereign debt crisis') on the pages of the *People's Daily*, we found 56 607 occurrences, predominantly in the sections 'Finance and economics' (20 783), 'International' (8938), and 'Chinese Communist Party news' (2953). One example of its coverage in social media is a detailed page devoted to this topic in the online *Baidu Encyclopedia* (*Bǎidù bǎikē* 百度百科, the Chinese answer to Wikipedia).[7] Other examples can be found in the *Zhihu* question and answer website (*Zhī hū* 知乎 'Do you know that?').[8] Among the comments on this topic, and in the reactions that appeared on social media, one post on the microblogging website Sina weibo (*Xīnlàng wēibó* 新浪微博) from the economist Hán Zhìguó 韩志国 is worth mentioning. Hán Zhìguó compared the possibility of the Chinese offering help during the European debt crisis to 'a sheep saving a wolf' (中国救欧洲是羊救狼). These comments and the reactions to them deserve to be taken into account, because echoes in the media and blogs[9] reflect the acutely ambivalent perception the Chinese have of Europe and their mixed feelings about it.

Spakowski (2013: 210) chose to make a study focusing on middle school textbooks because of their primal and shaping role in the formation of an image of Europe for Chinese people. And she underlined the mixed feelings that Chinese people express about Europe. She argued that the representation of Europe in China reflects two diametrically opposed perspectives. On the one hand, the Marxist reading stresses the colonial and imperialist aspects of European history. This reading foregrounds aspects of European societies that can be considered as antagonistic to non-Western civilizations, China included. On the other hand, what Spakowski calls 'the capitalist perspective' emphasizes the economic and technological progress of European countries. From 'the capitalist perspective', Europe is regarded as 'the origin of modernity ... and – to a certain degree – also as a model to learn from' (Spakowski 2013: 210).

A similar impression emerges when we consider other surveys and studies. A public survey entitled 'Chinese Views of the EU', carried out in spring and summer 2010 of 3019 urban residents across six cities in China (Beijing, Shanghai, Guangzhou, Xi'an, Chengdu, and Nanning) (Dekker and Van der Noll 2011), produced results which confirmed the hypothesis that the perception of Europe in China is ambivalent. How did the people questioned respond? According to this survey, those asked considered the situation in the EU 'better than in China in the domains of economic prospects, employment, environment, social welfare, and quality of life' (Dekker and Van der Noll 2011: 5). Moreover, the 'Chinese people favor the EU most, followed by Russia, the US and then Japan', the survey determined (see Wang and Popescu 2011: 2). However, more than half the respondents voiced concerns over the ideological divide between the EU and China, and spoke of a conflict of values between the two (see Dekker and Van der Noll 2011: 5). Wang and Popescu (2011: 3) also underlined that the history of European colonialism in Asia, and the differences between the political systems and cultural traditions are among the main factors that affect the way the Chinese perceive Europe and Europeans. It should be clear then that while the image of Europe and Europeans is largely positive, two things are still felt to divide Europe and China: ideological differences and the problematic heritage of Europe's dealings with China throughout history.

In the Chinese media and social media, European news has continued to figure highly, notably in recent years when it came to the 'European refugee crisis' (Ōuzhōu nànmín wéijī 欧洲难民危机) and Brexit (in Chinese Yīngguó tuō ōu 英国脱欧 or simply tuō'ōu 脱欧).

In the *People's Daily* we found 1161 results for 'European refugee crisis' (欧洲难民危机). A Google search on the sinophone web produced 459 000 results. Numerous questions and comments are posted on the European refugees on the question and answer (Q&A) website *Zhihu*.[10] These concern the causes of this wave of refugees, the way the refugees were to be distributed among the various Member States, and all the possible solutions concerning them. This interest can be seen all too clearly from the fact that the expression *Ōuzhōu nànmín wéijī* 欧洲难民危机 'European refugee crisis' has been listed as an entry in the *Baidu Encyclopedia*.[11]

Brexit gained even greater attention in the media and on social media. In the *People's Daily* we found 3869 results for the expression *tuō'ōu* 脱欧, 'Brexit', when it was accessed less than two months after the vote (11 August 2016). These were found mainly in the sections related to international and economic issues. In a Google search of this expression carried out on the same date 1 040 000 results were found.

Furthermore, 257 questions on the Q&A website *Zhihu* were devoted to Brexit,[12] with questions and comments ranging from the possible influence of Brexit on the Chinese economy and on the world economy, and Brexit's consequences for Chinese students abroad. Concerns were also voiced about opportunities and eventual benefits for China. These involved considering which cities might be likely to replace London as a financial centre.

The Brexit referendum (*Tuō ōu gōngtóu* 脱欧公投) has also been listed as a detailed entry on the *Baidu Encyclopedia*. It even figures among the ten most popular entries (热词 'hot words') on this website.[13] Brexit was also used as the subject of a cartoon image conceived by Lǐ Xiǎoguāi 李小乖 posted on 24 June 2016,[14] entitled *Ōu!* 欧! 'Europe!'. This illustration shows the decomposition of the character *ōu* 欧, whose left component '区'[15] separates to become British flag.

In Chinese, 'Europe' can form a verb; this makes it very much 'a process'. That is why it appeared to us important in our study of the keywords related to Europe to analyse the word *ōuhuà* 欧化 'Europeanization', or 'to Europeanize', mentioned in the quotation by Hé (1995) at the opening of this chapter. The word *ōuhuà* is widely used in academic discourse and in newspapers. This word is defined as *xīhuà* 西化 'Westernization' in the 2015 edition of the *Dictionary of Modern Chinese*. The previous edition, published in 2005, defined *ōuhuà* 欧化 as designating the imitation of European customs, languages, culture, and so forth (模仿欧洲风俗习惯、语言文化等).

How is the word used in the press? It is found quite frequently in the *People's Daily*, with 3353 occurrences. These entries break down as follows:

- 816 references relating to 'Cars';
- 191 references relating to the 'Chinese Communist Party news';
- 134 references relating to 'Culture'.

This word is also used quite frequently in the pages of the *People's Daily*. However, only eight occurrences could be found in the Corpus of Modern Chinese (*Xiàndài hànyǔ yǔliàokù* 现代汉语语料库, http://www.cncorpus.org/CCindex.aspx). What attitude is expressed when 'Europeanize' is used? At times the connotations are negative. This is certainly true, for example, when they speak of 'the shortcomings of Europeanized youth' (*ōuhuà qīngnián de máobìng*欧化青年的毛病). Other occurrences prove controversial. This is true of debates on the European influence on the Chinese language when phrases like 'Europeanized grammar' (*ōuhuà de yǔfǎ* 欧化的语法), or 'Europeanized sentences' (*ōuhuà jù*欧化句) are used. This is a hotly debated topic in modern Chinese linguistics, and as we will see, this subject has been given great consideration in academic literature. Various scholars have analysed the way the Chinese lexicon and Chinese syntactic structures have been modified because of European and Western influence (see for instance Kubler 1985; Hè 2008).

In other sources, the word *Ōuzhōu* 'Europe' can also be found: we found over 1000 references made to it in the above-mentioned Corpus of Modern Chinese (*Xiàndài hànyǔ yǔliàokù* 现代汉语语料库) in May 2015. In a total of 1158 references, the sources covered the period 1946 onwards. This cannot be considered very frequent, however, if compared with the occurrences of individual European countries, like 'United Kingdom' (*Yīngguó*英国), which in itself produced 1522 occurrences in the same corpus. 'France' (*Fǎguó* 法国) produced a similar number of occurrences (1227). 'Germany' (*Déguó* 德国) produced somewhat fewer occurrences (936). What does this tell us? It leads us to conclude that the impact of Europe as a whole appears to the Chinese to be somewhat less relevant than the impact of the various European countries. Europe still appears to represent a federation of nation states in the minds of the Chinese.

Among the occurrences of the word *Ōuzhōu* 'Europe', the examples are related to the following cultural and spiritual traditions:

- European culture and civilization, such as 'European cultural tradition' (*Ōuzhōu wénhuà chuántǒng* 欧洲文化传统);
- 'European civilization' (*Ōuzhōu wénmíng* 欧洲文明);
- 'European spiritual culture' (*Ōuzhōu jīngshén wénhuà* 欧洲精神文化) and 'the mother of European spiritual culture' (*Ōuzhōu jīngshén wénhuà zhī mǔ* 欧洲精神文化之母, referring to the Ancient Greece).

Other examples are related to European history, such as:

- 'the history of European democratic movements' (*Ōuzhōu mínzhǔ zhèngzhì yùndòng shǐ* 欧洲民主政治运动史);
- 'European feudal society' (*Ōuzhōu de fēngjiàn shèhuì* 欧洲的封建社会);
- 'European feudal system' (*Ōuzhōu de fēngjiàn zhìdù* 欧洲的封建制度);
- 'European industrial revolution' (*Ōuzhōu de chǎnyè gémìng* 欧洲的产业革命).

Various examples concern the recent history of the European Community and the European Union. For example, we find references to 'the great European market' (*Ōuzhōu dà shìchǎng* 欧洲大市场), 'the formal establishment of the European Economic Community' (*Ōuzhōu jīngjì gòngtóngtǐ zhèngshì chénglì* 欧洲经济共同体正式成立), and references to 'Europe's awakening' (*Ōuzhōu de juéxǐng* 欧洲的觉醒, a phrase which refers to the creation of a single unified market).

Negative connotations are attached to some of these references. This is the case of examples like 'the outbreak of European developed capitalist countries' (*Ōuzhōu fādá de zīběnzhǔyì guójiā bàofā* 欧洲发达的资本主义国家爆发), 'European contradictions' (*Ōuzhōu de máodùn* 欧洲的矛盾), and 'the gravity of European problems' (*Ōuzhōu wèntí zhī yánzhòng* 欧洲问题之严重).

In the BCC corpus (BCC 汉语语料库), we also find a high number of occurrences (95 710) for the word *Ōuzhōu*. Frequent collocations are related to European unification: 'European Union' (欧洲联盟, 2030), 'European unification' (欧洲统一, 369), 'European integration' (欧洲一体化, 297), 'European construction' (欧洲建设, 157). Nevertheless, the most frequent collocation is *Ōuzhōu guójiā* 欧洲国家 'European country' or 'European countries' (3231).

According to the results of this corpus, economic and cultural issues prevail in the perception of Europe.

Different collocations refer to the European economy: 'European economy' (欧洲经济, 859), 'European stock markets' (欧洲股市, 337),

'European debt' (欧洲债务, 224), 'European finance' (欧洲金融, 185), 'European enterprises' (欧洲企业, 144).

We can also identify collocations related to European culture, as 'European culture' (欧洲文化, 283), 'European movies' (欧洲电影, 202), 'European history' (欧洲历史, 177), 'European civilization' (欧洲文明, 171).

The word *Ōuzhōu*, 'Europe', and its related compounds and derived words are also widely used in contemporary Chinese academic discourse. Numerous Chinese academic writings are devoted to the European Union's history, and the European experience occupies a considerable place in intellectual debates. For instance, when on 13 July 2015 we searched for the word 'Europe' (*Ōuzhōu*欧洲) in the National Social Science Database (*Guójiā zhéxué shèhuì kēxué xuéshù qíkān shùjùkù* 国家哲学社会科学学术期刊数据库), we found a total of 178 252 academic publications, most of them related to economics and management (经济管理, 85 593 results). Somewhat less frequent were the references to cultural studies (文化科学, with 33 701 results), to politics and law (政治法律, 22 224), and to the arts (艺术, 12 108).

How frequently do academics speak of Europe and its parliament in China? A total of 48 874 results were found for the word *Ōuméng* 欧盟 'EU', the abridged form for 'European Union' (*Ōuzhōu liánméng* 欧洲联盟). These statistics can be broken down into subsections, and among these, economics and management (with 37 570 references), and politics and law (with 8 691) are the fields in which the word is most frequently encountered. These results can give us an overview of how frequently these words appear in different academic fields. It must be remembered, however, that the debates and writings on Europe greatly exceed the examples indexed in this database.

Among the numerous words and expressions currently used in Chinese academic writings, we chose to focus on:

- two words for 'Europeanization':
  - *ōuzhōuhuà* 欧洲化
  - *ōuhuà* 欧化;
- and two expressions :
  - 'European identity' (*Ōuzhōu rèntóng* 欧洲认同);
  - 'European model' (*Ōuzhōu móshì* 欧洲模式).

Both of these proved to be of great interest for our study of keywords.

The issue of a 'European identity' generates heated debates in Europe, but are the 'crises' that the European Member States frequently fret over of any interest to the Chinese? It would seem so. Far from regarding Europe's dramas and family infighting as self-absorbed introversion, what happens in Europe seems to matter to China. European issues certainly seem to be relevant for Chinese academics: our research came up with 1179 results for the expression *Ōuzhōu rèntóng* 欧洲认同 'European identity' when we consulted the National Social Science Database.

Among the numerous articles on this subject and the various points of views expressed, it is worth noting Yán and Shí's paper on EU cultural identity (*Ōuméng wénhuà rèntóng* 欧盟文化认同) and cultural integration (*wénhuà zhěnghé* 文化整合 published in 2012).[16] According to Yán and Shí (2012: 8), the 'European culture' (*Ōuzhōu wénhuà* 欧洲文化) and the 'pan-European cultural identity' (*fàn-ōu wénhuà rèntóng* 泛欧文化认同) belong to the 'elite culture' (精英文化) or 'high culture' (高雅文化), while this 'great tradition' (to use Redfield's 1956 expression) has only a limited impact on the 'common' European people (所谓泛欧文化认同或 "欧洲文化" 的基石充其量也只是属于精英文化或高雅文化的范畴，这种 "大传统" 对于欧洲普通民众的影响毕竟有限).

There are many other examples demonstrating that the Chinese are striving to understand what is happening in the arduous process of European integration. In one essay analysing the 'question of European identity' (*Ōuzhōu rèntóng wèntí* 欧洲认同问题) from the perspective of political participation, Fàn (2007) affirms that 'the concept of "identity" between the seventies and the eighties replaced the concept of "integration": "integration" was a keyword in the fifties and sixties' (在50、60年代显赫一时的《一体化》概念在70、80年代被《认同》概念所取代).

Keywords change, and 'identity' is the new keyword, in this reading of Europe's development. Fàn defines this identity as 'the comprehensive incarnation of the individual identity and the collective political identity of the European citizens, concretely manifested in the relations among individuals, nation-states and the EU' (欧洲公民个人认同和集体政治认同的一种综合体现，具体表现为个人与民族-国家和欧盟之间的关系). This essay is also of special interest for our study because it brings together two of our keywords, 'the people' and 'Europe', and considers how they work together. In this essay Fàn quotes the expression 'Europe of the people(s)' (*Rénmín de Ōuzhōu* 人民的欧洲), which is described as a goal to realize (实现《人民欧洲》的目标). Creating this 'Europe of the people(s)' is seen as the most important aspect of the European construction (建设 "人民的欧洲" 作为作为欧洲建设的重中之重。).

This idea is certainly a fertile one, all the more so because, to our knowledge, few political actors in Europe are considering how Europe should 'make Europeans'. In Europe, it has become customary to speak of Europe as an abstract whole, either an empty promise, or a bureaucratic institution. Rhetorically speaking, people in Europe speak more about what Europe is doing than what Europeans are doing. Europe tends to be personified; Europeans are objectified.

Fàn's intuition is worth taking into consideration in this respect, because Fàn grasped that only peoples can create a people, only unified groups can create a greater unity that has meaning not only as a whole but as a meaningful whole that reflects, in its common identity, the identities of the groups that contribute not only to creating it but also to sustaining it. This raises an interesting question for cross-cultural work: when outsiders represent cultures, do they see things that insiders miss?

The Chinese are subjecting European society to social analysis, and, once more, the findings prove both intriguing and perplexing for Europeans, who willingly admit they are searching somewhat lamely for a sense of identity. At any rate, several Chinese scholars voice interesting criticisms. Yì (2009: 114), for example, claims that the issue of cultural identity has been neglected in the European construction process for decades, overshadowed by economic and political questions (半个多世纪的欧盟建设似乎更多集中于经济层面的整合和政治层面的协调, 文化认同的推进却相对滞后。). Post-colonial scholars will appreciate Yì's analysis because he contextualizes Europe's own federating process within the context of an ongoing colonial heritage. According to this author, European identity has been constructed partially on the basis of the opposition between 'us' and 'the other' in the colonial context. For this reason, the author posits that it is important to avoid falling into what he calls 'Eurocentric flavor' ("Ōuzhōu zhōngxīnzhǔyì" de sècǎi "欧洲中心主义"的色彩) (Yì 2009: 121) by stressing a European 'us' defined as an ideal in opposition to a 'them'.

Zhāng (2007) also brings to bear a critique of Europe's very nature as a concept and ideal. He questions the very content of the word 'Europe'. In his terms:

> the word 'Europe' is not really concrete and definite, and the sentiment of 'Europeanism' constitutive of the cultural identity seems

to be lacking (《欧洲》一词就没有那么具体和确定, 也似乎缺乏形成文化认同的《欧洲主义》情绪). (Zhāng 2007)

In another study, the Chinese scholar, Niú (2009), proves much more optimistic about Europe, and sees in its integration process a source of inspiration. The level and speed of merging and integration has progressed slower than expected by politicians, Niú concedes (2009: 1) (尽管融合的程度和速度都低于政治家的期望). Nonetheless, from his perspective, over the past fifty years, the European Union has represented an example for peaceful multiculturalism (多元文化是可以和平相容的). Féng (2007) also investigates European integration (欧洲一体化) as a possible model, in this respect, for promoting a process of regional integration in East Asia. This remains to be seen, but from the European perspective, these words will be heart-warming not only for those struggling to create Europe, but also for those who are inclined to forget the advantages of Europe.

The National Social Science Database provides no less than 6236 results for the expression *Ōuzhōu móshì* 欧洲模式 'European model'. Among the various types of expressions, we found:

- 'European social model' (*Ōuzhōu shèhuì móshì* 欧洲社会模式);
- 'European welfare state model of development' (*Ōuzhōu fúlì guójiā fāzhǎn móshì* 欧洲福利国家发展模式);
- 'European (Union) model of social cohesion' (*Ōuméng shèhuì tuánjié móshì* 欧盟社会团结模式, for instance in Zhōu 2007: 98–100).

The expression *Ōuzhōu móshì* 欧洲模式 'European model' was also included in the title of the Chinese version of Giddens et al.'s (2006) *Global Europe, Social Europe*, which becomes *Ōuzhōu móshì: quánqiú Ōuzhōu, shèhuì Ōuzhōu* 《欧洲模式:全球欧洲,社会欧洲》 (lit. 'The European Model: Global Europe, Social Europe'). In times in which the social model is highly contested within Europe, and Europe's solidity and coherence as a unified global power seems hard for Europeans to grasp, this may well prove both insightful and uplifting. At any rate, the fact that these questions are considered sufficiently important to be translated into Chinese shows that the Chinese at least hold European values and questions to be worth paying attention to.

The specific nature of the European model has been debated in Chinese academic circles. In 2003, for example a congress was held in order to compare the European model (欧洲模式) and the American model (美国模式), a congress organized by the Chinese Academy of Social Sciences. The role of social dialogue, the welfare state, political balance, and multilateralism were analysed as constitutive elements of the European model (Zhōu et al. 2003). The differences in the social, economic, and political sectors and in the field of defence were regarded as the consequence of different ways of thinking and different ways of behaving, different cultural logics (不同的思维逻辑和行为逻辑). It was argued that they also resulted from different historical experiences (不同的历史经历). The results of this congress appeared in the section 'Opinions' of the widely diffused online version of the *People's Daily* (Zhōu et al. 2003), and this exposure bears witness to the impact of these studies and the ripple effect they are having beyond academic circles.

Various authors express admiration for the European model. In his essay analysing the 'European model' in international relations, Zhāng (2007: 147) also describes a model based on multilateralism and balance of power, which, according to the author, reduces conflicts and is useful for peacekeeping (同以双边外交和势力均衡为基础的国家秩序相比, "欧洲模式"减少了直接的冲突和对抗, 更有利于维护安全与和平).

Wǔ (2007: 122) gives a similarly positive appraisal of Europe, when he concludes his essay on the European model of social development by affirming that 'this social model deserves consideration and can be a source of inspiration for its theoretical and practical value' (这一社会模式在理论探索意义和现实参考价值等方面都将引发人们更多深思和可资借鉴的启示).

The fate of migrating meanings is always fascinating because of the curious ways concepts must be adapted to make them understood, and the way they take on new usages which partly redefine their original 'borrowed' meanings. The very metaphor of 'borrowing' begins to break down as soon as this process gets underway, because these migrating concepts set sail for a journey with no return. They are 'taken on', but they can't be 'given back'. Our findings induce us to conclude that 'Europe' means something very different for the Chinese, something very different from all the various meanings Europeans might ascribe to the word. This takes us to the core of comparative semantics and cross-lingual research. When we study other cultures, we ask what the world means for them. But this involves asking what we mean for them, as much as trying to understand what they mean for us. In studying languages and cultures, we must try to understand their perspective, their culture, their history, and their worldview. But their gaze includes us, our culture, and our Europe. So understanding them means we must take up the challenge of trying to grasp what we as Europeans mean for other cultures.

This is nowhere so clear as in the concept of 'Europeanization'. This word barely exists in the various forms of spoken English that have spread throughout the globe, but it has been regarded as a keyword by certain Chinese scholars (e.g. Hé 1995: 761).

A search for the term with the English spelling, 'europeanisation', in the 100 000 000 word British National Corpus provided only thirteen examples. And the word with the American spelling, 'europeanization', provided only three examples in the BNC in the search on the same day.

The COCA did, admittedly, provide thirty-eight examples of 'Europeanization', but the examples themselves proved interesting. Often the concept was in inverted commas, indicating that it was not a 'natural' concept for English-speakers in North America. Indeed, the sources were often foreign, either relating to the field of anthropology, or, more often, to foreign politics. In this respect the following example from Tibi Bassam, writing in the 2009 winter edition of the *Middle East Quarterly*, is fairly representative:

> European officials neglect or simply ignore cultural issues such as the identity of Europe and **Europeanization**. Compromising and power sharing are an essential part of democratic politics. (Tibi Bassam, Winter 2009, 16(1), 47–54, quoted in COCA; emphasis added)

Europeans do not speak about 'Europeanization' and neither do Americans, it would appear. Judging from the few examples we could find in English, Europeanization is not a project, a policy promoted by Europeans. It is a process that is perceived and defined by those who are living through it as passive objects or active partners in the process. Interestingly, fifteen of the thirty-eight examples of 'Europeanization' – just under half – in the COCA were from the same source, the *Middle East Quarterly*.

The importance of 'Europeanization' as a Chinese concept is amply proven by statistics, on the other hand. In the writings indexed in the National Social Science Database, we can find the two forms of 'Europeanization':

- *ōuhuà* 欧化;
- and *ōuzhōuhuà* 欧洲化.

In our search, we found a total of 1118 examples:

- 884 for *ōuhuà*;
- 234 for *ōuzhōuhuà*.

The relatively high frequency tends to indicate that these two have become keywords in various academic debates. Corpus analysis provides up-to-date results. Dictionaries have yet to catch up with the trend of speaking of Europeanization. And this is only to be expected. Only the form *ōuhuà* 欧化 was included in the sixth edition of the reference *Dictionary of Modern Chinese* (*Xiàndài hànyǔ cídiǎn* 现代汉语词典 2015). And the definition proves disappointing in the light of our textual analysis, because this reference edition defines *ōuhuà* only as a verb, and defines it as a synonym of *xīhuà* 西化 'to Westernize' or 'Westernization'.

The analysis of a corpus of academic writings provides a much more detailed account, showing that the words *ōuhuà* 欧化 and *ōuzhōuhuà* 欧洲化 are both used in academic discourse, but with slightly different connotations. Most of the results for the word *ōuhuà* 欧化 relate to foreign influence on the Chinese language. This includes European influence, and, more generally speaking, Western influence, the forms of which are described and analysed. Among the numerous articles on this topic, we can find various studies on the Europeanization of Chinese grammar (Xiè 2001; Hè 2004; Hè 2008). Some of the papers, for example, emphasize 'the exacerbation' (恶化) of this phenomenon (e.g. Wáng 2008). Nevertheless, the word *ōuhuà* 欧化 is not limited to the field of linguistic studies, and it is used by literary critics in their articles on the European influence on modern Chinese novels (e.g. Zōu 2012). Similarly it is used in historical essays on the relationship between 'national essence' (*guócuì* 国粹) and periods of 'Europeanization' in the late Qing period of China's history (Luō 2002).

The form *ōuzhōuhuà* 欧洲化 is used in somewhat different contexts. Authors often use this keyword in the field of European studies in order to describe the process of 'Europeanization' as the 'integration' of individual European countries into the European Union. In the same way, it is used to depict the different forms of 'Europeanization' as a process of convergence for European societies. Good examples include Hè's article (2015) on the accession processes of Croatia and Serbia, Wǔ and Wáng's article (2007), and Liú's 2011 essays on the political and institutional changes required by Member States because of the European integration. But Huán's study (2006) on the 'Europeanization' of 'green' political parties offers an equally good example.

This leaves us with the impression that *ōuzhōuhuà* 欧洲化 is used primarily to speak about the Europeanization of Europeans. But this is not necessarily the case. This term is also frequently used to define 'Europeanization' as the European impact on China (as in Xià and Pān's study (2004) on the history of European influence in China). Furthermore, the term is also applied to Europe's influence on other countries.

Concluding Remarks

What conclusions are we to draw from the complex development of our migrating meanings related to Europe and Europeanization? The questions we need to ask ourselves if we are to begin to understand this complex process of cultural renewal involving China's relationship with what it conceives of as 'Europe' include the words borrowed, the periods in which they took on meaning, and the adaptations and transformations they underwent. It is crucial to understand how those words reflect not only the way the Chinese think about Europe and Europeans, but the way they feel about them.

When did translations and adaptations of European words begin to enter into the Chinese worldview? The impact of European learning was particularly strong at the end of the Qing dynasty period (1644–1911). This period was characterized by a massive process of introduction and adaptation of words, concepts, and categories. The current Chinese word for 'Europe' and some of its derived words spread in the second half the Qing dynasty, a period in which Europe influenced China in various fields of activity.

Have European ideas or words influenced the Chinese language? To a certain extent, a case can be made for this. The introduction of European terms and their transformation in new Chinese expressions bears witness to this fact. There is a great deal of debate on how good this is for Chinese, but the Chinese have made many European concepts theirs, adopting them as new ways to modernize the country.

How frequently are these words related to Europe used, and how can we determine their frequency by using the corpora at our disposal? The words *Ōuzhōu* 欧洲 ('Europe') as well as the abridged form *ōu-* 欧 are relatively productive in Modern Chinese, forming numerous derived words, compound words, and expressions. As we have seen, these forms are found in various corpora, media sources, academic writings, and in official discourse. The findings of our textual analysis and corpus analysis proved that the words for Europe were central to many debates. The examples found in books and articles enabled us to ascertain in which fields of activities and spheres of Chinese life, Europe and European styles and practices were held to be of interest.

How do Chinese people react to Europe? Answering this question proved particularly hard, but all the more interesting for us, because we first have to grasp what 'Europe' means for China, and this did not prove easy for us as Europeans. Our research leads us to posit that the Chinese have various conflicting models of Europe, and these all contribute towards constructing a complex model for which many Chinese have ambivalent feelings. Europe attracts and repels.

We considered briefly tensions in Sino-European history, and asked how both the colonial projects of the European nations and the present-day defence of European interests and policies continues to affect the way the Chinese feel about Europe. The response to this proves challenging, because it forces us to face up to our own history and our colonial projects not from the perspective of conquering victors, but from the perspective of those that found themselves bearing the brunt of that colonizing drive, and accordingly forced to position themselves in relation to it. But more than this, it forces Europeans to look at themselves in the mirror, and question what it is that Europe is exporting today, and what it exported in the past.

In a very different way, it might not be an exaggeration to suggest that certain Chinese writers hold a mirror up to Europeans. This does not necessarily suggest they understand us better than Europeans do themselves. Perhaps they can, nonetheless, reveal aspects of the European culture and identity that they are eager to preserve. Like all cultures, there are shady aspects of history and politics that Europeans prefer to hide, from others, and most of all from themselves.

Europe has an ambivalent relationship with America and the West as a cultural project, but how are Europeans to define themselves in terms of a shared, specifically European project? Do Europeans have the conceptual tools, the terms, the concepts, the distinctions? It is possible that the Chinese perspective will prove enlightening in this respect, since certain Chinese authors do appear to be making interesting distinctions in defining the difference between Europeanization and Westernization, and explaining where the two words overlap and where they differ.

NOTES

1. See the cartoons that appeared in the press at the time: https://www.google.fr/search?dcr=0&biw=1909&bih=677&tbm=isch&sa=1&ei=ZXaEWrmEBYmMgAaL7I_oCw&q=helmut+kohl+fran%C3%A7ois+mitterrand+hand+in+hand+cartoons&oq=helmut+kohl+fran%C3%A7ois+mitterrand+hand+in+hand+cartoons&gs_l=psy-ab.3...6615.7850.0.8456.9.9.0.0.0.0.110.700.8j1.9.0....0...1c.1.64.psy-ab..0.0.0....0.47810gIWhmU
2. A previous and somewhat different version of this chapter was presented during the congress *Eurojos* in Puławy (Poland) in November 2014 and has been published under the title 'Europe, Europeanization and related words in Mandarin Chinese' (Gianninoto 2018).
3. See Corpus of Classical Chinese (*Gǔdài hànyǔ yǔliàokù* 古代汉语语料库, http://www.cncorpus.org/ACindex.aspx).
4. Quoted from the Corpus of Classical Chinese (*Gǔdài hànyǔ yǔliàokù*).
5. The *Nederlandsch-Chineesch Woordenboek met de Transcriptie der Chineesche Karakters in het Tsiang-Tsiu Dialekt* (Chinese title *Hé-huá wényǔ lèicān* 荷華文語類參) by G. Schlegel.
6. This word was used to designate Europe in the French *Dictionnaire de poche français-chinois, suivi d'un dictionnaire technique des mots usités à l'arsenal de Foutcheou* (Chinese title *Hàn-fǎ yǔhuì biànlǎn* 漢法語彙便覽, 1874) by G. Lemaire and P. Giquel (MCST).
7. http://baike.baidu.com/item/%E6%AC%A7%E5%80%BA%E5%8D%B1%E6%9C%BA/74525
8. https://www.zhihu.com/topic/19610149/hot
9. For instance see: http://business.sohu.com/20111029/n323830404.shtml, http://blog.sina.com.cn/s/blog_6601be1b01010cr1.html, http://finance.sina.com.cn/stock/stocktalk/20111028/142210713289.shtml http://www.investbank.com.cn/information/Detail.aspx?id=36864 http://blog.jsercvb.net/yjcl/3582.html
10. https://www.zhihu.com/search?type=content&q=%E6%AC%A7%E6%B4%B2%E9%9A%BE%E6%B0%91
11. http://baike.baidu.com/item/%E6%AC%A7%E6%B4%B2%E9%9A%BE%E6%B0%91%E5%8D%B1%E6%9C%BA/18767409
12. https://www.zhihu.com/search?type=content&q=+%E8%84%B1%E6%AC%A7
13. http://baike.baidu.com/view/10176445.htm

14. http://blogtd.org/2016/06/24/%E6%AC%A7%EF%BC%81/
15. A phonetic component. As an independent character, it means 'area', 'region', or 'district'.
16. This study was financed by the Chinese Ministry of Education within the framework of two founding programmes: 'Research into the cultural contradictions in the European integration process and their meaning' (欧洲一体化进程中的文化矛盾及启示研究) and 'Together but not the same: European Union cultural diversity policy and its meaning for China' (和而不同: 欧盟文化多样性政策及其对中国的启示).

A Final Word

We now come to the close of this book, and if summing our findings up in one single simple statement is difficult, it is because a work of this nature opens our eyes to the complexity and diversity of ways we understand everyday keywords. We hope we have proven that our objectives were coherent. And we would like to believe that our study of our four keywords has made a contribution to work in the fields of semantics, comparative linguistics, linguistic anthropology, ethnolinguistics, and translation studies.

Following Raymond Williams, who coined the term 'keywords', we have always sought to unravel who is speaking to whom, and who is protecting whose interests. When speakers claim, for example, that 'more importance will be given to individualism than to solidarity' in the future in Europe, we have taken this as an ideological interpretation of an ideological trend. When speakers claim they speak 'to the people as one of the people', we have tried to grasp how this works as an astute use of rhetoric serving to win others over to the speaker's own point of view, or induce them to follow courses of action conducive to the speaker's ends.

As linguists, the scope of our study goes much deeper than many accounts of keywords offered in philosophical or sociological dictionaries and encyclopaedias: we delve deep into grammar, semantics, and linguistic patterning. We have gone far beyond lexis in our study of our keywords. This is a Humboldtian strategy. Words are only one dimension of linguistic patterning that includes morphology, word compounds, collocations, phrases and expressions, semantic fields, associations, conceptual metaphors, and innovative metaphoric extensions.

In the eighteenth century, many people believed that the difference between languages lay in their different vocabularies. Later, it became more evident that the grammatical structures of languages were radically different. Finally, in the Herder-Humboldt revelation, it became clear that we inhabit different conceptual and semantic worlds. Languages are distinct worldviews, in a global world that we must share. Our languages open up to us their own unique ways of drawing the world of experience into the mind. And it is thanks to the conceptual organization of the world through the language system that we are able to learn to interact with others and negotiate our own place in social exchanges.

We either share the world with others in our language, or we translate our worlds into other modes of thinking and feeling in other languages. While our book should have demonstrated that translating and reconceptualizing keywords is complex, we are in no way sceptical about the possibilities of translating and sharing meanings. We believe we can learn to understand other languages, other people, and their worlds. But we have to get to grips with culture, traditions, religions, and ideologies. At first, English-speakers are, of course, perplexed when they come across expressions like, *niú guǐ shé shén* 牛鬼蛇神 'ox-monsters and snake-demons', an expression with its roots in Buddhist demonology, used to designate China's 'non-People' (Schoenhals 1994: 12). But analysing the context and the tradition helps to explain these expressions. Ultimately, they are no more absurd or obscure than the scenarios Europeans live through, when they represent Europe 'lurching from crisis to crisis', stories that may well appear absurd or incomprehensible, when viewed from outside Europe.

We hope the pages devoted to the '*peuple*' of France, to German '*Bürger*', and to Czech 'individualists' have not seemed out of place, but have enabled us to present a rich selection of Europe's cultural resources. Above all, we hope that our investigations into the complexity and the diversity of European concepts, and their dynamic changing natures, have prevented readers from forming a simplistic impression of one solid stable concept that is 'exported' or 'borrowed' from the West. As we made perfectly clear at the outset, this book is about 'migrating meanings'. We compare and contrast broadly similar concepts in several languages, and then we ask what happens to words that move from one linguistic tradition to another. As the keyword migrates, it takes on a new role in a new environment, and by competing with other words in that new context, the keyword is transformed and reconfigured. Once they leave home, keywords reinvent themselves.

As we pointed out in our introduction, we had a single aim that could best be described in terms of seven related objectives:

1. To understand the diverse facets of 'citizen', 'individual', 'Europe', and 'the people', more fully in English.
2. To understand the diversity of traditions in American, Scottish, and English English.
3. To compare the different traditions of those forms of English and to understand how they conditioned the way in which our keywords developed.
4. To compare the ways broadly similar keywords function in the linguistic patterning of other European languages.
5. To see how indigenous Chinese words like *mín* 民, *rénmín* 人民, and *guómín* 国民 were transformed when foreign borrowed words started to enter into usage, and Western interpretations of society began to have an impact on Chinese society.
6. To try to understand how borrowed words introduced new concepts into the Chinese worldview, and how the Chinese creatively modify and domesticate the concepts they adopt and integrate.
7. To understand the way that process of integration gives rise to transmutations, and the way transformed keywords open up new trajectories for the Chinese culture.

The question of the people, and who defends them, has always been the essential question in politics. Whether leaders should be part of the people remains an eternal question of paramount importance. This question will not go away, and those who make the mistake of forgetting the people are in for a rude awakening. Ancient and recent history alike prove this. Mencius was simply reiterating the truth that was enshrined in more ancient canonical texts when he reminded leaders not to neglect the people. This was something that Farage, Trump, and Le Pen knew all too well. But it is something that others – to their great regret – forgot. This explains the charm of populism, when the dialogue between the people and their leaders breaks down. Above all, it is the breakdown of that dialogue that endows populists and demagogues with such great power of persuasion at crucial moments in a country's history.

The question of citizenship and the rights of individuals takes us to the heart of our project. In a way they are inseparable, and by rights they should both be inseparable from 'the people'. But all too often, we carve up these concepts, just as we carve up people into 'full citizens', 'second-class citizens', 'non-citizens', and 'enemies of the people'.

We all know that we have to live together in what is increasingly a world community. Ecology, geopolitics, monetary transactions, employment, and resources leave us little alternative. But how are we to think together as a global community? There is no simple answer to this question. But the authors of this book belong to those who believe that simplistic reductive definitions will only serve to confuse people and manipulate debates: simplistic meanings are either imposed upon a culture from without, or willingly embraced by uncritical 'ideological converts'. We believe that conceptual shortcuts will be of little use to real people looking for real solutions to express their ideas, needs, desires, and aspirations regarding the essential questions of citizenship and individualism.

There is no shortage of works promising to unlock the secrets of the East. Our book, on the other hand, is not a celebration of *Alterity* or exotic traditions. It is neither a defence of Europe or the West, nor a celebration of China. It is not an ideological defence of any one system of thought. We wanted to produce a thought-provoking investigation into conceptual complexity and question terminological definitions. This means for us investigating both the strategies used to translate and assimilate keywords, and taking into account the way existing keywords in Chinese are modified or even radically revised with the introduction of new meanings and new modes of conceptualizing keywords. It is a rigorous analysis of the concepts we share, and what we understand about our differences: cultural differences, traditional differences, linguistic differences, political and ideological differences. And we have tried not to neglect those specific differences related to individual perspectives and personal sensibilities. In studying how our keywords, the citizen, the individual, and the people, are used in various European nations, we have sought to enter different worldviews: we have tried to find our bearings, to see more clearly, together. We have explored the associations related to the English concepts and logics and cultural narratives they are bound up in. And we have contrasted the way they are perceived with the way other peoples perceive their own analogous keywords within the framework of their own traditions.

Our friendship has deepened with this book, and our dialogue opened up as we discussed our ideas with scholars around Europe. During the course of writing this book, other concepts have come to haunt us, and we have worked on freedom, hearts, houses, walls, home, and homelands together (see Underhill 2015, http://rep.univ-rouen.fr/content/homeland-06 and Gianninoto 2015, http://rep.univ-rouen.fr/content/homeland-05), and with the key ethnolinguists of the Lublin School, Bartmiński (2015, http://rep.univ-rouen.fr/content/homeland-01), Abramowicz (2014, https://webtv.univ-rouen.fr/videos/le-terme-liberte-et-son-equivalent-polonais-par-maceij-abramovicz/), and Głaz (2015, http://rep.univ-rouen.fr/content/homeland-11). Our friends in Rouen, Lozano (2015, http://rep.univ-rouen.fr/content/homeland-08), Rabasso (2015, http://rep.univ-rouen.fr/content/homeland-07, and El Alaoui (2015, http://rep.univ-rouen.fr/content/homeland-10) have opened up our questions to new horizons, by taking us into the perspectives of the Spanish, the Catalans, and the Moriscos. Our great friend, Jürgen Trabant, has helped to explicate the Humboldtian conception of languages and worldviews, a conception of language and understanding that gives meaning and purpose to the work of the entire range of authors we have quoted. Humboldt reminds us why comparing concepts in languages is so exciting and so fundamental for human creativity and culture (see Trabant 2015, http://rep.univ-rouen.fr/content/films-trabant). And Irena Vaňková (2016, https://slideslive.com/38897480/clovek-v-jazyce-prostor-pribeh-prozitek-jazyky-mluvene-a-jazyky-znakove) brought us together in the summer of 2016 in Prague to speak of Europe and the kind of linguistics it needs to help us think through its unity in diversity. Since then, various meetings with international scholars, such as the leading sinologist working with the Natural Semantics Method, Zhengdao Ye (2018, https://webtv.univ-rouen.fr/permalink/v125a8ca692echodnk4f/), have enabled us to discuss the way we construct meaning out of words.

These meetings made it clear that we will continue to wonder about how we try to make sense of that world together, and how we live among a world of words. For the past few years, we have been dialoguing with Anna Wierzbicka, because we are fascinated by the way our words open up worlds for us, and because, like her, we believe the words of different languages open up different worlds to us. What stimulates us is the way people make sense of the world using language, 'thinking through language' (*Denken durch Sprache*), as Humboldt would say.

Even after forty years in Australia, Anna Wierzbicka is a migrant, like us. We have all tried to bear witness to the way meanings migrate from culture to culture. We are all concerned about where we come from and where we are going, as much as the origin and destinies of words. Because if we must make our home in language, it becomes crucial to understand the way – like us – migrating meanings take up new roots in foreign soil, allowing the people who use new words to express their own new relevant, heartfelt perspectives and affirm their positions among others, in society and in language.

Completed Christmas Day, 2017

Glossary

Affixoid Booji (2005: 114) defines affixoids (including prefixoids and suffixoids) as 'morphemes which look like parts of compounds, and ... occur as lexemes, but have a specific and more restricted meaning when used as part of a compound'. Novotná (1967; 1968; 1969) uses the term 'affix-like formative' to designate these forms in her study on Chinese word formation. In this work, we have used this term to refer to a form like *zhǔyì* 主义 'doctrine', 'principle', which can occur as an independent word, but is often used as in compound words as an equivalent of the English suffix '-ism' (for example in words like *gèrénzhǔyì* 个人主义 'individualism' and *shèhuìzhǔyì* 社会主义 'socialism').

Asia/Asian A concept of importance for history, culture and identity, but one that proves difficult to define in cultural, linguistic, or even geographic terms. In Europe, and the West in general, China and Japan are invariably considered to form part of Asia, but the countries lumped together in this group is indeterminate and the concept evoked by 'Asia' itself is always vague. Whether this confusion serves covert interests is open to debate. Western discursive strategies often define Asian cultures as forming part of a fairly homogenous cultural and geographic block, in contrast to 'the West'. This of course makes little sense to the Chinese, the Japanese, and the Koreans, who are understandably concerned about doing justice to their own cultural diversity. 'Asia' serves to position countries and cultures in an unequal opposition in which the non-Asian countries are positively defined in terms of their own interests. The definitions of those 'non-Asian' countries and cultures, does, however, inevitably, prove to be equally vague. In our book, we have striven to resist binary oppositions which promote simplistic impressions of Asian culture that can easily be assimilated by Westerners. See 'the East/Eastern', 'the West'.

British English   The standard English used in the press and in novels in Britain. The term 'British English' is used in contrast to 'American English' in this book. This distinction proves operational up to a point, but it breaks down when we begin to compare the way our keywords, 'citizen' and 'Europe' are used in the varieties of standard English used in the press and other publications in Scotland and England. For this reason, we distinguish between English English and Scottish English, when significant distinctions are found. Though the 'people' and 'citizen' exist in both languages, the patterning often proves richer and more extensive in Scottish English than English English, and this affects the rhetorical potential for political discussion that harnesses these two keywords in media debates and in the parliaments in Edinburgh and London.

The Chinese dream (中国梦)   'The Chinese dream' was advocated by the President Xí Jìnpíng 习近平, with the ambition of the 'Great renewal of the Chinese Nation' (中华民族的伟大复兴英文). The expression 'great dream of the renewal of the Chinese nation' (中华民族伟大复兴的中国梦) was used by Xí Jìnpíng in a speech given on 29 November 2012, at the National History Museum, in front of the exhibition 'The road toward Renewal' (复兴之路), retracing country's history over the last two centuries. 'The Chinese dream' has become a key expression in Xí's political discourse.

Concept   Term used in the present work to refer to a complex nexus of related meanings. While terms ideally have only one designated and clearly defined meaning, one that we try to elevate to universal usage, concepts often refuse to be curtailed and reduced to clearly defined limits. As deep and powerful resources, concepts animate language and culture. Their multifaceted meanings bear witness to their flexibility as resources for expressing meanings at various levels of everyday life and philosophical discussion. Concepts like 'love' and 'hate' may be translated into other languages, but the dimensions of these concepts, and the extent of their associations reaching throughout the language-culture, may prove impossible to translate. Concepts are clearly inseparable from keywords, but the two terms entail different approaches, each with their own methodology. Working from concepts to words is the standard philosophical approach. Working from keywords back to concepts is a semantic approach. We have adopted the semantic approach, and begun and ended with keywords, but we have at times adopted the philosophical method in order to question to what extent culture-specific keywords can be considered to have trans-European meanings, and to what extent Chinese modifies these meanings conceptually speaking.

Conceptual metaphor (Originally referred to by Lakoff and Johnson as 'protometaphor' (1980) and referred to before them by other scholars as 'root metaphor'). Term denoting an underlying metaphorical equation. If a man describes a woman as 'spicy', the expression can only be understood fully by virtue of the underlying conceptual metaphor which invites us to understand sexual congress as eating, and partners as food. Describing men as 'hunks' or 'beefcakes' in English, or describing them in French as '*alléchants*', a term which translates as 'lickable' or 'tasty', testifies to two facts: different languages can share the same conceptual metaphors, and such expressions are not gender-restrictive. Here the cognitive unconscious at work in both men and women operates with largely the same conceptual resources.

Corpus (pl. corpora) A collection of texts of a specific or varied nature designed to facilitate study usually of a linguistic kind. In recent decades, corpora have increasingly been electronic, but using a specific collection of texts as a whole for study purposes was long-established before the advent of the IT revolution. Electronic corpora have grown from the revolutionary British National Corpus with its 100 000 000 words which came out in the early 1990s, to the Corpus of American Colloquial English with 440 million words. Over the last decade, Google has been producing multi-billion word corpora, such as the Google Books corpora upon which the Ngram online word frequency tool is based. Despite the self-evident advantages of these corpora, the more-is-better philosophy that is generating these mega-corpora does have shortcomings. Formerly, philologists, linguists, and literary scholars would consult texts they were familiar with, and corpora study went hand in hand with discourse analysis. Massive electronic corpora present researchers with a much wider range of material, but though great progress has been made in contextualizing the words searched for, most people consulting electronic corpora find themselves quoting passages from books they have not read or phrases from video media they have not seen. This has a direct impact on interpretation. It becomes increasingly difficult to grasp the complexities of word use, and especially political or ironic uses of words. For this reason, it appeared to us essential to contrast the findings derived from electronic corpora with our own samples drawn from texts and authors with whom we were familiar. For this reason, we found it useful to produce our own much more restrained corpora (of around three million words) in order to ensure we had a firm grasp of the contexts within which words were used. We believe this enables us to grasp more fully the specific meaning or meanings individual authors are giving to our four keywords.

Cultural linguistics Modern currents in cultural linguistics converge with schools of linguistic anthropology and ethnolinguistics in stressing the importance of language for culture and culture for language. They therefore resist the reduction of language to an arbitrary means of communicating universal concepts. Like the neo-whorfians, and scholars working in the field of psycholinguistics, however, cultural linguists are more concerned with grammar than semantics. Seeking to use the deep structures of language as a doorway into the worldviews of foreign cultures, all of these various approaches are less interested in individual perspectives and the manifold diversity and dynamism of speech communities, than the underlying traditions that shape and frame speaking and thinking. Our corpus-based approach to debate and discourse, in contrast, seeks to understand the deeper frameworks of conceptualization of our keywords, as cultures evolve, and as individuals take their stance in dialogue and discussion.

Cultural mindset Term used in this work to designate that relatively stable way of seeing the world which frames our perception and conception of politics, society, history, behaviour, the individual's place in the world and the organizing conceptual frameworks of social relations. When groups and generations who speak the same language fail to understand each other, it is often because their cultural mindsets have grown into very different expressions of the world, although those differing expressions are derived from the same linguistic patterning that is inextricable from world-perceiving and world-conceiving. This patterning that organizes the language is shared by all groups within their linguistic community, but it is understood differently and mastered in varying degrees by individuals. The rights and the obligations of 'citizens' are understood differently in Western democracies depending upon whether we have a cultural mindset anchored in the left-wing or the right-wing. Similarly, royalists and egalitarians do not share the same conception of 'the people', its destiny, and its rights. Cultural mindsets often oppose one another within the same period, and the cultural mindset of one generation is often rejected by the next generation. Nevertheless, this rejection, contestation, debate, and opposition takes place within the language system, using shared concepts (the individual, the citizen, the people, and so forth). Cultural mindsets can never be disentangled from the language system and the shared modes of world-conceiving and world-perceiving of the linguistic community. Paradoxically, however, cultural mindsets can migrate. Religious and political worldviews are exported and imported. The task we set ourselves in the present work was to evaluate the ways in which we find contrasting and coinciding tendencies among cultures as words, ideas, and ideologies are exported and imported. Our questions became: How similar are the conceptual mindsets of different languages? And how are keywords transformed as various conceptual mindsets compete and displace one another? To what degree can we find a critique of individualism in both Czech and Chinese communist discourse, for example? Or on the other hand: To what degree is the traditional conception of the people in China transformed by the discourse strategies of bourgeois liberals, Marxists, and Post-Marxists, who all have their own cultural mindsets with their own specific understanding of the rights and vocation of the people?

Discourse Form or style of language which can be attributed to an individual, a group, an institution, or a period in a culture's history. It is, nevertheless, important to identify the way in which individual discourse contrasts with and resists reigning ideologies and cultural mindsets.

Discursive strategy Term used in the present work to designate the manner by which a speaker uses the concepts and modes of reasoning related to a conceptual mindset. This entails activating associations, and following time-worn arguments. In linguistic terms, this involves activating the patterning of the shared language, but doing so either with a conscious or unconscious intention to influence the people addressed. A discursive strategy can be considered an individual expression of rhetoric. Among contemporary cognitive linguists, Eubanks (2000) used the term, 'discursive strategy', in a distinct but related manner to denote the arguments and positions we formulate to serve our purposes and consolidate our positions. Conceptual metaphors are often harnessed in ways which bolster our discursive strategies.

East/Eastern Words with an unquestionable power for evoking cultural and historical associations. These words do, nonetheless, defy definition, and cannot be considered either as neutral terms or as objective concepts. The East begins in Morocco and stretches as far as Japan, thereby going beyond the boundaries of Europe itself on both sides. Culturally and linguistically speaking, these terms also prove to be of little use. Nonetheless, both the Chinese and the Europeans make use of the East–West dichotomy, and situate themselves within its terms. Identity cannot be fully understood if we abandon these terms as values. On the one hand, there is an unconscious supposition that *West is Best* in Europe, and this prejudice is arguably more pronounced in North America. On the other hand, the East is often held up as an aesthetic and cultural ideal, a bastion of tradition. This is, however, a conception that situates Asia in the past, and excludes it from modernity. Japan's high tech image and China's exports contradict this facile dichotomy between the East and the West, of course. Our hope is that our study of migrating meanings will contribute to helping us move beyond this reductive and misleading opposition. We have sought to understand the nature and the development of European cultures and Chinese history and contemporary society through the prism of four keywords. At any rate, we insist the findings of our study cannot be organized into a reductive East–West dichotomy. On the contrary, permeation and fusion are better paradigms for understanding how meanings migrate. The global world is not new, and cultures have long been engaged in sharing values and reappraising each other's cultures, innovations, and ideas.

English English The standard English used in English novels and the English press. Although we used the term British English in contrast to American English, it proved necessary to distinguish, in turn, between English and Scottish varieties of this common vernacular. Conceptions of 'the people' have both a patriotic and a political meaning in Scottish English, for example, which is rarely found in English sources.

Enlightened American individualism Term used in the present work to denote the philosophical position adopted by thinkers such as James and Dewey who saw the development and cultivation of individuality as a psychological, spiritual, and social necessity. Rather than pitting individuals against society, James and Dewey saw individuals as the source of a strong, entrepreneurial, and cultured society. At the same time, Dewey promoted a system of education and psychological institutions that would permit socialization through individuation. A healthy society should, he believed, enable children to develop into independent, free-thinking, well-balanced human beings: individuals. In contrast to this, the negative or excessive expression of individualism associated with the egotistical satisfaction of personal interests irrespective of the common good, the family, and society as a whole, has frequently been condemned by religious leaders and statesmen. Such an individualism would, from Dewey's perspective, be regarded as a stunted form of personal development in children who never outgrow their drives and desires or incorporate a faculty of empathy and sympathy.

Ethnolinguistics The school of linguistics considering the development of mankind within language and the relationship between culture and conceptualization in language. For ethnolinguists, we think and feel in language. In English-speaking linguistics, this term is often considered as a synonym for *linguistic anthropology*. Though it has as yet gained little recognition in English-speaking countries, the Lublin School of Poland has been developing a forceful analysis of language and culture in its school of ethnolinguistics since the 1980s. See Bartmiński in Polish, and, in English, Wierzbicka, who has managed to introduce a philological approach (the Natural Semantics Metalanguage) which preserves a concern for the interaction between literature and the language system. The German linguist Wilhelm von Humboldt (1767–1835) is often considered as the source of inspiration for ethnolinguistics, and the first thinker to launch the project to study the great variety of the world's worldviews as expressed by all the linguistic communities of mankind. See Trabant (2012), and Underhill (2009, 2012).

Europeanize, Europeanization *ōuhuà* 欧化 Term used to designate the influence of Europe and the espousal of Western ways of living and thinking. The Chinese scholar, Hé Jiǔyíng 何九盈, included the word *ōuhuà* 欧化 ('to 'Europeanize' or 'Europeanization') among the 'keywords' (*guānjiàncí* 关键词) in modern Chinese knowledge. The word 'Europeanization' can be considered as a quasi-synonym of 'Westernization'. Nonetheless, the use of this term, and the relevance it is attributed by Hé Jiǔyíng reflects the strong impact European culture had on the Chinese culture between the eighteenth and the early twentieth centuries. The concept and the term 'Europeanization' is, however, recent in English, and remains very rare. The COCA, for example, provides 231 examples of 'westernization', but only thirty-eight examples for 'europeanization', and it provides no results for 'europeanize' while the verb 'westernize' is commonly used in everyday English. For our study of migrating meanings, the term 'Europeanize' is of crucial importance, because it demonstrates the difficulty Europeans have in forming an overall impression of European identity and European ideals. It reveals the almost inescapable trap of ethnocentrism: Europeans apparently find it difficult to see themselves as a whole and as parts of a shared community. Consequently, it proves difficult to understand what Europe shares, politically, ideologically, and culturally, and what distinguishes European modes and lifestyles from other 'Western' or 'American' modes and lifestyles. Curiously, the examples found in the COCA for 'europeanization' did not refer to Europe's influence throughout the world. For the most part, the examples referred to problems outsiders were having adapting to life in European states: for example, the difficulties Muslims experienced in adapting to the cultural codes of their newly adopted countries. No trace of the conceptual distinction between 'Westernization' and 'Europeanization' could be found in the COCA or any other of our English sources.

Familism The term 'familism' denotes family feeling in the Chinese tradition, a notion close to the ancient Greek concept of *storgē* (στοργή), also called familial love. While familism was a fundamental value in the Chinese tradition, the influence of the West began to weaken the status of this binding social structure. Familism was a kind of social structure that holds the family's needs as a group and traditional collectivism to be paramount, and the individual's needs to be secondary. In contrast to this, many Chinese thinkers of the twentieth century criticized this form or social organization, claiming it was outdated and ill-adapted to modernity. Interestingly, it was not only those with liberal leanings that adopted this stance. Chén Dúxiù 陈独秀 (1879–1942), one of the co-founders of the Chinese Communist Party, played a key role in promoting the Western-inspired notions of the individual and individualism and disparaging familism. Chén Dúxiù staunchly advocated individualism in his essay *Dōng xī mínzú gēnběn sīxiǎng zhī chāyì* 东西民族根本思想之差异, 'The fundamental difference between the intellectual tradition of Eastern and Western peoples', published in December 1915 in *Youth* magazine. In that essay, Chén identified Western individualism as one of the West's strengths, while the Eastern tendency to value the family and the clan could, he believed, be a source of weakness. Chén, therefore, advocated 'replacing familism with individualism' (以个人本位主义易家族本位主义).

However, the family occupies a central place in Confucian thought and in Chinese culture. The family is regarded as the basis of the sociopolitical structure. This is summed up in the expression, *qí jiā zhì guó* 齐家治国 'to regulate the family and to rule the state'. The philosophy expressed by this principle is that social relations are interpreted with reference to the conceptual framework of the family, or 'familiarized' (see Lǚ 2003: 16).

Gèrénzhǔyì 个人主义 (individualism)   The current Chinese word used for individualism, *gèrénzhǔyì* 个人主义, came into use in late Qing China, in a period of great political and social change. For decades, it coexisted with rival synonyms. The various terms for individual and individualism were already central in intellectual debates and literary writings during the first decades of the twentieth century. They were associated with reformist, anti-traditionalist movements and campaigns, calling for national salvation and China's modernization. Among the numerous expressions related to individualism that were coined in those decades, we find Máo Zédōng's 'spiritual individualism' (in Chinese *jīngshén zhī gèrénzhǔyì* 精神之个人主义). In Mao's terms: 'this is an individualism of the spirit and may be called spiritual individualism' (此个人主义乃为精神的，可谓之精神之个人主义) ('*Lúnlǐxué yuánlǐ*' *pīzhù* 《伦理学原理》批注 'Marginal Notes to: Friedrich Paulsen, A System of Ethics', written by Máo between 1917 and 1918, according to and quoted in Wǔ and Jiāng (1996)). Chén Dúxiù, one of the co-founders of the Chinese Communist Party, praised 'the great spirit of the pure individualism' (*chúncuì gèrénzhǔyì zhī dà jīngshén* 纯粹个人主义之大精神), but a few years later (1920) criticized 'nihilistic individualism' (*xūwú de gèrénzhǔyì* 虚无的个人主义) (Lǐ 2008). It is also important to quote Hú Shì's (2015) distinction between 'false individualism' (*jiǎ de gèrénzhǔyì* 假的个人主义), which he considered to be equivalent to 'egoism' (*wèiwǒzhǔyì* 为我主义), and 'true individualism' (*zhēn de gèrénzhǔyì* 真的个人主义), characterized by 'independent thought' and involving the individual assuming 'full responsibility for the results or consequences of his own ideas and beliefs' (独立思想 […]二是个人对于自己思想信仰的结果要负完全责任). Hú also criticized what he called *dúshàn de gèrénzhǔyì* 独善的个人主义 'detached individualism' (Fung 2010: 154). According to Hú (2015), this form of individualism was a posture adopted by people who were disappointed by society, and unable to cope with it, people who turned their backs on society as a shared project, and simply desired to escape and pursue an ideal life outside of society (不满意于现社会，却又无可如何，只想跳出这个社会去寻一种超出现社会的理想生活). The words for individual and individualism were clearly perceived in negative terms for decades, especially after the foundation of the People's Republic ('individualism is the source of all evils', 个人主义是万恶之源). But a considerable change occurred after 1978. A new emerging narrative of the individual and individualism in Chinese contemporary society can be traced from then onwards. Individualism emerges in the contemporary Chinese worldview as a controversial keyword with multiple meanings. The individual appears to be perceived with a certain ambivalence, depending on who uses the word, in which sphere of society, and in what period of China's political and social history.

Gōngmín 公民   One of the three current Chinese words for the citizen. Goldman and Perry (2002: 4) underscore that 'the origins of the term *gongmin* lie in the Confucian celebration of the public service'. This term was already in use in the *Hán Fēizi* 韩非子 (III BCE), in which it designates the 'men who are concerned with public welfare', as opposed to 'those who think only of private interests' (*sīrén* 私人, see Watson 2003: 116). *Gōngmín* has become the prevalent term designating the citizen in contemporary Chinese, widely used not only in official and institutional discourse, but also in civil rights discourse, as well as in academic writings and newspapers. It is characterized by very positive connotations in all the wide range of sources we consulted, from newspapers to blogs, and from social media to academic writings.

Individualism   A controversial term that places the individual at the centre of political or economic activity. Individualism has had its defenders in European nations, and is currently enjoying a privileged status since the fall of the communism in Russia and the East European nations. On the whole, however, in English, many people have tended to use the 'individualism' as a pejorative term. Even the great defender of the individual's human rights and the right to free speech and free agency, John Stewart Mill, had little good to say of 'individualism'. He saw it as a form of egotism that was so lethal for society it would continue to encourage communist support as long as it was allowed to grow. In Chinese, Hú Shì (2015) distinguished between 'false individualism' (*jiǎ de gèrénzhǔyì* 假的个人主义), which he considered to be equivalent to 'egoism' (*wèiwǒzhǔyì* 为我主义), and 'true individualism' *(zhēn de gèrénzhǔyì* 真的个人主义). According to Hú, 'true individualism' is characterized by 'independent thought' and involves an individual assuming 'full responsibility for the results or consequences of his own ideas and beliefs' (独立思想 [...]二是个人对于自己思想信仰的结果要负完全责任). As the various authors quoted in this book demonstrate, individualism has been considered both an evil and an ideal. On the one hand, it became an ideal during the Cold War, a period in which the West claimed to protect and promote the freedom of the individual and, most of all, the freedom of individual expression, in contrast to repressive communist regimes which suppressed it. Arguments in favour of individualism tended to be consolidated following the fall of the communist regimes in Eastern Europe at the end of the 1980s. On the other hand, individualism had always been treated with suspicion by the both the Catholic and Protestant churches. Individualism is, nonetheless, well-anchored in the American tradition, and becomes an ideal for personal and cultural development with thinkers such as William James and John Dewey. Individualism remains an ideal for post-Cold War thinkers such as Francis Fukuyama (born 1952). Rifkin on the other hand, the contemporary American sociologist, is sceptical regarding the future of American frontier-style individualism. Rifkin sees the European Dream as a new ideal more adapted to the connected world of global communities. American-style individualism, the frontier spirit, and the American dream have served their time, Rifkin believes, and are no longer of much relevance to the way we work and live together today in societies and as world citizens. The various Chinese interpretations of European and Western individualism are crucial for this book on migrating meanings. The way the Chinese have appraised, rejected, or reformulated individualism demonstrates both the fundamental importance of the concept for understanding society and the way it develops, and the necessity of understanding the alternative forms of organizing social relations.

Individualization   Theory that posits that 'the individual is becoming the central unit of social life' and 'one's life is increasingly a reflexive or self-steered phenomenon' (Lair 2007). This 'individualization thesis' was proposed by Beck (1992).

Keyword Term borrowed from Raymond Williams, whose famous work by that name was first published in 1976. Williams defined 'keywords' as 'binding words in certain activities and their interpretation; they are significant indicative words in certain forms of thought' (Williams 1985: 15). Dealing exclusively with the English language, and more specifically the way it had changed over the course of the Second World War, Williams was interested in the way keywords frame debates and arguments about society and life in general. In the fields of ethnolinguistics and linguistic anthropology, Anna Wierzbicka, the famous Polish scholar based in Australia from the 1980s onwards, adopted the term and invented a cross-lingual approach for comparing keywords. Wierzbicka sees keywords as one of the ways of working our way into foreign worldviews to try to understand how they work. In the same vein, we have striven to follow the migration of meanings in order to uncover two things: the different natures of languages and worldviews, and the ways the introduction, adoption, and adaptation of keywords reveal the complex dynamics involved in restructuring linguistic patterning. For Williams, keywords are keys to unlocking ideologies, and the means of tracing society's transformations. For Wierzbicka, keywords are the keys to unlock foreign cultures, and the keys for showing the limits of the Anglo worldview which is organized and patterned in a culture-specific way. Our study of our four keywords, 'the people', 'citizen', 'individual', and 'Europe' has enabled us to follow the way Chinese, for example, welcome European concepts such as 'individual', and the way Chinese writers and thinkers critically reappraise existing keywords such as 'the people' (*mín/rénmín*). For us, it is essential to stress that keywords cannot be 'borrowed' without the migrating meaning being transformed. Not only do many of the facets of the keyword fail to take root in the new language, but borrowed keywords must also get to grips with existing words with which they compete. New keywords must come to terms with existing terms as rival synonyms or efface them. The concept of the citizen or the individual cannot be transplanted into the cultural mindset of the Chinese linguistic community without forcing the Chinese to reorder their own concepts and the relations between them. In the course of this process, semantic knots are untied and new knots are tied, binding together new conceptual clusters of meaning. At one stage in Chinese history, the individual was promoted as an agent of modernization and the saviour of the nation. At another, individualism was denigrated as 'source of all evils'.

Language-culture The idea that a language is defined by its culture, and its culture by its language, in an inseparably reciprocal manner. In the present work, we have tended to use the terms, language-culture and linguistic community, as synonyms.

lǎobǎixìng 老百姓 / *bǎixìng* 百姓 The words *bǎixìng* (lit. hundred surnames) and *lǎobǎixìng* both designate the 'ordinary people'. In his study of *lǎobǎixìng* discourse, Wang (2015: 203) states that: 'the concept of *laobaixing* has come to occupy a central position in contemporary Chinese social life. *Laobaixing*, often regarded as the "silent majority" in China, represents the governed and underprivileged individuals distant from power, wealth, and glory.'

Lemma In morphology, the canonical form of a word used as the heading in a dictionary.

Lexeme Term used to refer to the root form or the fundamental unit of the lexicon of a language. The lexeme is the smallest meaningful unit of language. The lexeme invariably refers to the unit that will be taken up as the dictionary entry: bring is the lexeme from which 'brings', 'bringing', and 'brought' all derive. This becomes somewhat more complicated with compound words formed by two lexemes.

lidé Czech term for a concept covered in English by various concepts (the people, people, folk). The full semantic resonance of this term is felt when it has to be translated back into English into a variety of related concepts which bear no morphological resemblance: communism with a 'human face' (*lidskýy tvář*), 'folk song' (*lidová písnička*), humane person (*lidský člověk*), people's art (*lidové umění*). English speakers can understand that a decent person could be 'human' or 'humane', but the Czech concept of a '*lidský člověk*', a decent/human person, makes little sense and taps into no networks of linguistic patterning shared by English-speakers. Arguably, it would be best translated as 'a man of the people' or 'a person close to the people', but the former draws us into another history and structure of feeling. At this stage, it becomes clear that we cannot simply translate Czech concepts into English concepts, but must start to get to grips with conceptualization as a historical and culture-specific phenomenon. Keywords prove inseparable from the development of the language as a shared medium for thinking, feeling, and expressing thoughts and feelings.

Linguistic anthropology The study of humankind in terms of linguistic and cultural communities. Closely related to ethnolinguistics. Linguistic anthropology maintains that humans are socialized into communities when they learn the language practices of their cultures. We learn to think and feel in communities and in language. The various American traditions in linguistic anthropology draw their inspiration from the German thinkers Johann Gottfried von Herder (1744–1803) and Wilhelm von Humboldt (1767–1835).

Linguistic worldview conception The worldview encapsulated in the language of a community. The crucial distinction is between ideological worldviews (referred to as cultural mindsets in the present work) and the underlying worldview that language offers to the speakers of a linguistic community. We can adopt or reject conceptual mindsets, but it proves much more difficult for us to question the more fundamental concepts and modes of relating them that we learn with our mother tongue. The concept of linguistic worldview conception was used by the Polish Ethnolinguistics School of Lublin and adopted by Czech scholars (see Vaňková 2001; 2007; Vaňková et al. 2005) who translate it as *world picture* (*obraz světa*). Jerzy Bartmiński (2012: 213) gives the following definition:

> The linguistic worldview conception is semantic, anthropological and cultural in nature. It is based on the assumption that language codes a certain socially established knowledge of the world and that this knowledge can be reconstructed and verbalised as a set of judgements about people, objects and events. The knowledge results from the subjective perception and conceptualisation of reality by the human mind; it is anthropocentric and relativised to languages and cultures.

Lud Polish term for a concept covered in English by various concepts (the people, people, folk, the nation). See Abramowicz and Bartmiński (1998).

Mín 民 This form can be considered as pivotal in the political lexicons of various Asian languages, such as Chinese, Japanese, and Korean (see Tsutsumibayashi 2012). It assumed different connotations related to the notions of 'the people', 'nation', and 'citizen' in Meiji Japan and in Late Qing (1644–1911) China (Burtscher 2012). Above all, *mín* was the dominant keyword designating 'the people' in Chinese political rhetoric for centuries. And it is still used in crystallized idiomatic expressions, such as *yōu guó ài mín* 忧国爱民 'be concerned with the country and love the people', *zhì guó ān mín* 治国安民 'rule the country and give the people stability' and *guó fù mín ān* 国富民安 'the country is rich, the people is pacified'.

Over-lexicalization Term referring to the coexistence of various quasi-synonyms. Wales (2014) underlines that 'over-lexicalization in a language occurs when a particular concept or a set of concepts are of vital concern to a culture'. Fowler (1991: 85) defines this phenomenon as 'the existence of an excess of quasisynonymous terms for entities or ideas that are a particular preoccupation or problem in the culture's discourse'. In our study, a great diversity of terms designating individualism and the individual in Chinese offers an example of over-lexicalization. We have tended to conclude that this indicates the fragile nature of the words that are introduced, debated, and often abandoned.

Patterning The linguistic paths along which thinking runs. Patterning involves harnessing concepts together. Language provides us with conventional paths for thinking, connections, and configurations. Since speech is by nature creative, it goes without saying that we can resist or break out of patterning. Nevertheless, discourse analysis seeks to uncover the strategies and interests which lie behind much linguistic patterning. The theory of patterning was best explained in English by Sapir and Whorf (see Lee on Whorf's unpublished works). In German, Humboldt used the expression *Wechselwirkung* to describe a largely similar concept of linguistic configuration, but he did not stress the political dimension, being primarily interested in the nature of culture as a whole and the way it was engendered by the worldview of the linguistic community (or what he called *Nation*). In the present work, the concept of linguistic patterning is closely linked with the forms of thought and the structures of feelings triggered by keywords as they were studied by Raymond Williams, and adapted in her cross-lingual comparative method by Anna Wierzbicka.

People/the People Distinguishing between a random number of individuals and an active self-defining, self-determining democratic force is perfectly possible for English-speakers. This is clear if we compare the following two sentences: 'There were a lot of people in the bar' and 'Power to the people!' Here we are clearly dealing with two different concepts. Although the fact that the same word is used to cover these two concepts complicated our electronic corpora research, that research did lead us to conclude that the latter concept relating to the democratic force was fairly rare or weak in English sources. This was true of both our own corpora and the established mega-corpora (BNC, COCA, Google Books). Compared with Czech, German, and even French, the discussion of what the people wants and what the people demands, proves rare in English English. This appears to be less the case in other forms of English (see Scottish or American English).

The people as root (民本)   This is a central metaphor in ancient Chinese political rhetoric. It can be found in the section 'Song of the five sons' (*Wǔ zǐ zhī gē* 五子之歌) of the Classic of Documents (*Shūjīng* 书经) and was developed by the early Chinese Confucian philosopher Mencius (Mèngzǐ 孟子 371–*c*.289 BCE). Sabattini (2012: 167) underlines that the 'people as the root' was an idea that 'experienced a revival in China starting from the early twentieth century, when it was introduced into the debate on democracy'. Points of view still diverge on the interpretation of the 'people as the root': for some scholars like Zhao (2001: 22), this must be considered a paternalistic conception of the political relationship, which 'excludes participation and denotes nothing more than a passive people and a benign ruler'. Other scholars, like Lǚ (2003: 19), see similarities between the theory of the people as the root and the participant political culture.

Perspective   Term used in this work to designate the changing nature of the way each human being perceives and conceives the world. An individual's 'perspective' changes as he or she moves through the world, interacting with others and discovering new and different experiences. In this, it contrasts with what might be called the individual's 'personal world', which can be said to be a more or less stable form of consciousness framing the individual's experience, worldview, and identity. Perspective is active, or rather interactive, and for that reason it is constantly changing. When we quote Mao, for example, at times we will highlight the specific position or stance he adopts (perspective), at times we will refer to his general approach to politics (personal world), and, at other times, he will be quoted as representing a certain ideological way of thinking (cultural mindset).

Quasi-synonyms Words designating the same concepts but which are not interchangeable in all contexts. In Chinese, Europeanize (欧化) and westernize (西化) can function as quasi-synonyms, although the two can be used to distinguish distinct processes in certain circumstances.

Regulated individualism Cheung and Pan (2006) adopt this term in describing the transformation of China's educational system, and underline that its emergence has replaced both the 'traditional' collectivism that existed before the Cultural Revolution, and 'radical collectivism' that emerged during the Cultural Revolution.

Rénmín 人民 The current Chinese word for 'the people'. The word *rénmín* was already being used in the pre-imperial period, even though it was the monosyllabic form *mín* 民 that designated 'the people' in political rhetoric for centuries before *rénmín* gradually began to assert itself. It was during the twentieth century that the form *mín* was replaced by the disyllabic word *rénmín*, and the political rhetoric about the people underwent a significant change. The word *rénmín* became inseparably linked to Chinese communist discourse and, most significantly, to the political rhetoric of Máo Zédōng. 'The people' – *rénmín* – can function as an inclusive as well as an exclusive category. Various categories were considered to belong to the people at different periods in history. At the same time, others were excluded and dubbed as 'enemies of the people' or 'non-people' (Schoenhals 1994). Throughout the communist period, the idea of 'the people' was associated with class and class conflict. In that period, the people were invested with both a historical role and a national vocation. The class-based dimensions of the concept of the people gradually began to fade in the period following 1976, however, as can be seen in the entries in dictionaries published in the recent decades. Nevertheless, *rénmín* remains a keyword in contemporary Chinese. Widely used in academic and journalistic discourses, it remains unshakably part of Chinese political and institutional discourse, as can be seen in the contemporary speeches of China's political leaders.

Return graphic loans Forms found in Classical Chinese, which have been adopted in Japanese to designate new concepts and are reintroduced with these new connotations in Chinese (see Masini 1993). For example, the form *gōngmín* 公民, the current word for citizen in Chinese, was attested in early sources (in the *Hán Fēizi* 韩非子 it designated the 'people who are concerned with public welfare'), but it acquired the new meaning of 'citizen' as a graphic loan from the Japanese word, *kōmin* 公民.

Rival synonym Term coined by the authors of this work and used to describe the process by which a new or alternative word begins to challenge a widely used word. Invariably, rival synonyms come into play when speakers or authors wish to highlight or downplay certain facets of an existing concept. Because they cover broadly similar meanings, rival synonyms compete with existing terms and can begin to encroach on them, overshadow them, or even force them into disuse. 'Folk' and 'the people' are to some degree rival synonyms in English. At one time, the two covered a similar range of meanings and could be used in various situations. But the origins of 'the people' contrasts with 'folk' in English. In Old Saxon, Old English, and even in Norman French, the term 'folk' originally referred to the followers, servants, or soldiers 'belonging' to a given leader. Despite being of Germanic origin, 'folk' never evolved into a democratic ideal in English, as '*Volk*' did in German. And today 'folk music' evokes very different associations to 'pop' music. One is popular – of the people. The other belongs to the past, to the culture of our folk traditions. *Rénmín* 人民 can be considered a rival synonym of *qún* 群 in late Qing China. The form *qún* took on a wide range of meanings in this period of Chinese history: it could refer to 'group' and 'grouping', to 'community', to the 'masses' as well as to 'the people'. This should help us to understand the usefulness of the term 'rival synonyms': the community, the masses, and the people can all be used to refer to the same group, but the ideological meaning we attribute to that group and the perspective we adopt in relation to it changes with each word used. In English, 'community' presents itself as a non-ideological term, where the masses either invites us into either a radical revolutionary stance, or invites us to stand outside and look down upon 'the people'. The people can be either an ideal or a source of fear, depending upon the perspective adopted. All of these perspectives, attitudes, values, meanings, and associations are negotiated when we adopt a word or its rival synonym in our discursive strategy.

Scottish English The standard English used in Scottish novels and the Scottish press. Although we used the term British English in contrast to American English, it proved necessary in our study of migrating meanings to distinguish, in turn, between English and Scottish varieties of this common vernacular. Indeed, it is not certain that the Scots and the English share the same definition of 'the people', 'citizenship', or 'Europe'. As forms of British English, English English and Scottish English appear to be patterned in much the same way. Their shared literature, philosophical histories, and cultures no doubt account for this. So, it might be claimed that distinguishing between two worldviews at the level of perceiving and conceiving is spurious when it comes to the Scots and the English. But at an ideological level, in terms of the way the two peoples perceive their own histories and their unfolding destinies, it would appear that crucial differences of perspectives are at stake. To what extent we can speak of a Scottish cultural mindset remains an open question. Nonetheless, it will be clear to everyone that different ways of viewing themselves, their nations, and the place of their peoples in Europe are currently being hotly debated in Scotland and England, and that those debates are not new, but express distinct histories and cultural heritages of the two 'peoples'.

Semantic colonization   Process of reinvesting an 'empty' word with a new meaning. When words lose their meaning (see 'semantic evacuation'), they will often be reinvested with new meanings. Populist movements champion an ideal of the people, but often in the absence of any real popular movements, demagogic movements that seek to harness resentments and manipulate what they see as 'the masses' will present themselves as 'champions of the people'. This was clearly the case in the ways 'the people' in English, and '*le peuple*' in French, were used in nationalist rhetoric in the 2010s. For example, in the 2017 French elections, Marine Le Pen presented her Eurosceptic nationalism with a racist subtext as a movement for the people of France. This was part of a discourse that has, over the past twenty years, presented the Front National, as a party that will get rid of immigrants, and close frontiers in order to put 'the French first' (*les français d'abord*).

Semantic evacuation   The emptying of a word's meaning. Linguistic patterning weaves complex networks of meaning around words, and especially around keywords that take on a special significance in discourse. Consequently, even after a keyword has ceased to resonate with any clear and vigorous meaning in the imagination of a linguistic community, expressions and phrases will continue to maintain it. Phrases like 'a friend to the people', and 'enemy of the people' may continue to exist as expressions long after the ideologies that promoted them have disappeared. However, since language, like nature, abhors a vacuum, often words emptied of their meaning will be colonized by parasitic uses. New meanings will be invested in the vacant spaces left by semantic evacuation. See 'semantic colonization'.

Semantics The study of meaning, terminology, and conceptualization in language. Because it stands at the cross-roads of disciplines which are not always on speaking terms, semantics as a discipline has been fought over by philosophy, psychology, cognitive science, and linguistics. The authors of the present work contend that semantics can be most profitably studied within the field of linguistics, on the condition that linguistics, as a human science, does not cut itself off from philosophic inquiry and questions related to understanding and perceiving the world around us. This makes semantics an important dimension of the Humboldtian project to consider languages as worldviews (*Weltansichten*), modes of perceiving and conceiving the world around us.

Sociolinguistics In recent decades, sociolinguistics has tended to study language within society, and language use and language forms within a given linguistic community, leaving the study of linguistic diversity within cultures and across cultures to ethnolinguistics. There is, however, nothing deterministic in this mode of working, and Dell Hymes, among others, defends a sociolinguistics that reaches beyond the limits of linguistic communities on the one hand, while investigating the specificity of subcultures within societies and their language practices, on the other (see Hymes 1974; Gumperz and Hymes 1986).

State-sanctioned individualism Beck and Beck-Gernsheim (2010: xviii) use this expression to describe modern Chinese society in which 'individuals are condemned to take their own initiatives, while the social safety nets of Chinese state socialism have disappeared'. These authors argue that 'this opens the door to the individual assignment of responsibility which is one of the general features of individualization'.

Term Word used to denote a clearly defined notion or idea. In the way we have used it, term contrasts with concept. A concept may be vague and complicated. It may have multiple paradoxical meanings. But those meanings are usually held to be related, often so much so that they are difficult to disentangle. A term, on the other hand, usually denotes a more restricted meaning that is felt to be shared by many people. Often terms are used exclusively in specific fields of knowledge and activities (science, technology, education, and so forth). Scientific terminology strives for a simplicity and precision which philosophical notions cannot hope to attain. Compare 'carbon' for example, to 'soul'. One is a simple label that can be translated from one language to the other, the other is a conceptual problem difficult to limit and define, and to translate. We have preferred to use 'keyword' when we refer to significant cultural concepts designated by words which may have multiple meanings often of a very different nature.

Tridemism (or 'Three principles of the people')   The three principles of the people *Sānmínzhǔyì* 三民主义: 'nationalism' (*mínzúzhǔyì* 民族主义), 'democracy' (*mínquánzhǔyì* 民权主义), and 'subsistence of the people' (*mínshēngzhǔyì* 民生主义) formed part of a doctrine promoted by the first president of the Republic of China, Sun Yat-sen (Sūn Yìxiān 孙逸仙 or Sūn Zhōngshān 孙中山). This tripartite doctrine was first recorded in 1903 (Fairbank 1989: 223), in the last years of the Qing empire (1644–1911). It was reformulated by Sun Yatsen after the end of the dynastic empire with the foundation of the Republic. This redefined doctrine was influenced by the Russian October Revolution (Liú and Lǐ 2003: 228).

das Volk   German term covering the English meanings of 'the people', 'folk', 'the nation', and 'the German-speaking peoples'. It is worth remembering the great productivity of this term in the German imagination and worldview. '*Volk*' is used as a noun, in its adjectival form, and in various agglutinative words, which English would translate as noun phrases ('*Volkslied*', folk song, for example). The great productivity of the concept of the people in German enables it to cover various related meanings, which are rendered as 'social', 'pop', 'popular', and 'folk' in English. The German worldview arguably holds the concept of the people together in a far greater semantic and morphological coherence than 'the folk' or 'the people' in English. At any rate, English-speakers must have recourse to more indirect paths when they weave together different words and ideas in order to establish broadly similar meanings. Unfortunately, German intellectuals often still feel uncomfortable with this keyword for historical reasons. The appropriation of the term by the National Socialists, with Hitler's claim for the need of '*Ein Reich, Ein Volk, Ein Führer*', has tended to produce a knee-jerk reaction among German-speaking intellectuals and educators. And it is true that in the Nazi era an adjectival innovation '*völkerisch*' came to mean 'racist'. The Nazis considered it an ideal rather than a pejorative term. This explains why, even to this day, certain German speakers are loath to discuss the meaning of the concept of '*das Volk*'. This attitude or unresolved trauma does, however, contrast starkly with the ongoing productivity of '*volk*' as adjective, noun, or as part of noun phrases in the German language.

The West   This term pertains to the countries of Europe and America regardless of whether they are further to the west than many of the countries said to be 'in the East' or referred to as 'Eastern' or 'Asian'. Russia, for example, will often be considered to be part of Europe, but not Turkey, though most of Russia is to the east of Turkey. This poses the question of perspective and neutrality when we speak of the East and the West. Moving towards the East or the West is often symbolic. Going to the East and towards the 'eastern promise' we are invited into traditions, into the past. Going west or going western has become assimilated with modernization. It is significant for our study that the word 'easternize' is not listed in the two volume 1985 version of the *OED*, though 'westernize' was: 'To make western in character: esp. to make (an Oriental race or country) Western in ideas, institutions, etc. (*OED*, 1985: volume 2: 2530). The *Merriam-Webster* online dictionary does list 'easternize', and gives the cursory definition 'to adopt Asian characteristics' (https://www.merriam-webster.com/dictionary/orientalize). But this is the second definition. The first definition refers to the emulation of the American East: 'to imbue with qualities native to or sometimes associated with residents of eastern U.S.' (https://www.merriam-webster.com/dictionary/easternize). The fact that COCA provides 31 999 references to 'eastern' but none for 'easternize' would seem to confirm that it is Westerners who speak about the East and eastern countries. To this extent, the terms 'east' and 'west' cannot be considered to be neutral terms relating to objective realities. They are invariably employed in situated discursive strategies. And the cultural bias and frameworks of thinking that these terms impose are difficult to escape. For our study of migrating meanings, it came as something of a revelation to realize the degree to which these terms proved 'ethnocentric' and 'Eurocentric'. Conversely, it was only by escaping the Anglo worldview that we realized the necessity of clearly distinguishing between various forms of 'west' and 'westernization'. This proved very much the case in the 'Westernize–Europeanize' distinction. See 'Europeanize'.

World-conceiving Term used in this work to designate one aspect of Humboldt's concept of 'worldview' (*Weltansicht*), namely the changing and developing manner in which we draw that world into the realm of thought to form concepts and frameworks to represent things and our experience of the world.

World-perceiving Term used in this work to denote one aspect of Humboldt's concept of *Weltansicht*, the linguistically shaped worldview, namely the changing way we perceive and feel about the world.

Worldview We have used this term in the present work to include both world-perceiving and world-conceiving: worldviews relate to the way we understand and perceive the world. Because we are socialized in society and learn to understand social relations by learning language and by interacting with others, we consider that worldviews are linguistic worldviews. The term 'worldview' is, however, more often used in English to refer to political, ideological, religious, or personal modes of constructing, understanding, and perceiving the world. The same claim can be made about '*vision du monde*' in French, '*Weltanschauung*' in German, and '*visón del mundo*' in Spanish, or '*obraz světa*' in Czech. Jürgen Trabant made a crucial distinction in German between 'cultural mindsets' or ideologies (*Weltanschauungen*), and linguistic worldviews (*Weltansichten*) (see Underhill 2009). Linguistic worldviews in the Humboldtian distinction involve cultivating the power of the imagination (*Einbildungskraft*) to enable humans to develop into socially interacting individuals capable of conceiving of the world conceptually and expressing ideas and impressions to other people who share the same language. Today, however, few people distinguish clearly between the concepts of worldview as an ideological and as a linguistic phenomenon. The Lublin School of Ethnolinguistics is something of an exception in this respect. This school makes a methodological distinction between worldview, '*obraz świata*', and linguistic worldview, '*językowy obraz świata*'.

Bibliography

CORPORA AND DATABASES

BCC (BLCU Chinese Corpus), Beijing Language and Culture University (*Běiyǔ hànyǔ yǔliàokù* 北语汉语语料库), http://bcc.blcu.edu.cn/

British National Corpus, http://www.natcorp.ox.ac.uk/

CCL (Center for Chinese Linguistics) Corpus, Peking University (*Běijīng dàxué hànyǔ yǔyánxué yánjiū zhōngxīn yǔliàokù* 北京大学汉语语言学研究中心语料库), http://ccl.pku.edu.cn:8080/ccl_corpus/

Chinese Text Project (中國哲學書電子化計畫), http://ctext.org/zh

Corpus of Classical Chinese (*Gǔdài hànyǔ yǔliàokù* 古代汉语语料库), State Language Commission Corpora (国家语委语料库), http://www.cncorpus.org/ACindex.aspx

Corpus of Contemporary American English, http://corpus.byu.edu/coca

Corpus of Modern Chinese (*Xiàndài hànyǔ yǔliàokù* 现代汉语语料库), State Language Commission Corpora (国家语委语料库), http://www.cncorpus.org/CCindex.aspx

Frantext, http://www.frantext.fr/

Lackner, Michael, Amelung, Iwo, Kurtz, Joachim (2001). *MCST (Modern Chinese Scientific Terminology) Database: An Electronic Repository of Chinese Scientific, Philosophical and Political Terms Coined in the Nineteenth and Early Twentieth Century*, http://mcst.uni-hd.de

Leipzig Wortschatz Corpus (consulted for its Czech, English, French, and German corpora), http://wortschatz.uni-leipzig.de/de

National Social Science Database (*Guójiā zhéxué shèhuì kēxué xuéshù qíkān shùjùkù* 国家哲学社会科学学术期刊数据库), http://www.nssd.org/, http://old.nssd.org/

Specially Compiled Corpora

Although the links for the vast majority of Project Gutenberg references are given in the text, the texts quoted from Project Gutenberg were generally compiled and studied in the form of five specially compiled corpora. The main advantage of this method was to avoid the limits of the most frequently used English corpora, BNC and COCA.

MyAmericanCorpus, a three million word electronic American English corpus of works compiled exclusively from texts in http://www.gutenberg.org. (In the text, individual authors and works are referenced followed by the specific http://www.gutenberg.org page.)

MyEnglishCorpus, a three million word electronic English corpus of works compiled exclusively from texts in http://www.gutenberg.org. (In the text, individual authors and works are referenced followed by the specific http://www.gutenberg.org page.)

MyHistIdeasCorpus, a nine million word electronic English corpus of works compiled exclusively from texts in http://www.gutenberg.org. (In the text, individual authors and works are referenced followed by the specific http://www.gutenberg.org page.)

MyFrenchCorpus, a three million word electronic French corpus of works compiled exclusively from texts downloaded from http://www.gutenberg.org. (In the text, individual authors and works are referenced followed by the specific http://www.gutenberg.org page.)

Scottish Corpus, a Scottish corpus of newspaper articles related to the Independence movement, taken from online and printed British press. Individual sources are given for each article.

BOOKS AND ARTICLES

Abramowicz, Maciej and Bartmiński, Jerzy, *Langues et peoples d'Europe Centrale et Orientale dans la culture française*, Paris: Institut d'Études Slaves, 1998.
Ackerman, Bruce, *We the People*, Harvard, Kindle ebook, 1993.
Ackerman, Bruno, *Denis Rougemont: une biographie intellectuelle*, 2 volumes, Geneva: Labor et Fides, 1996.

Almond, Gabriel A. and Verba, Sydney, *The Civic Culture: Political Attitudes and Democracy in Five Nations*, Princeton: Princeton University Press, 1963.
Andersson, Ruben, *Illegality, Inc.: Clandestine Migration and the Business of Bordering Europe*, Oakland: University of California Press, 2014.
Bacon, Francis, 'Of Goodness and Goodness of Nature', in *The Essays*, New York: Dolphin Books [1597], http://www.gutenberg.org/files/575/575-h/575-h.htm
Bacon, Francis, *The Essays of Francis Bacon*, New York: Dolphin Books [1597], http://www.gutenberg.org/files/575/575-h/575-h.htm
Bartmiński, Jerzy, *Aspects of Cognitive Ethnolinguistics*, trans. Adam Głaz, ed. Jörg Zinken, London: Equinox, 2012.
Bartmiński, Jerzy, 'The Cognitive Definition as a Method of Concept Explication', conference paper, Prague, 2016, https://slideslive.com/38897506/kognitivni-definice-jako-metoda-vykladu-pojmu
Bärtsch, Christine, 'Metaphernkonzepte in Pressetexten. Das Verhältnis der Schweiz zu Europa und der Europäischen Union', unpublished dissertation, Zurich University, 2004
Bastid-Bruguière, Marianne (*Bāsīdì* 巴斯蒂), 'Zhōngguó jìndài guójiā guānniàn sùyuán——guānyú Bólúnzhīlǐ 'guójiā lùn' de fānyì' 中国近代国家观念溯源——关于伯伦知理〈国家论〉的翻译, *Jìndàishǐ yánjiū* 近代史研究, 1997(4): 221–232.
Beck, Ulrich, *Risk Society: Towards a New Modernity*, London: Sage, 1992.
Beck, Ulrich and Beck-Gernshein, Elisabeth, 'Foreword: Varieties of Individualization', in Mette Halskov Hansen and Rune Svarverud (eds), *iChina: The Rise of the Individual in Modern Chinese Society*, Copenhagen: NIAS Press, 2010, pp. xiii–xx.
Bertuccioli, Giuliano and Masini, Federico, *Italia e Cina*, Bari: Laterza, 1996.
Billeter, Jean-François, *Chine trois fois muette*, Paris: Allia, 2000.
Blake, William, *Poetry and Prose* (1965), newly revised edition, edited by David V. Erdman, Blay, Michel (ed.), *Larousse grand dictionnaire de la philosophie*, Paris: Larousse, 2003. Berkeley: University of California Press, 1982.
Blumczynski, Piotr and Gillespie, John, (eds), *Translating Values: Evaluative Concepts in Translation*, London: Palgrave Macmillan, 2016.
Bonaparte, Napoléon, Tome deuième, C.L.F. Pankoucke, 1821, http://www.gutenberg.org/files/12782/12782-h/12782-h.htm

Booji, Geert, 'Compounding and Derivation: Evidence for Construction Morphology', in Dressler, Wolfgang et al. (eds), *Morphology and its Demarcations: Selected Papers from the 11th Morphology Meeting, Vienna 2004*, Amsterdam/Philadelphia: John Benjamins, 2005, pp. 109–132.

Bowie, R. and Fairbank, J., *Communist China 1955-1959: Policy Documents with Analysis*, Volume 1, Cambridge, MA: Harvard University Press, 1971.

Boxer, Charles Ralph, *South China in the Sixteenth Century (1550-1575). Being the narratives of Galeote Pereira, Fr. Gaspar da Cruz, O.P., Fr. Martin de Rada, O.E.S.A., (1550-1575)*, London: Hakluyt Society, 1953.

Brindley, Erica, *Individualism in Early China: Human Agency and the Self in Thought and Politics*, Honolulu: University of Hawai'i Press, 2010.

Brockey, Liam Matthew, *Journey to the East. The Jesuit Mission to China 1579-1724*, Harvard: Harvard University Press, 2008.

Brockhaus Enzyklopädie in vierundzwanzig Bänden, 19, Us-Wej, Mannheim: Brockhaus, 1994.

Bruce, Steve, *God save Ulster! The Religion and Politics of Paisleyism*, Oxford: Oxford University Press, 1990.

La Bruyère, *Charactères* (*Characters*, a translation and adaptation of Theophrastus' work), 1775, Paris, https://www.gutenberg.org/files/17980/17980-h/17980-h.htm

Buber, Martin, *Between Man and Man*, Glasgow: Fontana Press, 1973.

Buber, Martin, *Ich und Du*, Stuttgart: Reklam, 1995.

Buber, Martin, *I and Thou*, trans. Ronald Gregor Smith, Trowbridge, Cromwell Press, 1996.

Burtscher, Michael, 'Facing "the West" on Philosophical Grounds: A View from the Pavilion of Subjectivity on Meiji Japan', *Comparative Studies of South Asia, Africa and the Middle East*, 2006, 26(3), 367–376.

Burtscher, Michael, 'A Nation and a People? Toward a Conceptual History of the Terms Minzoku民族 and Kokumin國民in Early Meiji Japan', *Journal of Political Science and Sociology*, May 2012, 16, 47–106, http://koara.lib.keio.ac.jp/xoonips/modules/xoonips/download.php?file_id=64793

Lord Byron, *Childe Harold's Pilgrimage*, ed. J. M. Beach, North Charleston, SC: CreateSpace Independent Publishing Platform, 2012.

Casacchia, Giorgio and Gianinnoto, Mariarosaria, *Storia della linguistica cinese*, Venice: Libreria Editrice Cafoscarina, 2012.
Cassin, Barbara (ed.), *Vocabulaire européen des philosophes, Dictionnaires des intraduisibles*, Paris: Robert, 2004.
Cassin, Barbara (ed.), *Dictionary of Untranslatables: A Philosophical Lexicon*, trans. and ed. Emily Apter, Jacques Lezra and Michael Wood, Princeton: Princeton University Press, 2014.
Chappell, Hilary, 'Mandarin Semantic Primitives', in Cliff Goddard and Anna Wierzbicka (eds), *Semantic and Lexical Universals: Theory and Empirical Findings*, Amsterdam: John Benjamins, 1994, pp. 109–148.
Chappell, Hilary, 'The Universal Syntax of Semantic Primes in Mandarin Chinese', in Cliff Goddard and Anna Wierzbicka (eds), *Meaning and Universal Grammar – Theory and Empirical Findings*, vol. 1, Amsterdam: John Benjamins, 2002, pp. 243–322.
Chappell, Hilary and Peyraube, Alain, 'The History of Chinese Grammar in Chinese and Western Scholarly Tradition', *Language & History*, 2014, 57(2): 107–136.
Chén Chāo 陳超, *Jīngshén zhònglì yǔ gèrén cíyuán —Zhōngguó xiānfēng shīgē lùn* 精神重力與個人詞源 ——中國先鋒詩歌論, Běijīng: Rénmín wénxué chūbǎnshè, 2013.
Chén Guānglěi (ed.) 陈光磊, *Gǎigé kāifàng zhōng hànyǔ cíhuì de fāzhǎn* 改革开放中汉语词汇的发展, Shànghǎi: Rénmín chūbǎn shè, 2008.
Chen Xiaoming, *From the May Fourth Movement to Communist Revolution*, Albany: State University of New York, 2007.
Cheung, Kwok-Wah and Pan, Suyan, 'Transition of Moral Education in China: Towards Regulated Individualism', *Citizenship Teaching and Learning*, December 2006, 2(2), http://www.citized.info
Childers, Joseph and Hentzi, Gary (eds), *Columbia Dictionary of Modern Literary and Cultural Criticism*, New York: Columbia University Press, 1995.
Chilton, P. A. and Ilyin, M., 'Metaphors in Political Discourse: The Case of the Common European House', *Discourse and Society*, 1993, 4(1), 7–31.
Cíhǎi 辞海. Shànghǎi: Shànghǎi císhū chūbǎnshè, 1985.
Cíyuán 辞源, 4 vols, compiled by Guǎngdōng Guǎngxī Húnán Hénán Cí yuán xiūdìng zǔ 广东广西湖南河南辞源修订组 and Shāngwù yìn shūguǎn biānjíbù 商务印书馆编辑部, Běijīng: Shāngwù yìnshūguǎn, 1986.
Coccia, Filippo, 'La conoscenza delle scienze occidentali e il pensiero riformista nella Cina di fine '800', in G. Mantici, P. Paderni and

V. Varriano (eds), *Sulla Cina*, Naples: Istituto Universitario Orientale, 1998, pp. 491–506.

Dai, Bingran and Zhang, Shuangquan, 'EU Perceptions in China', in Martin Holland, Peter Ryan, Alojzy Z. Nowak and Natalia Chaban (eds), *The EU Through the Eyes of Asia*, Singapore: Asia-Europe Foundation, 2007, pp. 43–67.

De Bary, William Theodore, *Asian Values and Human Rights: A Confucian Communitarian Perspective*, Cambridge, MA and London: Harvard University Press, 1998.

Dekker, Henk and Van Der Noll, Jolanda, 'Chinese Citizens' Attitudes Towards the European Union and Their Origins', Nottingham: China Policy Institute, Briefing Series: Issue 70, 2011, http://www.nottingham.ac.uk/cpi/documents/briefings/briefing-70-chinese-views-of-eu.pdf

de Rougement, Denis, *Être un intellectuel*, 1971, https://www.youtube.com/watch?v=-ZLc-mC6DgQ)

Deulceux, Sandrine and Hess, Remi, *Lefebvre, Henri : vie, œuvres, concepts*, Paris: Ellipses, 2009.

Dewey, John, *Democracy and Education*, 1916, http://www.gutenberg.org/files/852/852-h/852-h.htm

Dictionnaire de la Philosophie, Encyclopædia Universalis, Paris: Albin Michel, 2000.

Djamouri, Redouane, 'Le chinois classique', in Emilio Bonvini, Joëlle Busuttil and Alain Peyraube (eds), *Dictionnaire des langues*, Paris: Presses Universitaires de France, 2011, pp. 984–995.

Eliot, T. S., *The Sacred Wood and Other Major Essays*, New York: Dover Publications, 1998.

Encyclopaedia Britannica, London: Encyclopaedia Britannica, 2005.

Encyclopaedia Universalis, Paris: Encyclopaedia Universalis, 2008.

Eubanks, Philip, *A War of Words in the Discourse of Trade: Rhetorical Constitution of Metaphor*, Carbondale: South Illinois University Press, 2000.

Fairbank, John, *La grande révolution chinoise 1800-1989* (original title: *The Great Chinese Revolution 1800-1989*), trans. Silvie Dreyfus, Paris: Flammarion, 1989.

Fàn, Yǒngpéng 范勇鹏, 'Rúhé kàndài Ōuzhōu rèntóng wèntí? Yǐ zhèngzhì cānyù wèi shìjiǎo' 如何看待欧洲认同问题？以政治参与为视角, *Ōuzhōu yánjiū* 欧洲研究, 2007, 6, 25–44.

Fāng Chan'an 方长安. 'Xíngchéng, tiáozhěng yǔ zhìbiàn——Zhōu zuòrén "rén de wénxué" guānyú Rìběn wénxué de guānxì' 形成、

调整与质变——周作人"人的文学"观与日本文学的关系, *Wénxué pínglùn* 文学评论, 2004, 3.

Fāng Zhìmǐn 方志钦 and Wáng Jié 王杰, *Kāng Yǒuwéi yǔ jìndài wénhuà* 康有为与近代文化, Kāifēng: Hénán dàxué chūbǎnshè, 2006.

Fauconnier, G., *Mental Spaces: Aspects of Meaning Construction in Natural Language*, Cambridge, MA: MIT Press, 1985.

Fauconnier, Gilles, and Turner, Mark, *The Way We Think: Conceptual Blending and the Mind's Hidden Complexities*, New York: Basic Books, 2003.

Féng, Shàoléi 冯绍雷, 'Zhōngguó kěyǐ cóng Ōuzhōu yìtǐhuà zhōng xuéxí shénme? —Cóng dìqū bǐjiào céngmiàn de yī zhǒng sīkǎo' 中国可以从欧洲一体化中学习什么?——从地区比较层面的一种思考, *Ōuzhōu yánjiū* 欧洲研究, 2007, 6, 1–11.

Fergusson, Rosalind, *The Penguin Dictionary of Proverbs*, London: Penguin Books, 1983.

Fidelius, Petr, *L'esprit post-totalitaire*, Paris: Bernard Grasset, 1986.

Fidelius, Petr, *Řeč komunistické*, Prague: Triada, 1998.

Fingl, J., et al., *Stručný Slovník Politický* [A Short Dictionary of Political Terms], Prague: Nakladatelsví Politické Literatury, 1962

Flew, Antony (ed.), *A Dictionary of Philosophy*, London: Macmillan Press, 1984.

Foucault, Michel, *Philosophie: Anthologie*, Paris: Gallimard, 2004.

Fowler, R., *Language in the News: Discourse and Ideology in the Press*, London: Routledge, 1991.

Fukuyama, Francis, *The End of History, and the Last Man*, New York: The Free Press, 1992.

Fumian, Marco, *Fendou: una parola chiave della Cina moderna*, in M. Abbiati and F. Greselin (eds), *Il liuto e i libri*, Venezia: Ca' Foscari, 2014, pp. 361–372.

Fung, Edmund S. K. *The Intellectual Foundations of Chinese Modernity: Cultural and Political Thought in the Republican Era*, Cambridge: Cambridge University Press, 2010.

Gāo Míngkǎi 高名凯 and Liú Zhèngtàn 刘正埮, *Hànyǔ wàiláicí cídiǎn* 汉语外来词词, Shànghǎi: Shànghǎi císhū chūbǎnshè, 1984.

Gardner, Daniel K., *The Four Books: The Basic Teachings of the Later Confucian Tradition*, Indianapolis: Hackett, 2007.

Gěng Yúnzhì 耿云志, '"Xīn qīngnián" yǔ "gèrén" de fā xiàn——jìniàn "Xīn qīngnián" chuàngkān yībǎi zhōunián' 《新青年》与"个人"的发现——纪念《新青年》创刊一百周年, *Hú Shì yánjiū tōngxùn* 胡适研究通讯, 2015, 3, 1–6.

Gianninoto, Mariarosaria, '*Qunxue* or *Shehuixue*: First Steps in the Introduction of Sociology into China and the Formation of Sociological Lexicon', in Jana S. Rošker and Nataša Vampelj Suhadolnik (eds), *Modernisation of Chinese Culture: Continuity and Change*, Newcastle upon Tyne: Cambridge Scholars Publishing, 2013, pp. 279–294.

Gianninoto, Mariarosaria, 'The Development of Chinese Grammars and the Classification of the Parts of Speech', *Language & History*, 2014a, 57(2), 137–148.

Gianninoto, Mariarosaria, 'Shíqī dào shíjiǔ shìjì zhōngwén yǔfǎshū: Zhōng-Xī yǔyánxué chuántǒng de rónghé' 十七到十九世纪中文语法书: 中西语言学传统的融合, *Lìshǐ yǔyánxué yánjiū* 历史语言学研究, 2014b, 8, 255–262.

Gianninoto, Mariarosaria, 'Western Grammars of the Chinese Language in the 18th and 19th Centuries', in V. Kasevich, Y. A. Kleiner and P. Sériot (eds), *History of Linguistics 2011*, Amsterdam/Philadelphia: John Benjamins, 2014c, pp. 53–61.

Gianninoto, Mariarosaria, '"When Boats Sail against the Current, Not Going Ahead Means Going Back": Proverbs, Metaphors and Slogans Chinese Political Discourse', in J. Szerszunowicz et al. (eds), *Linguocultural Research on Phraseology*, Bialystok: University of Bialystok publishing house, 2015a, pp. 359–374.

Gianninoto, Mariarosaria, 'When I Think of this Homeland of Yours/Mine/Ours: (我想起同我的家乡, 我们的庄严灿烂的祖国): Chinese Words for "Homeland"', Translating Heimat, Home and Homeland Conference, Rouen, 2015b, https://rep.univ-rouen.fr/content/homeland-05

Gianninoto, Mariarosaria, 'Da *xiǎojǐ* 小己 a *gèrén* 个人: alcune riflessioni sui termini per individuo e individualismo in cinese', in Clara Bulfoni (ed.), *Linguistica cinese: Tendenze e prospettive*, Milan: Unicopli, 2016a, pp. 89–101

Gianninoto, Mariarosaria, 'Translating the Terms for Citizen in Mandarin Chinese', Cultural Linguistics for Europe Conference, Prague, 2016b, https://slideslive.com/38898129/preklad-evropskych-pojmu-do-cinstiny-da-gongmin-or-xiao-shimi-nekolik-poznamek-o-terminech-oznacujicich-obcana-v-mandarinske-cinstine

Gianninoto, Mariarosaria, 'Hybridation des traditions linguistiques chinoise et occidentale: réflexions sur le lexique, la grammaire et la didactique', Habilitation thesis, Paris: École des hautes études en sciences sociales, 2017.

Gianninoto, Mariarosaria, 'Europe, Europeanization and Related Words in Mandarin Chinese', in Wojciech Chlebda (ed.), *Europa*, Lublin, Opole: UMCS Publishing House 2018, pp. 497–521.

Gianninoto, Mariarosaria, and Casacchia, G. 'Western Views of Chinese language', in Rint Sybesma et al. (eds), *Encyclopedia of Chinese Language and Linguistics*, Leiden and Boston: Brill, 2017, pp. 520–527.

Giddens, Anthony, Diamond, Patrick and Liddle, Roger (eds), *Global Europe, Social Europe*, Cambridge/Malden, MA: Polity, 2006.

Giles, H. (ed.), *A Chinese English Dictionary*, Shanghai: Kelly and Walsh, 1912.

Goatly, Andrew, *Washing the Brain: Metaphor and Hidden Ideology*, Amsterdam and Philadelphia: John Benjamins, 2007.

Goddard, Cliff and Ye, Zhengdao, 'Exploring "happiness" and "pain" across languages and cultures', in Cliff Goddard and Zhengdao Ye (eds), *"Happiness" and "Pain" across Languages and Cultures*, Amsterdam: John Benjamins Publishing Company, 2016, pp. 1–18.

Goldman, Merle, *From Comrade to Citizen: The Struggle for Political Rights in China*, Cambridge, MA: Harvard University Press, 2005.

Goldman, Merle and Perry, Elizabeth J., 'Introduction: Political Citizenship in Modern China', in Merle Goldman and Elizabeth J. Perry (eds), *Changing Meaning of Citizenship in Modern China*, Cambridge, MA: Harvard University Press, 2002, pp. 1–22.

Gōng Yáng 公羊 (ed.), *Sīcháo - zhōngguó 'xīn zuǒpài' jí qí yǐngxiǎng* 思潮 - 中国'新左派'及其影响, Běijīng: Zhōngguó shèhuì kēxué chūbǎnshè, 2003.

Goschler, Juliana, 'Embodiment and Body Metaphors', 2005, http://www.metaphorik.de/sites/www.metaphorik.de/files/journal-pdf/09_2005_goschler.pdf

Grady, J., 'Foundations of Meaning: Primary Metaphors and Primary Scenes', PhD thesis, Berkeley: University of California, 1997.

Grand Larousse, Lizy-sur-Ourcq: Jean Didier, 1992.

Gumperz, John, J. and Hymes, Dell, *Directions in Sociolinguistics: The Ethnography of Communication*, Oxford: Basel Blackwell [1972], 1986.

Guildin G. E., *The Saga of Anthropology in Cina*, Armonk, NY: M. E. Sharpe, 1994.

Guō Táihuī 郭台辉, 'Zhōng-rì de "guómín" yǔyì yǔ guójiā gòujiàn ———Cóng míngzhì wéixīn dào xīnhài gémìng' 中日的"国民"语义与国家构建——从明治维新到辛亥革命 ('Meanings of "guomin" and State-building in Early Modern China and Japan: From the Meiji

Japan to China's Revolution'), *Shèhuìxué yánjiū* 社会学研究, 2011, 4, 137–245.

Guō Zhōnghuá 郭忠华, 'Jìndài gōngmín gàiniàn yǔ fānyì de xiàndàixìng', 近代公民概念与翻译的现代性, *Zhōngguó shèhuì kēxué bào* 中国社会科学报, 2013.

Guō Zhōnghuá 郭忠华, 'Lìmín yǔ lìguó! Zhōngguó xiàndài guójiā gòujiàn zhōng de huàyǔ xuǎnzé' 立民与立国! 中国现代国家构建中的话语选择, *Wǔhàn dàxué xuébào* 武汉大学学报, 2014, 67(3), 56–62.

Harbsmeier, Chistoph, *Language and Logic. Science and Civilization in China, vol. VII:1*, Cambridge: Cambridge University Press, 1998.

Hansen, Chad, *Language and Logic in Ancient China*, Ann Arbor: University of Michigan Press, 1983.

Hansen, Chad, 'Individualism in Chinese Thought', in D. J. Munro (ed.), *Individualism and Holism: Studies in Confucian and Taoist Values*, Ann Arbor: Center for Chinese Studies. University of Michigan, 1985, pp. 35–56.

Harris, Peter, 'The Origins of Modern Citizenship in China', *Asia Pacific Viewpoint*, 2002, 43(2), 181–203.

Hè Gāng 贺刚, 'Shēnfèn jìnhuà yǔ Ōuzhōuhuà jìnchéng--Kèluódìyà hé Sài'ěrwéiyà liǎngguó rùméng jìnchéng bǐjiào yánjiū' 身份进化与欧洲化进程——克罗地亚和塞尔维亚两国入盟进程比较研究, *Ōuzhōu yánjiū* 欧洲研究, 2015, 1, 99–115.

Hé Jiǔyíng 何九盈, *Zhōngguó xiàndài yǔyánxué shǐ* 中国现代语言学史, Shāngwù yìnshūguǎn, 1995.

Hè, Yáng 贺阳, 'Xiàndài hànyǔ ōuhuà yǔfǎ xiànxiàng yánjiū', 现代汉语欧化语法现象研究, *Shìjiè hànyǔ jiàoxué* 世界汉语教学, 2008, 4, 16–31.

Hè, Yáng 贺阳, 'Cóng xiàndài hànyǔ jiècí zhōng de ōuhuà xiànxiàng kàn jiànjiē yǔyán jiēchù', 从现代汉语介词中的欧化现象看间接语言接触, *Yǔyán wénzì yìngyòng* 語言文字應用, 2004, 4, 82–89.

Hobbes, Thomas, *Leviathan* London: Penguin [1651], 1985.

Hon, Tze-ki, 'From Sheng Min 生民 to Si Min 四民: Social Changes in Late Imperial China', *Journal of Political Science and Sociology* (Keio University), May 2012, 16, 11–31.

Hooper, Beverly, 'The Consumer Citizen in Contemporary China', Working Papers in Contemporary Asian Studies, Centre for East and South-East Asian Studies, Lund University, 2005, http://www.ace.lu.se/images/Syd_och_sydostasienstudier/working_papers/Hooper.pdf

Hsü, Immanuel C. Y., *The Rise of Modern China*, New York/Oxford: Oxford University Press, 1970.

Hú Shì 胡适, *Hú Shì sǎnwén jīngxuǎn* 胡适散文精选, edited by Wáng Jiàn 王健, Nánchāng: Èrshíyī shìjì chūbǎn shè, 2013.

Hú Shì 胡适, *Rénshēng yǒu hé yìyì* 人生有何意义, Běijīng: Mínzhǔ yǔ jiànshè chūbǎnshè, [1920], 2015.

Huán, Qìngzhì 郇庆治, 'Lǜdǎng de ōuzhōuhuà yǔ Ōuzhōu mínzhǔ: gōngnéng yǔ júxiàn', 绿党的欧洲化与欧洲民主：功能与局限, *Ōuzhōu yánjiū* 欧洲研究, 2006, 6, 80–103.

Huáng Kèwǔ 黄克武, 'Gèrénzhǔyì de fānyì wèntí: cóng Yán Fù tán qǐ', 「個人主義」的翻譯問題:從嚴復談起, *Èrshíyī shìjì* 二十一世纪, 2004, 84, 40–51.

Huang Yibing, *Contemporary Chinese Literature: From the Cultural Revolution to the Future*, New York: Palgrave Macmillan, 2007.

Humboldt, Wilhelm von, *Schriften zur Sprache*, Stuttgart: Reklam, Universal-Bibliothek, 1995.

Humboldt, Wilhelm von, *On language: On the Diversity of Human Language Construction and its Influence on the Mental Development of the Human Species* (1836), trans. Peter Health, ed. Michael Losonsky, Cambridge: Cambridge University Press, 1999.

Humboldt, Wilhelm von, *Sur le caractère national des langues et autres écrits sur le langage*, trans. Denis Thouard, Paris: Seuil, 2000.

Humboldt, Wilhelm von, *Über die Verschiedenheit des menschlichen Sprachbaues/Über die Sprache*, Berlin: Fourier Verlag, 2003.

Hymes, Dell, *Foundations in Sociolinguistics: An Ethnological Approach*, Cinnaminson, University of Pennsylvania Press, 1974.

Ilie, Cornelia (ed.), *European Parliaments under Scrutiny: Discourse Strategies and Interaction Strategies*, Amsterdam and Philadelphia: John Benjamins, 2010.

James, William, *The Varieties of Religious Experience*, 1902, http://www.gutenberg.org/ebooks/621

James, William, *Pragmatism: A New Name for Some Old Ways of Thinking*, 1907, http://www.gutenberg.org/ebooks/5116

Jī Lěi 姬蕾, 'Lùn gèrénzhǔyì yǔ "Wǔ sì" xīn wénxué de yǐngxiǎng', 论个人主义与"五四"新文学的影响, *Dōngběi shī dà xuébào (zhéxué shèhuì kēxué bǎn)* 东北师大学报(哲学社会科学版), 2008, 5, 154–159.

Jīn Guāntāo 金观涛 and Liú Qīngfēng 刘青峰, *Guānniàn shǐ yánjiū— Zhōngguó xiàndài zhòngyào zhèngzhì shùyǔ de xíngchéng* 观念史研究—中国现代重要政治术语的形成, Xiānggǎng: Xiānggǎng zhōngwén dàxué chūbǎnshè, 2008.

Joseph, E. John, *Language and Identity: National, Ethnic, Religious*, New York: Palgrave Macmillan, 2004.
Joseph, John, E., *Language and Politics*, Edinburgh: Edinburgh University Press, 2006.
Joseph, John, E., ‚Wilhelm von Humboldt's Reception in the Anglosphere', Thinking Humboldt Now Conference, London, 2016, http://german.sllf.qmul.ac.uk/german/thinking-language-humboldt-now/symposium-videos/
Judge, Joan, 1994, 'Key Words in the Late Qing Reform Discourse: Classical and Contemporary Sources of Authority', Indiana East Asian Working Paper Series on Language and Politics in Modern China, Paper 5, Bloomington: Indiana University East Asian Studies Center, 1994, pp. 1–33,
Keane, Michael, 'Redefining Chinese Citizenship', *Economy and Society*, 2001, 30(1), 1–17.
Kimmel, Michael, 'Metaphors of the EU Constitutional Debate – Ways of Charting Discourse Coherence in a Complex Metaphor Field', 2009, http://www.metaphorik.de/de/autor/kimmel-michael.html
Kipnis, Andrew, '*Suzhi*: A Keyword Approach', *The China Quarterly*, June 2006, 186, 295–313.
Kubler, Cornelius, C., *A Study of Europeanized Grammar in Modern Written Chinese*, Taipei: Student Book, 1985.
Lackner, Michael, and Vittinghoff, Natascha, *Mapping Meanings: The Field of New Learning in Late Qing China*, Leiden: Brill, 2004
Lackner, Michael, Amelung, Iwo and Kurtz, Joachim, 'Introduction', in M. Lackner, I. Amelung and J.Kurtz (eds), *New Terms for New Ideas. Western Knowledge and Lexical Change in Late Imperial China*, Leiden: Brill, 2001a, pp. 1–12.
Lackner, Michael, Amelung, Iwo and Kurtz, Joachim, (eds), *New Terms for New Ideas. Western Knowledge and Lexical Change in Late Imperial China*, Leiden: Brill, 2001b.
Lair, Craig, D., 'Individualization (Beck)', in G. Ritzer (ed.), *The Blackwell Encyclopedia of Sociology*, Malden, MA/Oxford/Carlton, Australia: Blackwell Publishing, 2007.
Lakoff, George, *Women, Fire and Dangerous Things: What Categories Reveal about the Mind*, Chicago: University of Chicago Press, 1987.
Lakoff, George, *Moral Politics*, Chicago: University of Chicago Press, 1996.
Lakoff, George, and Johnson, Mark, *Metaphors We Live By*, Chicago: University of Chicago Press, 1980.

Lakoff, George and Turner, Mark, *More Than Cool Reason: A Field Guide to Poetic Metaphor*, Chicago: University of Chicago Press, 1989.
Lakoff, George and Johnson, Mark, *Philosophy in the Flesh*, Chicago: Chicago University Press, 1999.
Lefebvre, Henri, *La Production de l'espace*, Paris: Anthropos [1974], 2000.
Legge, James, 'The Ch'un ts'ew, with the Tso chuen', in *The Chinese Classics, with a Translation, critical and exegetical notes and copious indexes by J. Legge, vol V, part II, containing Dukes Seang, Ch'au, Ting, and Gae, with Tso's appendix; and the indexes*, Hong Kong: Lane, Crawford & Co; London: Trübner & Co, 1872. https://babel.hathitrust.org/cgi/pt?id=uc1.b000970399;view=1up;seq=254
Lemoine J., 'Ethnologues en Chine', *Diogène*, 1986, 133, 82–113.
Leonhardt, Katharina, 'Dem europäischen Körper eine europäische Seele. Körperkonzepte einer europäischen Identität' ('The European body has a European soul: The European Identity in Body Concepts', 2012, http://www.metaphorik.de/de/autor/leonhardt-katharina.html
Levi, Jean, 'Le père insuffisant. Remarques sur la phraséologie politique en Chine ancienne', *Extrême-Orient Extrême-Occident, Hors-série*, 2012, http://journals.openedition.org/extremeorient/208
Lǐ Dàzhāo 李大钊, 'Yóu jīngjì shàng jiěshì Zhōngguó jìndài sīxiǎng biàndòng de yuányīn' 由经济上解释中国近代思想变动的原因, *Xīn qīngnián* 新青年, 1920, 7(2), https://www.marxists.org/chinese/lidazhao/marxist.org-chinese-lee-19200101.htm
Lǐ Láiróng 李来容, 'Ōuhuà zhì běntǔhuà: Qīngmò Mínguó shíqí xuéshù dúlì guānniàn de méngfā yǔ shēnhuà', 欧化至本土化：清末民国时期学术独立观念的萌发与深化, *Xuéshù yánjiū* 学术研究, 2011, 11, 120–127.
Lǐ Míngmíng 李明明, 'Jùjué ōuzhōuhuà? Tǔ'ěrqí yíōuzhǔyì de xīngqǐ', 拒绝欧洲化？土耳其疑欧主义的兴起, *Guójì guānchá* 国际观察, 2011, 4, 73–79.
Lǐ Zéhòu 李泽厚, *Zhōngguó xiàndài sīxiǎng shǐ* 中国现代思想史, Běijīng: Sānlián shūdiàn, 2008.
Liang Qichao, 'On the Relationship between Fiction and the Government of the People', trans. Gek Nai Cheng, in Kirk A. Denton (ed.), *Modern Chinese Literary Thought: Writings on Literature, 1893-1945*, Stanford: Stanford University Press, 1996, pp. 74–81.
Lin, Wusun, 有关"八荣八耻"翻译的讨论和思考 ['Discussions and reflections on translation of "Eight Honours and Eight Shames"'], *Chinese Translators Journal*, 2006, 27(5), 80–81.

Link, E. Perry, *An Anatomy of Chinese: Rhythm, Metaphor, Politics*, Cambridge: Harvard University Press, 2013.

Littré: Dictionnaire de référence de la langue française, Paris: Garnier, 2007.

Liú, Jiā 刘佳, 'Ōuméng chéngyuánguó yǔ ōuzhōuhuà', 欧盟成员国与欧洲化, *Zhōngguó xībù kējì* 中国西部科技, 2011, 10, 71–72.

Liú Jiànqīng 刘健清 and Lǐ Zhènyà 李振亚, *Zhōngguó jìnxiàndài zhèngzhì sīxiǎng shǐ* 中国近现代政治思想史, Tiānjīn: Nánkāi dàxué chūbǎnshè, 2003.

Liu, Lydia, 'Translingual Practice: The Discourse of Individualism between China and the West', in Wimal Dissanayake (ed.), *Narratives of Agency: Self-making in China, India, and Japan*, Minneapolis/London: University of Minnesota, 1996, pp. 1–34.

Liu, Lydia H., *Translingual Practice. Literature, National Culture, and Translated Modernity—China, 1900-1937*, Stanford: Stanford University Press, 1995.

Liu, Lydia H., 'Legislating the Universal: The Circulation of International Law in the Nineteenth Century', in Lydia H. Liu, (ed.), *Tokens of Exchange: The Problem of Translation in Global Circulations*, Durham/London: Duke University Press, 1999, pp. 127–164.

Liú Zàifù 刘再复 and Lǐ Zéhòu 李泽厚, 'Gèrénzhǔyì zài Zhōngguó de chénfú' 个人主义在中国的沉浮, *Huáwén wénxué* 华文文学, 2010, 4, 58–62.

Locke, John, *An Essay Concerning Human Understanding* (1689), Glasgow: Fontana, Collins, 1964, http://www.gutenberg.org/ebooks/10615

Lǚ Xiǎobō 闾小波, *Zhōngguó jìndài zhèngzhì fāzhǎn shǐ* 中国近代政治发展史, Běijīng: Gāoděng jiàoyù chūbǎnshè, 2003.

Lu, Xing, *Rhetoric of the Chinese Cultural Revolution: The Impact on Chinese Thought, Culture and Communication*, Columbia: University of South Carolina Press, 2004.

Luō, Hòulì 罗厚立, 'Guócuì yǔ Ōuhuà: cóng Qīngjì dào Mínchū de guānniàn chuánchéng', 国粹与欧化：从清季到民初的观念传承, *Dúshū* 读书, 2002, 1, 52–58.

Mackerras, Colin, McMillen, Donald H. and Watson, Andrew, *Dictionary of the Politics of the People's Republic of China*, London and New York: Routledge, 1998.

Máo Zédōng 毛泽东, *Xīnmínzhǔzhǔyìlùn* 新民主主义论, 1940, https://www.marxists.org/chinese/maozedong/marxist.org-chinese-mao-194001.htm

Máo Zédōng毛泽东, *Wèi rénmín fúwù* 为人民服务, 1944a, http://cpc.people.com.cn/GB/64184/64185/66617/4488954.html

Máo Zédōng毛泽东, *Wèi rénmín fúwù* 为人民服务, 1944b (English translation) https://www.marxists.org/reference/archive/mao/selected-works/volume-3/mswv3_19.htm

Máo Zédōng毛泽东, *Lùn liánhé zhèngfǔ* 论联合政府, 1945, https://www.marxists.org/chinese/maozedong/marxist.org-chinese-mao-19450424aa.htm

Máo Zédōng毛泽东, *Lùn rénmín mínzhǔ zhuānzhèng* 论人民民主专政, 1949a, http://cpc.people.com.cn/GB/64184/64185/66618/4488978.html

Máo Zédōng毛泽东, *Máo zhǔxí kāimùcí* 毛主席开幕词, 1949b, http://www.people.com.cn/item/lianghui/zlhb/zx/1jie/newfiles/a1020.html

Máo Zédōng毛泽东, *Guānyú zhèngquè chǔlǐ rénmín nèibù máodùn de wèntí* 关于正确处理人民内部矛盾的问题, 1957, http://cpc.people.com.cn/GB/64184/64185/189967/11568204.html

Máo Zédōng毛泽东, 'On the Chungking Negotiations', *Selected Works of Mao Tse-tung: Vol. IV*, Beijing: Foreign Language Press, 1961, pp. 53–64.

Mao Zedong, 'Marginal Notes to: Friedrich Paulsen, A System of Ethics', in Stuart R. Schram trans. and ed. *Mao's Road to Power: Revolutionary Writings 1912–1949, vol. I, The Pre-Marxist Period, 1912–1920*, Armonk: M. E. Sharpe, 1992.

Masini, Federico, *The Formation of Modern Chinese Lexicon and its Evolution toward a National Language: The Period from 1840 to 1898*, Berkeley: Journal of Chinese linguistics: Monograph VI, 1993.

Masini, Federico, 'Different Chinese Perceptions of Italy from late Ming to late Qing', in Christina Neder, Heiner Roetz and Ines-Susanne Schilling (eds), *China in Seinen Biographischen Dimensionen/China and Her Biographical Dimensions: Gedenkschrift Fur Helmut Martin / Commemorative Essays for Helmut Martin*, Wiesbaden: Harrasowitz Verlag. 2001, pp. 567–577.

Médard, J. (ed.), *Vocabulaire français-chinois des sciences morales et politiques*, Tianjin: Société Française de Librairie et d'Édition, 1927.

Michelet, Jules, *Le Peuple*, Paris: Marcel Didier [1846], 1946.

Mill, John, Stuart, *On Liberty*, 1859, https://www.gutenberg.org/files/34901/34901-h/34901-h.htm

Mill, John Stuart (Yuēhàn•Mùlēi 约翰•穆勒), *Qún jǐ quán jiè lùn* 群己權界論, trans. Yán Fù 严复, Běijīng: Shāngwù yìnshūguǎn, 1981.

Musolff, Andreas, *Attitudes towards Europe: Language in the Unification Process*, Aldershot: Taylor & Francis, 2001.

Musolff, Andreas, *Metaphor and Political Discourse: Analogical Reasoning in Debates about Europe*, New York/Basingstoke: Palgrave Macmillan, 2004.

Musolff, Andreas, *Political Metaphor Analysis: Discourse and Scenarios*, London: Bloomsbury Press, 2016.

Musolff, Andreas, Schäffner, Christiana and Townson, Michael, *Conceiving of Europe, Diversity in Unity*, Aldershot: Dartmouth Publishing Company, 1996.

Nguyen, Etienne Van, 'Unité lexicale et morphologie en chinois mandarin. Vers l'élaboration d'un Dictionnaire Explicatif et Combinatoire du chinois', PhD dissertation, Université de Montréal, 2006.

Niebrzegowska-Bartmińska, Stanisława, 'On the Profiling of Concepts: Issues Debatable and Nondebatable', conference paper, Prague, 2016, https://slideslive.com/38897791/0-profilovani-pojmu-otazky-sporne-i-nesporne

Niú, Rǔjí 牛汝极, 'Kuàwénhuà shìjiǎo: Ōuzhōu rèntóng lǐlùn duì Zhōngguó xībù mínzú dìqū de qǐshì', 跨文化视角：欧洲认同理论对中国西部民族地区的启示, *Zhōngguó xīběi biānjiāng*中国西北边疆, 2009, 1, http://www.sinoss.net/qikan/uploadfile/2010/1130/8009.pdf

Novotná, Zdenka, 'Contribution to the Study of Loan-Words and Hybrid Words in Modern Chinese', *Archiv Orientální*, 1967, 35, 613–648.

Novotná, Zdenka, 'Contribution to the Study of Loan-Words and Hybrid Words in Modern Chinese', *Archiv Orientální*, 1968, 36, 295–325.

Novotná, Zdenka, 'Contribution to the Study of Loan-Words and Hybrid Words in Modern Chinese', *Archiv Orientální*, 1969, 37, 48–75.

Nuyen, A. T., 'Confucianism, the Idea of *Min-pen* and Democracy', *Copenhagen Journal of Asian Studies*, 2000, 14, 130–151.

Oster, Pierre, *Dictionnaire de citations françaises*, Tome I, Paris: Robert, 1990.

Oster, Pierre, *Dictionnaire de citations françaises*, Tome II, Paris: Robert, 1993.

Oxford Dictionary of Quotations, ed. Sara Tulloch, Oxford: Oxford University Press, 1992.

Oxford Dictionary of Sociology, ed. Gordon Marshall, Oxford: Oxford University Press, 1998.

Oxford-Duden German Dictionary, Oxford: Clarendon Press, 1994.
Pajevic, Marko, *Poetic Thinking*, TEDx Talk, 2015, https://www.youtube.com/watch?v=G6092qNTjNA
Pajevic, Marko, *Thinking Humboldt Now*, Royal Holloway University London, conference, 2016, http://german.sllf.qmul.ac.uk/german/thinking-language-humboldt-now/symposium-videos/
Péng Yǒngchūn 彭永春, 'Ōuzhōuhuà•běntǔhuà•duōyuánhuà--Měiguó wénxué lìchéng shùpíng', 欧洲化•本土化•多元化--美国文学历程述评, *Shàngráo shīfàn xuéyuàn xuébào* 上饶师范学院学报, 2002, 1, 75–78.
Perry, Elizabeth J. and Li, Xun, 'Revolutionary Rudeness: The Language of Red Guards and Rebel Workers in China's Cultural Revolution', Indiana East Asian Working Paper Series on Language and Politics in Modern China, Paper 2, Bloomington: East Asia Studies Center, Indiana University, 1993, pp. 1–18.
Picoche, Jacqueline, *Le Robert dictionnaire étymologique du français*, Paris: Robert, 1994.
Plato, *The Collected Dialogues*, eds Edith Hamilton and Huntington Cairns, Princeton: Princeton University Press, 1961.
Plato, *The Republic*, trans. Allan Bloom, New York: Basic Books, 1968.
Poldauf, Ivan, *Česko-anglický slovník*, 2nd edition, Prague: Státní pedagogické nakladatelství, 1986.
Poupard, Paul, *Dictionnaire des religions*, in two 1,000 page volumes, A–K, L–Z, Paris: Presses Universitaires de France, 1984.
Puntsch, Eberhard, *Das neue Zitatenhandbuch*, Köln: Area Verlag, 2007.
Redfield, Robert, *Peasant Society and Culture*, Chicago: University of Chicago, 1956.
Reining, Astrid, 'Conceptual Metaphor in Media Discourse about the European Constitution - An Evaluation of the Hamburg Metaphor Database', in Online Proceedings of the Third Interdisciplinary Workshop on Corpus-Based Approaches to Figurative Language, Birmingham, 14 July 2005.
Rey, Alain (ed.), *Le Robert Dictionnaire historique de la langue française*, in three volumes, Paris: Robert, 1992.
Rey-Debove, Josette and Rey, Alain, *Le Nouveau Petit Robert*, Paris: Robert, 1993.
Rey-Debove, Josette and Rey, Alain (eds), *Le Petit Robert*, Paris: Robert, 2000.
Ricoeur Paul, *La métaphore vive*, Paris: Seuil, 1975.

Richard, Timothy and MacGillivray, Donald, *A Dictionary of Philosophical Terms: Chiefly from the Japanese*, Shanghai: Christian Literature Society for China, 1913.

Riegel, Jeffrey, '*Shih-ching* Poetry and Didacticism in Ancient Chinese Literature', in Victor H. Mair (ed.), *The Columbia History of Chinese Literature*, New York: Columbia University Press, 2001, pp. 97–109.

Rifkin, Jeremy, *The European Dream: How Europe's Vision of the Future is Quietly Eclipsing the American Dream*, Tarcher Perigee, Kindle ebook, 2005.

Rifkin, Jeremy, *The European Dream*, conference paper, European Union, 2005, https://www.youtube.com/watch?v=h3XIavS7fZs

Riley, Philip, *Language, Culture and Identity*, London: Continuum, 2008.

Ripert, Pierre, *Dictionnaire des Citations de la langue française*, Paris: Booking International, 1993.

Robert-Collins Dictionary, Glasgow: Harper Collins Publisher, 1998.

Robertson, James, *Joseph Knight*, London: Harper Collins, 2003.

Roger, Philippe, *L'Ennemi américain: Généalogie de l'antiaméricanisme français*, Paris: Seuil, 2002.

Sabattini, Elisa, '"People as Root" (min ben) Rhetoric in the New Writings by Jia Yi (200-168)', *Extrême-Orient Extrême-Occident*, 2012, 34, http://extremeorient.revues.org/261

Said, Edward, W. *Orientalism*, London: Penguin, Modern Classics [1977], 2012.

Said, Edward, W., *Culture and Imperialism*, Kindle ebook, London: Vintage Digital Vintage Books [2012], 2014.

Sapir, Edward, *Language: An Introduction to the Study of Speech* (1921), New York: Harcourt, Brace & World Inc., 1949.

Sapir, Edward, *Selected Writings in Language, Culture, and Personality* (1949), ed. David G. Mandelbaum, Berkeley: University of California Press, 1985.

Schäffner, Christina, 'Die europäische Architektur. Metaphern der Einigung Europas in der deutschen, britischen und amerikanischen Presse', in Adi Gewenig (ed.), *Inszenierte Information. Politik und strategische Kommunikation in den Medien*, Opladen: Westdeutscher Verlag, 1993, pp. 13–30.

Schoenhals, Michael, '"Non-People" in the People's Republic of China: A Chronicle of Terminological Ambiguity', Indiana East Asian Working Paper Series on Language and Politics in Modern China, Paper 4, Bloomington: East Asia Studies Center, Indiana University, 1994, pp. 1–48.

Scholze-Stubenrecht, W. and Sykes, J. B., *The Oxford-Duden German Dictionary*, Oxford: Clarendon Press, 1999.
Scott, Sir Walter, *The Lay of the Last Minstrel, with Ballads, Songs, and Miscellaneous Poems*, New York: C. S. Francis and Co., 1845.
Shakespeare, William, *Henry IV*, Parts One and Two, in *The Complete Oxford Shakespeare, in Three Volumes, (Histories, Comedies, and Tragedies)*, eds Stanley Wells and Gary Taylor, London: Guild, 1987a.
Shakespeare, William, *Henry V*, in *The Complete Oxford Shakespeare, in Three Volumes, (Histories, Comedies, and Tragedies)*, eds Stanley Wells and Gary Taylor, London: Guild, 1987b.
Shakespeare, William, *Henry VI*, Parts One, Two, and Three, in *The Complete Oxford Shakespeare, in Three Volumes (Histories, Comedies, and Tragedies)*, eds Stanley Wells and Gary Taylor, London: Guild, 1987c.
Shakespeare, William, *Macbeth*, in *The Complete Oxford Shakespeare, in Three Volumes, (Histories, Comedies, and Tragedies)*, eds Stanley Wells and Gary Taylor, London: Guild, 1987d.
Shakespeare, William, *Twelfth Night*, in *The Complete Oxford Shakespeare, in Three Volumes, (Histories, Comedies, and Tragedies)*, eds Stanley Wells and Gary Taylor, London: Guild, 1987e.
Shun Kwong-loi, 'Conception of the Person in Early Confucian Thought', in Kwong-loi Shun and David B. Wong (eds), *Confucian Ethics: A Comparative Study of Self, Autonomy, and Community*, Cambridge: Cambridge University Press, 2004, pp. 183–199.
Sima, Yangzi and Pugsley, Peter, 'The Rise of A "Me Culture" in Postsocialist China', *The International Communication Gazette*, 2010, 72(3), 287–306.
Smith, Adam, *An Inquiry into the Nature and Causes of the Wealth of Nations*, 1775, https://www.gutenberg.org/files/3300/3300-h/3300-h.htm
Spakowski, Nicola, 'From Antagonist to Model? The Function and Place of Europe in Chinese Middle School Textbooks', in Dong Lisheng, Wang Zhengxu and Henk Dekker (eds), *China and the European Union*, London: Routledge, 2013, pp. 210–230.
Staiger, Brunhild, 'Preface', in *Timeline of Chinese-European Cultural Relations*, edited by the Institute of Asian Affairs, Gütersloh: Bertelsmann Foundation, 2004, pp. 1–2.
Staines, Judith, *Mapping Existing Studies on EU-China Cultural Relations*, EENC (European Expert Network on Culture) Short

Report, March 2012, http://www.eenc.info/wp-content/uploads/2013/01/JStaines-Mapping-Existing-Studies-on-EU-China-Cultural-Relations.pdf

Strauss, Julia C., '*Wenguan* ("Lettered Official"), *Gongwuyuan* ("Public Servant"), and *Ganbu* ("Cadre"): The Politics of Labelling State Administrators in Republican China', Indiana East Asian Working Paper Series on Language and Politics in Modern China, Paper. 6, Bloomington: East Asia Studies Center, Indiana University, 1995, pp. 25–56.

Svarverud, Rune, 'The Notions of "Power" and "Rights" in Chinese Political Discourse', in Michael Lackner, Iwo Amelung and Joachim Kurtz (eds), *New Terms for New Ideas: Western Knowledge and Lexical Change in Late Imperial China*, Leiden, Boston and Cologne: Brill. 2001, pp. 125–143.

Svarverud, Rune, 'Individual Self-Discipline and Collective Freedom in the Minds of Chinese Intellectuals', in Mette Halskov Hansen and Rune Svarverud (eds), *iChina: the Rise of the Individual in Modern Chinese Society*, Copenhagen: NIAS Press, 2010, pp. 193–225.

Tang Tsou, *The Cultural Revolution and Post-Mao Reforms: A Historical Perspective*, Chicago: University of Chicago Press, 1986.

Tang Xiaobing, *Global Space and the Nationalist Discourse of Modernity: The Historical Thinking of Liang Qichao*, Stanford: Stanford University Press, 1996.

Thoraval, Joël, 'Le concept chinois de nation est-il obscur? À propos du débat sur la notion de "*minzu*" dans les années 1980', *Bulletin de sinologie*, 1990, 65, 24–41.

Thoraval, Joël, 'Sur la transformation de la pensée néo-confucéenne en discours philosophique moderne. Réflexions sur quelques apories du néo-confucianisme contemporain', *Extrême-Orient Extrême-Occident*, 2005, 27, 91–121.

Toolan, Michael (ed.) *Critical Discourse Analysis: Critical Concepts in Linguistics* (Vol II: Leading Advocates), London: Routledge, 2002.

Townsend, James R., *Political Participation in Communist China*, Berkeley: University of California Press, 1969.

Trabant, Jürgen, *Weltansichten: Wilhelm von Humboldts Sprachprojekt*, München: C. H. Beck, 2012.

Trabant, Jürgen, The Jürgen Trabant Wilhelm von Humboldt Lectures, Rouen 2015, http://rep.univ-rouen.fr/content/films-trabant

Tsien Tsuen-hsuin, 'Western Impact in China through Translation', *Far Eastern Quarterly*, 1954, 13(3), 305–327.

Tsutsumibayashi, Ken, 'Preface to the Special Issue on the EAP Tokyo Workshop', *Journal of Political Science and Sociology*, May 2012, 16, 1–11, http://koara.lib.keio.ac.jp/xoonips/modules/xoonips/download.php?file_id=64787

Underhill, James, W., 'The Switch: Metaphorical Representation of the War in Iraq from September 2002 – May 2003', http://www.metaphorik.de/fr/autor/underhill-james-william.html, 2003.

Underhill, James, W., *Humboldt, Worldview, and Language*, Edinburgh: Edinburgh University Press, 2009.

Underhill, James W., *Creating Worldviews: Metaphor, Ideology, and Language*, Edinburgh: Edinburgh University Press, 2011.

Underhill, James W., *Ethnolinguistics and Cultural Concepts: Truth, Love, Hate, and War*, Cambridge: Cambridge University Press, 2013.

Underhill, James, W., 'Who Wants Walls? An Ethnolinguistics of Insides and Outsides', in Piotr Blummczynski and John Gillespie (eds), *Translating Values: Evaluative Concepts in Translation*, London: Palgrave Macmillan, 2016a, pp. 11–36.

Underhill, James, W., 'Individuals or Peoples for Europe?', conference paper, Prague, 2016b, https://slideslive.com/38897474/jednotlivci-nebo-narody-pro-evropu

Underhill, James, 'Beyond Barriers and Borders', in Alicja Witalisz, and Władysław Witalisz (eds), *Across Borders: The West Looks East*, Krosno: Drukarnia Eikon Plus, 2017, pp. 11–40.

Urmson, J. O. and Rée, Jonathan, *The Concise Encyclopedia of Western Philosophy and Philosophers*, London: Unwin & Hyman, 1991.

Vaňková, Irena (ed.), *Obraz světa v jazyce* (The Picture of the World in Language), Prague: Desktop Publishing, FF UK, 2001.

Vaňková, Irena, *Nádoba plná řeči* [*Dishes Full of Speech*], Prague: Karolinum, 2007.

Vaňková, Irena, Nebeská, Iva, Římalová, Saicová, Lucie and Šlédrová, Jasňa, *Co na srdci, to na jazyku* [*What's on Your Heart is on the Tip of Your Tongue*], Prague: Karolinum, 2005.

Vaňková, Irena, Macurová, Alena and Hynková Dingová, Naďa, *Man in Language: Spaces, Stories, States of Mind – Experience* (spoken and sign languages), 2016, https://slideslive.com/38897480/clovek-v-jazyce-prostor-pribeh-prozitek-jazyky-mluvene-a-jazyky-znakove

Vlasák, Vaclav and Lyer, Stanislav, *Česko-Francouský Slovník*, Prague: Státní Pedagogické Nakladatelství, 1987.

Von Racknitz, Ines, 'Chinese Perceptions of Europe before 1949. Perspectives from the Qing Dynasty (1644- 1911)', NFG Working Paper No. 8, Berlin: Freie Universität Berlin, 2013.

Wales, Katie, *A Dictionary of Stylistics*, New York: Routledge, 2014.

Wàn Qízhōu 万齐洲 and Féng Tiānyú 冯天瑜, '"Rénmín" cíyì de biànqiān——zhèngzhì shùyǔ "rénmín" zhī lìshǐ wénhuà kǎochá' 人民"词义的变迁——政治术语"人民"之历史文化考察, *Wǔhàn lǐgōng dàxué xuébào (shèhuì kēxué bǎn)* 武汉理工大学学报(社会科学版), 2007, 3, 387–390.

Wang, Ban, 'Understanding the Chinese Revolution through Words: An Introduction', in Ban Wang (ed.), *Words and Their Stories: Essays on the Language of the Chinese Revolution*, Leiden: Brill, 2011a, pp. 1–14

Wang, Ban (ed.), *Words and Their Stories: Essays on the Language of the Chinese Revolution*, Leiden: Brill, 2011b.

Wang, Helen, *Chairman Mao Badges: Symbols and Slogans of the Cultural Revolution*, British Museum Research Publications, London: British Museum Press, 2008.

Wang, Hui, 'Zhang Taiyan: The Individual and Modern Identity in China', *The Stockholm Journal of East Asian Studies*, 1996, 7, 89–124.

Wang, Wei, 'Uncovering How Identities of *laobaixing* are Constructed in China's Most Read Magazine', in Dwi Noverini Dejnar, Ahmar Mahboob and Ken Cruikshank (eds), *Language and Identity across Modes of Communication*, Berlin: Mouton de Gruyter, 2015, pp. 202–223.

Wáng, Yàn 王艳, 'Shì xī "ōuhuà" xiànxiàng de èhuà' 试析"欧化"现象的恶化, *Zhōngguó kējì fānyì* 中国科技翻译, 2008, 3, 40–43.

Wang, Zhengxu and Popescu, Bogdan G, 'Knowledge Breeds Affects: Understanding EU's Internal Complexities Help Increase Chinese Perception of the EU and Europe', Nottingham: China Policy Institute, Briefing Series – Issue 71, 2011, http://www.nottingham.ac.uk/cpi/documents/briefings/briefing-71-chinese-views-eu-internal-complexities.pdf

Watkins, Calvert, *The American Heritage Dictionary of Indo-European Roots*, Boston: Houghton Mifflin, 2000.

Watson, Burton (trans.), *Han Feizi: Basic Writings*, New York: Columbia University Press, 2003.

Weber, Max, *The Protestant Ethic and the Spirit of Capitalism*, New York: Routledge, 2012.

Wedell-Wedellsborg, Anne, 'Between Self and Community: The Individual in Contemporary Chinese Literature', in Mette Halskov

Hansen and Rune Svarverud (eds), *China: the Rise of the Individual in Modern Chinese Society*, Copenhagen: NIAS Press, 2010, pp. 164–192.

Wheaton, Henry, *Elements of International Law*, London: Sampson Low, Son & Company, [1836], 1866.

Wheaton, Henry (Huì Dùn 惠顿), *Wànguó Gōngfǎ* 万国公法, trans. Martin A. P. William (Dīng Wěiliáng 丁韪良), Shànghǎi: Shànghǎi shūdiàn chūbǎnshè, [1864], 2002.

Whitson, Roger and Whittaker, Jason, *William Blake and the Digital Humanities: Collaboration, Participation, and Social Media*, New York: Routledge, 2013.

Whorf, Benjamin Lee, *Language, Thought and Reality: Selected Writings*, edited by John B. Caroll, Cambridge, MA: MIT Press [1956], 1984.

Wierzbicka, Anna, *Semantics, Culture and Cognition: Universal Human Concepts in Culture-Specific Configurations*, New York: Oxford University Press, 1992.

Wierzbicka, Anna, *Understanding Cultures through their Key Words*, Oxford: Oxford University Press, 1997.

Wierzbicka, Anna, *Experience, Evidence and Sense: The Hidden Cultural Legacy of English*, Oxford: Oxford University Press, 2010.

Wierzbicka, Anna, *Imprisoned in English: The Hazards of English as a Default Language*, Oxford: Oxford University Press, 2014.

Wilhelm, Richard, *Deutsch-Englisch-Chinesisches Fachwörterbuch*, Tsingtau (Qīngdǎo): Deutsch-chinesische Hochschule, 1911.

Williams, Raymond, *Keywords*, New York. Oxford University Press [1976], 1985.

Witalisz, Alicja, and Witalisz, Władysław, (eds), *Across Borders: The West Looks East*, Krosno: Drukarnia Eikon Plus, 2017.

Wong, Reuben, 'The Issue of Identity in the EU-China Relationship', *Politique européenne*, 2013, 39(1), 158–185.

Wright, David, 'Yan Fu and the Tasks of the Translator', in Michael Lackner, Iwo Amelung and Joachim Kurtz (eds), *New Terms for New Ideas: Western Knowledge and Lexical Change in Late Imperial China*, Leiden: Brill, 2001, pp. 235–256.

Wú, Jiàxiáng吴稼祥, *Lùn rénmín*论人民, 2013, http://wujiaxiang.blog.21ccom.net/?p=55, http://wujiaxiang.blog.21ccom.net/?p=56

Wǔ, Mǎnguì 武满贵 and Jiāng Píng江萍, 'Lüèlùn qīngnián Máo Zédōng réngé dúlìzìzhǔ sīxiǎng' 略论青年毛泽东人格独立自主思想, *Máo Zédōng Dèng Xiǎopíng lǐlùn yánjiū* 毛泽东邓小平理论研究, 1996, 2, 69–72.

Wǔ, Yíkāng 伍贻康, 'Yī zhǒng shèhuì fāzhǎn xīn móshì de tànsuǒ shíjiàn —Ōuzhōu yìtǐhuà xīn lùn' 一种社会发展新模式的探索实践——欧洲一体化新论, *Ōuzhōu yánjiū qiányán bàogào* 欧洲研究前沿报告, 2007, 110–122.

Wǔ, Zhìchéng 吴志成 and Wáng, Xiá 王霞, 'Ōuzhōuhuà jí qí duì chéngyuánguó zhèngzhì de yǐngxiǎng' 欧洲化及其对成员国政治的影响, *Ōuzhōu yánjiū* 欧洲研究, 2007, 4, 38–52.

Xià Ruìchūn 夏瑞春 and Pān Lín 潘琳, 'Ōuzhōuhuà Zhōngguó: Guòqù hé wèilái' 欧洲化中国：过去和未来, *Zhōngguó wénhuà yánjiū* 中国文化研究, 2004, 3, 41–61.

Xiàndài hànyǔ cídiǎn 现代汉语词典, compiled by *Zhōngguó shèhuì kēxuéyuàn yǔyán yánjiūsuǒ cídiǎn biānjíshì* 中国社会科学院语言研究所词典编辑室, 5th edition, Běijīng: Shāngwù yìnshūguǎn, 2005.

Xiàndài hànyǔ cídiǎn 现代汉语词典, compiled by *Zhōngguó shèhuì kēxuéyuàn yǔyán yánjiūsuǒ cídiǎn biānjíshì* 中国社会科学院语言研究所词典编辑室, 6th edition, Běijīng: Shāngwù yìnshūguǎn, 2015.

Xiè, Yàojī 谢耀基, 'Hànyǔ yǔfǎ ōuhuà zòngshù', 汉语语法欧化综述, *Yǔwén yánjiū* 语文研究, 2001, 1, 17–22.

Xīnhuá cídiǎn 新华词典, compiled by Xīnhuá cídiǎn biānzuǎnzǔ 新华词典编纂组, Běijīng: Shāngwù yìnshūguǎn [1988], 1997.

Xīnhuá cídiǎn 新华词典, compiled by Shāngwù yìnshūguǎn císhū yánjiū zhōngxīn 商务印书馆辞书研究中心, Běijīng: Shāngwù yìnshūguǎn, 2001.

Xīnhuá cídiǎn 新华词典, compiled by Shāngwù yìnshūguǎn císhū yánjiū zhōngxīn 商务印书馆辞书研究中心, Běijīng: Shāngwù yìnshūguǎn, 2009.

Xú Bāngzhì 徐邦治, 'Xuānbù "Zhōngguó rénmín cóngcǐ zhàn qǐláile" bùshì zài kāiguó dàdiǎn shàng', 宣布"中国人民从此站起来了"不是在开国大典上, *Rénmínwǎng* 人民网, 7 March 2007, http://media.people.com.cn/GB/22114/49489/78505/5447793.html

Yan, Lianke, *Servir le peuple*, trans. Claude Payen, Arles: Philippe Picquier, 2006.

Yán, Shuǐshēng 颜水生 and Wáng Jǐngkē 王景科, '"Gèrénzhǔyì" yǔ Zhōngguó xiàndài sǎnwén' 个人主义"与中国现代散文, *Shāndōng shīfàn dàxué xuébào* 山东师范大学学报, 2011, 6.

Yán, Tiānqīn 严天钦 and Shí, Jiān 石坚, 'Ōuzhōu yìtǐhuà jìnchéng zhōng de wénhuà zhěnghé', 欧洲一体化进程中的文化整合, *Xīnán mínzú dàxué xuébào* 西南民族大学学报, 2012, 1, 7–11.

Yan, Yunxing, 'Introduction: Conflicting Images of the Individual and Contested Process of Individualization', in M. Halskov Hansen and

Rune Svarverud (eds), *China: The Rise of the Individual in Modern Chinese Society*, Copenhagen: NIAS Press, 2010, pp. 1–38.

Yáng Zhēndé 楊貞德, 'Zìyóu yǔ zìzhì Liáng Qǐchāo zhèngzhì sīxiǎng zhōng de `gèrén', 自由與自治梁啟超政治思想中的「個人」, *Èrshíyī shìjì* 二十一世紀, 2004, pp. 26–39, 84.

Ye, Zhengdao, 'Eating and Drinking in Mandarin and Shanghainese: A Lexical-Conceptual Aanalysis', in Cathryn Donohue, Shunichi Ishihara and William Steed (eds), *Quantitative Approaches to Problems in Linguistics: Studies in Honour of Phil Rose*, Munich: Lincom Europa, 2012, pp. 265–280.

Ye, Zhengdao, 'Understanding the Conceptual Basis of the "old friend" Formula in Chinese Social Interaction and Foreign Diplomacy: A Cultural Script Approach', *Australian Journal of Linguistics*, 2013, 33(3), 365–385.

Ye, Zhengao, 'The Meaning of "Happiness" (xingfu) and "Emotional Pain" (tongku) in Chinese', *International Journal of Language and Culture*, 2014, 1(2), 194–215.

Ye, Zhengdao, 'On Chinese "Happiness": A Semantic Perspective', conference held at the École des hautes études en sciences sociales, Paris, 16 January 2018.

Yì, Dān 易丹, 'Èryuán duìlì zhōng de Ōuzhōu rèntóng' 二元对立中的欧洲认同, *Sìchuān dàxué xuébào* 四川大学学报, 2009, 4, 114–121.

Yu, Hua, *La Chine en dix mots*, trans. Isabelle Rabut and Angel Pino, Arles: Actes Sud, 2010.

Yu Hua, *China in Ten Words*, trans. Allan H. Barr, London: Duckworth Overlook, 2013.

Yu Keping (ed.), *Democracy and the Rule of Law in China*, Leiden and Boston: Brill, 2010.

Zarrow, Peter G., 'Introduction: Citizenship in China and in the West', in Joshua A. Fogel and Peter G. Zarrow (eds), *Imagining the People, Chinese Intellectuals and the Concept of Citizenship 1890-1920*, New York and London: M. E. Sharpe, 1997, pp. 3–38.

Zarrow, Peter G., *After Empire: The Conceptual Transformation of the Chinese State, 1885-1924*, Stanford: Stanford University Press, 2012.

Zhāng, Jùn 张浚, 'Cóng Yà-Ōu huìyì jìnchéng kàn fāzhǎn guójì guānxì de Ōuzhōu móshì' 从亚欧会议进程看发展国际关系的欧洲模式, *Ōuzhōu yánjiū qiányán bàogào* 欧洲研究前沿报告, 2007, http://ies.cass.cn/wz/yjcg/ozzz/201207/t20120731_2458284.shtml

Zhāng, Wéirán 张未然, 'Jīyú rènzhī xíngtàixué de lèicízhuì gòucí yánjiū' 基于认知形态学的类词缀构词研究, PhD dissertation, Běijīng and Paris: Peking University and Université Paris Sorbonne Cité, 2016.

Zhāng, Wéiwèi 张维为, 'Mínběnzhǔyì shì gè hǎo dōngxī', 民本主义是个好东西, *Huánqiú shíbào* 环球时报, *Rénmín wǎng* 人民网, 19 September 2014, http://opinion.people.com.cn/n/2014/0919/c1003-25693067.html/.

Zhao Yuezhi, *Media, Market, and Democracy in China: Between the Party Line and the Bottom Line*, Urbana and Chicago: University of Illinois Press, 1998.

Zhao Yuezhi, 'Media and Elusive Democracy in China', *The Public*, 2001, 8(4), 21–44.

Zhao Yuezhi, *Communication in China: Political Economy, Power, and Conflict*, Lanham: Rowman & Littlefield, 2008.

Zhong, Yong. 'The Making of a "Correct" Translation-Showcasing the Official Chinese Discourse of Translation', *Meta: Journal des traducteurs [Meta: Translators' Journal]*, 2011, 56(4), 796–811.

Zhōu, Hóng 周弘, 'Ōuméng shèhuì tuánjié móshì yǔ Ōuméng fāzhǎn zhànlüè' 欧盟社会团结模式与欧盟发展战略, 欧洲研究前沿报告, 2007, 98–109.

Zhōu, Hóng 周弘 et al., '"Dān tiāo": Ōuzhōu móshì vs Měiguó móshì' "单挑": 欧洲模式vs美国模式, *Rénmínwǎng* 人民网, 2003, http://www.people.com.cn/GB/guandian/183/6103/7942/2014617.html

Zōu, Lǐ 邹理, 'Zhōu Lìbō xiǎoshuō de ōuhuà qīngxiàng', 周立波小说的欧化倾向, *Wénxué pínglùn* 文学评论, 2012, 1, 173–181.

WEBSITES

Daily Mail, British daily newspaper, http://www.dailymail.co.uk
Der Spiegel, German weekly magazine, http://www.spiegel.de
El País, http://elpais.com
Europa, Bulgarian EU website, https://europa.eu/european-union/index_bg
Europa, Czech EU website, https://europa.eu/european-union/index_cs
Europa, English EU website, https://europa.eu/european-union/index_en
Europa, French EU website, https://europa.eu/european-union/index_fr

Europa, German EU website, https://europa.eu/european-union/index_de
Europa, Spanish EU website, https://europa.eu/european-union/index_es
Europa, Polish EU website, https://europa.eu/european-union/index_pl
Le Nouvel Observateur, French weekly political magazine, http://tempsreel.nouvelobs.com
Libération, French daily newspaper, http://www.liberation.fr
Lidové Noviny, Czech daily newspaper, http://www.lidovky.cz/
Merriam-Webster Dictionary, http://www.merriam-webster.com
Metaphorik.de, a forum for scientific exchange concerning questions about metaphor and metonymy, http://www.metaphorik.de/
Oxford English Dictionary (*OED*), http://www.oed.com
Project Gutenberg, http://www.gutenberg.org
Rénmín wǎng 人民网, Chinese newspaper, http://www.people.com.cn
Rouen Ethnolinguistics Project, forum for international online conferences founded and directed by James Underhill, http://rep.univ-rouen.fr/
The Guardian, British daily newspaper, http://www.theguardian.com/uk
The Herald, Scottish daily newspaper, http://www.heraldscotland.com
The New York Times, American daily newspaper, http://www.nytimes.com,
The Scotsman, Scottish daily newspaper, http://www.scotsman.com
The Statesman, British weekly political magazine, http://www.thestatesman.com/
The Sun, British daily newspaper, http://www.thesun.co.uk
Wikipedia, Czech, https://cs.wikipedia.org/wiki/Hlavn%C3%AD_strana
Wikipedia, English, https://en.wikipedia.org/wiki/Main_Page
Wikipédia, French, https://fr.wikipedia.org/wiki/Wikip%C3%A9dia:Accueil_principal
Wikipedia, German, https://de.wikipedia.org/wiki/Wikipedia:Hauptseite
YouTube, English, https://www.youtube.com/
YouTube, French, https://www.youtube.com/?hl=fr&gl=FR
Zàixiàn xīnhuá zìdiǎn 在线新华字典, http://xh.5156edu.com/html5/370560.html

Index

Abramowicz, M., 20, 55–6, 59, 61, 65, 338, 353
American English, 29, 40, 41, 126, 210, 341
Austen, J., 50–1

Bartmiński, J., 20, 55–6, 59, 61, 65, 338, 353, 246, 353
Burns, R., 52

Chén, Dúxiù, 196, 247, 249, 250, 251, 252, 348
conceptual metaphor, 75, 136, 268, 294–300
Corneille, P., 6–23, 168
cultural mindset, 5, 8, 26, 55, 109, 134, 202, 221, 224, 343, 344, 351

Dèng, Xiǎopíng, 14, 253, 316
Dewey, J., 17, 200, 205, 228, 235–6, 237, 345
Dickens, Ch., 50, 64, 207, 286

enemies of the people, 78, 97, 98, 101, 108, 337, 356
English English, 51–2, 54, 119, 125, 142, 336, 341
Europa, EU website, 132, 147, 196, 204, 205, 237, 268, 280, 300–3
Europeanism, 309, 325
Europeanization, 306, 308–10, 315, 316, 317, 320, 328–32, 346, 347

familism, 249–50
Farage, N., 24–5, 76–80, 82, 83, 84, 293

Hobbes, 17, 118, 161, 163–5, 169, 205, 228–30
Hollande, F., 70–3
Hú, Jǐntāo, 105, 106
Hú, Shì, 243, 247, 250, 348, 350
Humboldt, W. von, 6, 20, 117, 133, 156, 234–5, 238, 346

James, W., 200, 228, 223–4, 235, 237
Jiāng, Zémín, 103, 107, 112

Kāng, Yǒuwéi, 177
Keyword, 4, 5, 8, 12, 261–2, 306, 310, 311, 320, 324, 328, 334–6, 337, 341–2, 343, 345, 349, 351, 351
Kimmel, M., 296–300
Kundera, M., 212–16

Lakoff, G., 294, 342
Le Pen, M. 25, 73–6, 80, 82
Lǐ, Zéhou, 248, 249, 259
Liáng, Qǐchāo, 86, 90, 175, 177, 178, 244, 375
Liu, Lydia, 18, 21, 177, 178, 181, 240, 242, 243, 244, 245, 246, 251, 252
Locke, J., 17, 118, 162–3, 169, 235, 286

Macron, E., 23, 74–5, 203, 294, 302, 304
Máo, Zédōng, 86, 91, 95, 96, 97, 99, 100, 101, 102, 103, 107, 108, 112, 181, 182, 239, 240, 243, 348, 356
May, Th., 89, 90
Mélenchon, J-L., 25, 69–75, 80
mencius *(Mèngzǐ)*, 88, 92, 109, 110, 111, 355
Michelet, J., 60, 61, 63, 70, 177
Mill, J. S., 16, 168, 201, 206, 211, 232–3, 235–6, 238, 241–2, 247

people as the root, 87–9, 108, 195, 355
Plato, 162, 226

return graphic loan, 176, 177, 246, 356
rival synonym, 50, 118, 124, 311, 315, 348, 351, 357
Rouen Ethnolinguistics Project, 4, 395

Sarkozy, N., 67–71, 131, 273
Scottish English, 2, 10, 17, 55, 66, 141–4, 293, 305, 347, 351, 357

semantic colonization, 68, 81, 358, 359
semantic evacuation, 68, 81, 358, 359
serve the people, 41, 85, 86, 95, 98, 100, 103–7
Shakespeare, W., 30, 49, 121, 133, 166, 168, 225, 237, 286
Smith, A., 17, 118, 134, 164–5, 205, 231–2
Sūn, Zhōngshān (Sun Yat-sen), 86, 90, 360

Trabant, J., 344, 352, 368

Underhill, J. W., 8, 9, 14, 75, 78, 79, 156, 267, 289, 294, 304, 338, 346

Wierzbicka, A., 1, 20, 338, 351
Williams, R., 8, 3, 20, 25, 115, 288, 340, 351

Xí, Jìnpíng, 106, 113, 253, 341

Yán, Fù, 241, 242
Ye, Zhengdao, 13, 14, 338
Yú, Huá, 85, 105

EU representative:
Easy Access System Europe
Mustamäe tee 50, 10621 Tallinn, Estonia
Gpsr.requests@easproject.com